Stanley Gibbons

Great Britain

Specialised Stamp Catalogue
Volume 5

**Wreathed Machin Head as used
for Special Issues**

Stanley Gibbons

Great Britain

Specialised Stamp Catalogue

Volume 5
Queen Elizabeth II
Decimal Special Issues

First Edition

Stanley Gibbons Publications Ltd
London and Ringwood

By Appointment to H.M. the Queen
Stanley Gibbons Ltd, London
Philatelists

Published by Stanley Gibbons Publications Ltd.
Editorial, Sales Offices and Distribution Centre:
5 Parkside, Christchurch Road, Ringwood,
Hants BH24 3SH

© Stanley Gibbons Publications Ltd 1988

ISBN 0–85259–202–7

1st separate edition—September 1988

Item No. 2891 (88)

Typeset by The Whitefriars Press Ltd, Tonbridge, Kent
Printed in Great Britain by Black Bear Press Ltd, Cambridge

Contents

COMPLETE YOUR SET

No stamp collector likes to have incomplete sets – whether you are talking about Tudor Crowns, St Edward Crowns or the Crown of the SG Catalogue range – the **Great Britain Specialised Catalogue**.

Volume 1	(item 0285)	**Queen Victoria** – new edition due early 1989.
Volume 2	(item 0286)	**King Edward VII to King George VI**
Volume 3	(item 2810)	**Queen Elizabeth II pre-decimal issues**
Volume 4	(item 2820)	**Queen Elizabeth II decimal definitive issues**
Volume 5	(item 2891)	**Queen Elizabeth II decimal special issues**

HOW TO KEEP RIGHT UP TO DATE

A handbook-catalogue such as this volume can only be published every two or three years. For more simplified but up to date details of the current GB market it is wise to augment the information provided in the Great Britain Specialised Catalogue with

Collect British Stamps (item 0289) – published each November. The World's most successful Catalogue, published in full colour.

Great Britain CONCISE Stamp Catalogue (item 2887) – published each May. A one-volume Catalogue based on the GB listing in Part I with a host of additional information.

THE MAGAZINE FOR THE GB COLLECTOR

Each month **Gibbons Stamp Monthly** contains a 16-page 'British Stamps' section with regular coverage of new issues, Machins, varieties and books, including the supplements to the Great Britain Specialised Catalogue. Feature articles cover a variety of topics from Queen Victoria line-engraved to modern postal history and a varied selection of advertisements provide the very latest in market information.

Please send for a free specimen copy and subscription details to **Hugh Jefferies, Stanley Gibbons Magazines, Parkside, Ringwood, Hampshire BH24 3SH**.

Preface

The seventeen years since the introduction of decimal currency in Great Britain has witnessed a revolution in stamp design and production. The evolution of the Machin definitives into one of the most complex issues ever has overshadowed, but not completely obscured, advances in the design and production of the Special issues for which the British Post Office has achieved a world-wide reputation.

The twin strands of modern British philately are now recognised by the publication of separate volumes in the Specialised range for the Decimal Definitives and Decimal Special Issues. The definitives continue as the Specialised Volume 4, a new edition of which appeared in March of this year, and the Special stamps will form a new Volume 5.

Since the first set of the decimal period, 1971 Ulster Paintings, the special issues have undergone a metamorphosis which is just as far-reaching in its implications as anything in the Machin issues. The last seventeen years have seen the introduction of new stamp formats and printing processes, coupled with major changes in the design concept. In 1971 no one would have predicted the introduction of miniature sheets and year books, the high standard achieved in the continuing series of Flora and Fauna stamps or the inclusion in the new issue programme of such innovative designs as the 1986 Halley's Comet or 1988 Sports Organisations issues. The actual production of Special stamps has also changed radically. The introduction of the Jumelle press from November 1972 has virtually eliminated missing colour errors and has resulted in such improvements to the condition of the printing cylinders that the incidence of minor flaws has dropped so dramatically as to make it no longer worthwhile to record them. We do, however, continue to illustrate and price the few larger cylinder flaws which have occurred.

The use of the APS perforator has also resulted in the occasional part-perforated sheet from which listable imperforate pairs come. The advances in technology have also extended to the stamp paper with the unannounced introduction, as early as the 1983 Christmas series, of the Advanced Coated Paper type. This new volume of the Specialised Catalogue provides details of all these technical differences or sheet stamps, together with the booklets and sheetlet packs containing special issues.

Since the last Specialised listing of the stamps in 1984 many prices have risen quite considerably, in particular the errors which remain in constant demand. Some basic sets, especially those with thematic subjects are also becoming harder to find in bulk and such movements are also reflected in the pricing for this edition.

A helpful design index, together with background notes for every issue are also provided up to and including the 1988 Transport and Communications ("EUROPA") issues.

We are grateful to the many collectors and dealers who have shown us errors and varieties or supplied information to assist in the preparation of this edition. Particular thanks are due to Mr. Alan Bond (plate and cylinder blocks). Addresses of the three specialist societies dealing with Great Britain stamps will be found on page viii.

Supplements to the *Great Britain Specialised Catalogue Volumes 4 and 5* will be found each month in *Gibbons Stamp Monthly*.

D. J. Aggersberg
R. H. Oliver

Stanley Gibbons Addresses

HEAD OFFICE, 399 STRAND, LONDON WC2R 0LX

Auction Room and Specialist Stamp Departments. Open Monday–Friday, 9.30 a.m. to 5 p.m.

Shop. Open Monday–Friday 9.30 a.m. to 6 p.m. and Saturday 10 a.m. to 4 p.m.
Telephone 01 836 8444 and Telex 28883 for all departments.

RINGWOOD OFFICE

Stanley Gibbons Publications and Promotions, 5, Parkside, Christchurch Road, Ringwood, Hants BH24 3SH. Telephone 0425 472363. Telex: 41271.

OVERSEAS BRANCHES

Stanley Gibbons Australia Pty. Ltd., P.O. Box 863J, Melbourne 3001, Australia. Telephone (01 0613) 670 3332 and Telex AA 37223.

Stanley Gibbons (Pty.) Ltd., P.O. Box 930, Parklands 2121, R.S.A.

Stanley Gibbons (Singapore) Pte. Ltd., Maxwell Road P.O. Box 1372, Singapore 9027, Republic of Singapore.

Stanley Gibbons Publications Ltd. has overseas agents and distributors for Australia, Belgium, Canada, Denmark, Finland, France, West Germany, Hong Kong, Israel, Japan, Luxembourg, Netherlands, New Zealand, Norway, South Africa, Sweden, Switzerland, United States and West Indies. Please contact the Ringwood address for details.

Great Britain Philatelic Societies

The Great Britain Philatelic Society. Hon. Membership Secretary: A. J. Walker, 42 Jesmond Road, Newcastle-upon-Tyne, Tyne & Wear, NE2 4PQ.

The British Decimal Stamps Study Circle. The Secretary: P. Daniels, 70 Moor Park Close, Rainham, Gillingham, Kent ME8 8QT.

The Great Britain Decimal Stamp Book Study Circle. Hon. Membership Secretary: A. J. Wilkins, 3 Buttermere Close, Brierley Hill, West Midlands DY5 3SD.

Introductory Notes

Detailed Introductory Notes

Before using the catalogue it is most important to study the "General Notes" as these detail the technical background of the issues in question. These "General Notes" will be found at the beginning of each section and also indicate some of the areas which are beyond the scope of this work.

Catalogue Numbering

Basic catalogue numbers bear the prefix letter which denotes its Section of the catalogue. This is followed by the related number in the 1989 edition of the *Part I (British Commonwealth)* and 1988 *G.B. Concise Catalogues*.

Varieties have a letter identification, *e.g. a.* Phosphor omitted, *b.* (short description of cylinder variety) and related varieties to item *b.* will be listed as *ba., bb.,* etc.

Booklet panes containing special stamps have numbers prefixed with the letters WP, listed under the relevant set. The booklets have the same numbers and prefix letters as are used in the *G.B. Concise Catalogue.*

Prices

Prices quoted in this Catalogue are those which Stanley Gibbons Ltd. estimate will be their selling prices at the time of publication. They are for stamps of fine condition for the particular issue, unless otherwise indicated; those of lesser quality may be offered at lower prices.

In the case of unused stamps, our prices are for stamps unmounted mint. Prices for used stamps refer to postally used copies.

All prices are subject to change without prior notice and Stanley Gibbons Ltd. may from time to time offer stamps below catalogue price in consequence of special purchases or particular promotions. Subscribers to new issues are asked to note that the prices charged for them contain an element for the service rendered and so may exceed the prices shown when the stamps are subsequently catalogued.

No guarantee is given to supply all stamps priced, since it is not possible to keep every catalogued item in stock.

Cases can exist where a particular stamp shows more than one of the listed varieties. It might, for example, have a cylinder flaw as well as a broad phosphor band, both of which are listed but priced separately. It is not practical to cover every possible combination but the value of such items may be established by adding the *difference* between the price of the basic stamp and the dearest variety to the catalogue price of the cheapest variety.

Plate and cylinder blocks are priced according to the type of perforator used. This takes account of the state of the perforations on all four sides of the sheet, not just the corner where the cylinder number appears. Note that a full specification of a cylinder block should quote the basic number of the stamp; cylinder number; phosphor cylinder number and displacement if any; with or without dot; perforation type; and type of paper and gum wherever such alternatives exist.

Prices for *cylinder flaws* are for single stamps and extra stamps required to make up positional blocks would be charged as normals. However all cylinder flaws and other varieties listed under *booklet panes* are priced for the complete pane.

Prices for *cylinder blocks containing listed varieties* are indicated by an asterisk and include the cost of the variety.

The prices quoted for *folded booklet panes* are for panes with good perforations and complete with the binding margin. Prices for complete booklets are for those containing panes with average perforations.

Items Excluded

In dealing with *varieties* we record only those for which we can vouch, namely items we have seen and verified for ourselves. It should be recognised, however, that some flaws described as constant may be transient: they may develop in size to be sufficiently noticeable to be worth retouching.

To qualify for listing, *imperforate errors* must show no sign of indentation, i.e. blind perforations, on any side of a pair. Such part-perforated varieties can occur in "Jumelle" printings after re-starting the press during a run and are caused by the pins on the Kampf perforating drum only gradually coming into contact with the female cylinder so that some rows will show signs of indentation.

Colour shifts due to faulty registration range from minor shifts to quite spectacular varieties. As it is very difficult to draw a line between major and minor shifts we have not listed any.

We likewise exclude: doctor blade flaws; paper creases; partially omitted colours; and misplaced perforations.

We do not quote for traffic light blocks, gutter margins or positional blocks showing various sheet markings other than cylinder blocks but when available they will be supplied at appropriate prices.

Finally, we make no mention whatever of unusual items in a form not issued by the Post Office. In recent years many philatelic items have been prepared privately, with or without Post Office authority, some having postal validity. Many are made for laudable purposes, such as for the promotion of philatelic events, exhibitions and society anniversaries, or for charitable causes, but others have been purely commercial productions. They can be such things as legitimate postal issues with overprints in the margins, black prints, specially prepared packs and booklets made up from sheet stock. Their variety seems endless and their status is arguable.

Correspondence

Letters should be addressed to the Catalogue Editor, Stanley Gibbons Publications Ltd., 5, Parkside, Christchurch Road, Ringwood, Hants BH24 3SH, and return postage is appreciated when a reply is sought. New information and unlisted items for consideration are welcomed.

Please note we do not give opinions as to the genuineness of stamps, nor do we identify stamps or number them by our Catalogue.

To order from this Catalogue

Always quote the *Specialised Catalogue* number, mentioning *Volume 5, 1st Edition,* and where necessary specify additionally the precise item wanted.

Guarantee

All stamps supplied by Stanley Gibbons Ltd., are guaranteed originals in the following terms:

If not as described, and returned by the purchaser, we undertake to refund the price paid to us in the original transaction. If any stamp is certified as genuine by the Expert Committee of the Royal Philatelic Society, London, or by B.P.A. Expertising Ltd., the purchaser shall not be entitled to make any claim against us for any error, omission or mistake in such certificate.

Consumers' statutory rights are not affected by the above guarantee.

Expertisation

We do not give opinions as to the genuineness of stamps. Expert Committees exist for this purpose and enquiry can be made of the Royal Philatelic Society, 41 Devonshire Place, London W1N 1PE or B.P.A. Expertising Ltd., P.O. Box 163, Carshalton Beeches, Surrey SM5 4QR. They do not undertake valuations under any circumstances and fees are payable for their services.

National Postal Museum Archive Material

During 1984 and 1985 surplus GB material from the National Postal Museum archives was included in three auction sales. The lots offered were mostly imprimaturs, which were handstamped on the reverse to indicate origin, and specimen overprints. All the material offered in these auction sales was issued before decimalization and does not affect the listings in this volume.

Symbols and Abbreviations

†	(in price column) does not exist.
—	(in price column) exists, but no market price is known. (a blank in the used price column conveys the same meaning).
*	(against the price of a cylinder block) price includes a listed variety.
Cyl.	Cylinder (photo. or typo. printings).
FCP	Fluorescent coated paper.
GA	Gum arabic.
mm.	Millimetres.
No.	Number.
OCP	Original coated paper.
Phos.	Phosphor.
PHQ	Postcard-size reproductions of special or commemorative stamps. Each card has a "PHQ" serial number and are usually on sale shortly before the date of issue of the stamps. There is no officially designated "first day".
Pl.	Plate (litho. printings).
ptg.	Printing.
PVA	Polyvinyl alcohol (gum).
PVAD	Polyvinyl alcohol (gum) with dextrin added.
R.	Row (thus "R. 6/4" indicates the fourth stamp from the left in the sixth horizontal row from the top of a sheet of stamps).

Whether you Collect Definitives or Commemoratives

You need the Stanley Gibbons Uvitec Micro Ultra Violet Lamp.

As all GB collectors know, the current 'Machin' definitives have been through quite a number of changes since they were first issued; with some of the combinations of paper, gum and phosphor type being extremely hard to find; moreover such varieties are not confined only to the definitives with a number of useful items to be found in the commemorative listings.

Unfortunately not all of these desirable items can be spotted with the naked eye, many of them requiring the aid of a shortwave ultra violet lamp for positive identification.

Following exhaustive research and tests Stanley Gibbons believe that they have come up with the perfect answer to the collectors prayer.

The Stanley Gibbons Uvitec Micro Short Wave Ultra Violet Lamp.
EXCLUSIVE – designed to meet the needs of today's collector and produced for us by the leading manufacturer of UV Lamps in the UK.

NEW IMPROVED VERSION – with up to 30% more power.
EFFECTIVE – detects phosphors, paper and ink variations, fakes, forgeries and repairs.
SAFE – the specially designed hood protects the eyes from direct UV light.
SMART and ROBUST – well designed plastic casing built to withstand regular use.
CONVENIENT – battery powered, ideal for taking to stamp shops and fairs.
EASY TO USE – simple press button, on-off operation.
SMALL and LIGHT – slips easily into the pocket. Weighs less than 6oz (with batteries) and therefore suitable for prolonged use.
VERSATILE – comes with its own detachable viewing hood allowing effective daylight use. Suitable for studying individual stamps or for 'sweeping'.
CLEAR INSTRUCTIONS – are provided with every lamp.
THE PRICE – not only one of the best ultra violet lamps on the market but also one of the least expensive.

SECTION W
Machin Decimal Special Issues
1971–88. Sheet and Booklet Stamps

General Notes

PRINTERS. With the exception of the issues noted below Harrison & Sons have printed all special issues by photogravure. The 1975 Sailing, 1978 Commonwealth Heads of Government, 1982 Maritime Heritage, 1984 Royal Mail and 1987 Victorian Britain stamps were printed by photogravure and recess. The "London 1980" stamp was printed in recess and the border of the miniature sheet was printed in photogravure.

Bradbury, Wilkinson printed the 1973 issues commemorating Inigo Jones and the Commonwealth Parliamentary Conference. The latter was printed by a combination of recess and typography and the former by lithography and typography.

The House of Questa printed the 1980 Sports, 1982 British Motor Industry, 1984 British Meridian, 1986 Industry Year, Commonwealth Parliamentary Association Conference and 1987 St. John Ambulance issues by lithography.

John Waddington printed the 1981 Duke of Edinburgh Award scheme, 1983 British Garden and 1985 Safety at Sea issues.

All the stamps printed by Harrison were issued in Post Office sheets of 100 arranged 10 × 10; but those printed on the "Jumelle" press, first introduced for the 1972 Silver Wedding issue, were arranged in two panes of 50 with a gutter margin, with the single exception of the 1973 Cricket issue which was in sheets of 10 × 10.

During 1971–73 most issues were printed in sheet-fed single panes with the exception of the values for second class postage which were needed in larger quantities and these were generally printed in reel-fed double panes (no dot and dot). From 1974 onwards all issues have been printed in double panes on the "Jumelle" press.

This information is given under "Sheet Details" after the listing of each issue.

GUTTER MARGINS. The reason for the gutter margins arises from the need to relate the circumference of the perforating drum to that of the printing cylinders. Since the stamp size of the special issues had already been standardised to meet the requirements of the designers this could not be varied.

The circumference of the perforating drum for special issues was fixed at 45·15″. If it were to be any smaller the pins would enter the mating holes at an acute angle which would cause them to be bent or possibly broken. The ratio of the circumference of the perforating drum to that of the printing cylinders was fixed at 4:7 so that the circumference of the printing cylinders had to be 45·15″ × 4/7 = 25·8″.

With standard-sized horizontal format special issues the vertical measurement of complete sheets of 200 would be 23·6″, leaving a gap of 2·2″. Therefore the stamp images had to be spaced evenly round the cylinders in four panels of 50 stamps separated by gutter margins to take account of the 2·2″ gap (vertical format stamps are printed sideways).

Thus with each revolution of the perforating drum seven panes of 50 stamps are perforated in precise register with the printed design. The reel is then guillotined to produce counter sheets of 100 stamps in two panes of 50. Further information is contained in the *Philatelic Bulletin* for April 1978, from which this information was drawn.

The issues printed by Questa have narrow gutter margins between two panes of 50 stamps.

Gutter margin pairs, like other multiples from special positions in the sheet, are outside the scope of this catalogue. We list the cylinder blocks because of the information they give and for identifying the perforators.

PRINTING PRESSES. Harrisons printed the sheet-fed special issues on the Rembrandt press and the reel-fed issues on the Woods machine until the "Jumelle" machine was introduced, with its characteristic sheet markings and layout. There was a single exception when the Halley machine was brought back into use for part of the printing of the 3p. 1972 Silver Wedding. The 1978 British Architecture and 1979 Sir Rowland Hill miniature sheets were printed on the Rembrandt press.

Bradbury, Wilkinson printed the 1973 Inigo Jones and Commonwealth Parliamentary Conference issues on a sheet-fed machine.

Stamps printed by Questa, in lithography, were printed on a sheet-fed Heidelberg press and those by John Waddington on a sheet-fed Falcon press.

QUEEN'S PORTRAIT. The silhouette profile from Arnold Machin has been used where appropriate except for the 1972 General Anniversaries Nos. W221 (3p.) W222 (7½p.), 1973 Inigo Jones and 1974 U.P.U. Centenary when the profile used was from the coinage design by Mrs. Mary Gillick, adapted by David Gentleman.

PAPER. All Special Issues are on unwatermarked chalk-surfaced paper with the exception of the 1972 Churches issue (Nos. W224/8) which are on ordinary paper. The original off-white coated paper (OCP) was used for all 1971 issues and also the 1972 Churches issue (Nos. W224/8). All other issues from the 1972 British Polar Explorers onwards are on the whiter fluorescent coated paper (FCP). The chalk-surfacing is not apparent on stamps having "all-over" phosphor and only shows in the sheet margins outside the phosphor area.

1

There has been one instance where the coating has been omitted. The 1976 Christmas 11p. (No. W351a) does not respond to the chalky test (applying silver to see if it will produce a black line) and may be further distinguished from the normal chalk-surfaced paper by the fibres which clearly show on the surface, resulting in a rougher impression and less definition to the screening dots. Stamps showing signs of poor impression due to insufficient ink (which are known as "dry prints") are sometimes confused with uncoated paper.

Phosphorised (fluorescent coated) paper, which has the phosphor incorporated into the paper coating was used for the 1977 Rackets issue as an experiment. It was again introduced in 1979 for the Direct Elections to the European Assembly stamps and was then used for all special issues from the 1979 Police issue onwards.

Phosphorised (advanced coated) paper. In order to resolve the problem of ink absorption in the drying process, the chemists at the printer's laboratories developed a different method of combining phosphor with fluorescence. It became necessary to increase the amount of fluorescent brightener to reduce longwave ultra violet sensitivity. Under ultra violet light the improved fluorescent property in the paper coating gives a stronger result than before. The first special stamp to appear on this paper was the 1983 Christmas 16p. value but it was not until the 1985 Famous Trains issue that all values appeared on this paper. Stamps in lithography continued on fluorescent paper until the 1986 Parliamentary Association Conference stamp (No. W671) when the phosphorised (advanced coated) paper was used by Questa.

All the phosphorised paper used includes a fluorescent additive which can be detected using an ultra violet lamp. Occasionally the fluorescent additive in the coating is omitted in error and these stamps give a dull response under ultra-violet light. They are distinguished in the lists as fluorescent brightener omitted.

GUM. PVA gum was used for all issues up to the 1973 Commonwealth Parliamentary Conference issue. PVAD was introduced for the 1973 Royal Wedding stamps and PVAD, PVA and gum arabic were all used for the 1973 Christmas stamps. Thereafter PVAD was employed for all issues but occasionally part of a printing appeared on PVA gum, which could be due to using up old stocks of paper or the dextrin may have been omitted in error. Stamps having more than one type of gum are listed in full.

UNDERPRINTS. Symbols, printed in pale blue ink over the gum, denote that the stamp was issued in a booklet or special folder and sold at a discount rate. The stamps thus marked were identifiable for post office accounting purposes.

PERFORATION. All stamps are perforated 15 × 14 or 14 × 15 in the case of vertical designs. Stamps printed by John Waddington are perforated 14 and those by Questa 14½ × 14 for horizontal designs, or 14 × 14½ for vertical. Stamps printed by Harrison in a changed format and size were perforated 14½ × 14 ("London 1980", 1986 Nature, 1987 Flowers, Pottery, 1988 Welsh Bible) 14 × 14½ (1985 Composers); 14 × 15 (1982 Information Technology) or 14½ (1984 Heraldry, 1985 Films, 1986 RAF, 1987 Scottish Heraldry, 1988 Sports). Cylinder numbers are listed according to the perforation types used and these are described in Appendix I.

PHOSPHOR. A single phosphor band was used for the second class mail values of the Christmas issues and two bands were employed on the rest until this was superseded by "all-over" phosphor, first used for the 3p. 1972 Royal Silver Wedding stamp, the 20p. having no phosphor. "All-over" phosphor extends into the left and right margins of the sheet. There is some evidence that the phosphor was not always printed last. Missing phosphor varieties on "all-over" phosphor issues can only be distinguished under ultra violet light.

Misplaced Phosphor Bands. Phosphor bands are sometimes found misplaced but they are not listed unless they affect the number of bands, i.e. one broad band instead of two bands. These are very popular with collectors and are described as one broad band left, right or centre but we do not make these distinctions. Nor do we list misplaced centre or side bands as a general rule as this can be a matter of degree.

PHOSPHOR CYLINDER NUMBERS. These normally appear on the cylinder blocks but are sometimes displaced through being unsynchronised, inverted or omitted in error. The known examples of these variations are listed under the cylinder blocks.

CYLINDER VARIETIES. We have only listed or recorded those we have actually seen and know to be constant in the position given. Others have been reported and may be added in future editions as specimens become available for inspection.

MULTICOLOURED STAMPS. Colour descriptions are taken from the traffic lights to identify the colours of the cylinder numbers and also missing colour errors. Where colours are superimposed one over another, the colours that result will be different from those described.

PRE-RELEASE DATES. It sometimes happens that stamps are mistakenly issued in advance of the official date of issue at individual post offices, or even by the Edinburgh Philatelic Bureau.

Such items, when found on cover, are recorded in footnotes where they have been brought to our notice.

It is possible, however, to obtain postmarks a day early quite legitimately by posting covers on mail trains at intermediate stations in the small hours of the morning of the date of issue, when they are postmarked with the T.P.O. cancellation of the day before, when the train journey started. These datestamps are not altered en route. As these "pre-releases" are not due to error and, could be obtained for any issue, we do not record them.

WITHDRAWAL DATES. About a month's supply or less of the Special Issues is normally supplied to post offices but it is the practice to keep them on sale for one year at the Philatelic Bureau and Philatelic Sales Counters, unless previously sold out. The dates quoted are those on which the stamps were withdrawn at the Philatelic Bureau.

QUANTITIES SOLD. These figures are supplied by the Post Office and we understand they refer to the quantities issued from the Post Office Stores Department to post offices plus the nett sales at the Philatelic Bureau and Philatelic Sales Counters and through foreign agents to stamp dealers abroad, after deducting stocks remaining unsold on the withdrawal dates. The separate figures given for Presentation Packs and Souvenir Packs are already included in the figures for the numbers sold of the individual values.

The figures supplied by the Post Office for issues after 1975 are to the nearest ten thousand. More detailed figures are not available due to changes in internal accounting.

PRESENTATION PACKS. Packs as issued in this country but sold by Post Office Agencies in Germany or Japan and containing printed cards with text in German or Japanese are noted where they exist.

BLACK PRINTS, UNLISTED PRESENTATION PACKS, ETC. See notes under "Items Excluded" in the Introductory Notes at the beginning of the volume.

SHEET MARKINGS. We give below the various markings found on the sheets of the special stamps. They are helpful in establishing the position of varieties where marginal blocks are available and in identifying the perforator used or the type of machine employed for printing etc.

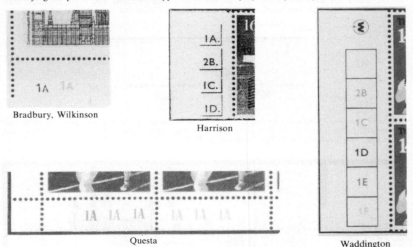

Bradbury, Wilkinson

Harrison

Questa   Waddington

Plate and Cylinder Numbers. In the listing of cylinder number blocks for stamps printed in more than one colour we give the colour of each cylinder number in order, reading downwards. The information is sometimes helpful in connection with varieties and flaws where more than one cylinder has been used for the same colour in combination with others.

Examples from the four printers are as shown. For the row position see under "Sheet Details". Stamps printed in lithography or recess are described as having plate numbers.

Varieties in Cylinder Blocks. Where a cylinder block contains a listed variety the price is adjusted accordingly and bears an asterisk.

3

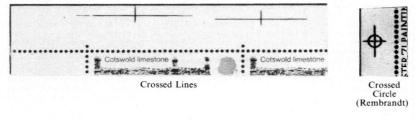

Crossed Lines

Crossed
Circle
(Rembrandt)

"Jumelle" markings:

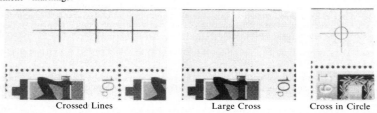

Crossed Lines   Large Cross   Cross in Circle

Colour Register Marks. These are superimposed coloured crosses of very fine lines, one for each colour. The first two types illustrated appear on sheet-fed issues. Reel-fed sheets had no register marks until the "Jumelle" machine was brought into use. Sheets from "Jumelle" bear several superimposed crosses joined together on both panes and an additional larger cross at one side on no dot or dot pane. From the 1977 Racket Sports issue onwards, this cross appeared over a circle in various sizes. The Bradbury, Wilkinson issues are sheet-fed but have no colour register marks.

Coloured Crosses. These serve as trimming lines and so occur on the edges of sheet margins and are usually partly trimmed off. They may appear on both sheet-fed and reel-fed issues but ceased to be used on issues printed by the "Jumelle" machine.

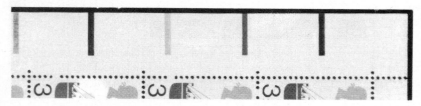

Autotron Marks. These are scanners designed to adjust the registration on a continuous length of paper and operate by temporarily disengaging the offending cylinder from the paper reel in order to adjust small register deviations. This gives rise to missing colour errors found on only three or four rows of stamps, depending upon the size of the stamp.

They therefore occur only on reel-printed stamps on one of the panes only; their first use was on the 2½p. 1972 Christmas stamp which, together with the 3p. 1973 Christmas stamp, were printed on the Wood press. They have the bars arranged vertically in the side margins. On the "Jumelle"-printed vertical format 3p. 1973 British Paintings in sheets of 10 × 10 without gutter, the marks are also vertical in the side margin. All other "Jumelle" printings are in sheets with gutter margins and the marks are horizontal in the side margins on horizontal format issues and vertical in the top margins on vertical format stamps.

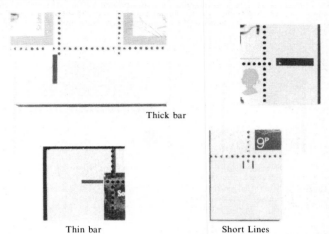

Thick bar

Thin bar   Short Lines

Perforation Register Marks. These were introduced in 1974, generally on issues which have no defined frame lines or where the frame colours bleed off over the perforation holes; they are a means for checking the registration of the perforations. Two types have been used, a thick bar and a smaller thinner bar, placed close to a row of perforations at some point in the sheet. Sometimes the bar adjoins the middle of the stamp but its exact position does not invalidate its effectiveness.

Two short lines, one on either side of the first extension hole in top and bottom margins were introduced in the 1977 Coronation Anniversary issue and were used again on the 1981 British Butterflies and 1983 Commonwealth Day issues.

Quality Control Marks. These were introduced in 1974 for checking the accuracy of the carbon tissue recess process before etching. These vertical bars occur in eight positions on each pane as indicated in the text. Sometimes one or more colours are superimposed over another. Sometimes they occur at the foot of the row instead of the top.

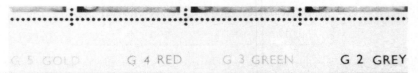

G 5 GOLD   G 4 RED   G 3 GREEN   **G 2 GREY**

Colour Designations. These consist of colour names, usually preceded by a figure and the letter "G" which stands for "Gear". They are usually trimmed off but sometimes appear, complete or in part, on extra wide right-hand margins on issues printed by the "Jumelle" machine. They are to indicate on which side the cylinder should be fitted and aligned with the colour gear in the press. They are not always shown in the colour indicated. Naturally we have only been able to record those we have seen.

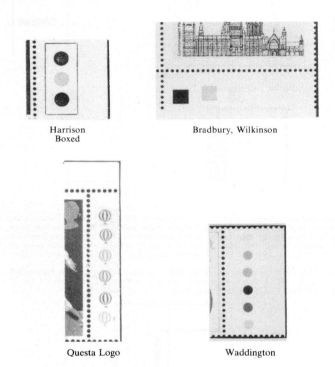

Harrison   Bradbury, Wilkinson
Boxed

Questa Logo   Waddington

"Traffic Lights". This term is used to denote the coloured check dots as a means for checking sheets for missing colours before delivery to the Post Office. They appeared twice on each pane until the 1979 Christmas issue after which they appear once in the side margin. We quote the colours in the order of their appearance reading downwards. Sometimes they are in the same order as the cylinder numbers in which case we state this to save space.

Embossed Head. In some issues in the period 1971–73 the Queen's head was printed in gold and then embossed. This gave rise to missing embossing varieties which are listed, although we do not list misplaced embossing. Provision was made for an embossed dot in the traffic lights, either within or outside the box.

Imprint. Special stamps printed by the House of Questa carry the firm's imprint at the right-hand bottom margin.

Marginal Arrows. These occur in the middle rows of the sheet as an aid to Post Office clerks when breaking up sheets and are printed in the colour of the stamp from the same cylinder.

Marginal Rules. These were discontinued on Special Issues before decimal stamps were introduced.

Perforation Guide Holes. These occur only on reel-fed sheets with the exception of those printed on the "Jumelle" press.

Positioning Lines. These consist of one short and one long line at right angles to indicate the corner of the sheet for trimming purposes. They are not seen complete but these lines may show in between a dot and a no dot pane at both corners of a sheet.

Printer's Logo. Issues printed by Questa and Waddington have the logo in the margin and these are illustrated in the notes for cylinder numbers and "traffic lights". The sheets printed by Harrison did not show a logo until the 1982 Youth Organizations issue. The logo is usually printed in black or other colours if black has not been employed in that particular value.

Sheet numbers. Most sheets are serially numbered in black after printing for checking purposes but the numbers are liable to be placed anywhere in the margins and so are of no use for identifying a position. They are not of much help in establishing whether a sheet occurred early or late in a printing either, as a particular printing was not necessarily numbered from 1 and several machines may have been used.

Total Sheet Values. As an aid to counter clerks in stocktaking and in selling stamps by the sheet, the "TOTAL SHEET VALUE" and amount is printed in the margins, four times in the sheet as described under "Sheet Details".

Harrison logo   Miscut gutter margin
pair ($\frac{3}{4}$ *linear size*)

Miscut Panes. Special issues printed by the "Jumelle" press and issued in double pane sheets of 100 in two panes of 50 (5 × 10 or 10 × 5) with gutter margin are sometimes miscut so that the markings appear transposed, i.e. on the wrong pane. Examples are the 3½p. Royal Wedding, 7p. Sailing, 16p. British Cattle and 28p. Urban Renewal. The Post Office authorities do not regard these as errors and issue them in the ordinary way and we record their existence in footnotes. They are best collected in sheet value inscription gutter margin pairs.

Checkers' Marks. These are small encircled numbers applied with a rubber stamp in a variety of colours. They are applied by Post Office checkers when counting the sheets delivered by the printer. As with sheet numbers they are liable to be placed anywhere in the sheet margins.

DESIGN INDEX

This index gives an easy reference to the inscriptions and designs of the Special Stamps. Where a complete set shares an inscription or type of design, then only the catalogue number of the first stamp is shown. Paintings are indexed under the name of the artist, where this is shown on the stamp.

W197 "A Mountain Road"
(T. P. Flanagan)

W198 "Deer's Meadow"
(Tom Carr)

W199 "Slieve na brock"
(Colin Middleton)
(Layout des. Stuart Rose)

1971 (16 JUNE). "ULSTER '71" PAINTINGS

This issue featuring paintings by contemporary artists living and working in Belfast marks the "Ulster '71" Festival aimed at tourists and industrialists.

Two phosphor bands.

W201 (=S.G.881)	**W197**	3p.	yell-buff, pale yell, Venetian red, blk, bl & drab	10	10
		a.	Phosphor omitted	3·25	
W202 (=S.G.882)	**W198**	7½p.	olive-brown, brownish grey, pale olive-grey, deep blue, cobalt and grey-blue	75	80
		a.	Pale olive-grey omitted*	60·00	
		b.	Phosphor omitted	18·00	
		c.	One broad band	5·00	
W203 (=S.G.883)	**W199**	9p.	greenish yellow, orange, grey, lavender-grey, bistre, black, pale ochre-brown and ochre-brown	75	80
		a.	Orange omitted	£150	
		b.	Phosphor omitted	15·00	
		c.	One broad band	15·00	

First Day Cover (W201/3) .. .. †			1·75
Presentation Pack (W201/3) .. .. 2·75			†
Pack also exists with a German insert card.			

* This only affects the boulder in the foreground, which appears whitish, and it only applied to some stamps in the sheet.

A used example of the 3p. has been seen with the Venetian red omitted.

Cylinder Numbers (Blocks of Six)

Cyl. Nos. (No dot)	Perforation Type A(T)
3p. 2A (black)–1B (yellow-buff)–1C (pale yellow)–2D (blue)–1E (Venetian red)–1F (drab)–P14 (phosphor)..	1·00
7½p. 1A (brownish grey)–1B (cobalt)–2C (deep blue)–1D (grey-blue)–1E (olive-brown)–1F (pale olive-grey)–P18 (phosphor) ..	5·50
9p. 1A (black)–2B (grey)–1C (lavender-grey)–1D (pale ochre-brown)–1E (ochre-brown)–1F (bistre)–1G (greenish yellow)–1H (orange)–P18 (phosphor)	5·50

W   1971.   Literary Anniversaries

Sheet Details

Sheet size: 100 (10 × 10). Single pane sheet-fed (cylinders arranged sideways)
Sheet markings:
Cylinder numbers: Opposite rows 8/9, left margin, boxed
Marginal arrows: At top, bottom and sides
Colour register marks: Crossed circle type opposite rows 1 and 19 at both sides. The 3p. has
  two in each position and the others one
Coloured crosses: 3p. Opposite rows 7/8 at both sides. Others: Opposite rows 6/8 at both sides
Sheet values: Above and below vertical rows 2/4 and 6/8 reading left to right in top margin
  and right to left (upside-down) in bottom margin
Traffic lights (boxed):
3p. Drab, yellow-buff, black, blue, Venetian red, pale yellow opposite rows 8/9 right margin;
  also in same order reading from left to right in top margin above vertical rows 9/10
7½p. Brownish grey, cobalt, deep blue, grey-blue, olive-brown, pale olive-grey opposite rows
  8/10 right margin; also in same order reading from left to right in top margin above
  vertical rows 9/10
9p. Grey, lavender-grey, pale ochre-brown, ochre-brown, black, bistre, greenish yellow, orange
  opposite rows 8/10 right margin; also in same order reading from left to right in top
  margin above vertical rows 9/10

Quantities Sold 3p. 63,214,628; 7½p. 7,868,543; 9p. 5,878,989; Pack 100,257

Withdrawn 15.6.72

W200 John Keats

W201 Thomas Gray

W202 Sir Walter Scott
(Des. Rosalind Dease)
(Printed in photogravure with the Queen's head in gold and then embossed)

1971 (28 JULY). LITERARY ANNIVERSARIES

The 3p. stamp commemorates the 150th Anniversary of the death of the poet John Keats. The 5p. stamp commemorates the Bicentenary of the death of Thomas Gray (poet) and the 7½p. the Bicentenary of the birth of Sir Walter Scott (novelist). All bear their signatures.

Two phosphor bands

W204 (=S.G.884)	**W200**	3p.	black, gold and greyish blue	..	..	..	10	10
		a.	Gold (Queen's head) omitted		..	..	75·00	
		b.	Phosphor omitted ..	..	..	..	2·50	
W205 (=S.G.885)	**W201**	5p.	black, gold and yellow-olive	..	..	..	75	80
		a.	Gold (Queen's head) omitted		..	..	£160	
		b.	Phosphor omitted ..	..	..	..	27·00	
		c.	White nick in hair line	..	..	..	3·50	
W206 (=S.G.886)	**W202**	7½p.	black, gold and yellow-brown	..	..	..	75	80
		a.	Embossing omitted ..	..	..	..	25·00	
		b.	Phosphor omitted ..	..	..	..	17·00	

First Day Cover (W204/6)	..	..	..	..	†	1·60
Presentation Pack (W204/6)	..	..	..	..	2·40	†
Pack also exists with a German or Japanese insert card.						

All values are known on first day covers from the Philatelic Bureau, Edinburgh, bearing the postmark for the "Ulster '71" Paintings issue dated 16 June 1971.

Listed Variety

White nick in line of hair above forehead (R.7/4)

W205*c*

Cylinder Numbers (Blocks of Four)

	Cyl. Nos. (No dot)		Perforation Type A(T)
3p.	1A (greyish blue)–1B (black)–1C (gold)–P13 (phosphor)	..	60
5p.	1A (yellow-olive)–1B (black)–1C (gold)–P13 (phosphor)	..	3·75
7½p.	1A (yellow-brown)–1B (black)–1C (gold)–P13 (phosphor)	..	3·75

Sheet Details

Sheet size: 100 (10 × 10). Single pane sheet-fed

Sheet markings:
Cylinder numbers: Opposite row 9, left margin, boxed
Marginal arrows: 3p. and 7½p. At top, bottom and sides. 5p. None
Colour register marks: Crossed circle type opposite rows 1 and 10 at both sides
Coloured crosses: Opposite rows 6/8 at both sides
Sheet values: Above and below vertical rows 2/4 and 7/9 reading left to right in top margin and right to left (upside down) in bottom margin
Traffic lights (boxed): Opposite rows 9/10 right margin; also in same order reading from left to right in top margin above vertical row 9:
3p. Greyish blue, black, gold and embossing
5p. Yellow-olive, black, gold and embossing
7½p. Yellow-brown, black, gold and embossing

Quantities Sold   3p. 61,635,564; 5p. 9,767,700; 7½p. 7,678,266; Pack 104,724

Withdrawn   27.7.72

W203 Servicemen and Nurse
of 1921

W204 Roman Centurion

W205 Rugby Football, 1871
(Des. Fritz Wegner)

1971 (25 AUGUST).   BRITISH ANNIVERSARIES

This issue commemorates three important anniversaries and the events are described on the stamps.

Two phosphor bands

W207 (=S.G.887)	**W203**	3p. red-orange, grey, deep blue, olive-green, olive-brown, black, rosine and violet-blue	..	..	10	10
		a. Deep blue omitted* ..	..	..	£750	
		b. Red-orange (Nurse's cloak) omitted	..	..	£300	
		c. Olive-brown (Faces, etc.) omitted ..	..	..	£160	
		d. Black omitted	..	..	£10000	
		e. Phosphor omitted ..	..	..	1·25	
		f. One broad band ..	..	..	10·00	
W208 (=S.G.888)	**W204**	7½p. grey, yellow-brown, vermilion, mauve, grey-black, black, silver, pale ochre and ochre	..	..	80	90
		a. Grey omitted	..	..	80·00	
		b. Phosphor omitted ..	..	..	6·50	
		c. One broad band	..	..	8·50	
W209 (=S.G.889)	**W205**	9p. new blue, myrtle-green, grey-black, lemon, olive-brown, magenta and yellow-olive ..	..	..	90	1.00
		a. Olive-brown omitted	..	..	£110	
		b. New blue omitted ..	..	..	£1400	
		c. Myrtle-green omitted	..	..	£1200	
		d. Phosphor omitted	..	..	£500	
		e. One broad band	..	..	9·00	
		f. Rose leaves in very pale green (R.2/9)	..	..	5·50	
		g. White spot under U and diagonal line	..	..	4·50	

First Day Cover (W207/9)	..	..	..	..	†	1·75
Presentation Pack (W207/9) ..	..	..	..	2·75	†
Pack also exists with a German or Japanese insert card.				

*The effect of the missing deep blue is shown on the sailor's uniform which appears as grey. A used example of the 3p. has been seen with the grey omitted.

14

Listed Variety

Large white spot under U of UNION
and coloured diagonal line just to the
right by topmost boot (R.3/8)

W209*g*

Cylinder Numbers (Blocks of Six)

	Cyl. Nos. (No dot)	Perforation Type A(T)

3p. 1A (black)–1B (violet-blue)–1C (olive-brown)–1D (grey)–1E
(red-orange)–1F (rosine)–1G (olive-green)–1H (deep blue)–P21
(phosphor) ..   ..   1·00

7½p. 1A (grey-black)–1B (yellow-brown)–1C (vermilion)–1D (grey)–
1E (ochre)–1F (mauve)–1G (silver)–1H (pale ochre)–1J (black)–
P20 (phosphor)   ..   ..   5·50

9p. 2A (myrtle-green)–1B (yellow-olive)–1C (lemon)–1D (olive-
brown)–1E (new blue)–2F (myrtle-green)–2G (magenta)–P20
(phosphor) ..   ..   6·50

Sheet Details

Sheet size: 100 (10 × 10). Single pane sheet-fed

Sheet markings:

Cylinder numbers: 3p. and 9p. Opposite rows 8/9, left margin boxed. 7½p. Opposite rows 8/10, left margin boxed

Marginal arrows: At top, bottom and sides

Colour register marks: Crossed circle type, twice, opposite rows 1 and 10 at both sides

Coloured crosses: 3p. and 7½p. Opposite rows 6/8 at both sides. 9p. Opposite rows 7/8 at both sides

Sheet values: Above and below vertical rows 2/4 and 7/9 reading left to right in top margin and right to left (upside down) in bottom margin

Traffic lights (boxed): In the same order as the cylinder numbers opposite rows 8/10 (7½p. rows 9/10 only) right margin; also in same order reading from left to right above vertical rows 9/10

Quantities Sold   3p. 55,211,706; 7½p. 7,026,973; 9p. 5,705,637; Pack 94,059

Withdrawn   24.8.72

W206 Physical Sciences Building,
University College of Wales,
Aberystwyth

W207 Faraday Building,
Southampton University

W208 Engineering Department,
Leicester University

W209 Hexagon Restaurant,
Essex University

(Des. Nicholas Jenkins)

1971 (22 SEPTEMBER). BRITISH ARCHITECTURE (UNIVERSITY BUILDINGS)

This continuation of the British Architecture series is devoted to depicting some of our modern University buildings.

Two phosphor bands

W210 (=S.G.890)	**W206**	3p. olive-brown, ochre, lemon, black and yellow-olive	10	10
		a. Lemon omitted £450		
		b. Black (windows) omitted		
		c. Phosphor omitted .. .. 3·75		
		d. One broad band		
W211 (=S.G.891)	**W207**	5p. rose, black, chestnut and lilac	20	25
		a. Phosphor omitted .. .. 55·00		
W212 (=S.G.892)	**W208**	7½p. ochre, black and purple-brown	80	80
		a. Phosphor omitted .. .. 7·00		
W213 (=S.G.893)	**W209**	9p. pale lilac, black, sepia-brown and deep blue ..	1·60	1·75
		a. Phosphor omitted .. .. 16·00		

First Day Cover (W210/13) .. .. †	2·50	
Presentation Pack (W210/13) .. .. 3·50	†	
Pack also exists with a German or Japanese insert card.		

The 3p. is known postmarked at Darlington on 21 September and the complete set on First Day Cover postmarked 25 August 1971, the date of the previous commemorative issue.
No. W210d exists showing a major shift of the lemon colour.

Cylinder Numbers (Blocks of Four)

Cyl. Nos. (No dot) Perforation Type A(T)
3p. 1A (yellow-olive)–1B (ochre)–1C (lemon)–1D (olive-brown)–1E
(black)–P12 (phosphor) 60
5p. 2A (lilac)–1B (chestnut)–1C (rose)–1D (black)–P12 (phosphor) 1·00

7½p. 2A (purple-brown)–1B (ochre)–1C (black)–P12 (phosphor)   ..   4·00
9p. 4A (deep blue)–1B (pale lilac)–3C (sepia-brown)–1D (black)–P12
(phosphor) ..   ..   8·00

Sheet Details

Sheet size: 100 (10 × 10). Single pane sheet-fed

Sheet markings:
  Cylinder numbers: Opposite row 9, left margin, boxed
  Marginal arrows: At top, bottom and sides
  Colour register marks: Crossed circle type
  3p. In corner of top margin and opposite row 10 at both sides with a second partial impression
      in bottom corner at both sides. Others: Opposite rows 1 and 10 at both sides
  Coloured crosses: Opposite rows 7/8 at both sides
  Sheet values: Above and below vertical rows 2/4 and 7/9 reading left to right in top margin
      and right to left (upside down) in bottom margin
  Traffic lights (boxed):
  3p. Yellow-olive, ochre, lemon, olive-brown, black and phosphor opposite rows 8/9 right
      margin; also in same order reading from left to right in top margin above vertical rows
      9/10
  5p. Lilac, chestnut, rose and black with the phosphor printed over it opposite row 9 right
      margin; also in same order reading from left to right in top margin above vertical rows
      9/10
  7½p. Purple-brown, ochre, black and phosphor opposite row 9 right margin; also in same
      order reading from left to right in top margin above vertical row 10
  9p. Deep blue, pale lilac, sepia-brown, black and phosphor opposite rows 8/9 right margin;
      also in same order reading from left to right in top margin above vertical rows 9/10

Quantities Sold   3p. 57,975,114; 5p. 9,843,757; 7½p. 7,640,465; 9p. 5,628,511; Pack 87,159

Withdrawn   21.9.72

1971 (29 SEPTEMBER).   COLLECTORS PACK 1971

WCP4 Comprises Nos. W195/7 and W198/200 (1970 "Philympia" and 1970
    Christmas) and Nos. W201/13 (Sold at £1·15)   35·00
Pack also exists with a German insert card.

Quantity Sold   42,500

Withdrawn   31.3.72

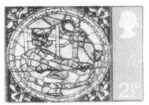

W210 "Dream of the Wise Men"   W211 "Adoration of the Magi"

W212 "Ride of the Magi"
(Des. Clarke-Clements-Hughes design team)
(Printed in photogravure with the Queen's head in gold and then embossed)

1971 (13 OCTOBER). CHRISTMAS

The designs are taken from stained-glass windows in Canterbury Cathedral.
One 4 mm. centre phosphor band (2½p.) or two 9·5 mm. phosphor bands (others)

W214 (=S.G.894)	W210	2½p. new blue, black, lemon, emerald, reddish violet, carmine-red, carmine-rose and gold	..	8	8
		a. Imperforate (pair)		£450	
W215 (=S.G.895)	W211	3p. black, reddish violet, lemon, new blue, carmine-rose, emerald, ultramarine and gold	..	10	10
		a. Gold (Queen's head) omitted		£250	
		b. Carmine-rose omitted		£275	
		c. Lemon omitted		60·00	
		d. New blue omitted		†	—
		e. Embossing omitted		5·00	
		f. Phosphor omitted		1·60	
		g. Embossing and phosphor omitted ..		50·00	
W216 (=S.G.896)	W212	7½p. blk, lilac, lemon, emer, new bl, rose, grn & gold		90	1·00
		a. Gold (Queen's head) omitted		90·00	
		b. Lilac omitted		£500	
		c. Emerald omitted		£190	
		d. Embossing omitted		30·00	
		e. Embossing and phosphor omitted.. ..		20·00	
		f. Embossing double*		30·00	
		g. Phosphor omitted		8·00	
		h. Phosphor omitted but one broad band at back ..		30·00	
		i. One vertical broad band		7·50	
		j. Broad diagonal phosphor band		25·00	
		k. Extra black line on horse's mane		2·50	

First Day Cover (W214/16) .. .. †	2·00
Presentation Pack (W214/16) .. .. .. 3·25 †	
Pack also exists with a German or Japanese insert card.	

*The embossing in the normal position was faint so the sheet was put through the machine again and received a much heavier second embossing misplaced.

The 3p. is known with reddish violet and embossing omitted (used in Llandudno) and with lemon and carmine-rose both omitted (used in Falkirk).

It has been claimed that the 3p. and 7½p. exist on fluorescent coated paper from certain cylinder combinations. We do not recognise this distinction as the so-called fluorescent paper is not as white as that employed for the next issue and two different papers cannot be visually recognised in the Christmas issue.

Listed Variety

Extra horizontal black line in mane of middle horse (Cyl. 1B, R.2/9)

W216*k*

Cylinder Numbers (Blocks of Six)

(a) Double pane, reel-fed

	Cyl. Nos.	Perforation Type A(T)	
		No dot	Dot
2½p.	1A (carmine-red)–2B (black)–1C (lemon)–2D (reddish violet)–1E (new blue)–1F (carmine-rose)–1G (emerald)–1H (gold)–P23 (phosphor)	80	80
	1A (carmine-red)–3B (black)–1C (lemon)–2D (reddish violet)–1E (new blue)–1F (carmine-rose)–1G (emerald)–1H (gold)–P23 (phosphor)	80	80
	1A (carmine-red)–4B (black)–1C (lemon)–2D (reddish violet)–1E (new blue)–1F (carmine-rose)–1G (emerald)–1H (gold)–P23 (phosphor)	80	80
3p.	2A (ultramarine)–7B (black)–2C (new blue)–2D (lemon)–2E (emerald)–2F (carmine-rose)–2G (reddish violet)–3H (gold)–P19 (phosphor)	1·10	1·10

(b) Single pane, sheet-fed

		No dot
3p.	1A (ultramarine)–1B (black)–1C (new blue)–1D (lemon)–1E (emerald)–1F (carmine-rose)–1G (reddish violet)–1H (gold)–P15 (phosphor)	1·00
	1A (ultramarine)–2B (black)–1C (new blue)–1D (lemon)–1E (emerald)–1F (carmine-rose)–1G (reddish violet)–1H (gold)–P15 (phosphor)	1·10
	1A (ultramarine)–3B (black)–1C (new blue)–1D (lemon)–1E (emerald)–1F (carmine-rose)–1G (reddish violet)–1H (gold)–P15 (phosphor)	1·10
	1A (ultramarine)–5B (black)–1C (new blue)–1D (lemon)–1E (emerald)–1F (carmine-rose)–1G (reddish violet)–1H (gold)–P15 (phosphor)	1·10
	1A (ultramarine)–5B (black)–1C (new blue)–1D (lemon)–1E (emerald)–1F (carmine-rose)–3G (reddish violet)–1H (gold)–P15 (phosphor)	30·00
	1A (ultramarine)–8B (black)–1C (new blue)–3D (lemon)–1E (emerald)–1F (carmine-rose)–3G (reddish violet)–1H (gold)–P15 (phosphor)	1·10

7½p. 1A (green)–1B (black)–1C (lemon)–1D (lilac)–1E (rose)–1F
(emerald)–1G (new blue)–1H (gold)–P16 (phosphor) .. .. 6·50
1A (green)–1B (black)–2C (lemon)–1D (lilac)–1E (rose)–1F
(emerald)–1G (new blue)–1H (gold)–P16 (phosphor) .. .. 6·50
2A (green)–1B (black)–2C (lemon)–1D (lilac)–1E (rose)–1F
(emerald)–1G (new blue)–1H (gold)–P16 (phosphor) .. .. 6·50
2A (green)–2B (black)–2C (lemon)–1D (lilac)–1E (rose)–1F
(emerald)–1G (new blue)–1H (gold)–P16 (phosphor) .. .. 6·50
3A (green)–1B (black)–2C (lemon)–1D (lilac)–1E (rose)–1F
(emerald)–1G (new blue)–1H (gold)–P16 (phosphor) .. .. 50·00
3A (green)–2B (black)–2C (lemon)–1D (lilac)–1E (rose)–1F
(emerald)–1G (new blue)–1H (gold)–P16 (phosphor) .. .. 6·50
3A (green)–3B (black)–2C (lemon)–1D (lilac)–1E (rose)–1F
(emerald)–1G (new blue)–1H (gold)–P16 (phosphor) .. .. 15·00
4A (green)–4B (black)–2C (lemon)–1D (lilac)–1E (rose)–1F
(emerald)–1G (new blue)–1H (gold)–P16 (phosphor) .. .. 20·00
4A (green)–4B (black)–2C (lemon)–1D (lilac)–1E (rose)–1F
(emerald)–2G (new blue)–1H (gold)–P16 (phosphor) .. .. 8·00

Single stamps of the 3p. from reel-fed sheets can be distinguished by the gold Queen's head which is slightly smaller than that on the sheet-fed stamps.

It has been reported that some reel-fed sheets were experimentally perforated through top and bottom margins but we do not know whether this applies to both values.

Sheet Details

Sheet size: 100 (10 × 10)
  2½p. and 3p. Double pane reel-fed
  3p. and 7½p. Single pane sheet-fed
Sheet markings:
  Cylinder numbers: Opposite rows 8/9, left margin, boxed
  Guide holes:
    2½p. and 3p. Reel-fed: Opposite row 5 at both sides, boxed (closely trimmed)
    3p. and 7½p. Sheet-fed: None
  Marginal arrows: At top, bottom and sides
  Colour register marks:
    2½p. and 3p. Reel-fed: None
    3p. and 7½p. Sheet-fed: Crossed circle type, twice, opposite rows 1 and 10 at both sides
  Coloured crosses:
    2½p. and 3p. Reel-fed: Opposite rows 2/5 at both sides (closely trimmed)
    3p. and 7½p. Sheet-fed: Opposite rows 6/7 at both sides
  Autotron marks: None
  Sheet values: Above and below vertical rows 2/4 and 7/9 reading from left to right in top margin
    and from right to left (upside down) in bottom margin
  Traffic lights (boxed):
    2½p. Black, carmine-red, lemon, reddish violet, new blue, carmine-rose, emerald, gold and
      embossing opposite rows 8/9 right margin; also in same order reading from left to right
      in top margin above vertical rows 9/10
    3p. Black, new blue, lemon, emerald, carmine-rose, reddish violet, ultramarine, gold and
      embossing opposite rows 8/10 right margin; also in same order reading from left to right
      in top margin above vertical rows 9/10
    7½p. Black, lemon, lilac, rose, emerald, new blue, green, gold and embossing opposite rows
      8/10 right margin; also in same order reading from left to right in top margin above
      vertical rows 9/10

Quantities Sold 2½p. 339,218,365; 3p. 217,033,884; 7½p. 18,777,401; Pack 113,276

Withdrawn 12.10.72

W213 Sir James Clark Ross

W214 Sir Martin Frobisher

W215 Henry Hudson

W216 Captain Scott

(Des. Marjorie Saynor)

(Printed in photogravure with the Queen's head in gold and then embossed)

1972 (16 FEBRUARY). BRITISH POLAR EXPLORERS

Sir James Clark Ross established the North magnetic pole and discovered the sea named after him. Sir Martin Frobisher first entered the Arctic Circle in 1576 in search of a North-West passage. Henry Hudson also searched for the passage and in 1610 discovered the bay named after him. Captain Scott died with his party returning from the South Pole in 1910.

Two phosphor bands

W217 (=S.G.897)	**W213**	3p.	yellow-brown, indigo, slate-black, flesh, lemon, rose, bright blue and gold	8	8
			a. Gold (Queen's head) omitted	60·00	
			b. Slate-black (hair etc.) omitted	£1250	
			c. Lemon omitted		
			d. Embossing omitted	25·00	
			e. Gold (Queen's head) and embossing omitted ..	70·00	
			f. Embossing and phosphor omitted..	20·00	
			g. Phosphor omitted	5·00	
W218 (=S.G.898)	**W214**	5p.	salmon, flesh, purple-brown, ochre, black & gold	20	20
			a. Gold (Queen's head) omitted	90·00	
			b. Gold and phosphor omitted	£110	
			c. Embossing omitted	12·00	
			d. Phosphor omitted	7·00	
			e. Embossing and phosphor omitted		
W219 (=S.G.899)	**W215**	7½p.	reddish violet, blue, deep slate, yellow-brown, buff, black and gold	60	65
			a. Gold (Queen's head) omitted	£200	
			b. Phosphor omitted	16·00	
W220 (=S.G.900)	**W216**	9p.	dull blue, ultramarine, black, greenish yellow, pale pink, rose-red and gold	1·00	1·10
			a. Phosphor omitted	£300	

21

First Day Cover (W217/20) .. .. † 2·00
Presentation Pack (W217/20) .. .. 3·25 †
Pack also exists with a German or Japanese insert
card.

A copy of the 3p. has been seen used on piece with the flesh colour omitted.

In all values there is an extension of the design of about 2 mm. into all four sheet margins. As multipositives comprise more rows of images than are required in the printing cylinders (in order to provide a choice), the extensions into the sheet margins are from the adjoining images.

Cylinder Numbers (Blocks of Four)

	Cyl. Nos. (No dot)	Perforation Type A(T)
3p.	1A (yellow-brown)–1B (flesh)–1C (lemon)–6D (slate-black)–1E (indigo)–2F (rose)–1G (gold)–1J (bright blue)–P24 (phosphor)	50
5p.	2A (black)–1B (ochre)–2C (flesh)–1D (salmon)–1E (purple-brown)–1G (gold)–P24 (phosphor)	1·00
7½p.	1A (deep slate)–1B (reddish violet)–1C (yellow-brown)–1D (buff)–1E (blue)–1F (black)–1G (gold)–P24 (phosphor) ..	3·00
9p.	2A (black)–1B (dull blue)–1C (pale pink)–1D (greenish yellow)–2E (rose-red)–1F (ultramarine)–1G (gold)–P24 (phosphor) ..	5·00

The above are with sheets orientated showing head to left.

Sheet Details

Sheet size: 100 (10 × 10). Single pane sheet-fed

Sheet markings:
 Cylinder numbers: Opposite rows 9/10, left margin, boxed
 Marginal arrows: At top, bottom and sides
 Colour register marks: Crossed circle type, twice, above and below vertical rows 1 and 10
 Coloured crosses: Above and below vertical rows 3/4
 Sheet values: Opposite rows 2/4 and 7/9 reading up at left and down at right
 Traffic lights (boxed): Opposite rows 9/10 right margin; also in same order reading from right to left in top margin above vertical rows 9/10:
  3p. Flesh, yellow-brown, lemon, indigo, slate, rose, bright blue, gold and embossing
  5p. Ochre, flesh, salmon, black, purple-brown, gold and embossing
  7½p. Reddish violet, deep slate, yellow-brown, buff, blue, black, gold and embossing
  9p. Dull blue, pale pink, greenish yellow, rose-red, black, ultramarine, gold and embossing.

Quantities Sold   3p. 53,630,000; 5p. 8,843,000; 7½p. 7,191,000; 9p. 5,488,300; Pack 103,676

Withdrawn 15.2.73

W217 Statuette of Tutankhamun
(Des. Rosalind Dease)

W218 19th-Century Coastguard
(Des. Fritz Wegner)

W219 Ralph Vaughan Williams and Score (Sea Symphony)
(Des. Clive Abbott)
(Printed in photogravure with the Queen's head in gold and then embossed
on 7½p. and 9p.)

1972 (26 APRIL).   GENERAL ANNIVERSARIES

The 3p. commemorates the 50th Anniversary of the discovery of the tomb of Tutankhamun by Howard Carter and Lord Carnarvon. The 7½p. celebrates the 150th Anniversary of the formation of H.M. Coastguard. The 9p. honours the Birth Centenary of the composer Ralph Vaughan Williams.

Two phosphor bands

W221 (=S.G.901)	**W217**	3p.	black, pale grey, gold, dull bistre-brown, blackish brown, pale stone and light brown		8	8
			a. Imperf. between stamp and bottom margin ..		£650	
W222 (=S.G.902)	**W218**	7½p.	pale yell, new bl, slate-bl, vio-bl, slate & gold ..		70	80
			a. Embossing omitted			
			b. Phosphor omitted		£300	
			c. Telescope flaw		3·25	
W223 (=S.G.903)	**W219**	9p.	bistre-brown, black, sage-green, deep slate, yellow-ochre, brown and gold		70	65
			a. Gold (Queen's head) omitted		£550	
			b. Brown (facial features) omitted		£1500	
			c. Deep slate omitted		£7500	
			d. Phosphor omitted		27·00	

First Day Cover (W221/3)	†	2·00
Presentation Pack (W221/3)	3·25	†
Pack also exists with a German or Japanese insert card.		

No. W221*a* was imperforate at base due to a perforation comb misplacement.

23

Listed Variety

W222c Dark spot under lower end of telescope
(No dot, R. 1/5)

Cylinder Numbers (Blocks of Six)

	Cyl. Nos.	Perforation Type A(T)	
		No dot	Dot
3p.	2A (black)–2B (pale grey)–3C (gold)–2E (dull bistre-brown)–2F (blackish brown)–2G (pale stone)–2H (light brown)–P27 (phosphor) ..	80	80
7½p.	1A (pale yellow)–1B (new blue)–1C (slate-blue)–1D (violet-blue)–1E (slate)–2F (gold)–P26 (phosphor)	5·00	†
9p.	1A (bistre-brown)–1B (black)–2C (sage-green)–1D (deep slate)–2E (yellow-ochre)–1F (brown)–1G (gold)–P26 (phosphor) ..	5·00	†

In the 3p. the dot phosphor cylinder number appears on the no dot pane and the no dot phosphor number on the dot pane.

Sheet Details

Sheet size: 100 (10 × 10)
   3p. Double pane reel-fed
   7½p. and 9p. Single pane sheet-fed
Sheet markings:
Cylinder numbers: Opposite rows 8/9, left margin, boxed
Guide holes:
   3p. Opposite row 5 at both sides, boxed (closely trimmed). 7½p. and 9p. None
Marginal arrows: At top, bottom and sides
Colour register marks:
   3p. None
   7½p. Crossed circle type, once, opposite rows 1 and 10 at both sides
   9p. Crossed circle type, twice, opposite rows 1 and 10 at both sides
Coloured crosses:
   3p. Opposite rows 1/5 at both sides
   7½p. Opposite rows 7/8 at both sides
   9p. Opposite rows 6/8 at both sides
Autotron marks: None
Sheet values: Above and below vertical rows 2/4 and 7/9 reading from left to right in top margin and from right to left (upside down) in bottom margin
Traffic lights (boxed):
   3p. Pale stone, pale grey, gold, dull bistre-brown, blackish brown, black, light brown opposite rows 8/9, right margin; also in same order reading from right to left in top margin above vertical rows 9/10
   7½p. Gold, slate, violet-blue, slate-blue, new blue, pale yellow opposite rows 8/9, right margin; also in the same order reading from left to right with the addition of the embossing outside the box, next to the pale yellow, in top margin above vertical rows 9/10
   9p. In the same order as the cylinder numbers with the addition of the embossing, within the box, opposite rows 8/10, right margin; also in the same order reading from left to right, but without the embossing, in top margin above vertical rows 8/9

Quantities Sold   3p. 60,602,200; 7½p. 7,182,300; 9p. 5,468,900; Pack 89,113

Withdrawn   25.4.73

| W220 St. Andrew's, Greensted-juxta-Ongar, Essex | W221 All Saints, Earls Barton, Northants | W222 St. Andrew's, Letheringsett, Norfolk |

W223 St Andrew's,
Helpringham,
Lincs

W224 St. Mary the Virgin,
Huish Episcopi,
Somerset

(Des. Ronald Maddox)
(Printed in photogravure with the Queen's head in gold and then embossed)

1972 (21 JUNE). BRITISH ARCHITECTURE (VILLAGE CHURCHES)
ORIGINAL COATED PAPER

This continuation of the British Architecture series is devoted to village churches in England.
Two phosphor bands

W224 (=S.G.904)	**W220**	3p. violet-blue, black, light yellow-olive, emerald-green, orange-vermilion and gold	8	8
		a. Gold (Queen's head) omitted .. .. .. 75·00		
		b. Gold and phosphor omitted £110		
		c. Embossing and phosphor omitted.. .. .. 10·00		
		d. Embossing omitted .. .. 20·00		
		e. Phosphor omitted .. .. 3·50		
		f. Broken line .. .. 1·00		
W225 (=S.G.905)	**W221**	4p. deep yell-olive, bl, emer, vio-bl, orge-verm & gold	20	20
		a. Gold (Queen's head) and phosphor omitted .. £2500		
		b. Violet-blue omitted £110		
		c. Embossing omitted .. .. 6·00		
		d. Phosphor omitted .. .. 10·00		
		e. White spur on parapet .. .. .. 1·75		

25

W226 (=S.G.906)	W222	5p. deep emerald, black, royal blue, light emerald-green, orange-vermilion and gold	20	25
		a. Gold (Queen's head) and phosphor omitted ..	£150	
		b. Embossing omitted	25·00	
		c. Phosphor omitted	20·00	
W227 (=S.G.907)	W223	7½p. orge-red, blk, dp yell-ol, royal bl, light emer & gold	1·40	1·50
		a. Phosphor omitted	10·00	
		b. Steeple flaw	3·00	
		c. Tower flaw	3·50	
W228 (=S.G.908)	W224	9p. new blue, black, emerald-green, deep yellow-olive, orange-vermilion and gold	1·60	1·75
		a. Embossing omitted	12·00	
		b. Phosphor omitted	16·00	
		c. Gap in tower	3·25	
		d. Tree and bird flaws	3·25	

First Day Cover (W224/8) .. .. † 3·50
Presentation Pack (W224/8) .. .. 5·00 †
Pack also exists with a German or Japanese insert card.

In all values there is an extension of the design of about 2 mm. into all four sheet margins which comes about as explained in the note after Nos. W217/20.

Listed Varieties

W224f
Break in line of boarding
(Cyl. 2A, R. 2/9)

W225d
White spur on parapet
(R. 1/6)

W227b
Black spots under window
in steeple (R. 3/6)

W227c
Extra spot right of lower
window in tower (R. 6/2)

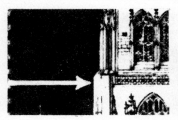

W228c
Gap in vertical shading
on tower (R. 1/6)

W228d
Missing topmost branch on left
tree and smaller bird over right tree
(R. 10/3)

Cylinder Numbers (Blocks of Four)

	Cyl. Nos. (No dot)	Perforation Type A(T)
3p.	2A (violet-blue)–1B (black)–1C (light yellow-olive)–1D (emerald-green)–1E (orange-yellow)–1F (gold)–25 (phosphor) ..	50
	3A (violet-blue)–1B (black)–1C (light yellow-olive)–1D (emerald-green)–1E (orange-yellow)–1F (gold)–25 (phosphor) ..	50
	3A (violet-blue)–1B (black)–1C (light yellow-olive)–1D (emerald-green)–1E (orange-yellow)–1F (gold)–25 (phosphor) ..	*
4p.	1A (deep yellow-olive)–2B (black)–1C (emerald)–1D (violet-blue)–1E (orange-vermilion)–1F (gold)–25 (phosphor)	1·00
5p.	1A (deep emerald)–2B (black)–1C (royal blue)–1D (light yellow-olive)–1E (orange-vermilion)–1F (gold)–25 (phosphor)..	1·00
7½p.	1A (orange-red)–2B (black)–1C (deep yellow-olive)–1D (royal-blue)–1E (light emerald)–1F (gold)–25 (phosphor)	7·00
9p.	1A (new blue)–1B (black)–1C (emerald-green)–1D (deep yellow-olive)–1E (orange-vermilion)–1F (gold)–25 (phosphor).. ..	8·00

*This was fed in reverse producing a cylinder block with left margin imperforate. Probably only a few sheets were affected.
The above are with sheets orientated showing head to left.
Some cylinder blocks of the 3p. from cylinder 3A have the 3 partially and in some cases completely omitted and the same applies to the 1 of cylinder 1D.

Sheet Details

Sheet size: 100 (10 × 10). Single pane sheet-fed
Sheet markings:
Cylinder numbers: Opposite rows 9/10, left margin, boxed
Marginal arrows: At top, bottom and sides
Colour register marks: Crossed circle type, twice, above and below vertical rows 1 and 8/9
Coloured crosses: Above and below vertical rows 3/4
Sheet values: Opposite rows 2/4 and 7/9 reading up at left and down at right
Traffic lights (boxed): All opposite rows 9/10, right margin; also in same order reading from right to left in top margin above vertical rows 9/10:
3p. Black, violet-blue, light yellow-olive, emerald-green, orange-vermilion, gold and embossing
4p. Black, deep yellow-olive, emerald, violet-blue, orange-vermilion, gold und embossing
5p. Black, deep emerald, royal blue, light yellow-olive, orange-vermilion, gold and embossing
7½p. Black, orange-red, deep yellow-olive, royal blue, light emerald, gold and embossing
9p. Black, new blue, emerald-green, deep yellow-olive, orange-vermilion, gold and embossing

Quantities Sold   3p. 53,929,600; 4p. 7,757,400; 5p. 7,834,400; 7½p. 7,065,600; 9p. 5,463,700; Pack
109,512
Withdrawn   20.6.73

1972 (24 JUNE). "BELGICA '72" SOUVENIR PACK

WSP5 Comprises Nos. W214/6 (1971 Christmas) and Nos. W224/8
(Sold at 60p.)   16·00

This pack was specially produced for sale at the "Belgica '72" Stamp Exhibition, held in Brussels between 24 June and 9 July. It contains information on British stamps with a religious theme, with text in English, French and Flemish, and was put on sale at Philatelic Bureaux in Britain on 26 June.

Quantity Sold   20,672

Sold Out   12.72

W225 Microphones, 1924–69   W226 Horn Loudspeaker

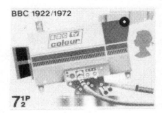

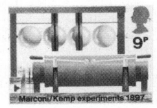

W227 T.V. Camera, 1972   W228 Oscillator and Spark
                                 Transmitter, 1897

(Des. David Gentleman)

1972 (13 SEPTEMBER). BROADCASTING ANNIVERSARIES

The 9p. value commemorates the 75th Anniversary of the first successful radio tests (across the Bristol Channel) conducted by Marconi with the assistance of George Kemp, an engineer seconded by the Post Office. The remaining values celebrate the beginning of daily broadcasting in the U.K. by the British Broadcasting Company in November 1922 from Savoy Hill.

Two phosphor bands

W229 (= S.G.909)	**W225**	3p. grey, pale brn, blk, brownish slate & greenish yell	10	8
		_a._ Greenish yellow (terminals) omitted	£400	
W230 (= S.G.910)	**W226**	5p. brownish slate, black, salmon, lake-brown, red-		
		brown and light brown	20	20
		_a._ Phosphor omitted	3·50	
		_b._ Phosphor bands printed on gum only	30·00	
W231 (= S.G.911)	**W227**	7½p. blk, violet-grey, light grey, mag & brownish slate	95	1·00
		_a._ Brownish slate (Queen's head) omitted*	†	—
		_b._ Phosphor omitted	7·00	
		_c._ One broad band	10·00	
W232 (= S.G.912)	**W228**	9p brownish slate, deep brownish slate, lemon,		
		bluish slate, brown and black ·	95	1·00
		_a._ Brownish slate (Queen's head) omitted	£600	
		_b._ Phosphor omitted ·.	20·00	
		_c._ One broad band	25·00	
		_d._ Phosphor bands printed on gum only	75·00	

First Day Cover (W299/32)	..	..	..	..	†	2·00
Presentation Pack (W229/32)	..	..	..	..	3.25	†
Pack also exists with German or Japanese insert card.						
Special BBC Pack (W229/31)	..	..	..	..	35·00	†

The Special Pack, inscribed "1922–72", was specially produced as a memento of the 50th Anniversary of the BBC. It was presented to BBC staff with the good wishes of the Chairman of the Board of Governors, the Director-General and Board of Management.

* The 7½p. with the brownish slate (Queen's head) omitted has been seen used on a First Day Cover with a Philatelic Bureau, Edinburgh postmark.

Cylinder Numbers (Blocks of Six)

	Cyl. Nos.	Perforation Type A(T)	
		No dot	Dot
3p.	2A (grey)–2B (pale brown)–2C (black)–1D (brownish slate)–1E (greenish yellow)–P31 (phosphor)..	5·50	5·50
	2A (grey)–2B (pale brown)–3C (black)–1D (brownish slate)–1E (greenish yellow)–P31 (phosphor)..	1·00	1·00
5p.	2A (brownish slate)–1B (black)–1C (salmon)–1D (lake-brown)–1E (red-brown)–1F (light brown)–P30 (phosphor) ..	1·50	†
7½p.	2A (black)–2B (violet-grey)–1C (light grey)–1D (magenta)–4E (brownish slate)–P30 (phosphor) ..	6·50	†
9p.	2A (brownish slate)–2B (deep brownish slate)–1C (lemon)–2D (bluish slate)–1E (brown)–1F (black)–P30 (phosphor) ..	6·50	†

Sheet Details

Sheet size: 100 (10 × 10)
   3p. Double pane reel-fed. Others: Single pane sheet-fed

Sheet markings:
   Cylinder numbers: Opposite rows 8/9, left margin, boxed
   Guide holes: 3p. Opposite row 5 at both sides, boxed (closely trimmed). Others: None
   Marginal arrows: At top, bottom and sides
   Colour register marks:
      3p. None. Others: Crossed circle type, once, opposite rows 1 and 10 at both sides
   Coloured crosses: 3p. None. Others: Opposite rows 6/7 at both sides
   Autotron marks: None
   Sheet values: Above and below vertical rows 2/4 and 7/9 reading from left to right in top margin and from right to left (upside down) in bottom margin
   Traffic lights (boxed):
      3p. Pale brown, black, grey, brownish slate, greenish yellow opposite rows 8/9, right margin; also in same order reading from left to right in top margin above vertical row 9
      5p. Black, salmon, lake-brown, red-brown, light brown, brownish slate opposite rows 9/10, right margin; also in same order reading from left to right in top margin above vertical rows 9/10
      7½p. Violet-grey, light grey, magenta, black, brownish slate opposite rows 8/9, right margin; also in same order reading from left to right in top margin above vertical rows 9/10
      9p. Deep brownish slate, lemon, bluish slate, brown, black, brownish slate opposite rows 9/10, right margin; also in same order reading from left to right in top margin above vertical rows 9/10

Quantities Sold   3p. 51,704,000; 5p. 8,201,800; 7½p. 6,632,000; 9p. 5,364,800; Pack 99,453

Withdrawn   12.9.73

W229 Angel holding Trumpet

W230 Angel playing Lute

W231 Angel playing Harp

(Des. Sally Stiff)

(Printed in photogravure and embossed)

1972 (18 OCTOBER).   CHRISTMAS

The designs, based on early Italian paintings of angels, were created by building up pieces of fabric and other material of different textures into a set of reliefs which were then photographed. The outlines of the angels are embossed.

One 4 mm. centre phosphor band (2½p.) or two 9·5 mm. phosphor bands (others)

W233 (=S.G.913)	**W229**	2½p.	cerise, pale reddish brown, yellow-orange, orange-vermilion, lilac, gold, red-brown and deep grey ..	8	8
			a. Gold omitted	£375	
			b. Deep grey omitted		
			c. Embossing omitted	6·00	
			d. Phosphor omitted	7·00	
			e. Left margin imperforate	£275	
			f. Broken ribbon	1·25	
W234 (=S.G.914)	**W230**	3p.	ultramarine, lavender, light greenish blue, bright green, gold, red-brown and bluish violet	8	8
			a. Red-brown omitted	£400	
			b. Bright green omitted	70·00	
			c. Bluish violet omitted	75·00	
			e. Embossing omitted	2·50	
			f. Embossing and phosphor omitted..	6·00	
			g. Phosphor omitted	2·25	
W235 (=S.G.915)	**W231**	7½p.	blackish brown, pale lilac, light cinnamon, ochre, gold, red-brown and slate-purple	40	50
			a. Ochre omitted	55·00	
			b. Embossing omitted	7·50	
			c. Embossing and phosphor omitted..	16·00	
			d. Phosphor omitted	7·00	

First Day Cover (W233/5)	†	1·25
Presentation Pack (W233/5)	2·00	†
Pack also exists with a German or Japanese insert card.		

The gold printing on the 3p. is from two cylinders, 1E and 1F. Examples have been seen with the gold of the 1F cylinder omitted, but these are difficult to detect on single stamps.

Listed Variety

Broken ribbon and scratch across Queen's head
causing deformed lip (Dot, R. 7/8)

W233*f*

Cylinder Numbers (Blocks of Four)

Cyl. Nos.	Perforation Type A(T)	
	No dot	Dot
2½p. 4A (cerise)–1B (pale reddish brown)–1C (yellow-orange)–1D (orange-vermilion)–1E (deep lilac)–1F (gold)–1G (red-brown)–1H (deep grey)–P32 (phosphor)	75	75
3p. 2A (ultramarine)–1B (lavender)–1C (light greenish blue)–1D (bright green)–1E (gold)–1F (gold)–1G (red-brown)–1H (bluish violet)–P35 (phosphor)	1·00	†
2A (ultramarine)–1B (lavender)–1C (light greenish blue)–1D (bright green)–1E (gold)–1F (gold)–2G (red-brown)–1H (bluish violet)–P35 (phosphor)	1·50	†
7½p. 1A (blackish brown)–1B (pale lilac)–1C (light cinnamon)–1D (ochre)–1E (gold)–1F (red-brown)–1G (slate-purple)–P35 (phosphor)	2·00	†

The above are with sheets orientated showing head to left.

Sheet Details

Sheet size: 100 (10 × 10)
2½p. Double pane reel-fed
3p. and 7½p. Single pane sheet-fed
Sheet markings:
Cylinder numbers: Opposite rows 9/10, left margin, boxed
Guide holes:
2½p. Above and below vertical row 6, boxed (closely trimmed). 3p. and 7½p. None
Marginal arrows: At top, bottom and sides
Colour register marks:
2½p. None. 3p. and 7½p. Crossed circle type, twice, above and below vertical rows 1 and 8/9
Coloured crosses:
2½p. Above and below vertical rows 2/4
3p. and 7½p. Above and below vertical rows 3/4
Autotron marks:
2½p. Opposite rows 1/5, right margin, in dot pane: deep grey, red-brown, gold, yellow-orange, orange-vermilion, cerise, deep lilac, pale reddish brown. 3p. and 7½p. None
Sheet values: Opposite rows 2/4 and 7/9 reading up at left and down at right
Traffic lights (boxed): All opposite rows 9/10, right margin; also in same order reading from left to right in top margin above vertical rows 9/10
2½p. Pale reddish brown, yellow-orange, cerise, orange-vermilion, deep lilac, gold, red-brown, deep grey and embossing
3p. Embossing, bluish violet, red-brown, gold, gold, bright green, ultramarine, light greenish blue, lavender
7½p. Embossing, blackish brown, red-brown, gold, slate-purple, ochre, light cinnamon, pale lilac

Quantities Sold   2½p. 323,277,200; 3p. 130,877,400; 7½p. 17,086,600; Pack 105,740

Withdrawn   17.10.73

W232 Queen Elizabeth and
Duke of Edinburgh
(Des. Jeffery Matthews from photograph by Norman Parkinson)

1972 (20 NOVEMBER). ROYAL SILVER WEDDING

In addition to the event commemorated, this issue is notable for the fact that the "Jumelle" press was used for the first time by Harrison's for printing part of the supply of the 3p. value. The 3p. was also the first special issue to have "all-over" phosphor printed on the stamp. "All-over" phosphor (3p.) and without phosphor (20p.)

A. "REMBRANDT" MACHINE

W236 (=S.G.916)	**W232**	3p. brownish black, deep blue and silver	..	..	10	10
		a. Silver (value and inscription) omitted	..	..	£300	
		b. Phosphor omitted	..	..	27·00	
		c. Phosphor on back and front	..	..		
		d. Eyebrow patch	..	..	2·25	
W237 (=S.G.917)	**W232**	20p. brownish black, reddish purple and silver	..	70	70
		a. Scratch under value ..	..	..	4·25	

First Day Cover (W236/7)	.. ..	†	1·25
Presentation Pack (W236/7)	.. .. ..	2·00	†
Pack also exists with a German insert card.			
Presentation Pack (Japanese) (W236/7)	..	4·50	†
Souvenir Book (W236/7) (Sold at 40p.)	.. ..	3·50	†

B. "JUMELLE" MACHINE

W238 (=S.G.918)	**W232**	3p. brownish black, deep blue and silver	..	..	20	25
		a. Horiz. pair with gutter margin	..	..	1·00	
		b. As a but showing traffic lights (row 9)	..	20·00		
		c. As a but showing phos. cyl. P33 (row 10)	..	30·00		

3p. stamps from the "Jumelle" machine can be positively identified when in gutter pairs and all marginal copies can be distinguished by the differences between the perforators used and some also by variations in the marginal markings, such as the coloured rectangles under the bottom row of the "Jumelle" stamps. Stamps from the "Rembrandt" machine were printed horizontally from the right and the phosphor cylinder has a 150 screen. Those from the "Jumelle" machine were printed horizontally from the left and the phosphor has a 250 screen; in these Prince Philip's face has a clearer, harder outline. The "Jumelle" printing is in a lighter shade of brownish black but on its own this is not a reliable test.

It is also known that between the "Jumelle" and Rembrandt printings the Halley press was also brought into use for two days but we know of no means of distinguishing this printing.

The Japanese Presentation Pack has inscriptions in Japanese and was produced for sale in Japan but it was also on sale at the Philatelic Bureau in Edinburgh.

The Souvenir Book is a twelve-page booklet containing photographs of the Royal Wedding and other historical events of the royal family and accompanying information.

Listed Varieties

W236d
White patch by Duke's eyebrow
(R. 9/6)

W237a
Scratch below value to Duke's head
(R. 9/6)

The 20p. variety is cleverly retouched in the corresponding position of the 3p. which also contains the white patch variety

Cylinder Numbers (Blocks of Four)

Cyl. Nos.

Perforation Type A (T)

A. "Rembrandt"

(No dot)

3p. 3A (silver)–1B (deep blue)–11C (brownish black)–P36 (phosphor)   60

20p. 1A (silver)–1B (reddish purple)–11C (brownish black) .. ..   3·50

B. "Jumelle"

                                   A

                        No dot   Dot

3p. 1A (silver)–1B (deep blue)–3C (brownish black)   ..   ..   1·50   1·00

The above are all with sheets orientated showing head to right.

Sheet Details

Sheet size:

"Rembrandt": 100 (10 × 10). Single pane sheet-fed

"Jumelle": 100 (2 panes each 5 × 10, separated by vertical gutter). Double pane reel-fed

Sheet markings:

Cylinder numbers: Opposite row 9, left margin, boxed

Guide holes: None

Marginal arrows: At top, bottom and sides

Colour register marks:

"Rembrandt": Crossed circle type, single, above and below vertical rows 1 and 10

"Jumelle": Crossed lines type, above vertical row 2 and below vertical rows 1/2

Coloured crosses:

"Rembrandt": Above and below vertical rows 7/8. "Jumelle": None

Autotron marks (solid):

"Rembrandt": None. "Jumelle": Oppoite rows 5/6, right margin, on dot pane

Vertical coloured oblongs:

"Rembrandt": None. "Jumelle": In brownish black in bottom margin under all stamps

Mark resembling arrow:

"Jumelle": Pointing left in gutter margin opposite row 6

Sheet values: Opposite rows 2/4 and 7/9 reading up at left and down at right. In the bottom left inscription of the 3p. in both printings "£20.00" was engraved in error but this was partially removed and replaced by "3·00".

Traffic lights:

"Rembrandt": In cylinder block opposite row 10; also in reverse order reading from left to right in top margin over vertical row 10—3p. Silver, deep blue, brownish black; 20p. Silver, reddish purple, brownish black

"Jumelle": In gutter margin in row 9; also in same order reading from left to right in top margin over vertical row 9—3p. Silver, deep blue, brownish black

Phosphor Cylinder number:

"Jumelle": P33 in box, sideways reading down, in gutter margin in row 10, dot pane. (This was added later as not all sheets show it and it was evidently inserted because there was not enough room for it in the upright position in the narrow sheet margins.)

Quantities Sold   3p. (W236 and 238 combined), 59,147,800; 20p. 7,241,300; Pack 140,050; Souvenir Pack 65,425

Withdrawn   19.11.73

1972 (20 NOVEMBER).   COLLECTORS PACK 1972

WCP6 Comprises Nos. W217/37 (Sold at £1·50)   38·00
Pack also exists with a German insert card.

Quantity Sold   33,380

Withdrawn   30.3.73

W233 "Europe"
(Des. Peter Murdoch)

1973 (3 JANUARY).   EUROPEAN COMMUNITIES

This issue marks Britain's entry into the European Communities.
The two 5p. values were issued together in horizontal *se-tenant* pairs throughout the sheet.
Two phosphor bands

W239 (=S.G.919)	**W233**	3p.	dull orge, bright rose-red, ultram, light lilac & blk	10	10
W240 (=S.G.920)	**W233**	5p.	new blue, bright rose-red, ultram, cobalt-bl & blk	25	35
			a. Pair. Nos. W240/1 ..	1·50	1·60
W241 (=S.G.921)	**W233**	5p.	light emerald-green, bright rose-red, ultramarine,		
			cobalt-blue and black	25	35

First Day Cover (W239/41)	†	1·50
Presentation Pack (W239/41)	2·50	†
Pack also exists with a German insert card.		

All values were inadvertently released at a Walthamstow, London, sub-office on 27 December and commercial mail franked with these stamps posted in Wood Green has been seen postmarked 28 December. A Post Office first day cover is reported from Edinburgh postmarked 28 December but not with the Edinburgh Philatelic Bureau "First Day of Issue" cancellation.

Cylinder Numbers (Blocks of Four)

			Perforation Type A(T)	
	Cyl. Nos.		No dot	Dot
3p. 3A (light lilac)–4B (black)–3C (dull orange)–2D (bright rose-red)–2E (ultramarine)–P40 (phosphor)			60	60
5p. 2A (cobalt-blue)–4B (black)–5C (light emerald-green)–2D (bright rose-red)–2E (ultramarine)–3F (new blue)–P40 (phosphor)..			3·50	3·50

The above are with sheets orientated showing head to left.

The 5p. also exists in sheets without extension hole in bottom margin (right-hand margin when sheets orientated with head to left). It is not known whether this is perforator Type F(T) modified or if it is the product of a different perforator. (*Price of cylinder block of four, no dot or dot, £7*).

Cylinder No. 5C on the dot pane of the 5p. has the dot to left of 5.

Sheet Details
Sheet size: 100 (10 × 10). Double pane reel-fed
Sheet markings:
  Cylinder numbers: Opposite rows 9/10, left margin, boxed
  Guide holes: Above and below vertical row 6, boxed (closely trimmed)
  Marginal arrows: At top, bottom and sides
  Colour register marks: None
  Coloured crosses: Above and below vertical rows 1/2
  Autotron marks: None
  Sheet values: Opposite rows 3/4 and 7/9 reading up at left and down at right
  Traffic lights (boxed): Opposite rows 9/10, right margin; also in same order reading from left
    to right in top margin above vertical rows 9/10
  3p. Black, light lilac, dull orange, bright rose-red, ultramine
  5p. Black, cobalt-blue, light emerald green, bright rose-red, ultramarine, new blue

Quantities Sold 3p. 54,812,900; 5p. (both together), 11,868,500; Pack 105,850

Withdrawn 2.1.74

W234 Oak Tree (*Quercus robur*)
(Des. David Gentleman)

1973 (28 FEBRUARY). TREE PLANTING YEAR

This stamp was issued as a contribution to Tree Planting Year 1973 and also as the first of
an occasional series of British Trees. A stamp depicting a Horse Chestnut tree was issued on
27 February 1974 but no other tree stamps have appeared in this series.
Two phosphor bands

W242 (= S.G.922) **W234**   9p. brownish black, apple-green, deep olive, sepia,
                                     blackish green and brownish grey   35   30
                               a. Brownish black (value and inscr.) omitted   ..   £550
                               b. Brownish grey (Queen's head) and phosphor omit-
                                     ted £400
                               c. Phosphor omitted £100
                               d. One broad band   ..   ..   18·00
                               e. Broken k in Oak   ..   ..   3·75

First Day Cover (W242)	†	70
Presentation Pack (W242)	2·50	†
Pack also exists with a German insert card.		

Listed Variety

Broken left leg of k (R. 9/2)

W242*e*

35

W 1973. British Explorers

Cylinder Numbers (Blocks of Six)

Cyl. Nos. (No dot)   Perforation Type A(T)
9p. 1A (brownish black–1B (apple-green)–1C (deep olive)–1D
(sepia)–1E (blackish green)–1F (brownish grey)–P41 (phosphor)   6·50*

Sheet Details
Sheet size: 100 (10 × 10). Single pane sheet-fed
Sheet markings:
  Cylinder numbers: Opposite rows 7/9, left margin, boxed
  Marginal arrows: At top, bottom and sides
  Colour register marks: Crossed circle type, twice, opposite rows 1 and 10 at both sides
  Coloured crosses: Opposite rows 7/8 at both sides
  Traffic lights (boxed); Opposite rows 9/10, right margin; also in same order reading from right
    to left in top margin above vertical row 10 in brownish black, apple-green, sepia, deep olive,
    blackish green and brownish grey

Quantities Sold   9p. 5,875,100; Pack 96,722

Withdrawn   17.2.74

W235 David Livingstone   **W236** H. M. Stanley
The above were printed horizontally *se-tenant* within the sheet

W237 Francis Drake   **W238** Walter Raleigh   **W239** Charles Sturt
                              (Des. Marjorie Saynor)
(Printed in photogravure with the Queen's head in gold and then embossed)

1973 (18 APRIL).   BRITISH EXPLORERS

Following the stamps commemorating British Polar Explorers issued in 1972, also designed by Marjorie Saynor, the *se-tenant* 3p. values appropriately depict Dr. David Livingstone who discovered the Victoria Falls and Sir Henry Morton Stanley, who went in search of Dr. Livingstone and found him at Ujiji. Sir Francis Drake was the first Englishman to circumnavigate the world; Sir Walter Raleigh is noted for his expeditions to the West Indies and North America and his expedition to the Orinoco; while Charles Sturt led many expeditions in Australia, discovering and opening up many rivers for water communication.

"All-over" phosphor

W243 (=S.G.923) **W235**	3p.	orange-yellow, light orange-brown, grey-black, light turquoise-blue, turquoise-blue and gold	..	25	20
	a.	Pair. Nos. W243/4 ..	.. .. ..	1·60	1·90
	b.	Gold (Queen's head) omitted	.. .. ..	32·00	
	c.	Gold and phosphor omitted	.. ..	35·00	
	d.	Turquoise-blue (background & inscr.) omitted	..	£450	
	e.	Light orange-brown omitted	.. .. ..	£350	
	f.	Embossing and phosphor omitted..	.. ..	25·00	
	g.	Embossing omitted ..	.. .. ..	20·00	
	h.	Phosphor omitted ..	.. .. ..	22·00	
	i.	Shirt variety ..	.. ..	1·50	
W244 (=S.G.924) **W236**	3p.	orange-yellow, light orange-brown, grey-black, light turquoise-blue, turquoise-blue and gold	..	25	20
	b.	Gold (Queen's head) omitted	.. .. ..	32·00	
	c.	Gold and phosphor omitted	.. ..	35·00	
	d.	Turquoise-blue (background & inscr.) omitted	..	£450	
	e.	Light orange-brown omitted	.. .. ..	£350	
	f.	Embossing and phosphor omitted..	.. ..	25·00	
	g.	Embossing omitted ..	.. .. ..	20·00	
	h.	Phosphor omitted ..	.. .. ..	22·00	
W245 (=S.G.925) **W237**	5p.	light flesh, chrome-yellow, orange-yellow, sepia, brownish grey, grey-black, violet-blue and gold ..		30	30
	a.	Gold (Queen's head) omitted	.. .. ..	90·00	
	b.	Grey-black omitted ..	.. .. ..	£550	
	c.	Sepia omitted	.. ..	£450	
	d.	Embossing and phosphor omitted..	.. ..	27·00	
	e.	Embossing omitted ..	.. .. ..	6·50	
	f.	Phosphor omitted ..	.. .. ..	7·00	
	g.	Grey-black and phosphor omitted..	.. ..	£550	
W246 (=S.G.926) **W238**	7½p.	light flesh, reddish brown, sepia, ultramarine, grey-black, bright lilac and gold	.. .. ..	35	30
	a.	Gold (Queen's head) omitted	.. ..		
	b.	Ultramine (eyes) omitted ..	.. .. ..	—	£350
	c.	Phosphor omitted ..	.. .. ..	£200	
W247 (=S.G.927) **W239**	9p.	flesh, pale stone, grey-blue, grey-black, brown-grey, Venetian red, brown-red and gold ..	..	40	40
	a.	Gold (Queen's head) omitted	.. .. ..	90·00	
	b.	Brown-grey double*	.. .. .. *from*	£100	
	c.	Grey-black omitted ..	.. .. ..	£275	
	d.	Embossing omitted ..	.. .. ..	22·00	
	e.	Phosphor omitted ..	.. .. ..	27·00	

First Day Cover (W243/7)	.. ..	† 2·50
Presentation Pack (W243/7)	.. .. ..	4·00 †
Pack also exists with a German insert card.		

3p. *Prices for major errors in pairs*

Gold	.. ..	70·00
Gold and phosphor	.. ..	75·00
Turquoise-blue	.. ..	£1000
Light orange-brown	.. ..	£850
Embossing and phosphor omitted	.. ..	55·00
Embossing omitted	.. ..	45·00
Phosphor omitted	.. ..	50·00

*The double printing of the brown-grey (cylinder 1F) on the 9p. is a most unusual type of error to occur in a multicoloured photogravure issue. Two sheets are known and it is believed that they stuck to the cylinder and went through a second time. This would result in the following two sheets missing the colour but at the time of going to press this error has not been reported.

The second print is slightly askew and more prominent in the top half of the sheets. Examples from the upper part of the sheet showing a clear double impression of the facial features are worth a substantial premium over the price quoted.

Caution is needed when buying missing gold heads in this issue as they can be removed by using a hard eraser, etc., but this invariably affects the "all-over" phosphor. Genuine copies have the phosphor intact. Used copies off cover cannot be distinguished as much of the phosphor is lost in the course of floating.

In the 5p. value the missing grey-black affects the doublet, which apears as brownish grey, and the lace ruff design, which is entirely missing. The missing sepia only affects Drake's hair, which appears much lighter.

As with the previous explorers issue all values have an extension of the design of about 2 mm. into all four sheet margins. See note after Nos. W217/20.

Listed Variety

Line down left of shirt is
missing or very weak
(R. 3/7)

W243*i*

Cylinder Numbers (Blocks of Four)

	Cyl. Nos. (No dot)	Perforation Type A(T)
3p.	1A (grey-black)–2B (pale turquoise-blue)–1C (orange-yellow)–1D (light orange-brown)–2E (turquoise-blue)–2F (gold)–P36 (phosphor)	4·00
	1A (grey-black)–2B (pale turquoise-blue)–1C (orange-yellow)–1D (light orange-brown)–2E (turquoise-blue)–2F (gold)–P46 (phosphor)	4·50
5p.	1A (grey-black)–1B (violet-blue)–1C (brownish grey)–1D (light flesh)–1E (orange-yellow)–1F (sepia)–1G (chrome-yellow)–1H (gold)–P36 (phosphor)	1·50
7½p.	3A (grey-black)–1B (bright lilac)–1C (light flesh)–1D (sepia)–1E (ultramarine)–1F (reddish brown)–1H (gold)–P36 (phosphor)..	1·75
9p.	1A (grey-black)–1C (Venetian red)–1C (brown-red)–1D (flesh)–1E (pale stone)–1F (brown-grey)–1G (grey-blue)–1H (gold)–P36 (phosphor)	2·00

The above are with sheets orientated showing head to left.

Sheet Details

Sheet size: 100 (10 × 10). Single pane sheet-fed

Sheet markings:
    Cylinder numbers: Opposite rows 9/10, left margin, boxed
    Marginal arrows: At top, bottom and sides
    Colour register marks: Crossed circle type, twice, above and below vertical rows 1 and 10
    Coloured crosses: Above and below vertical rows 3/4
    Sheet values: Opposite rows 3/5 and 7/9 reading up at left and down at right
    Traffic lights (boxed): Opposite rows 9/10, right margin; also in same order reading from right to left in top margin above vertical rows 8/10:
        3p. Pale turquoise-blue, orange-yellow, light orange-brown, turquoise-blue, grey-black, gold and embossing
        5p. Embossing, gold, chrome-yellow, grey-black, sepia, orange-yellow, light flesh, brownish grey, violet-blue
        7½p. Embossing, gold, reddish brown, grey-black, ultramarine, sepia, light flesh, bright lilac
        9p. Embossing, gold, grey-blue, grey-black, brown-grey, pale stone, flesh, brown-red, Venetian red

Quantities Sold   3p. 56,262,800; 5p. 8,502,300; 7½p. 6,572,700; 9p. 5,229,900; Pack 102,950

Withdrawn   17.4.74

W240   W241   W242

Sketches of W. G. Grace by Harry Furniss
(Des. Edward Ripley)
(Printed in photogravure with the Queen's head in gold and then embossed)

1973 (16 MAY).   COUNTY CRICKET 1873–1973

This issue marks the Centenary of meetings in 1872/3 of delegates from first-class cricketing counties (in which W.G. Grace participated) to formulate the rules which established that a cricketer could only play for one county in any season which could be that of his birth, his family home or his residence for two years. The designs are taken from a series of a hundred sketches by Harry Furniss entitled "A Century of Grace".

"All-over" phosphor

W248 (=S.G.928)	**W240**	3p. black, ochre and gold	8	8
		a. Gold (Queen's head) omitted £2500		
		b. Embossing omitted .. .. 7·00		
		c. Broken 7 in 1973 .. .. 2·00		
		d. Short i in Cricket .. .. 2·25		
		e. Broken c in Cricket .. .. 2·25		
W249 (=S.G.929)	**W241**	7½p. black, light sage-green and gold .. .. .. 1·25	1·40	
		a. Embossing omitted .. .. 16·00		
		b. Phosphor omitted .. .. 80·00		
		c. Broken 7 in 1973 .. .. 3·00		
		d. Spot on shirt.. .. .. 3·25		
		e. Break in hat and streak behind eye .. .. 4·00		
W250 (=S.G.930)	**W242**	9p. black, cobalt and gold .. .. .. 1·25	1·40	
		a. Embossing omitted .. .. 50·00		
		c. Broken 7 in 1973 .. .. 3·00		

First Day Cover (W248/50)	†	2·50
Presentation Pack (W248/50)	3·50	†
Pack also exists with a German insert card.		
Souvenir Book (W248/50) (Sold at 60p)	8·00	†
PHQ Card (W248)	60·00	£150

The souvenir book is a 24-page illustrated booklet containing a history of County Cricket with text by John Arlott.

The PHQ Card was not issued until July 1973.

Listed Varieties

W248/50c   W248d   W248e
Break in 7 of 1973   Short i   Broken c
(No dot, R. 4/9)   (No dot, R. 1/3)   (No dot, R. 10/7)

W249*d*	W249*e*
Black spot on shirt above belt (Dot and no dot, R. 9/1)	Break in hat outline and streak of white behind eye (No dot, R. 5/10)

Cylinder Numbers (Blocks of Six)

Cyl. Nos.	Perforation Type A(T)	
	No dot	Dot
3p. 2A (ochre)–1B (black)–1C (gold)–P48 (phosphor)	80	80
7½p. 2A (light sage-green)–1B (black)–1C (gold)–P48 (phosphor) ..	11·00*	11·00*
9p. 1A (cobalt)–1B (black)–1C (gold)–P48 (phosphor)	9·00	9·00

The above are with sheets orientated with head to left.

Printed on the "Jumelle" machine.

Sheet Details

Sheet size: 100 (10 × 10). Double pane reel-fed

Sheet markings:
Cylinder numbers: Opposite row 9, left margin, boxed
Guide holes: Above and below vertical row 6, boxed
Marginal arrows: At top, bottom and sides
Colour register marks: Crossed lines type, above and below vertical row 1
Coloured crosses: None
Autotron marks: Opposite rows 5/6, right margin on no dot panes:
3p. gold, ochre, black; 7½p. gold, light sage-green, black; 9p. gold, cobalt, black
Sheet values: Opposite rows 3/5 and 7/9 reading up at left and down at right
Traffic lights (boxed): Opposite rows 9/10, right margin; also in same order reading from left
to right in top margin above vertical rows 9/10:
3p. Ochre, black, gold and embossing
7½p. Light sage-green, black, gold and embossing
9p. Cobalt, black, gold and embossing

Quantities Sold   3p. 45,861,200; 7½p. 6,657,900; 9p. 5,289,600; Pack 97,870; Souvenir Pack 28,576

Withdrawn   15.5.74

W243 "Self-portrait"
(Reynolds)

W244 "Self-portrait"
(Raeburn)

W245 "Nelly O'Brien"
(Reynolds)

W246 "Rev. R. Walker (The
Skater)" (Raeburn)

(Des. Stuart Rose)
(Printed in photogravure with the Queen's head in gold and then embossed)

1973 (4 JULY).   BRITISH PAINTINGS

The 3p. and 7½p. commemorate the 250th Anniversary of the birth of Sir Joshua Reynolds, founder and first president of the Royal Academy; the others mark the 150th Anniversary of the death of Sir Henry Raeburn, the eminent Scottish portrait painter.

"All-over" phosphor

W251 (=S.G.931)	W243	3p. rose, new blue, jet-black, magenta, greenish yellow, black, ochre and gold	.. ..	8	8
		a. Gold (Queen's head) omitted	.. ..	60·00	
		b. Gold and embossing omitted	.. ..	65·00	
W252 (=S.G.932)	W244	5p. cinnamon, greenish yellow, new blue, light magenta, black, yellow-olive and gold	.. ..	20	25
		a. Gold (Queen's head omitted)	.. ..	75·00	
		b. Greenish yellow omitted	.. .. ..	£350	
		c. Phosphor omitted	.. ..	11·00	
W253 (=S.G.933)	W245	7½p. greenish yellow, new blue, light magenta, black, cinnamon and gold ..	.. .. ..	60	70
		a. Gold (Queen's head) omitted	.. ..	75·00	
		b. Cinnamon omitted ..	.. .. ..	£700	
		c. Embossing omitted ..	.. .. ..	12·00	
		d. Phosphor omitted ..	.. .. ..	7·00	
W254 (=S.G.934)	W246	9p. brownish rose, black, dull rose, pale yellow, brownish grey, pale blue and gold	.. ..	80	90
		a. Brownish rose omitted*	.. .. ..	30·00	
		b. Embossing and phosphor omitted..	.. ..	£100	
		c. Phosphor omitted ..	.. .. ..	90·00	

41

First Day Cover (W251/4)	..	..	..	..	†	1·90
Presentation Pack (W251/4)	..	..	..	..	2·40	†
Pack also exists with a German insert card.						

*This only affects the face which is paler.

Examples of No. W251a also exist with the embossing misplaced.

Yellow Phosphor In 1973 the violet phosphor became contaminated with an inorganic phosphor based on zinc sulphide of a type used by certain overseas postal administrations. This was a weak mixture which had no effect on the normal reaction of the letter facing machinery. It is possible that the whole printing of the 7½p. and 9p. values had this mixture but it has not been seen on the 5p. The yellow phosphor reacts after irradiation by longwave ultra violet light at 3650 Ångstroms and is distinct from the violet phosphor which only responds briefly to shortwave UV light. Examination should take place in darkness after allowing some minutes for the eyes to adjust to the dark. Irradiation should take place with the eyes closed and then opened after the lamp has been switched off when the phosphorescence should be visible for a period of up to 15 seconds. This longwave reaction can be seen using a shortwave lamp if the stamp is covered by a piece of plastic (such as the transparent material from a Hawid strip) to absorb and eliminate the shortwave UV light.

Cylinder Numbers (Blocks of Six)

	Cyl. Nos.	Perforation Type A(T)	
		No dot	Dot
3p.	3A (black)–1B (greenish yellow)–1C (rose)–3D (magenta)–2E (new blue)–1F (ochre)–1G (gold)–3J (jet-black)–P49 (phosphor)	80	80
5p.	1A (black)–1B (gold)–1D (greenish yellow)–1E (cinnamon)–1F (light magenta)–1G (new blue)–1H (yellow-olive)–P46 (phosphor) ..	1·50	†
7½p.	1A (black)–2B (gold)–1D (greenish yellow)–1E (cinnamon)–1F (light magenta)–1G (new blue)–P46 (phosphor)..	4·25	†
9p.	2A (black)–2B (gold)–1D (pale yellow)–1E (pale blue)–1F (dull rose)–1G (brownish rose)–1H (brownish grey)–P46 (phosphor)	5·50	†

The above are with sheets orientated with head to left.

The 3p. was printed on the "Jumelle" machine.

Sheet Details

Sheet size: 100 (10 × 10)

3p. Double pane reel-fed. Others: Single pane sheet-fed

Sheet markings:

Cylinder numbers: 3p. Opposite rows 8/10; others, rows 9/10, left margin, boxed

Guide holes: 3p. Above and below vertical row 5, boxed. Others: None

Marginal arrows: At top, bottom and sides

Colour register marks:

3p. None. Others: Crossed circle type, twice, above and below vertical rows 1 and 8/9

Coloured crosses: 3p. Above and below vertical rows 2/5. Others: None

Autotron marks:

3p. Opposite rows 1/5, right margin on dot panes: gold, ochre, new blue, black, jet-black, magenta, rose, greenish yellow. Others: None

Sheet values:

3p. Opposite rows 3/5 at both sides and rows 7/8 at left and 7/9 at right, reading up at left and down at right. Others opposite rows 3/5 and 7/9 at both sides

Traffic lights (boxed):

3p. Opposite rows 9/10, right margin; also in same order reading from left to right above vertical rows 8/10. Others: In same position except that they are above vertical rows 9/10

3p. Greenish yellow, rose, magenta, black, new blue, ochre, gold, embossing, jet-black.

5p. Yellow-olive, black, new blue, light magenta, cinnamon, greenish yellow, gold and embossing

7½p. Black, new blue, light magenta, cinnamon, greenish yellow, gold, and embossing

9p. Black, brownish grey, brownish rose, dull rose, pale blue, pale yellow, gold and embossing

Quantities Sold 3p. 52,330,100; 5p. 8,372,500; 7½p. 6,674,200; 9p. 5,306,500; Pack 104,830

Withdrawn 3.7.74

W247 Court Masque
Costumes

W248 St. Paul's Church,
Covent Garden

W249 Prince's Lodging,
Newmarket

W250 Court Masque
Stage Scene

Types **W247/8** and **W249/50** were printed horizontally *se-tenant* within the sheet
(Des. Rosalind Dease)
(Printed by lithography and typography by Bradbury, Wilkinson)

1973 (15 AUGUST). INIGO JONES

This issue honours the 400th Birth Anniversary of Inigo Jones. His most celebrated architectural work is St. Paul's Church, Covent Garden, which was commissioned to be built cheaply and no better than a glorified barn. The Prince's Lodging, Newmarket, demolished in the 1660s. Inigo Jones was also a great innovator in stage design and the costumes and stage scene are from his original designs for Ben Johnson's masque, "Oberon and the Faery Prince".

"All-over" phosphor

W255 (= S.G.935)	**W247**	3p. deep mauve, black and gold	..	..	..	10	15
		a. Pair. Nos. W255/6 ..	..	..	..	35	40
		b. Phosphor omitted ..	..	..	..	£250	
		c. 9 mm phosphor band*	..	..	..	10·00	
W256 (= S.G.936)	**W248**	3p. deep brown, black and gold	..	..	..	10	15
		b. Phosphor omitted ..	..	..	..	£250	
W257 (= S.G.937)	**W249**	5p. blue, black and gold	..	..	..	40	45
		a. Pair. Nos. W257/8 ..	..	..	..	2·40	2·40
		b. Phosphor omitted ..	..	..	..	£225	
		c. 9 mm phosphor band*	..	..	..	20·00	
		d. Missing serif to n ..	..	..	..	2·50	
W258 (= S.G.938)	**W250**	5p. grey-olive, black and gold ..	..	..	..	40	45
		b. Phosphor omitted ..	..	..	..	£225	

First Day Cover (W255/8)	..	..	..	†	2·50
Presentation Pack (W255/8)	..	..	..	2·75	†
Pack also exists with a German insert card.					
PHQ Card (W256)	..	..	..	..	£140	70·00

*On part of the printing of both values the "all-over" phosphor missed the first vertical row and a 9 mm. phosphor band was applied to correct this. The cylinder combinations affected were 1-1-1-2 and 1-1-2-2 3p., and 1A (×4) 5p.

A 24 mm. misplacement of the black cylinder resulted in several copies of the 3p. having the inscription "Inigo Jones 1572–1652" at the foot of the stamp. The stamps in the top row of the sheet had no denomination and showed parts of the top margin sheet value inscription.

Listed Variety

W257*d*

5p. Newmarket. Missing right serif to left leg of n in designer (Black cyl. 1A, R. 9/1)

Note. The right serif to right leg of n is omitted on all stamps in the sheet on the 3p. Court Masque Costumes stamp.

Cylinder Numbers (Blocks of Four)

	Cyl. Nos. (No dot)		Perforation Type G(L)
3p.	1 (deep mauve)–1 (deep brown)–1 (gold)–2 (black)	.. ..	1·00
	1A (deep mauve)–1A (deep brown)–1A (gold)–2A (black)	..	1·50
	1 (deep mauve)–1 (deep brown)–2 (gold)–2 (black)	.. ..	7·50
	1A (deep mauve)–1A (deep brown)–2A (gold)–2A (black)	..	7·50
5p.	1 (blue)–1 (grey-olive)–1 (gold)–1A (black)	.. .. ..	7·00*
	1A (blue)–1A (grey-olive)–1A (gold)–1A (black)	.. ..	8·50*

Sheet Details

Sheet size: 100 (10 × 10). Double pane sheet-fed (Cyls. 1 and 1A side by side)

Sheet markings:
Cylinder numbers: Bottom margin below vertical row 1
Marginal arrows: At top, bottom and sides
Colour register marks: None
Coloured crosses: Single crosses, all in black, above and below vertical rows 4/5 and 6/7 and at rows 4/5 and 6/7 at both sides
Sheet values: Above and below vertical rows 3 and 8 reading from left to right in top margin and from right to left (upside down) in bottom margin
Traffic lights (square, unboxed): Bottom margin below vertical row 2:
  3p. Deep mauve, deep brown, gold, black
  5p. Blue, grey-olive, gold, black

Quantities Sold 3p. 21,296,500 pairs; 5p. 5,337,300 pairs; Pack 99,320

Withdrawn 14.8.74

W251 Palace of Westminster
seen from Whitehall

W252 Palace of Westminster
seen from Millbank

(Des. Richard Downer)
(Recess printed and typographed by Bradbury, Wilkinson)

1973 (12 SEPTEMBER). COMMONWEALTH PARLIAMENTARY CONFERENCE

The 19th Annual Conference of the Commonwealth Parliamentary Association was held in London. Great Britain was last host to the Conference in September 1961 when two stamps were issued. In 1973 it had a membership of 93 Commonwealth legislatures.

"All-over" phosphor

W259 (=S.G.939)	**W251**	8p.	black, brownish grey and stone	..	..	..	30	30
W260 (=S.G.940)	**W252**	10p.	gold and black	..	..	..	40	40

First Day Cover (W259/60)	†	1·25
Presentation Pack (W259/60)	2·00	†
Pack also exists with a German insert card.		
Souvenir Book (W259/60) (Sold at 60p.)	9·00	†
PHQ Card (W259)	42·00	90·00

The souvenir book is a 24-page booklet containing a history of the Palace of Westminster.

Cylinder Numbers (Blocks of Four)

	Cyl. Nos. (No dot)	Perforation Type G(L)
8p.	1 (black)–1 (brownish grey)–1 (stone)	1·50
	1A (black)–1A (brownish grey)–1A (stone)	4·00
	2 (black)–1 (brownish grey)–1 (stone)	2·00
	2A (black)–1A (brownish grey)–1A (stone)	4·00
10p.	1 (gold)–1 (black)	4·00
	1A (gold)–1A (black)	2·00
	2 (gold)–1 (black)	4·00
	2A (gold)–1A (black)	4·00

Sheet Details

Sheet size: 100 (10 × 10). Double pane sheet-fed (Cyls. 1 and 1A etc. side by side)

Sheet markings:
Cylinder numbers: Bottom margin below vertical row 1
Marginal arrows: At top, bottom and sides
Colour registration marks: None
Coloured crosses: Above or below vertical rows 1 and 10
Sheet values: Above and below vertical rows 3 and 8 reading from left to right in top margin and from right to left (upside down) in bottom margin
Traffic lights (square, unboxed): Bottom margin below vertical row 2:
  8p. Black, brownish grey, stone
  10p. Gold, black

Quantities Sold 8p. 7,461,100; 10p. 6,481,500; Pack 86,010; Souvenir Pack 17,920

Withdrawn 11.9.74

W253 Princess Anne and Capt. Mark Phillips
(Des. Collis Clements and Edward Hughes)
(Printed in photogravure with the Queen's head in silver and then embossed)

1973 (14 NOVEMBER).   ROYAL WEDDING

The design for this Royal Wedding issue was taken from a photograph by Lord Lichfield, cousin to the Queen. This was the first special issue to be printed as well as rotary perforated by the "Jumelle" press in the now characteristic double-pane Post Office sheets.

"All-over" phosphor

W261 (=S.G.941)	W253	3½p. dull violet and silver	..	..	..	..	10	10
		a. Imperforate (pair)* ..	..	..	..	..	£900	
		b. Phosphor omitted	..	..	..	..	80·00	
		c. Eye retouch ..	..	..	..	..	2·25	
W262 (=S.G.942)	W253	20p. deep brown and silver	..	..	..	..	75	75
		a. Silver omitted†	..	..	..	..	£900	

First Day Cover (W261/2)	..	..	..	..	†	1·25
Presentation Pack (W261/2)	..	..	..	2·00	†	
Pack also exists with a German insert card.						
PHQ Card (W261)	..	..	..	..	12·00	22·00

*This comes from a sheet having the bottom row completely imperforate thus producing only five imperforate pairs.

†This affected the third row of a pane (ten copies) and although the silver was completely missing, it was probably due to a dry print.

Miscut Pane. Part of the printing of the 3½p. had the sheets miscut so that the bottom pane appeared at the top and vice versa. See under General Notes, page 7. (*Price for gutter pair showing sheet margin inscription* £20.)

Listed Variety

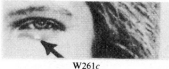

Retouch under Princess Anne's left eye
(No dot, R. 2/4)

W261c

Cylinder Numbers (Blocks of Four)

	Perforation	Type R*
Cyl. Nos.	No dot	Dot
3½p. 4A (dull violet)–2B (silver)–1C (embossing)–P5(0) (phosphor, on no dot only)	60	60
4A (dull violet)–2B (silver)–1C (embossing)	5·50	†
20p. 3A (deep brown)–2B (silver)–1C (embossing)–P5(0) (phosphor, on no dot only)	3·75	3·75

On the dot pane of the 20p. the dot is missing after 3A.

Sheet Details

Sheet size: 100 (2 panes 10 × 5). Double pane reel-fed

Sheet markings:
Cylinder numbers: Opposite rows 9/10, left margin, boxed
Marginal arrows: In centre, at top and bottom of each pane
Colour register marks (crossed lines type):
    3½p. Opposite rows 1/2 at both sides. 20p. Opposite row 8 at both sides
Autotron marks:
    3½p. In top margin, silver above vertical row 6, violet above vertical row 7
    20p. In bottom margin, silver below vertical row 6, brown below vertical row 7
Perforation register marks: Thick bar opposite rows 3/4, right margin in dot pane
Sheet values: Above and below vertical rows 2/4 and 7/9 reading from left to right in top margin
    and from right to left (upside down) in bottom margin
Traffic lights (boxed): Opposite rows 9/10, right margin; also in same order reading from left
    to right in gutter margin in vertical row 2:
    3½p. Dull violet, silver and embossing
    20p. Deep brown, silver and embossing

Quantities Sold   3½p. 54,034,900; 20p. 7,723,600; Pack 130,390

Withdrawn   13.11.74. Pack sold out 8.74

W254

W255

W256

W257

W258

The above depict the carol "Good King Wenceslas" and were
printed horizontally *se-tenant* within the sheet

W259 "Good King Wenceslas, the Page and Peasant"
(Des. David Gentleman)

1973 (28 NOVEMBER). CHRISTMAS

This issue is complicated by reason of the use of three types of gum, two types of perforator and a wide range of cylinders needed to produce very large quantities with each value employing nine colours.

3p. One 4 mm. centre phosphor band (position varies).   3½p. "All-over" phosphor

A. PVAD

W263 (=S.G. 943) **W254**	3p.	grey-black, blue, brownish grey, light brown, bright rose-red, turquoise-green, salmon-pink and gold ..	15	15
	a.	Strip of 5. Nos. W263/7	3·00	2·75
W264 (=S.G. 944) **W255**	3p.	grey-black, blue, brownish grey, light brown, bright rose-red, rosy mauve, turquoise-green and gold ..	15	15
	b.	Rosy mauve omitted		
	c.	Retouch under 3	3·00	
W265 (=S.G. 945) **W256**	3p.	grey-black, blue, brownish grey, light brown, bright rose-red, rosy mauve, turquoise-green and gold ..	15	15
	b.	Rosy mauve omitted		
	c.	Weak printing of salmon pink*	3·50	
W266 (=S.G. 946) **W257**	3p.	grey-black, blue, brownish grey, light brown, bright rose-red, rosy mauve, turquoise-green and gold ..	15	15
	b.	Rosy mauve omitted		
W267 (=S.G. 947) **W258**	3p.	grey-black, blue, brownish grey, light brown, bright rose-red, rosy mauve, turquoise-green and gold ..	15	15
	b.	Rosy mauve omitted		
W268 (=S.G. 948) **W259**	3½p.	salmon-pink, grey-black, red-br, bl, turquoise-grn, bright rose-red, rosy mve, lavender-grey & gold..	15	15
	a.	Imperforate (pair)	£450	
	b.	Bright rose-red (King's robe) omitted ..	75·00	
	c.	Blue (leg, robes) omitted	£125	
	d.	Blue and rosy mauve omitted	£250	
	e.	Salmon-pink omitted	70·00	
	f.	Red-brown (logs, basket, etc.) omitted ..		
	g.	Grey-black (value and inscr., etc.) omitted ..	75·00	
	h.	Phosphor omitted	10·00	

First Day Cover (W263/8)	†	2·75
Presentation Pack (W263/8)	3·25	†
Pack also exists with a German insert card.		

3p. *Price for missing colour error in strip of five:*
   Rosy mauve (boy's costume in last four stamps) £2500
Naturally the Presentation Packs may contain stamps with any of the gums.

*The salmon-pink (1H cylinder) affects the floor tiles and was very weak or completely omitted but the cylinder was re-etched and the colour is present on the latter part of the printing.

B. GA

W269	**W254**	3p.	As W263	20	
		a.	Strip of 5. Nos. W269/73	3·50	
		ab.	Imperforate (horiz. strip of 5 Nos. W269/73)		
W270	**W255**	3p.	As W264	20	
W271	**W256**	3p.	As W265	20	
W272	**W257**	3p.	As W266	20	
W273	**W258**	3p.	As W267	20	

The missing grey-black on this printing is due to a dry print and it is not completely omitted.

C. PVA

W274	**W259**	3½p.	As W268	25
		a.	Imperforate (pair)	£450
		b.	Grey-black (value and inscr., etc.) omitted ..	75·00
		c.	Rosy mauve (robe at right) omitted	80·00
		d.	Bright rose-red (King's robe) omitted	75·00
		e.	Blue and rosy mauve omitted	£250
		f.	Phosphor omitted	9·00

A copy of the 3½p. with the gold background colour omitted has been seen used on cover. Also a used copy of the 3½p. with the turquoise-green colour omitted and another with the lavender-grey colour omitted, both on pieces.

Listed Variety

Strong retouch under 3
(Cyl. 1B dot, R. 8/7)

W264c

Cylinder Numbers (Blocks of 15 (3p.) or Four (3½p.))

	Cyl. Nos.	Perforation Type A(T)	
		No dot	Dot

A. PVAD

3p.   2A (grey-black)–1B (blue)–1C (brownish grey)–1D (light brown)
–1E (bright rose-red)–1F (rosy mauve)–1G (turquoise-green)–1H
(salmon-pink)–1J (gold)–P50 (phosphor)..   ..   ..   12·00   12·00

2A (grey-black)–1B (blue)–1C (brownish grey)–1D (light brown)
–1E (bright rose-red)–1F (rosy mauve)–1G (turquoise-green)–1H
(salmon-pink)–2J (gold)–P50 (phosphor)..   ..   ..   10·00   10·00

3½p.   4A (grey-black)–4B (lavender-grey)–2C (salmon-pink)–2D (blue)
–2E (rosy mauve)–3F (bright rose-red)–2G (turquoise-green)–2H
(gold)–5J (red-brown)–P52 (phosphor) ..   ..   ..   5·00   †

4A (grey-black)–5B (lavender-grey)–2C (salmon-pink)–2D (blue)
–2E (rosy mauve)–3F (bright rose-red)–2G (turquoise-green)–2H
(gold)–5J (red-brown)–P52 (phosphor) ..   ..   ..   3·00   †

4A (grey-black)–5B (lavender-grey)–2C (salmon-pink)–2D (blue)
–2E (rosy mauve)–3F (bright rose-red)–2G (turquoise-green)–3H
(gold)–5J (red-brown)–P52 (phosphor)   90   †

B. GA   Perforation Type R*(X)

3p.   2A (grey-black)–1B (blue)–1C (brownish grey)–1D (light brown)
–1E (bright rose-red)–1F (rosy mauve)–1G (turquoise-green)–1H
(salmon-pink)–1J (gold)–P50 (phosphor)..   ..   ..   15·00   15·00

                                            Perforation Type A (T)

3p.   2A (grey-black)–1B (blue)–1C (brownish grey)–1D (light brown)
–1E (bright rose-red)–1F (rosy mauve)–1G (turquoise-green)–1H
(salmon-pink)–1J (gold)–P50 (phosphor)..   ..   ..   12·00   12·00

C. PVA

3½p.   5A (grey-black)–3B (lavender-grey)–1C (salmon-pink)–1D (blue)
–3E (rosy mauve)–1F (bright rose-red)–1G (turquoise-green)–1H
(gold)–3J (red-brown)–P51 (phosphor) ..   ..   ..   1·25   1·25

5A (grey-black)–3B (lavender-grey)–1C (salmon-pink)–1D (blue)
–3E (rosy mauve)–1F (bright rose-red)–1G (turquoise-green)–4H
(gold)–3J (red-brown)–P51 (phosphor) ..   ..   ..   55·00   55·00

4A (grey-black)–4B (lavender-grey)–2C (salmon-pink)–2D (blue)
–2E (rosy mauve)–3F (bright rose-red)–2G (turquoise-green)–3H
(gold)–4J (red-brown)–P52 (phosphor) ..   ..   ..   25·00   †

4A (grey-black)–5B (lavender-grey)–1C (salmon-pink)–1D (blue)
–2E (rosy mauve)–3F (bright rose-red)–2G (turquoise-green)–3H
(gold)–5J (red-brown)–P52 (phosphor) ..   ..   ..   25·00   †

4A (grey-black)–5B (lavender-grey)–2C (salmon-pink)–2D (blue)
–2E (rosy mauve)–3F (bright rose-red)–2G (turquoise-green)–2H
(gold)–5J (red-brown)–P52 (phosphor) ..   ..   ..   5·00   †

4A (grey-black)–5B (lavender-grey)–2C (salmon-pink)–2D (blue)
–2E (rosy mauve)–3F (bright rose-red)–2G (turquoise-green)–3H
(gold)–4J (red-brown)–P52 (phosphor) ..   ..   ..   40·00   †

4A (grey-black)–5B (lavender-grey)–2C (salmon-pink)–2D (blue)
–2E (rosy mauve)–3F (bright rose-red)–2G (turquoise-green)–3H
(gold)–5J (red-brown)–P52 (phosphor) ..   ..   ..   3·00   †

Methods of Printing and Perforating

Value	Gum	Panes	Machine-fed	Perf.-fed	Perf. Type	Guide Holes
3p.	GA	Double	Reel	Sheet	A(T)	Possible
	GA	Double	Reel	Reel	R*(X)	None
	PVAD	Double	Reel	Sheet	A(T)	Present
3½p.	PVA	Double	Reel	Sheet	A(T)	Possible
	PVA	Single	Sheet	Sheet	A(T)	None
	PVAD	Single	Sheet	Sheet	A(T)	None

49

Sheet Details

Sheet size: 100 (10 × 10)

Sheet markings:
Cylinder numbers:
  3p. Opposite rows 8/10, left margin, boxed
  3½p. Opposite rows 9/10, left margin, boxed
Guide holes:
  3p. PVAD: Opposite row 5, left margin, and row 6, right margin, both boxed. Others: See under "Methods of Printing and Perforating" above
Marginal arrows: At top, bottom and sides
Colour register marks:
  3p. Crossed lines type, above and below vertical rows 1/2
  3½p. Crossed lines type, opposite rows 1/3 at both sides
  3½p. Crossed circle type in addition below vertical rows 1 and 10 but only on single pane PVA and PVAD sheet-fed printings
Coloured crosses:
  3p. None
  3½p. Opposite rows 7/8 at both sides on single pane PVA and PVAD sheet-fed printings only
Coloured vertical oblongs:
  3p. In blue under all stamps in bottom margin. 3½p. None
Autotron marks:
  3p. In order of traffic lights reading down opposite rows 1/7, in left margin on no dot panes and in right margin on dot panes. 3½p. None
Sheet values:
  3p. Above and below vertical rows 3/4 and 7/9 reading from left to right in top margin and from right to left (upside down) in bottom margin
  3½p. As 3p. but above and below vertical rows 2/4 instead of 3/4
Traffic lights (boxed):
  3p. In cylinder block opposite rows 8/10. Also in same order reading from left to right in top margin above vertical rows 9/10: Grey-black, gold, salmon-pink, turquoise-green, rosy mauve, bright rose-red, light brown, brownish grey, blue
  3½p. Opposite rows 9/10, right margin. Also in same order reading from right to left in top margin above vertical rows 9/10: Lavender-grey, salmon-pink, blue, rosy mauve, bright rose-red, turquoise-green, gold, light brown, grey-black

Quantities Sold   3p. 46,088,200 of each design; 3½p. 110,558,200; Pack 107,070

Withdrawn   27.11.74

1973 (28 NOVEMBER).   COLLECTORS PACK 1973

WCP7 Comprises Nos. W239/62 and one set containing any of Nos. W263/74 (Sold at £1·80)   32·00

Pack also exists with a German insert card.

Quantity Sold   25,683

Withdrawn   30.3.74

W260 Horse Chestnut (*Aesculus hippocastanum*)
(Des. David Gentleman)

1974 (27 FEBRUARY). BRITISH TREES

This issue continues the theme of British Trees initiated by the Oak Tree issued in 1973 to mark Tree Planting Year. The Horse Chestnut was introduced into Western Europe from Istanbul in the 16th Century and it is said that it derives its name from the practice in eastern countries of using its fruit to cure horses of the cough.

"All-over" phosphor

W275 (=S.G.949) **W260**   10p. light emerald, bright green, greenish yellow, brown-olive, black and brownish grey   35   35

First Day Cover (W275)	..	..	..	..	†	1·00
Presentation Pack (W275)	..	..	..	..	2·25	†
Pack also exists with a German insert card						
PHQ Card (W275)	..	..	..	..	£160	65·00

Covers are known postmarked First Day of Issue in Salisbury dated 27 February 1973 instead of 1974.

Cylinder Numbers (Blocks of Six)

	Cyl. Nos.	Perforation Type R*
		No dot Dot

10p. 1A (black)–1B (bright green)–1C (light emerald)–1D (brn-olive)–
1E (greenish yellow)–1F (brownish grey)–P5(0) (phosphor)   ..   2·40   2·40
There is no phosphor cylinder number on the dot pane.

Sheet Details

Sheet size: 100 (2 panes 10 × 5). Double pane reel-fed

Sheet markings:
Cylinder numbers: Opposite rows 8/10, left margin, boxed
Marginal arrows: In centre, at top and bottom of each pane
Colour register marks: Crossed lines type, opposite rows 6/8 at both sides on no dot pane
Autotron marks: Dot pane not examined
Perforation register mark: Thick bar opposite rows 3/4, right margin on no dot pane
Sheet values: Above and below vertical rows 2/4 and 7/9 reading from left to right in top margin
   and from right to left (upside down) in bottom margin
Traffic lights (boxed): Opposite rows 8/10, right margin; also in same order reading from left
   to right in gutter margin in vertical row 2:
Bright green, light emerald, black, brown-olive, greenish yellow, brownish grey

Quantities Sold   10p. 7,245,200; Pack 93,680

Withdrawn   26.2.75

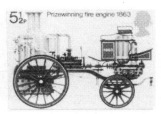

W261 First Motor Fire-engine, 1904   **W262** Prize-winning Fire-engine, 1863

W263 First Steam Fire-engine, 1830   **W264** Fire-engine, 1766

(Des. David Gentleman)

1974 (24 APRIL). FIRE ENGINES

This issue marks the Bicentenary of the Fire Service (Metropolis) Act of 1774 and the designs show historical fire-fighting appliances. The 3½p. depicts the first motor-powered fire-engine to be used, made by Merryweather & Sons of Greenwich for the Finchley brigade. The horse-drawn appliance on the 5½p. is the Sutherland fire-engine which won first prize for steam-operated pumps at Crystal Palace in 1863; also made by Merryweathers, it was still in use until 1918 and is now the oldest steam fire-engine in existence and is on view at the Science Museum, London. The first steam-powered fire-engine shown on the 8p. was invented by John Braithwaite in 1830. The 10p. shows a manual fire-engine made by Samuel Phillips in 1766.

"All-over" phosphor

A. PVAD

W276 (=S.G.950)	**W261**	3½p. grey-black, orange-yellow, greenish yellow, dull rose, ochre and grey		8	8
		a. Imperforate (pair)		£500	
		b. Broken connecting rod		2·25	
		c. Breaks in ladder		1·75	
W277 (=S.G.951)	**W262**	5½p. greenish yellow, deep rosy magenta, orange-yellow, light emerald, grey-black and grey		25	25
		a. Phosphor omitted		6·00	
		b. Broken handrail		2·50	
W278 (=S.G.952)	**W263**	8p. greenish yellow, light blue-green, light greenish blue, light chestnut, grey-black and grey		60	60
W279 (=S.G.953)	**W264**	10p. grey-black, pale reddish brown, light brown, orange-yellow and grey		80	80

First Day Cover (W276/9)		†	3·00
Presentation Pack (W276/9)		2·00	†
Pack also exists with a German insert card.			
PHQ Card (W276)		£160	60·00

B. PVA

W280	**W261**	3½p. grey-black, orange-yellow, greenish yellow, dull rose, ochre and grey		5·50
		a. Broken connecting rod		8·50
		b. Breaks in ladder		8·50

Listed Varieties

W276b, W280a	W276c, W280b	W277b
Broken connecting rod to right of chain-drive wheel (No dot, R. 4/10)	Ladder broken in three places (Dot, R. 7/1)	Broken handrail (No dot, R. 5/10)

Cylinder Numbers (Blocks of Six)

	Cyl. Nos.	Perforation Type R*	
		No dot	Dot

A. PVAD

3½p. 3A (grey-black)–1B (greenish yellow)–1C (dull rose)–1D (orange-yellow)–1E (grey)–1F (ochre)–P57 (phosphor) 80 80

3A (grey-black)–1B (greenish yellow)–1C (dull rose)–1D orange-yellow)–1E (grey)–1F (ochre) .. .. † 5·00

5½p. 3A (grey-black)–1B (greenish yellow)–1C (light emerald)–1D (orange-yellow)–1E (grey)–2F (deep rosy magenta)–P57 (phosphor) .. .. 1·75 1·75

8p. 1A (grey-black)–2B (light greenish blue)–1C (greenish yellow)–1D (light blue-green)–1E (grey)–2F (light chestnut)–P57 (phosphor) .. .. 4·25 12·00

1A (grey-black)–2B (light greenish blue)–1C (greenish yellow)–1D (light blue-green)–1E (grey)–2F (light chestnut) .. † 4·25

10p. 4A (grey-black)–1B (pale reddish brown)–1C (light brown)–1D (orange-yellow)–1E (grey)–P57 (phosphor) .. .. .. 5·50 5·50

B. PVA

3½p. 3A (grey-black)–1B (greenish yellow)–1C (dull rose)–1D (orange-yellow)–1E (grey)–1F (ochre)–P57 (phosphor) .. .. .. 45·00 45·00

The phosphor cylinder number occurs on dot cylinders only but is omitted on some dot sheets of the 3½p., this being listed above.

Sheet Details

Sheet size: 100 (2 panes 10 × 5). Double pane reel-fed

Sheet markings:
  Cylinder numbers: Opposite rows 8/10, left margin, boxed
  Marginal arrows: In centre, at top and bottom of each pane
  Colour register marks (crossed lines type):
    No dot panes: Opposite rows 1/3 at both sides
    Dot panes: Opposite rows 6/7 at both sides
  Autotron marks: In order of traffic lights reading down opposite rows 1/4, left margin on dot panes only (except 5½p. where magenta appears first instead of last)
  Perforation register marks; Thick bar opposite rows 3/4, right margin on no dot pane
  Sheet values: Above and below vertical rows 2/4 and 7/9 reading from left to right in top margin and from right to left (upside down) in bottom margin
  Traffic lights (boxed): Opposite rows 9/10, right margin, also in same order reading from right to left in gutter margin in vertical row 2:
    3½p. Greenish yellow, dull rose, grey-black, orange-yellow, grey, ochre
    5½p. and 8p. In same order as cylinder numbers
    10p. Pale reddish brown, light brown, grey-black, orange-yellow, grey

Quantities Sold 3½p. 47,526,900; 5½p. 7,393,600; 8p. 6,737,600; 10p. 6,631,300; Pack 118,010

Withdrawn 23.4.75

W265 P & O Packet, *Peninsular*, 1888

W266 Farman Biplane, 1911

W267 Airmail-blue Van
and Postbox, 1930

W268 Imperial Airways "C"
Class Flying-boat, 1937

(Des. Rosalind Dease)

1974 (12 JUNE).   U.P.U. CENTENARY

The Universal Postal Union was founded on 9th October 1874 and this issue marking its centenary shows steps in the development of oversea mail. The postmarks reproduced show the Southampton "Packet Letter" cancellation of 1896 (3½p.), the first "Aerial Post" cancellation on the London–Windsor flights of 1911 (5½p.), the London "F.S. Air Mail" cancellation of 1931 (8p.) and the Southampton "Air Port" cancellation of 1937 (10p.).

"All-over" phosphor

W281 (=S.G.954)	**W265**	3½p. deep brownish grey, bright mve, grey-blk & gold		8	8
		a. Pennant staff flaw	2·50		
W282 (=S.G.955)	**W266**	5½p. pale orange, light emerald, grey-black and gold ..		15	25
		a. "Bomb-burst" on wheels	3·25		
W283 (=S.G.956)	**W267**	8p. cobalt, brown, grey-black and gold ..		25	35
W284 (=S.G.957)	**W268**	10p. deep brownish grey, orange, grey-black and gold		40	40

First Day Cover (W281/4) .. .. †	2·00
First Day Cover (Basle) (W281/4) .. .. .. †	15·00
Presentation Pack (W281/4) .. .. 2·00   †
Pack also exists with a German insert card.

12 June was Great Britain Day at the U.P.U. Centenary International Exhibition at Basle and the British Post Office stand sold first day covers with the Basle "INTERNABA" cachet which, with the addition of a Swiss stamp, could then be posted.

Listed Varieties

W281*a*
Staff of pennant on bow is
almost missing
(No dot, R. 8/1)

W282*a*
"Bomb-burst" damage to
wheels at left
(No dot, R. 6/4)

Cylinder Numbers (Blocks of Six)

	Cyl. Nos.	Perforation Type R*	
		No dot	Dot
3½p.	1A (grey-black)–2B (grey-black)–1C (deep brownish grey)–1D (bright mauve)–1E (gold)–P57 (phosphor)	11·00*	8·50
	1A (grey-black)–2B (grey-black)–1C (deep brownish grey)–1D (bright mauve)–2E (gold)–P57 (phosphor)	3·25*	80
5½p.	2A (grey-black)–1B (grey-black)–1C (pale orange)–1D (light emerald)–1E (pale gold)–P57 (phosphor) on no dot	50·00	50·00
	2A (grey-black)–1B (grey-black)–1C (pale orange)–1D (light emerald)–2E (silvery gold)–P57 (phosphor) on no dot ..	10·00	10·00
	2A (grey-black)–1B (grey-black)–1C (pale orange)–1D (light emerald)–2E (dark gold)–P57 (phosphor) on no dot	10·00	10·00
	2A (grey-black)–1B (grey-black)–1C (pale orange)–1D (light emerald)–2E (dark gold)–P57 (phosphor) on dot	1·25	1·25
8p.	2A (grey-black)–1B (grey-black)–1C (cobalt)–1D (brown)–2E (gold)–P57 (phosphor)	1·75	1·75
10p.	1A (grey-black)–1B (grey-black)–1C (deep brownish grey)–1D (orange)–2E (gold)–P57 (phosphor)	2·75	2·75

The phosphor cylinder numbers of the 3½p., 8p. and 10p. occur on dot cylinders only. On the 5½p. they occur as stated above.

On the 5½p. the original gold cylinder 1E gave a pale gold head and when Cylinder 2E was introduced it gave a silvery gold. When this weakness was discovered the gold colour was strengthened, giving a darker and more distinct head.

Sheet Details

Sheet size: 100 (2 panes 10 × 5). Double pane reel-fed

Sheet markings:
Cylinder numbers: Opposite rows 8/9, left margin, boxed
Marginal arrows: In centre, at top and bottom of each pane
Colour register marks (crossed lines type):
  No dot panes: Opposite rows 1/3 at both sides
  Dot panes: Opposite rows 6/7 at both sides
Autotron marks: In order of traffic lights opposite rows 1/4, left margin on dot panes only
Perforation register marks: Thick bar opposite rows 3/4, right margin on dot panes
Sheet values: Above and below vertical rows 2/4 and 7/9 reading from left to right in top margin and from right to left (upside down) in bottom margin
Traffic lights (boxed): Opposite rows 9/10, right margin; also in same order reading from right to left in gutter margin in vertical row 2:
  3½p. Grey-black, deep brownish grey, bright mauve, grey-black, gold
  5½p. Grey-black, pale orange, light emerald, grey-black, gold
  8p. Grey-black, cobalt, brown, grey-black, gold
  10p. Grey-black, deep brownish grey, orange, grey-black, gold

Quantities Sold   3½p. 38,880,800; 5½p. 7,414,300; 8p. 6,450,000; 10p. 6,593,800; Pack 105,550

Withdrawn   11.6.75

W269 Robert the Bruce

W270 Owain Glyndwr

W271 Henry the Fifth

W272 The Black Prince

(Des. Fritz Wegner)

1974 (10 JULY). GREAT BRITONS–MEDIEVAL WARRIORS

The 4½p. honours Robert the Bruce, Earl of Carrick who won independence for Scotland from Edward I of England at the Battle of Bannockburn, 1314, and was crowned King of Scotland. This issue is centred on the 700th Anniversary of his birth. Owain Glyndwr (5½p.) was proclaimed Prince of Wales in 1400. He united the independent divisions of Wales and summoned two All-Wales Parliaments but was not heard of after 1416 and his life became a legend. King Henry the Fifth (8p.) won the famous Battle of Agincourt in 1415 and conquered Normandy, after which he was proclaimed heir to the French throne but died at the early age of 35. The Black Prince (10p.) was the eldest son of Edward III and a famous soldier who had many victories in France, including the capture of Calais in 1347 and Poitiers in 1356.

"All-over" phosphor

W285 (=S.G.958)	**W269**	4½p. greenish yellow, vermilion, slate-blue, red-brown, reddish brown, lilac-grey and gold	10	10
		a. Break in u of Bruce	1·50	
		b. Spot on horse's tail	1·50	
W286 (=S.G.959)	**W270**	5½p. lemon, vermilion, slate-blue, red-brown, reddish brown, olive-drab and gold	20	25
		a. Serif to 4 of 1416	1·50	
W287 (=S.G.960)	**W271**	8p. deep grey, vermilion, greenish yellow, new blue, red-brown, deep cinnamon and gold	90	90
W288 (=S.G.961)	**W272**	10p. vermilion, greenish yellow, new blue, red-brown, reddish brown, light blue and gold	90	90
		a. Line below a of Black	3·00	

First Day Cover (W285/8) .. .. †		2·00	
Presentation Pack (W285/8) .. .. 3·25		†	
Pack also exists with a German insert card.			
PHQ Cards (W285/8) .. .. 35·00		25·00	

All values are known pre-released at Dulverton, Somerset, postmarked 9 July.

The values and inscriptions are weaker on the first supplies which were issued in the packs but this is probably due to dry prints owing to insufficient ink.

Listed Varieties

W285*a*
Break in u of Bruce
(Dot, R. 10/6)

W285*b*
White spot on
horse's tail
(Dot, R. 7/5)

W286*a*
Serif to left of 4 of 1416
(No dot, R. 4/1)

W288*a*
Curved line joins a of
Black to horse's tail
(Dot, R. 7/2)

Cylinder Numbers (Blocks of Six)

	Cyl. Nos.	Perforation No dot	Type R* Dot
4½p.	1A (red-brown)–1B (greenish yellow)–1C (vermilion)–1D (slate-blue)–1E (lilac-grey)–2F (reddish brown)–2G (gold)	1·00	1·00
5½p.	3A (red-brown)–1B (lemon)–1C (vermilion)–1D (slate-blue)–1E (olive-drab)–2F (reddish brown)–2G (gold)	3·00	3·00
	3A (red-brown)–1B (lemon)–1C (vermilion)–1D (slate-blue)–1E (olive-drab)–2F (reddish brown)–2G (gold)	1·50	1·50
8p.	1A (red-brown)–1B (greenish yellow)–1C (vermilion)–1D (new blue)–2E (deep cinnamon)–1F (deep grey)–1G (gold)	6·50	6·50
10p.	1A (red-brown)–2B (greenish yellow)–2C (vermilion)–2D (new blue)–3E (light blue)–1F (reddish brown)–2G (gold)	6·50	6·50

No phosphor cylinder numbers occur on this issue.

Sheet Details
Sheet size: 100 (2 panes 10 × 5). Double pane reel-fed
Sheet markings:
    Cylinder numbers: Opposite rows 8/9, left margin, boxed
    Marginal arrows: In centre, at top and bottom of each pane
    Colour register marks (crossed lines type):
        No dot panes: Not examined
        Dot panes: Opposite rows 6/8 at both sides
    Autotron marks: In order of traffic lights opposite rows 1/5, left margin on dot panes only.
        Additionally the deep grey (8p.) and reddish brown (others) occur in left margin opposite
        gutter margin
    Perforation register marks: Thick bar opposite rows 3/4, right margin on dot panes
    Sheet values: Above and below vertical rows 2/4 and 7/9 reading from left to right in top margin
    and from right to left (upside down) in bottom margin
    Traffic lights (boxed): Opposite rows 9/10, right margin; also in same order reading from right
    to left in gutter margin in vertical row 2:
        4½p. Greenish yellow, vermilion, slate-blue, lilac-grey, reddish brown, gold, red-brown
        5½p. Lemon, vermilion, slate-blue, olive-drab, reddish brown, gold, red-brown
        8p. Greenish yellow, vermilion, new blue, deep cinnamon, deep grey, gold, red-brown
        10p. Greenish yellow, vermilion, new blue, light blue, reddish brown, gold, red-brown

Quantities Sold   4½p. 41,949,300; 5½p. 9,207,800; 8p. 7,243,600; 10p. 7,467,500; Pack 130,600
Withdrawn   9.7.75

W273 Churchill in Royal
Yacht Squadron Uniform

W274 Prime Minister, 1940

W275 Secretary for War
and Air, 1919

W276 War Correspondent,
South Africa, 1899

(Des. Collis Clements and Edward Hughes)

1974 (9 OCTOBER).   CHURCHILL CENTENARY

This issue celebrating the Centenary of the birth of Sir Winston Churchill, covers his career from 1899 to 1942. The 10p. shows him in the uniform of the South African Light Horse in 1899 when he was a war correspondent. The 8p. depicts him in 1919 when he was Secretary for War and Air. On the 5½p. he is shown when he first became Prime Minister in 1940. Finally on the 4½p. he appears in the uniform of the Royal Yacht Squadron.

"All-over" phosphor

A. PVAD

W289 (=S.G.962)	**W273**	4½p. Prussian blue, pale turquoise-green and silver	..	12	12
		a. Severed ear	..	2·25	
		b. Torn coat	..	2·25	
W290 (=S.G.963)	**W274**	5½p. sepia, brownish grey and silver	.. ..	20	25
		a. Phosphor omitted	..	2·50	
		b. White spot over 1	..	2·50	
		c. White spot over 5	..	2·25	
W291 (=S.G.964)	**W275**	8p. crimson, light claret and silver	.. ..	45	45
		a. Cut below left eye	..	3·50	
W292 (=S.G.965)	**W276**	10p. light brown, stone and silver	.. ..	45	45

First Day Cover (W289/92)	..	†	1·60
Presentation Pack (W289/92)	..	1·50	†
Pack also exists with a German insert card.			
Souvenir Book (W289/92) (Sold at 50p.)	..	2·75	†
PHQ Card (W290)	..	7·50	10·00

B. PVA

W293   **W275**   8p.   crimson, light claret and silver   ..   ..   .. 1·50
The souvenir book includes a fully illustrated biography of Churchill, the stamps being contained in raised plastic wallets on the front cover.
The 5½p. has been reported on thinner paper and the 8p. with thick PVAD gum.

Listed Varieties

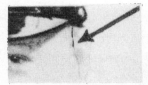

W289a	W290b	W290c
Vertical cut severing ear (Dot, R. 1/6)	White spot over 1 of ½ (Dot, R. 4/2)	White spot over 5 (Dot, R. 10/7)

W289b
Blue line across coat
(emphasised in illustration)
(No dot, R. 10/3)

W291a, W293a
Cut below Churchill's left eye
(Dot, R. 2/3)

Cylinder Numbers (Blocks of Four)

	Cyl. Nos.	Perforation No dot	Type R* Dot
A. PVAD			
4½p. 2A (Prussian blue)–1B (pale turquoise-green)–1C (silver)–P57 (phosphor) ..		75	75
5½p. 1A (sepia)–1B (brownish grey)–1C (silver)–P57 (phosphor) ..		1·00	1·00
8p. 1A (crimson)–1B (light claret)–1C (silver)–P57 (phosphor) ..		2·25	2·25
10p. 2A (light brown)–1B (stone)–1C (silver)–P57 (phosphor) ..		2·25	2·25
B. PVA			
8p. 1A (crimson)–1B (light claret)–1C (silver)–P57 (phosphor) ..		7·50	7·50

The phosphor cylinder numbers occur on dot cylinders only.
The above are with sheets orientated with head to left.

Sheet Details

Sheet size: 100 (2 panes 5 × 10). Double pane reel-fed

Sheet markings:
Cylinder numbers: In top margin above vertical rows 1/2, boxed
Marginal arrows: In centre, opposite rows 5/6 at each side and at each side of vertical gutter
Colour register marks (crossed lines type):
No dot panes: Above and below vertical rows 8/9
Dot panes: Above and below vertical rows 4/5
Autotron marks: In order of traffic lights in top margin above vertical rows 6/7 on dot panes only
Perforation register marks: Thick bar below vertical row 8 on dot panes
Sheet values: Opposite rows 2/4 and 7/9 reading up at left and down at right

Traffic lights (boxed): In bottom margin below vertical row 2; also in same order reading down in row 2 in gutter margin:
4½p. Silver, Prussian blue, pale turquoise-green
5½p. Silver, sepia, brownish grey
8p. Silver, crimson, light claret
10p. Silver, light brown, stone

Quantities Sold 4½p. 54,000,000; 5½p. 9,110,900; 8p. 7,925,000; 10p. 7,752,800; Pack 146,050; Souvenir Pack 40,630

Withdrawn
5½p. Presentation Pack and Souvenir Pack: 9.75
4½p., 8p. and 10p.: 8.10.75

W277 "Adoration of the Magi"
(York Minster, *c.* 1355)

W278 "The Nativity"
(St. Helen's Church, Norwich, *c.* 1480)

W279 "Virgin and Child"
(Ottery St. Mary Church, *c.* 1350)

W280 "Virgin and Child"
(Worcester Cathedral, *c.* 1224)

(Des. Peter Hatch Partnership)

1974 (27 NOVEMBER). CHRISTMAS

This issue features scenes depicted by medieval craftsmen on church roof bosses.
One 4 mm. centre phosphor band

W294	W277	3½p. gold, light new bl, light brn, grey-blk & light stone	50	25

One 4 mm. phosphor band at right

W295 (=S.G.966)	W277	3½p. gold, light new bl, light brn, gry-blk & light stone	8	8
		a. Phosphor omitted	7·00	
		b. Light stone (background shading) omitted		

"All-over" phosphor

W296 (=S.G.967)	W278	4½p. gold, yellow-orange, rose-red, light brown, grey-black and light new blue	10	10
		a. Reversed Q for O	1·60	
W297 (=S.G.968)	W279	8p. blue, gold, light brn, rose-red, dull grn & grey-blk	35	35
W298 (=S.G.969)	W280	10p. gold, dull rose, grey-black, light new blue, pale cinnamon and light brown	35	35

First Day Cover (W295/8)		†	1·40
Presentation Pack (W295/8)	1·50	†	
Pack also exists with a German insert card.			

The phosphor band on the 3½p. was first applied down the centre of the stamp but as this gave a poor phosphor response this was deliberately placed to the right between the roof boss and value, although intermediate positions due to shifts, are known. Naturally either stamp can occur on the first day covers and in the presentation packs.

Listed Variety

Reversed "Q" FOR "O" in date
(Dot, R. 1/8)

W296a

Cylinder Numbers (Blocks of Six)

	Cyl. Nos.	Perforation Type R*
		No dot Dot

One phosphor band

3½p. Centre band
2B (light-stone)–1C (light new blue)–1D (gold)–1E (light brown)–2F (grey-black)–P58 (varnish)–P59 (phosphor)   ..   3·50   5·00

3½p. Band at right
2B (light stone)–1C (light new blue)–1D (gold)–1E (light brown)–2F (grey-black)–P58 (varnish)–P59 (phosphor)   ..   80   80
2B (light stone)–1C (light new blue)–1D (gold)–1E (light brown)–2F (grey-black)–P58 (varnish)   ..   ..   2·50   2·50
2B (light stone)–1C (light new blue)–1D (gold)–1E (light brown)–2F (grey-black)–P59 (phosphor)..   ..   ..   ..   2·00   2·00
2B (light stone)–1C (light new blue)–1D (gold)–1E (light brown)–2F (grey–black)   ..   ..   2·50   3·50
2B (light stone)–1C (light new blue)–2D (gold)–1E (light brown)–2F (grey-black)–P58 (varnish)–P59 (phosphor)   ..   6·00   6·00
2B (light stone)–1C (light new blue)–2D (gold)–1E (light brown)–2F (grey-black)–P59 (phosphor)..   ..   ..   ..   5·00   5·00

"All-over" phosphor
4½p. 1B (light new blue)–1C (yellow-orange)–1D (rose-red)–1E (gold)–1F (light brown)–1G (grey-black)–P58 (phosphor)   ..   1·00   1·00
1B (light new blue)–1C (yellow-orange)–1D (rose-red)–1E (gold)–1F (light brown)–1G (grey-black)..   ..   ..   2·50   2·50

8p. 2A (grey-black)–1B (blue)–1C (dull green)–1D (rose-red)–2E (gold)–1F (light brown)–3G (grey-black)..   ..   ..   ..   2·50   2·50

10p. 1A (grey-black)–3B (pale cinnamon)–2C (dull rose)–3D (light new blue)–2E (gold)–2F (light brown)–2G (grey-black)   ..   2·50   2·50

On the 3½p. cylinder P58 was used to apply a varnish roller in order to improve the gold overlay and this gives no phosphor reaction. The P58 shown in the cylinder blocks for the 4½p. was used for the "all-over" phosphor and probably also for the 8p. and 10p., although the number was not engraved on the cylinder.

The phosphor cylinder P59 used for the centre band on the 3½p. was inverted to produce the band at right and the inverted cylinder number appears in the right margin by the traffic lights. Another "P59" was engraved on the left-hand side just above its box on the dot panes and opposite the gutter margin on the no dot panes.

Sheet Details

Sheet size: 100 (2 panes 10 × 5). Double pane reel-fed

Sheet markings:
Cylinder numbers: Opposite rows 8/10, left margin, boxed
Marginal arrows: In centre, at top and bottom of each pane
Colour register marks (crossed lines type):
No dot panes: Opposite rows 2/3 at both sides
Dot panes: Opposite rows 7/8 at both sides
Autotron marks: In order of traffic lights opposite rows 1/4, left margin on dot panes only

Perforation register marks: Thick bar opposite rows 3/4, right margin on dot panes. Also black horizontal bar in vertical row 5 in gutter margin and again in top or bottom margin partly trimmed off on both panes. This is to check registration when using a rotary perforator as a separate operation from the "Jumelle" machine

Quality control marks: Opposite rows 1, 5, 6 and 10 at both sides on both panes

Sheet values: Above and below vertical rows 2/4 and 7/9 reading from left to right in top margin and from right to left (upside down) in bottom margin

Traffic lights (boxed): Opposite rows 9/10, right margin in order of colours of cylinder numbers; also in same order reading from right to left in gutter margin in vertical row 2 (3½p. and 4½p.) or rows 2/3 (8p. and 10p.)

Colour designations seen: 8p. "G4 GOLD G6 BLACK G7 BLACK" reading down opposite rows 7/10 on dot pane

Quantities Sold   3½p. 234,783,700; 4½p. 12,902,200; 8p. 11,648,400; 10p. 12,046,000; Pack 129,020

Withdrawn   26.11.75

1974 (27 NOVEMBER).   COLLECTORS PACK 1974

WCP8 Comprises Nos. W275/98 (Sold at £1·60)   10·00
Pack also exists with a German insert card.

Where stamps exist PVA as well as PVAD either may occur in the pack, although PVAD is the more likely.

Quantity Sold   42,860

Withdrawn   9.75

W281 Invalid in Wheelchair
(Des. Philip Sharland)

1975 (22 JANUARY).   HEALTH AND HANDICAP CHARITIES

Responding to public pressure the Post Office issued, as an experiment, the first Charity stamp ever to appear for Great Britain. The Trustees of the Charity Stamp Fund were selected by the National Council of Social Service and charities working in the fields of health and the handicapped were to benefit from the proceeds of the premium charged on the stamp.

"All-over" phosphor

W300 (= S.G.970)   **W281**   4½p. + 1½p. azure and grey-blue   10   12

| First Day Cover (W300)   ..   ..   60 |

Cylinder Numbers (Blocks of Four)

	Cyl. Nos.	Perforation Type R*	
		No dot	Dot
4½p. + 1½p.	1A (grey-blue)–1B (azure)–P60 (phosphor)	60	60

The P60 was erroneously engraved opposite row 4 by mistake and then erased and correctly engraved opposite row 10.

W   1975.   Turner Bicentenary

Sheet Details

Sheet size: 100 (2 panes 10 × 5). Double pane reel-fed

Sheet markings:
Cylinder numbers: Opposite rows 9/10, left margin, boxed
Marginal arrows: In centre, at top and bottom of each pane
Colour register marks (crossed lines type):
No dot pane: Not examined
Dot pane: Opposite rows 7/8 at both sides
Autotron marks: In azure and grey-blue respectively opposite rows 4/5, left margin on dot pane only
Perforation register mark: Thick bar opposite rows 4/5, right margin on dot pane
Quality control marks: Opposite rows 1, 5, 6 and 10 at both sides on both panes
Sheet values: Above and below vertical rows 2/4 and 7/9 reading from left to right in top margin and from right to left (upside down) in bottom margin. Inscriptions read "TOTAL SHEET VALUE £4·50 + £1·50 CHARITY"
Traffic lights (boxed): Opposite row 10, right margin (azure and grey-blue) and in same order reading from left to right in gutter margin in vertical row 2

Quantity Sold   7,000,000
It is understood that 30,000,000 were printed and it was announced that sales during the four weeks when the stamp was on sale at post offices were 5½ million. The premium on these sales (excluding later sales at philatelic counters and the Philatelic Bureau) realised £84,000. The experiment involved the Post Office in additional costs amounting to £31,000 which were to be set off against the proceeds. As a gesture of goodwill the Post Office made a contribution of £4,000. Thus a net balance of £57,000 remained and this was paid to the Charity Trustees.

Withdrawn   21.1.76

W282 "Peace–Burial at Sea"

W283 "Snowstorm–Steamer off a Harbour's Mouth"

W284 "The Arsenal, Venice"

W285 "St. Laurent"

(Des. Stuart Rose)

63

1975 (19 FEBRUARY). TURNER BICENTENARY

Continuing the British Painters series this issue celebrates the Bicentenary of the birth of J. M. W. Turner. The paintings depicted are from the collections in the British Museum and Tate Gallery.

"All-over" phosphor

W301 (=S.G.971)	W282	4½p. grey-black, salmon, stone, blue and grey..	..	10	10
W302 (=S.G.972)	W283	5½p. cobalt, greenish yell, light yell-brn, grey-blk & rose		15	15
		b. Apostrophe before 1851		2·50	
		c. "18.51"		3·00	
W303 (=S.G.973)	W284	8p. pale yellow-orange, greenish yellow, rose, cobalt and grey-black		20	25
W304 (=S.G.974)	W285	10p. deep blue, light yellow-ochre, light brown, deep cobalt and grey-black		30	35

First Day Cover (W301/4)	..	..	..	..	† 1·40
Presentation Pack (W301/4)	..	..	..	1·50	†
PHQ Card (W302)	..	..	..	..	32·00 10·00

Listed Varieties

W302*b*
Apostrophe before 1851
(No dot, R. 6/5)

W302*c*
Stop between 18 and 51
(No dot, R. 8/5)

Cylinder Numbers (Blocks of Six)

	Cyl. Nos.	Perforation Type R*
		No dot Dot
4½p. 4A (grey)–1B (salmon)–1C (stone)–1D (grey-black)–1E (blue)–1F (grey-black)–P58 (phosphor)		1·00 1·00
5½p. 1A (grey-black)–2B (rose)–1C (greenish yellow)–1D (cobalt)–2E (grey-black)–1F (light yellow-brown)–P58 (phosphor)		1·25 1·25
8p. 2A (grey-black)–1B (rose)–1C (greenish yellow)–2D (pale yellow-orange)–1E (cobalt)–4F (grey-black)–P58 (phosphor) ..		1·50 1·50
10p. 1A (grey-black)–6B (deep cobalt)–1C (light yellow-ochre)–1D (deep blue)–1E (light brown)–P58 (phosphor)		2·10 2·10

Sheet Details

Sheet size: 100 (2 panes 10 × 5). Double pane reel-fed

Sheet markings:
Cylinder numbers: Opposite rows 8/9, left margin, boxed
Marginal arrows: In centre, at top and bottom of each pane
Colour register marks (crossed lines type):
No dot panes: Opposite rows 1/3 at both sides and opposite rows 6/7 in left margin only
Autotron marks and perforation register marks: Dot panes not examined
Quality control marks: Opposite rows 1, 5, 6 and 10 at both sides on both panes
Sheet values: Above and below vertical rows 2/4 and 7/9 reading from left to right in top margin and from right to left (upside down) in bottom margin, except on 8p. where inscriptions occur above and below vertical rows 3 and 8
Traffic lights (boxed): Opposite rows 8/9, right margin; also in same order reading from left to right in gutter margin in vertical rows 1/2 (4½p.) or row 2 (others):
4½p. Grey-black, salmon, stone, grey-black, blue, grey
5½p. Rose, greenish yellow, cobalt, grey-black, light yellow-brown, grey-black
8p. Rose, greenish yellow, pale yellow-orange, cobalt, grey-black, grey-black
10p. Deep cobalt, light yellow-ochre, deep blue, light brown, grey-black
Colour designations seen: 5½p. "G6 GREY G5(?)G3 BLUE" opposite rows 1/3 right margin on no dot pane; 10p. "G3 BLUE" opposite row 1 on no dot pane

Quantities Sold   4½p. 47,920,000; 5½p. 8,690,000; 8p. 7,200,000; 10p. 7,100,000

Withdrawn   18.2.76

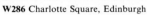

W286 Charlotte Square, Edinburgh   **W287** The Rows, Chester
The above were printed horizontally *se-tenant* within the sheet

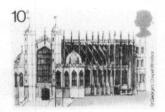

W288 Royal Observatory, Greenwich   **W289** St. George's Chapel, Windsor

W290 National Theatre, London
(Des. Peter Gauld)

1975 (23 APRIL).   EUROPEAN ARCHITECTURAL HERITAGE YEAR

The issue marks the culmination of a three-year campaign promoted by the Council of Europe
to awaken interest in our common architectural heritage. Charlotte Square, Edinburgh, designed
by Robert Adam in 1791 and The Rows, Chester, medieval double-storeyed shopping streets shown
on the *se-tenant* 7p. stamps are two of the conservation pilot projects which have been adopted.
The Old Royal Observatory, Flamsteed House, designed by Sir Christopher Wren, was intended
as a habitation for the first Astronomer Royal rather than as an observatory. St. George's Chapel,
Windsor, is a fine example of medieval church architecture. The 12p. depicts the only modern
building in the set, the new National Theatre on the South Bank, designed by Denys Lasdun.
It contains three separate auditoriums, the main one being the Lyttleton Theatre which opened
on 16 March 1976 with a performance of *Hamlet*.
"All-over" phosphor

W305 (=S.G.975) **W286**	7p. greenish yellow, bright orange, grey-black, red-brown, new blue, lavender and gold	..	..	20	20
	a. Pair. Nos. W305/6 ..	..	..	..	..	60	70
	b. Missing chimney outlines ..	..	..	2·25	
	c. Missing outline of left chimney	..	..	1·75	
W306 (=S.G.976) **W287**	7p. grey-black, greenish yellow, new blue, bright orange, red-brown and gold	..	..	..	20	20
	b. Thick T in The ..	..	..	..	..	2·25	

65

W307 (= S.G.977)	**W288**	8p. magenta, deep slate, pale magenta, light yellow-olive, grey-black and gold	20	25
W308 (= S.G.978)	**W289**	10p. bistre-brown, greenish yellow, deep slate, emerald-green, grey-black and gold	20	25
W309 (= S.G.979)	**W290**	12p. grey-black, new blue, pale magenta and gold ..	30	35

First Day Cover (W305/9)	†	1·60
Presentation Pack (W305/9)	2·00	†
PHQ Cards (W305/7)	8·50	9·00

Listed Varieties

W305*b*
Outlines to both chimneys almost missing
(Dot, R. 8/1)

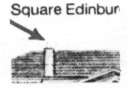

W305*c*
Outline of left chimney missing
(No dot, R. 1/1)

W306*b*
Thick T
(No dot, R. 4/6)

Cylinder Numbers (Blocks of Six)

		Perforation	Type R*
	Cyl. Nos.	No dot	Dot
7p.	3A (grey-black)–2B (lavender)–2C (greenish yellow)–1D (bright orange)–1E (new blue)–1F (red-brown)–1G (gold)	2·25	4·25*
	3A (grey-black)–2B (lavender)–2C (greenish yellow)–1D (bright orange)–1E (new blue)–1F (red-brown)–1G (gold)–P58 (phosphor)	†	15·00*
8p.	1A (grey-black)–1B (deep slate)–1C (pale magenta)–1D (light yellow-olive)–1E (magenta)–1F (gold)–P58 (phosphor).. ..	1·50	1·50
10p.	1A (grey-black)–1B (greenish yellow)–1C (bistre-brown)–1D (emerald-green)–1E (deep slate)–1F (gold)–P58 (phosphor) ..	1·60	1·60
12p.	1A (grey-black)–2B (grey-black)–2C (new blue)–1D (pale magenta)–1F (gold)..	2·10	2·10

On the 7p. the phosphor cylinder was inverted so that the phosphor number appeared in the right-hand margin opposite row 10 on no dot panes. It has also been found on dot panes opposite row 9 with P58 printed upright. On the 12p. the phosphor number has been seen displaced, appearing opposite row 5. It was probably engraved in that position by mistake.

Sheet Details

Sheet size: 100 (2 panes 10 × 5). Double pane reel-fed

Sheet markings:
Cylinder numbers: Opposite rows 8/9, left margin, boxed
Marginal arrows: In centre, at top and bottom of each pane
Colour register marks (crossed lines type):
No dot panes: Opposite rows 1/3 at both sides and also opposite row 4 in left margin only
Dot panes: Opposite rows 6/8 at both sides
Autotron marks: In order of traffic lights opposite rows 1/5 (7p. and 10p.) or rows 4/6 (12p.) left margin only on dot panes only. 8p. sheet not examined
Perforation register marks: Thick bar opposite row 3, right margin on dot pane
Quality control marks: Opposite rows 1, 5, 6 and 10 both sides on both panes
Sheet values: Above and below vertical rows 2/4 and 7/9 reading from left to right in top margin and from right to left (upside down) in bottom margin
Traffic lights (boxed): Opposite rows 8/9, right margin; also in same order reading from left to right in gutter margin in vertical row 2:
7p. and 12p. In order of colours of cylinder numbers
8p. Deep slate, pale magenta, light yellow-olive, magenta, grey-black, gold
10p. Greenish yellow, bistre-brown, emerald-green, deep slate, grey-black, gold
Colour designations seen: 7p. "G1 BLACK" reading up opposite rows 7/8, right margin on no dot pane; 10p. "G6 GOLD G5(?) G4 GREY" + (?) reading opposite rows 1/4, right margin on dot pane

Quantities Sold   7p. 40,950,000; 8p. 6,640,000; 10p. 5,560,000; 12p. 5,450,000

Withdrawn   22.4.76

W291 Sailing Dinghies   **W292** Racing Keel Boats

W293 Cruising Yachts   **W294** Multihulls
(Des. Andrew Restall)
(Printed in photogravure with outlines, waves and rigging recess-printed in black)

1975 (11 JUNE). SAILING

Issued on the occasion of the Bicentenary of the Royal Thames Yacht Club and the Centenary of the Royal Yachting Association and other club anniversaries, these stamps were designed to span the spectrum of sailing from dinghies and racing keel boats to cruising yachts and modern multihulls.

This was also the first occasion when Harrisons combined photogravure with recess-printing, achieving this with a single run through the "Jumelle" machine. Unfortunately this coincided with a period when there was a dispute in the printing trade in consequence of which difficulties arose over manning the machine between "recess staff" and "photogravure staff". Not only was a substantial part of the printing lost, especially of the 12p. which was sold out within days, but the quality of the printing also suffered. This applied particularly to the recess-printing in black of the outlines, waves and rigging where loss of ink frequently occurred; moreover it is easy to remove black lines just using a thumbnail. Hence most minor varieties of the recess-printed black colour are not constant.

"All-over" phosphor

W310 (=S.G.980)	**W291**	7p.	black, bluish vio, scar, orange-verm, orge & gold	20	20
		a.	Grey Moon flaw	2·75	
		b.	"Knot" in margin .. .. *Pair*	2·50	
W311 (=S.G.981)	**W292**	8p.	black, orange-vermilion, orange, lavender, bright mauve, bright blue, deep ultramarine and gold ..	20	20
		a.	Black omitted	60·00	
W312 (=S.G.982)	**W293**	10p.	black, orange, bluish emerald, light olive-drab, chocolate and gold	25	25
		a.	Faint ribs upper right of middle sail	1·75	
		b.	Broken ribs above ball on middle sail	1·75	
		c.	Broken ribs upper centre of aft sail	1·75	
		d.	Broken ribs lower right of aft sail	2·25	
		e.	2nd ptg. Paler orange	25	25
		ea.	As W312*a*	1·75	
		eb.	As W312*b*	1·75	
		ec.	As W312*c*	1·75	
		ed.	As W312*d*	2·25	
W313 (=S.G.983)	**W294**	12p.	black, ultramarine, turquoise-blue, rose, grey, steel-blue and gold	35	45
		a.	Phosphor omitted		

First Day Cover (W310/3)	..	..	..	..	†	1·40	
Souvenir Cover (W310/3)	..	..	..	..	†	1·25	
Presentation Pack (W310/3)	..	..	..	..	1·25	†	
PHQ Card (W311)	..	..	..	..	..	4·00	9·00

In No. W311*a* the recess-printed black colour is completely missing.

Five sheets of the 8p. value had the gold apparently omitted from the tenth vertical row. However, residual specks of gold lead us to believe that this may have been due to a dry print.

The 12p. exists with the rose colour partially omitted, also with black partially omitted.

The printing of the 10p. was interrupted because the orange colour was unstable and could be rubbed off. In the second printing a sealer was applied (using cylinder P58) resulting in a paler, duller orange.

Miscut Pane. Part of the printing of the 7p. had the sheets miscut so that the bottom pane appeared at the top and vice versa. See under General Notes (page 7). (*Price for gutter pair showing sheet margin inscription* £50.)

The Post Office Souvenir cover was not generally available until a few weeks after the date of issue. Hence first day covers are not usually the Post Office Souvenir covers; these are known with later dates of the London Chief Office or Trafalgar Square cancellations.

The Presentation Pack contains the first printing of the 10p.

Listed Varieties

Light grey Moon-shaped flaw at top of red sail at left
(No dot, R. 9/1)

W310*a*

W310*b*

Black "knot" in stamp margin, sometimes extending
into left-hand stamp

No. W310*b* occurs in the margin between vertical rows 3/4 on five adjoining stamps in either rows 1/5 no dot or dot or rows 6/10 no dot or dot. It is not known on more than one pane in the same sheet. It derives from the black recess plate which comprises seven panes of 50 stamps so that any constant flaw can occur in four positions in the complete printer's sheet.

Short black horizontal lines above the corners of 7p. stamps are not varieties but guide lines which were introduced in error. They normally occur in the stamp margins at right above vertical row 1, at left above vertical row 10 and at left and right in all the intervening vertical rows as well as in the sheet margin at left and at right. When displaced upwards or downwards they are liable to occur on the stamps.

W312*a* and *ea*
Faint ribs at upper right of
ball in middle sail
(Dot, R. 3/8)

W312*b* and *eb*
Broken ribs above ball in
middle sail
(Dot, R. 4/3)

W312*c* and *ec*
Broken ribs at upper centre
of aft sail
(Dot, R. 6/3)

W312*d* and *ed*
Broken ribs at lower right
of aft sail
(Dot, R. 8/8)

69

Cylinder Numbers (Blocks of Six)

Cyl. Nos.	Perforation No dot	Type R* Dot
7p. 1A (black)–1B (scarlet)–1C (orange)–1D (orange-vermilion)–1E (bluish violet)–1F (gold)–P61 (phosphor)	6·00*	3·50
1A (black)–1B (scarlet)–1C (orange)–1D (orange-vermilion)–1E (bluish violet)–1F (gold) (no phosphor)	4·00*	1·50
8p. 2A (lavender)–1B (orange)–1C (bright blue)–1D (orange-vermilion)–1E (bright mauve)–1G (deep ultramarine)–1F (gold)–P58 (phosphor) (row 8) ..	5·00	5·00
2A (lavender)–1B (orange)–1C (bright blue)–1D (orange-vermilion)–1E (bright mauve)–1G (deep ultramarine)–1F (gold)–P58 (phosphor) (row 10)	5·00	5·00
2A (lavender)–1B (orange)–1C (bright blue)–1D (orange-vermilion)–1E (bright mauve)–1G (deep ultramarine)–1F (gold) ..	1·50	1·50
10p. 1A (orange)–2B (bluish emerald)–2C (light olive-drab)–1D (chocolate)–1F (gold)–P61 (phosphor)	7·50	7·50
1A (orange)–2B (bluish emerald)–2C (light olive-drab)–1D (chocolate)–1F (gold)–P61 (phosphor) (2nd printing)	1·75	1·75
12p. 1A (grey)–1B (rose)–1C (ultramarine)–1D (turquoise-blue)–1E (steel-blue)–1F (gold)	2·50	2·50

There were no plate numbers for the black recess-printed plates.

Phosphor Cylinder Numbers

7p. P61 normally occurs opposite row 9 but is also known opposite rows 4 and 7 and above row 1. On miscut sheets it is found opposite centre gutter or row 2 on dot panes only
    P58 is known opposite row 6
8p. P58 is found opposite rows 8 or 10 on dot panes and opposite rows 8/10 or 10/10 on no dot panes
10p. P61 occurs opposite row 10. In the second printing the P58 sealer is found inverted opposite row 10/10 on no dot panes only
12p. P61 is found opposite rows 2 or 7

Sheet Details

Sheet size: 100 (2 panes 10 × 5). Double pane reel-fed

Sheet markings:
    Cylinder numbers: Opposite rows 8/9, left margin, boxed
    Marginal arrows: In centre, at top and bottom of each pane
    Colour register marks (crossed lines type):
      No dot panes: Opposite rows 1/3 at both sides and opposite row 4 in left margin only
      Dot panes: Opposite rows 6/8 at both sides
    Autotron marks: In order of traffic lights opposite rows 1/4 (2/4 for 10p.), left margin on dot panes only.
    Additional similar gold horizontal bar in vertical row 4 in gutter margin and at top and bottom margin at cutting line and black bar in same positions in vertical row 5 on both panes in all values. These autotron marks were for adjusting the registration of the intaglio unit.
    Perforation register marks: Thick bar opposite rows 3/4, right margin in dot panes
    Quality control marks: Opposite rows 1, 5, 6 and 10 at both sides on both panes
    Sheet values: Above and below vertical rows 2/4 and 7/9 reading from left to right in top margin and from right to left (upside down) in bottom margin
    Traffic lights (boxed): Opposite rows 3/4 (7p. and 12p.) and rows 8/9 (8p. and 10p.), right margin; also in same order reading from right to left in gutter margin in vertical row 2 (rows 1/2 on 8p.):
    7p. Gold, bluish violet, orange-vermilion, orange, scarlet, black
    8p. Gold, deep ultramarine, bright mauve, orange-vermilion, lavender, bright blue, orange
    10p. Gold, chocolate, orange, light olive-drab, bluish emerald
    12p. Not examined

Quantities Sold   7p. 17,000,000; 8p. 4,320,000; 10p. 3,620,000; 12p. 2,470,000

Withdrawn   12p. Sold out 6.75; remainder 10.6.76

W295 Stephenson's "Locomotion" 1825

W296 "Abbotsford", 1876

W297 "Caerphilly Castle", 1923

W298 High-speed Train, 1975

(Des. Brian Craker)

1975 (13 AUGUST).   PUBLIC RAILWAYS

This issue celebrates the 150th Anniversary of the inauguration of the first public steam railway, the Stockton to Darlington line, on which Stephenson's "Locomotion" was first used. This could haul a 90-ton train up to a speed of 15 miles per hour. The "Abbotsford" engine, designed by Dugald Drummond, became one of the North British Railway's Waverley Class and could attain a speed of 80 mph. The "Caerphilly Castle", one of the Great Western Railway's Castle Class, was designed by C. B. Collett to pull the heavier trains. British Rail's High Speed Train went into service in 1975 and is designed to reach speeds of 125 mph.

"All-over" phosphor

W314 (=S.G.984)	W295	7p. red-brown, grey-black, greenish, yell, grey & silver	30	35
		a. Broken R in Railway	2·25	
W315 (=S.G.985)	W296	8p. brown, orange-yell, verm, grey-blk, grey & silver	30	40
W316 (=S.G.986)	W297	10p. emerald-green, grey-black, yellow-orange, vermilion, grey and silver	40	45
		a. Serif omitted from 1 of Class	2·25	
		b. Orange glow in driver's cab	2·50	
W317 (=S.G.987)	W298	12p. grey-black, pale lemon, vermilion, bl, grey & silver	50	60
		a. "Obstruction" on line	4·50	
		b. Missing serif to n	2·50	

First Day Cover (W314/7)	†	2·50
Presentation Pack (W314/7)	2·25	†
Souvenir Book (W314/7) (Sold at 85p.)	3·50	†
PHQ Cards (W314/7)	60·00	25·00

The souvenir book includes a fully illustrated history of the railways, the stamps being contained in raised plastic wallets on the front cover.

The 8p. is known with misplaced horizontal perforations resulting in the four top rows of the sheet having the brown line at foot instead of at top and in the bottom row the brown line was completely omitted.

Listed Varieties

Railway   Class   Train

W314a	W316a	W317b
Broken R in Railway (No dot, R. 1/9)	Top Serif omitted from 1 of Class (Dot, R. 1/10)	Missing bottom serif to n (Dot, R. 5/8)

'ice HST

W316b	W317a
Orange glow in driver's cab (No dot, R. 6/4)	Grey "obstruction" on line in front of engine (No dot, R. 5/9)

Cylinder Numbers (Blocks of Six)

Cyl. Nos.	Perforation No dot	Type R* Dot
7p. 1A (grey-black)–1B (grey)–1C (greenish yellow)–1D (red-brown)–1E (silver)–P61 (phosphor)	2·10	2·10
8p. 1A (grey-black)–1B (grey)–1C (orange-yellow)–1D (brown)–1E (silver)–1F (vermilion)–P61 (phosphor)	2·25	2·25
1A (grey-black)–1B (grey)–1C (orange-yellow)–1D (brown)–1E (silver)–1F (vermilion)–(no phosphor)*	2·25	2·25
10p. 1A (grey-black)–1B (grey)–1C (yellow-orange)–1D (vermilion)–1E (silver)–1F (emerald-green)–P61 (phosphor)	2·75	2·75
12p. 1A (grey-black)–1B (grey)–1C (pale lemon)–1D (vermilion)–1E (silver)–1F (blue)–P61 (phosphor)	3·50	3·50

*The cylinder block of the 8p. without phosphor number results from the use of phosphor cylinder P58 which exists in two forms: upright opposite R. 10/1 on dot pane and inverted opposite R. 10/10 on no dot pane.
Phosphor cylinder No. P61 occurs in row 8 on the 8p. and in row 10 on the other values.

Sheet Details
Sheet size: 100 (2 panes 10 × 5). Double pane reel-fed
Sheet markings:
    Cylinder numbers: Opposite rows 8/9 (7p.), 8/10 (others), left margin, boxed
    Marginal arrows: In centre, at top and bottom of each pane
    Colour register marks (crossed lines type):
        No dot panes: Opposite rows 1/3 at both sides and opposite row 4 in left margin only
        Dot panes: Opposite rows 6/8 at both sides
    Autotron marks: In order of traffic lights opposite rows 1/4, left margin on dot panes only
    Perforation register marks: Thick bar opposite rows 3/4, right margin on dot panes
    Quality control marks: Opposite rows 1, 5, 6 and 10 at both sides (8p. and 10p. at right only) on both panes
    Sheet values: Above and below vertical rows 1/2 and 9/10 reading from left to right in top margin and from right to left (upside down) in bottom margin

W   1975.   62nd Inter-Parliamentary Union Conference

Traffic lights (boxed): Opposite rows 8/9, right margin; also in same order reading from left to right in gutter margin in vertical rows 2/3:
7p. Grey-black, grey, greenish yellow, red-brown, silver
8p. Grey-black, grey, orange-yellow, brown, vermilion, silver
10p. Grey-black, grey, yellow-orange, vermilion, emerald-green, silver
12p. Blue, grey-black, grey, pale lemon, vermilion, silver

Quantities Sold   7p. 47,160,000; 8p. 9,900,000; 10p. 10,530,000; 12p. 8,690,000

Withdrawn   12.8.76

W299 Palace of Westminster
(Des. Richard Downer)

1975 (3 SEPTEMBER).   62nd INTER-PARLIAMENTARY UNION CONFERENCE

The Inter-Parliamentary Union was founded in 1889 by an Englishman, William Cremer, and a Frenchman, Frederick Passey who shared an enthusiasm for the ideal of peace through international arbitration. The last occasion when the Annual Conference was held in London was in 1957 when a special stamp was also issued.

"All-over" phosphor

W318 (= S.G.988)   **W299**   12p. light new blue, black, brownish grey and gold   ..   35   35

First Day Cover (W318)	..	..	..	..	†	65
Presentation Pack (W318)	..	..	..	..	1·00	†

Cylinder Numbers (Blocks of Four)

	Cyl. Nos.			Perforation Type R*	
				No dot	Dot
12p. 1A (brownish grey)–1B (light new blue)–1C (black)–1D (gold)–P61 (phosphor) (row 9)				1·75	1·75

Sheet Details

Sheet size: 100 (2 panes 10 × 5). Double pane reel-fed

Sheet markings:
Cylinder numbers: Opposite row 9, left margin, boxed
Marginal arrows: In centre, at top and bottom of each pane
Colour register marks (crossed lines type):
  No dot pane: Opposite rows 3/4 at both sides and opposite row 5 in left margin only
  Dot pane: Opposite rows 7/8 at both sides
Autotron marks: In order of traffic lights opposite rows 2/4, left margin on dot pane only
Perforation register marks: Thick bar opposite row 4, right margin on dot pane
Quality control marks: Opposite rows 1, 5, 6 and 10 at both sides on both panes
Sheet values: Above and below vertical rows 1/2 and 9/10 reading from left to right in top margin and from right to left (upside down) in bottom margin
Traffic lights (boxed): Opposite row 9, right margin; also in same order reading from left to right in gutter margin in vertical row 2: light new blue, brownish grey, black, gold
Colour designations seen: "G4 GOLD G3 BLACK G2 GREY" reading up opposite rows 1/3 on dot pane

Quantity Sold   12p. 5,770,000

Withdrawn   2.9.76

W300 "Emma and Mr Woodhouse"
(*Emma*)

W301 "Catherine Morland"
(Northanger Abbey)

W302 "Mr. Darcy"
(*Pride and Prejudice*)

W303 "Mary and Henry Crawford"
(*Mansfield Park*)

(Des. Barbara Brown)

1975 (22 OCTOBER).   JANE AUSTEN

This issue is in honour of the Bicentenary of the birth of Jane Austen and the stamps depict characters from her novels as indicated in the captions. Apart from Royalty, Jane Austen is only the second woman to be commemorated on British stamps, the first being Florence Nightingale in the 1970 Anniversaries issue.

"All-over" phosphor

W319 (=S.G.989)	**W300**	8½p.	blue, slate, rose-red, light yellow, dull green, grey-black and gold	20	20
			a. Break in bottom frame	2·10	
			b. Break in top frame	1·90	
W320 (=S.G.990)	**W301**	10p.	slate, bright magenta, grey, light yellow, grey-black and gold	25	25
			a. Spot to J	2·25	
			b. Magenta dots left of Queen's head	1·90	
W321 (=S.G.991)	**W302**	11p.	dull blue, pink, olive-sepia, slate, pale greenish yellow, grey-black and gold	40	45
			a. Dotted line through pedestal	2·40	
W322 (=S.G.992)	**W303**	13p.	bright magenta, light new blue, slate, buff, dull blue-green, grey-black and gold	40	40
			a. Break in bottom frame	2·75	

First Day Cover (W319/22)				†	1·40
Presentation Pack (W319/22)				2·00	†
PHQ Cards (W319/22)				15·00	15·00

Listed Varieties

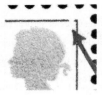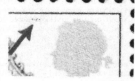

W319*b*	W320*a*	W320*b*
Break in top frame (No dot, R. 9/10)	Spot to the lower tail of J (No dot, R. 7/9)	Magenta dotted line (Dot, R. 10/7)

W319*a*. The break in the bottom frame occurs in the same place as that on the 13p. (W322*a*) but the position is No dot, R. 2/5.

W321*a*
Black dotted line through pedestal
(No dot, R. 2/4)

W322*a*
Break in bottom frame
(No dot, R. 3/2)

Cylinder Numbers (Blocks of Six)

	Cyl. Nos.	Perforation No dot	Type R* Dot
8½p.	1A (grey-black)–1B (blue)–1C (light yellow)–4D (rose-red)–1E (dull green)–1F (gold)–1G (slate)–P61 (phosphor)	5·00	5·00
	1A (grey-black)–1B (blue)–1C (light yellow)–4D (rose-red)–1E (dull green)–1F (gold)–1G (slate) (no phosphor)*	1·50	1·50
10p.	2A (grey-black)–1B (grey)–2C (light yellow)–1D (bright magenta) –1E (slate)–1F (gold)	1·75	1·75
11p.	1A (grey-black)–1B (dull blue)–1C (pale greenish yellow)–1D (pink)–1E (olive-sepia)–1F (gold)–2G (slate)	2·75	2·75
13p.	1A (grey-black)–4B (light new blue)–3C (buff)–1D (bright magenta)–1E (dull blue-green)–1F (gold)–1G (slate)–P61 (phosphor)..	5·50	5·50
	1A (grey-black)–4B (light new blue)–3C (buff)–1D (bright magenta)–1E (dull blue-green)–1F (gold)–1G (slate) (no phosphor)* ..	2·75	2·75

The above are with sheets orientated with head to left

Phosphor Cylinder Numbers

8½p.* On no dot pane P61 normally occurs in top margin over R. 1/3 but when displaced it appears in the right-hand gutter. On dot panes it is usually displaced in right-hand margin and has been found opposite R. 10/3–4, R. 10/4–5 and R. 10/8

10p. On no dot and dot panes P61 occurs in top margin above R. 1/7

11p. On no dot panes P61 occurs in vertical gutter next to R. 10/6 and on dot panes it appears in left margin opposite R. 10/1

13p.* On no dot panes P61 normally occurs in top margin above R. 1/1 but when displaced it appears above R. 1/6. On dot panes it usually occurs above R. 1/4

75

W 1975. Christmas

Sheet Details

Sheet size: 100 (2 panes 5 × 10). Double pane reel-fed

Sheet markings:
Cylinder numbers: In top margin above vertical rows 2/3, boxed
Marginal arrows: In centre, opposite rows 5/6 at each side and at each side of vertical gutter
Colour register marks (crossed lines type):
No dot panes: Above and below vertical rows 8/10 and at vertical row 7 in top margin only
Dot panes: Above and below vertical rows 3/5
Autotron marks: Vertical bars in order of traffic lights reading from left to right above vertical rows 6/10 on dot panes only
Perforation register marks: Thick vertical bar below vertical row 7 on dot panes
Quality control marks: Horizontal bars above and below vertical rows 1, 5, 6 and 10 on both panes
Sheet values: Opposite rows 3/5 and 7/9 reading up at left and down at right
Traffic lights (boxed): In bottom margin below vertical rows 2/3; also in same order reading up in gutter margin in rows 2/3:
8½p. Gold, slate, grey-black, dull green, rose-red, light yellow, blue
10p. Gold, slate, grey-black, bright magenta, light yellow, grey
11p. Gold, slate, grey-black, olive-sepia, pink, pale greenish yellow, dull blue
13p. Gold, slate, grey-black, dull blue-green, bright magenta, buff, light new blue
Colour designations seen: 8½p. "G6 BLACK G6 GOLD G5 GREY G4 GREEN G3 RED G2" below vertical rows 8/10 extending to the edge of the sheet on dot pane. The "G6 BLACK" is superimposed over the "G6 GOLD". Also continued onto no dot pane "YELLOW G1 BLUE" below vertical row 1

Quantities Sold   8½p. 44,040,000; 10p. 8,280,000; 11p. 7,600,000; 13p. 6,920,000

Withdrawn   Pack, sold out 9.76; remainder 21.10.76

W304 Angel with Harp and Lute

W305 Angel with Mandolin

W306 Angel with Horn

W307 Angel with Trumpet

(Des. Richard Downer)

1975 (26 NOVEMBER).   CHRISTMAS

This is the second Christmas series depicting angels and musical instruments. The first appeared in 1972 designed by Sally Stiff. In this issue there is a new departure in the use of phosphor on the 8½p. value where it is mixed with the light turquoise-green ink used for the background colour. It reacts bright green under an ultra violet lamp. No doubt this was an experiment.

A. PVAD

One 4 mm. phosphor band at left

W323 (=S.G.993)	**W304**	6½p.	bluish vio, bright reddish vio, light lavender & gold	20	15

Phosphorised turquoise-green ink

W324 (=S.G.994)	**W305**	8½p.	turquoise-green, bright emerald-green, slate, light turquoise-green and gold	20	20

"All-over" phosphor

W325 (=S.G.995)	**W306**	11p.	vermilion, cerise, pink and gold	40	50
W326 (=S.G.996)	**W307**	13p.	drab, brown, bright orange, buff and gold ..	40	45

First Day Cover (W323/6)	..	..	..	..	†	1·25
Presentation Pack (W323/6)	..	..	..	..	2·00	†

B. PVA

One 4 mm. phosphor band at left

W327	**W304**	6½p.	bluish vio, bright reddish vio, light lavender & gold	75

The 6½p. PVAD exists with mottled toned gum.

The 6½p. value exists cancelled 25 November 1976 at Newport, I.O.W. but this may be due to incorrect use of the date stamp.

Cylinder Numbers (Blocks of Six)

	Cyl. Nos.	Perforation No dot	Type R* Dot
A. PVAD			
6½p. 1A (light lavender)–1B (bluish violet)–P63 (phosphor)–1D (bright reddish violet)–1E (gold) (a)		1·50	1·50
1A (light lavender)–1B (bluish violet)–1C (phosphor)–1D (bright reddish violet)–1E (gold) (b)*		15·00	15·00
1A (light lavender)–1B (bluish violet)–1C (phosphor)–1D (bright reddish violet)–1E (gold) (c)*		15·00	15·00
8½p. 1A (light turquoise-green)–1B (turquoise-green)–1C (bright emerald-green)–1D (slate)–1E (gold)		1·60	1·60
11p. 1A (pink)–1B (vermilion)–1C (cerise)–1D (cerise)–1E (gold)–P61 (phosphor)		5·00	5·00
1A (pink)–1B (vermilion)–1C (cerise)–1D (cerise)–1E (gold) (no phosphor)		2·75	2·75
13p. 1A (buff)–1B (drab)–1C (bright orange)–1D (brown)–1E (gold)–P61 (phosphor)		5·50	5·50
1A (buff)–1B (drab)–1C (bright orange)–1D (brown)–1E (gold) (no phosphor)		2·75	2·75
B. PVA			
6½p. 1A (light lavender)–1B (bluish violet)–P63 (phosphor)–1D (bright reddish violet)–1E (gold) (a)		8·50	6·50

Phosphor Cylinder Numbers

In the 6½p value variations in the positioning of the phosphor cylinder numbers occurred because the no dot phosphor cylinder was sometimes synchronised with the dot ink cylinders and vice versa owing to the dot cylinder being above the no dot cylinder. Moreover "P63" exists large and small and in addition there is a phosphor "1C". The variations are as follows:—

(a) No dot Small P63 below 1B and an inverted and reversed 1C in bottom left-hand corner
    Dot   Large P63 below 1B and an upright 1C in bottom left-hand corner
(b) No dot Upright 1C below 1B and large P63 displaced opposite R. 7/1
    Dot   Inverted and reversed 1C below 1B and small P63 displaced opposite R. 7/1
(c) No dot Inverted and reversed 1C below 1B and large P63 displaced opposite R. 7/1
    Dot   Upright 1C below 1B and large P63 displaced opposite R. 7/1

*Types (b) and (c) need to be collected in blocks of eight.

The 11p. and 13p. have P61 on the cylinder blocks opposite R. 10/1 but this has not been seen on the 13p. no dot where it exists inverted in the right margin opposite R. 2/10.

Sheet Details

Sheet size: 100 (2 panes 10 × 5). Double pane reel-fed

Sheet markings:

Cylinder numbers: Opposite rows 8/9, left margin, boxed

Marginal arrows: In centre, at top and bottom of each pane

Colour register marks (crossed lines type):

No dot panes: Opposite rows 1/3 at both sides and opposite row 4 in left margin only

Dot panes: Opposite rows 6/8 (6/7 on 13p.), at both sides

Autotron marks: In order of traffic lights opposite rows 2/4 (6½p.) or 1/4 (others), in left margin on dot panes only

Perforation register marks: Thick bar opposite row 4, right margin no dot panes

Quality control marks: Opposite rows 1, 5, 6 and 10 at both sides on both panes

Sheet values: Above and below vertical rows 2/4 and 7/9 reading from left to right in top margin and from right to left (upside down) in bottom margin

Traffic lights (boxed): In order of cylinder numbers opposite row 8 (13p.) or 9 (others), right margin; also in same order reading from left to right in gutter margin in vertical row 2

Colour designations seen:

6½p. "G5 GOLD G4 BLACK" reading up opposite rows 3/5, right margin on dot pane

11p. "G1 PINK" reading up opposite row 10, right margin on no dot pane

13p. "G5 GOLD G4 LINE G3 ORANGE G2 BROWN G1 LIGHT ORANGE", reading up oppositite rows 1/4, right margin on no dot pane and "OON (Maroon)/RED G3 RED/MAUVE G2 ORANGE/RED" reading up opposite rows 1/3 on dot pane

Quantities Sold   6½p. 215,530,000; 8½p. 108,340,000; 11p. 13,850,000; 13p. 12,610,000

Withdrawn   25.11.76

1975 (26 NOVEMBER). COLLECTORS PACK 1975

WCP9 Comprises Nos. W300/26 (Sold at £2·65)   9·00

This pack also contains background notes on the subjects depicted in the issues.

Although this pack was quickly sold out at post offices owing to the demand for the 12p. Sailing stamp and was withdrawn from the Philatelic Bureau in January 1976, it was put back on sale there in April 1976.

Sold Out   9.76

W308 Housewife

W309 Policeman

.**W310** District Nurse

W311 Industrialist

(Des. Philip Sharland)

1976 (10 MARCH).   TELEPHONE CENTENARY

This issue celebrates the first telephone communication made on 10 March 1876 by Alexander Graham Bell and the designs highlight the importance of the telephone to the community.
"All-over" phosphor

W328 (=S.G.997)	**W308**	8½p. greenish blue, deep rose, black and blue	20	20
		a. Deep rose omitted	£2250	
		b. Imperf. between stamp and bottom margin ..		
		c. Spot in upper lip	1·40	
		d. Eye in Queen's head	1·75	
W329 (=S.G.998)	**W309**	10p. greenish blue, black and yellow-olive ..	25	25
		a. Small 3 in upper margin (*vert. pair*) ..	2·25	
		b. Large blob right of telephone	3·50	
W330 (=S.G.999)	**W310**	11p. greenish blue, deep rose, black and bright mauve	40	45
		a. Imperf. between stamp and bottom margin ..		
W331 (=S.G.1000)	**W311**	13p. olive-brown, deep rose, black and orange-red ..	40	45
		a. Bump at back of Queen's head	2·75	

First Day Cover (W328/31)	†	1·25
Presentation Pack (W328/31)	2·00	†

Listed Varieties

W328*c*
Dark spot in housewife's
upper lip
(No dot, R. 3/5)

W328*d*
Blue spot in Queen's head
appearing as an eye
(No dot, R. 5/3)

W329*a*
Flaw in upper margin
appearing as a very small 3
(No dot, R. 8/3)

W329*b*
Large blob between
telephone and
policeman's sleeve
(Dot, R. 3/2)

W331*a*
Large bump at back of
Queen's head
(No dot, R. 8/2)

Cylinder Numbers (Blocks of Four)

Cyl. Nos.	Perforation Type R*

	No dot	Dot
8½p. 2A (blue)–1B (greenish blue)–1C (black)–1D (deep rose)–P62 (phosphor)	1·00	1·00
10p. 1A (yellow-olive)–1B (greenish blue)–1C (black)–P62 (phosphor)	1·25	1·25
11p. 1A (bright mauve)–1B (greenish blue)–1C (black)–1D (deep rose)–P62 (phosphor)	2·00	2·00
13p. 2A (orange-red)–1B (olive-brown)–1C (black)–1D (deep rose)–P62 (phosphor)	2·10	2·10

The phosphor cylinder number appears opposite row 9 in both panes

Sheet Details

Sheet size: 100 (2 panes 10 × 5). Double pane reel-fed

Sheet markings:
Cylinder numbers: Opposite rows 8/9, left margin, boxed
Marginal arrows: In centre, at top and bottom of each pane
Colour register marks (crossed lines type):
No dot panes: Opposite rows 1/2 at both sides and opposite row 4 in left margin only
Dot panes: Opposite rows 6/7 at both sides
Autotron marks: In reverse order of traffic lights opposite rows 1/4, left margin on dot panes only
Perforation register marks: Thick bar opposite row 4, right margin on dot panes
Quality control marks: Opposite rows 1, 5, 6 and 10 at both sides on both panes
Sheet values: Above and below vertical rows 2/4 and 7/9 reading from left to right in top margin and from right to left (upside down) in bottom margin
Traffic lights (boxed): Opposite row 9 (10p.) and rows 8/9 (others), right margin; also in same order reading from left to right in gutter margin in vertical row 2 (10p.) and rows 1/2 (others):
8½p. Deep rose, black, blue, greenish blue
10p. Black, yellow-olive, greenish blue
11p. Deep rose, black, bright mauve, greenish blue
13p. Deep rose, black, orange-red, olive-brown
Colour designations seen: All reading up in right margin on no dot panes:
10p. "G2 GREEN" (row 10), "BLACK G3" (row 8)
11p. "G2 BACKGROUND" (row 10), "BLACK G3" (row 8), "G4 RED" (rows 6/7)
13p. "G2 ORANGE" (row 10), "BLACK G3" (row 8), "G4 PINK" (row 6)

Quantities Sold   8½p. 41,350,000; 10p. 8,660,000; 11p. 7,540,000; 13p. 7,130,000

Withdrawn   27.4.77

W312 Hewing Coal
(Thomas Hepburn)

W313 Machinery
(Robert Owen)

W314 Chimney Cleaning
(Lord Shaftesbury)

W315 Hands clutching Prison Bars
(Elizabeth Fry)

(Des. David Gentleman)

1976 (28 APRIL). SOCIAL REFORMERS

This issue pays tribute to British poineers of social reform in the 19th century and the designer employed the symbolic use of hands as a common theme.

Thomas Hepburn formed the first miners' union at Hetton in the Tyne and Wear district in 1831, calling a strike over the bond of service whereby men could be sacked and evicted from their houses for trifling offences. Robert Owen, shocked at conditions in the cotton mills, purchased the New Lanark Mills in 1799 and made them a model for a better industrial system, introducing schools and co-operative communities. Lord Shaftesbury pioneered many reforms, such as the 1843 Mines Act, which excluded women and children under 13 from working in mines, houses for workers, free elementary education and changing the public attitude to mental illness but he is best known for the abolition of chimney sweeping by climbing boys. Elizabeth Fry was a Quaker who dared to visit the two cells in Newgate Prison where 300 women cooked, ate and slept on the bare floor. She introduced women supervisors, separation of regular offenders from petty criminals, education and employment and her ideas were imitated in prisons throughout Europe.

"All-over" phosphor

W332 (= S.G.1001)	W312	8½p. lavender-grey, grey-black, black and slate-grey ..	20	20
		a. White patches in coal	1·40	
W333 (= S.G.1002)	W313	10p. lavender-grey, grey-black, grey and slate-violet ..	25	25
W334 (= S.G.1003)	W314	11p. black, slate-grey and drab	40	45
W335 (= S.G.1004)	W315	13p. slate-grey, black and deep dull green	40	45

First Day Cover (W332/5)	..	..	..	†	1·25
Presentation Pack (W332/5)	..	..	..	2·00	†
PHQ Card (W332)	..	..	..	6·00	7·00

In all values there is an extension of the design of about 2 mm. into all four sheet margins which comes about as explained in the note after Nos. W217/20.

The 8½p. value is known with horizontal perforations displaced about 6 mm. upwards, resulting in the first and sixth rows having no face value and stamps in the remaining rows having it at the top of the design. It is not known how many sheets were issued.

The 10p. is also known with horizontal perforations displaced about 8 mm. upwards, resulting in the value appearing near the top of the stamp.

Major colour shifts are frequently seen in this issue.

W   1976.   Social Reformers

Listed Variety

Two small white patches on piece of coal
(No dot, R. 10/1)

W332*a*

Cylinder Numbers (Blocks of Six)

	Cyl. Nos.	Perforation Type R*	
		No dot	Dot
8½p.	1A (slate-grey)–1B (black)–1C (grey-black)–1D (lavender-grey)–2E (black)–P62 (phosphor)	2·75*	1·50
10p.	1A (grey-black)–1B (slate-violet)–4C (lavender-grey)–2D (grey)–P62 (phosphor)	1·75	1·75
11p.	1A (black)–1B (drab)–1C (slate-grey)–1D (black)–P62 (phosphor)	2·75	2·75
13p.	2A (black)–2B (deep dull green)–1C (black)–1D (slate-grey)–2E (black)–P62 (phosphor)	2·90	2·90

Sheet Details

Sheet size: 100 (2 panes 10 × 5). Double pane reel-fed
Sheet markings:
  Cylinder numbers: Opposite rows 8/9 (8½p., 13p.) or 8 (10p., 11p.), left margin, boxed
  Marginal arrows: In centre at top and bottom of each pane
  Colour register marks (crossed lines type):
    No dot panes: Opposite rows 1/2 at both sides and opposite rows 6/7 in left margin only
    Dot panes: Opposite rows 6/8 at both sides
  Autotron marks: In order of traffic lights opposite rows 2/5 (8½p.) or 3/5 (others), left margin
    on dot panes only
  Perforation register marks: Thin bar in left margin opposite bottom row of perforations on
    no dot panes and opposite top row on dot panes
  Quality control marks: None
  Sheet values: Above and below vertical rows 2/4 and 7/9 reading from left to right in top margin
    and from right to left (upside down) in bottom margin
  Traffic lights (boxed): Opposite rows 8/9 (8½p.) or 8 (others), right margin, also in same order
    reading from left to right in gutter margin in vertical row 2:
    8½p. Slate-grey, black, grey-black, lavender-grey, black
    10p. Slate-violet, grey-black, lavender-grey, grey
    11p. Black, drab, slate-grey, black
    13p. Deep dull green, black, black, slate-grey, black
  Colour designations seen: All reading up in right margin on dot panes:
    8½p. "G1 GREY G2 BLACK G3 BROWN BLACK" (rows 2/5)
    10p. "G2 LIGHT BROWN" (rows 1/2)

Quantities Sold   8½p. 41,260,000; 10p. 8,630,000; 11p. 7,510,000; 13p. 7,090,000

Withdrawn   27.4.77

82

W316 Benjamin Franklin
(Des. Philip Sharland after bust by Jean-Jacques Caffieri at the
Royal Society of Arts, London)

1976 (2 JUNE). BICENTENNIAL OF AMERICAN INDEPENDENCE

Benjamin Franklin attempted to mediate between the British Government and the American colonies before the final break on 4 July 1776. When the American Continental Congress adopted the Declaration of Independence he signed it and became one of the "founding fathers" of the new republic. Formerly the Postmaster of Philadelphia, he later became Deputy Postmaster General under the British colonial administration and then Postmaster General under the independent American Government.

"All-over" phosphor

W336 (=S.G.1005)   **W316**   11p. pale bistre, slate-violet, pale blue-grn, blk, & gold   30   30

First Day Cover (W336)	..	..	..	..	†	60
Presentation Pack (W336)	..	..	..	..	1·00	†
PHQ Card (W336)	..	..	..	..	﹐4·00	8·50

Cylinder Numbers (Blocks of Six)

	Perforation	Type R*
Cyl. Nos.	No dot	Dot

11p. 1A (black)–1B (pale bistre)–1C (pale blue-green)–4D (slate-
violet)–1E (gold)–P62 (phosphor) ..   ..   2·10   2·10
The above are with sheet orientated with head to left.

Sheet Details

Sheet size: 100 (2 panes 5 × 10). Double pane reel-fed

Sheet markings:
 Cylinder numbers: In top margin above vertical rows 2/3, boxed
 Marginal arrows: In centre, opposite rows 5/6 at each side and at each side of vertical gutter
 Colour register marks (crossed lines type):
  No dot pane: Above and below vertical rows 9/10 and at vertical row 7 in top margin only
  Dot pane: Above and below vertical rows 4/5
 Autotron marks: Vertical bars in order of traffic lights above vertical rows 6/8 on dot pane
  only
 Perforation register mark: Thick bar below vertical row 7 in dot pane only
 Sheet values: Opposite rows 2/4 and 7/9 reading up at left and down at right
 Traffic lights (boxed): In bottom margin below vertical row 2; also in same order reading up
  in gutter margin in row 2: Gold, black, slate-violet, pale blue-green, pale bistre
 Colour designations seen: "G£ GOLD" below gutter margin and "G3 GREY" below vertical
  rows 4/5 on dot pane

Quantity Sold 11p. 9,970,000

Withdrawn 1.6.77. Pack sold out 2.77

W317 "Elizabeth of Glamis"   **W318** "Grandpa Dickson"

W319 "*Rosa Mundi*"   **W320** "Sweet Briar"

(Des. Kristin Rosenberg)

1976 (30 JUNE).   ROSES

This set, marking the centenary of the Royal National Rose Society, shows respectively a floribunda, a tea rose, a shrub rose and a briar. "Elizabeth of Glamis" was named after the Queen Mother, who is Patron of the society.

"All-over" phosphor

W337 (=S.G.1006)	**W317**	8½p.	bright rose-red, greenish yellow, emerald, grey-black and gold	20	20
W338 (=S.G.1007)	**W318**	10p.	greenish yellow, bright green, reddish brown, grey-black and gold	30	30
W339 (=S.G.1008)	**W319**	11p.	bright magenta, greenish yellow, emerald, grey-blue, grey-black and gold	35	40
W340 (=S.G.1009)	**W320**	13p.	rose-pink, lake-brown, yellow-green, pale greenish yellow, grey-black and gold	35	35
		a.	Value omitted*		

First Day Cover (W337/40)	..	..	..	†	1·50
Presentation Pack (W337/40)	..	..	..	2·25	†
PHQ Cards (W337/40)	..	..	..	30·00	14·00

*The value was not engraved in one position (R.1/9) of the dot cylinder but the error was discovered before issue and most examples were removed from the sheets. Three examples have been reported and, of these, one mint example is in private hands. The Royal Collection contains mint and used examples, the latter is postmarked at Dover, Kent.

A single used copy of the 8½p. has been seen with the bright rose-red colour omitted but we do not regard this as a missing colour as the roses appeared in orange, a colour which was not employed and we can only assume that the colours were faded.

Two different types of phosphor were used. The second type was applied to the 10p. and 11p. and about 40% of the printing of the 13p. There is no difference to the naked eye but under ultra-violet light the second type gives a stronger and longer afterglow compared with the normal type used on the 8½p. It also responds to a broader waveband of ultra-violet light.

Cylinder Numbers (Blocks of Six)

	Cyl. Nos.	Perforation Type R*	
		No dot	Dot
8½p.	1A (grey-black)–1B (greenish yellow)–3C (bright rose-red)–1D (grey-black)–1E (emerald)–1F (gold)–P62 (phosphor*).. ..	1·50	1·50
	1A (grey-black)–1B (greenish yellow)–3C (bright rose-red)–1D (grey-black)–1E (emerald)–1F (gold)	3·00	3·00
10p.	1A (grey-black)–1B (greenish yellow)–1C (reddish brown)–1D (grey-black)–1E (bright green)–1F (gold)–P62 (phosphor) ..	2·10	2·10
11p.	1A (grey-black)–2B (greenish yellow)–1C (bright magenta)–1D (grey-blue)–1E (emerald)–1F (gold)–P62 (phosphor)	2·40	2·40
13p.	1A (grey-black)–1B (pale greenish yellow)–1C (lake-brown)–2D (rose-pink)–1E (yellow-green)–1F (gold)–P62 (phosphor) ..	2·50	2·50

The above are with sheets orientated with head to left.

*On the 8½p. the phosphor number appears on the no dot and dot panes (just above 1F). Both panes have been seen with part P62 phosphor number and with part phosphor inset at the extreme top and bottom of the phosphor margin.

Sheet Details

Sheet size: 100 (2 panes 5 × 10). Double pane reel-fed

Sheet markings:
Cylinder numbers: In top margin above vertical rows 2/3, boxed
Marginal arrows: In centre, opposite rows 5/6 at both sides and at each side of vertical gutter
Colour register marks (crossed lines type):
No dot panes: Above and below vertical rows 8/10 and large cross at vertical row 7 in top margin only
Dot panes: Above and below vertical rows 3/5
Autotron marks: Vertical bars in order of traffic lights reading from left to right above vertical rows 6/9 on dot panes only
Perforation register marks: Vertical thick bar below vertical row 7 on dot panes of 8½p. and 11p. (10p. not examined)
Quality control mark: Horizontal bar below vertical row 6 on dot pane of 13p.
Sheet values: Opposite rows 2/4 and 7/9 reading up at left and down at right
Traffic lights (boxed). In bottom margin below vertical rows 2/3; also in same order reading up in gutter margin in rows 2/3:
8½p. Gold, emerald, grey-black, bright rose-red, greenish yellow, grey-black
10p. Gold, bright green, grey-black, reddish brown, greenish yellow, grey-black
11p. Gold, emerald, grey-blue, bright magenta, greenish yellow, grey-black
13p. Gold, yellow-green, rose-pink, lake-brown, pale greenish yellow, grey-black
Colour designation seen: "G6? G5? G4 GREY G3 RED G2 YE" below vertical rows 8/10 on dot pane of 11p. and "LLOW G1 BLACK" on the no dot pane. "G6 GOLD G5 GREEN G4 PINK G3 BROWN G2 YEL" below vertical rows 8/10 on dot pane of 13p. and "G1 BLACK" below vertical row 1 on no dot pane. There is also something below vertical row 1 on no dot pane of the 10p.

Quantities Sold 8½p. 39,760,000; 10p. 8,940,000; 11p. 7,990,000; 13p. 7,410,000

Withdrawn 29.6.77

W321 Archdruid   **W322** Morris Dancer

W323 Scots Piper   **W324** Welsh Harpist

(Des. Marjorie Saynor)

1976 (4 AUGUST).   BRITISH CULTURAL TRADITIONS

The 8½p. and 13p. values celebrate the 800th anniversary of the Royal National Eisteddfod, whilst the 10p. stamp marks Morris Dancing and the 11p. a Highland Gathering.

"All-over" phosphor

W341 (=S.G.1010)	**W321**	8½p.	yellow, sepia, bright rose, dull ultram, blk & gold				20	20
W342 (=S.G.1011)	**W322**	10p.	dull ultramarine, bright rose-red, sepia, greenish yellow, black and gold	..	..	..	30	30
			a. Phosphor omitted ..	..	..	..	£350	
			b. Brown mark on handkerchief	..	..	2·10	
			c. Brown line ..	..	..	..	2·40	
W343 (=S.G.1012)	**W323**	11p.	bluish green, yellow-brown, yellow-orange, black, bright rose-red and gold	..	..	..	35	35
W344 (=S.G.1013)	**W324**	13p.	dull violet-blue, yellow-orange, yellow-brown, black, bluish green and gold	..	..	35	35
			a. Short serif ..	..	..	..	2·50	
			b. Broken 2nd harp-string	..	..	2·25	
			c. Broken 8th harp-string	..	..	2·25	

First Day Cover (W341/4)	..	..	..	..	†	1·25
Presentation Pack (W341/4)	..	..	..	2·00	†
PHQ Cards (W341/4) ..	..	..	..	..	16·00	8·50

Listed Varieties

W342*b*	W342*c*	W344*a*
Brown mark on hand-kerchief (No dot, R. 1/5)	Brown line between handkerchief and ribbon. Stamp also shows yellow and red line on dancer's right arm (No dot, R. 3/5)	Short serif to first 1 (Dot, R. 3/1)

W344*b*	W344*c*
Broken 2nd harp-string (Dot, R. 3/3)	Broken 8th harp-string (No dot, R. 6/1)

Cylinder Numbers (Blocks of Six)

	Cyl. Nos.	Perforation No dot	Type R* Dot
8½p.	1A (black)–1B (yellow)–1C (sepia)–1D (bright rose)–1E (dull ultramarine)–1G (gold)–P62 (phosphor)	1·50	1·50
	1A (black)–1B (yellow)–1C (sepia)–1D (bright rose)–1E (dull ultramarine)–1G (gold)	4·00	4·00
10p.	4A (black)–1B (sepia)–4C (bright rose-red)–1D (dull ultramarine)–1E (greenish yellow)–1F (gold)	2·10	2·10
11p.	1A (black)–1B (yellow-brown)–1C (bluish green)–1D (yellow-orange)–1E (bright rose-red)–1F (gold)	2·40	2·40
13p.	3A (black)–1B (dull violet-blue)–1C (bluish green)–1D (yellow-orange)–1E (yellow-brown)–1F (gold)	2·50	2·50

The above are with sheets orientated with head to left.

The phosphor cylinder No. P62 is displaced on the 10p., 11p. and 13p. values.

Both 8½p. panes have been seen with part P62 phosphor number and part phosphor inset at the extreme top and bottom of the phosphor margin.

Sheet Details

Sheet size: 100 (2 panes 5 × 10). Double pane reel-fed

Sheet markings:

Cylinder numbers: In top margin above vertical rows 2/3, boxed

Marginal arrows: In centre, opposite rows 5/6 at both sides and at each side of vertical gutter

Colour register marks (crossed lines type):—

No dot panes: Above and below vertical rows 8/9 and large cross in top margin above vertical rows 6/7

Dot panes: Above and below vertical rows 3/5

Autotron marks: Vertical bars in order of traffic lights reading from left to right above vertical rows 6/9 on dot panes only

Perforation register marks: Vertical thick bar below vertical row 7 on dot panes
Sheet values: Opposite rows 2/4 and 7/9 reading up at left and down at right
Traffic lights (boxed): Below vertical rows 1/2; also in same order reading up in gutter margins in row 2:
8½p. Gold, black, dull ultramarine, bright rose, sepia, yellow
10p. Gold, black, dull ultramarine, bright, rose-red, sepia, greenish yellow
11p. Gold, bright rose-red, yellow-orange, bluish green, black, sepia
13p. Gold, black, yellow-brown, yellow-orange, bluish green, dull violet-blue
Colour designations seen: "G6 GOLD G5 ? G4 BLUE G3 RED G2 BROWN G1 YELLOW" below vertical rows 3/8 on dot pane of 8½p. "G6 GOLD G5 ? G4 BROWN G3 FLESH G2 GREEN G1 BLUE" below vertical rows 4/10 on dot pane of 13p.

Quantities Sold   8½p. 38,250,000; 10p. 8,360,000; 11p. 7,410,000; 13p. 6,920,000

Withdrawn   3.8.77

William Caxton 1476   8½ᵖ

W325 Woodcut from *The Canterbury Tales*

William Caxton 1476   10ᵖ

W326 Extract from *The Tretyse of Love*

William Caxton 1476   11ᵖ

W327 Woodcut from *The Game and Playe of Chesse*

William Caxton 1476   13ᵖ

W328 Early Printing Press

(Des. Richard Gay)
(Printed in photogravure with the Queen's head in gold and then embossed)

1976 (29 SEPTEMBER).   500th ANNIVERSARY OF BRITISH PRINTING

This issue is a tribute to William Caxton who first introduced printing to England in 1476. He set himself up as a successful merchant in Flanders and translated books into English in his leisure hours and it is likely that he thought of printing as an alternative to having his popular translations laboriously copied out. The first book ever printed in English was his translation of Le Fevre's history, produced late in 1473 in Bruges. He returned to England in 1476 and the first piece of jobbing printing in England was an indulgence in December 1476, which can still be seen at the Public Record Office.

"All-over" phosphor

W345 (= S.G.1014)	**W325**	8½p.	black, light new blue and gold	..	..	..	20	20
			a. Broken fingers	..	..	..	..	2·50
			d. Gap in shading	..	..	..	..	2·00
			c. Break in shoe	.:	..	..	..	2·00
			d. Mark under 8	..	..	..	..	2·00
W346 (= S.G.1015)	**W326**	10p.	black, olive-green and gold	..	..	..	25	30
W347 (= S.G.1016)	**W327**	11p.	black, brownish grey and gold	..	..	..	35	40
			a. Imperf. between stamp and left margin	..	..	£450
W348 (≐ S.G.1017)	**W328**	13p.	chocolate, pale ochre and gold	..	..	..	40	45

First Day Cover (W345/8)	..	..	..	..	†	1·25
Presentation Pack (W345/8)	..	..	..	..	2·10	†
PHQ Cards (W345/8)	..	..	..	..	14·00	8·50

The descriptive text for the presentation packs, on postcards and inside first day covers relating to the Caxton issue wrongly ascribes the design of the 8½p. value as depicting the woodcut as representing the Knight instead of the Squire.

Listed Varieties

W345a	W345b	W345c	W345d
Broken fingers	Gap in shading by	Rider's pointed shoe	Blue mark under 8
(Dot, R. 1/1)	horse's hind leg	broken at tip	(Dot, R. 9/8)
	(Dot, R. 3/6)	(Dot, R. 9/5)	

Cylinder Numbers (Blocks of Four)

Cyl. Nos.	Perforation Type R*	
	No dot	Dot
8½p. 1A (black)—1B (light new blue)—2C (gold)—P62 (phosphor)	1·00	3·25*
1A (black)—1B (light new blue)—2C (gold)	4·00	6·00*
10p. 1A (black)—1B (olive-green)—1C (gold)—P62 (phosphor) ..	1·25	1·25
11p. 1A (black)—1B (brownish grey)—2C (gold)—P62 (phosphor)	1·75	1·75
1A (black)—1B (brownish grey)—2C (gold)	5·00	†
13p. 1A (chocolate)—1B (pale ochre)—1C (gold)—P62 (phosphor)	2·00	2·00

The above are with sheets orientated with head to left.

The same cylinder 1B was used for the background of all values so that any flaws on this are likely to occur on all values. It is understood that this is the first time a cylinder has been used in different colours for all values in a special issue.

W 1976. Christmas.

Sheet Details

Sheet size: 100 (2 panes 5 × 10). Double pane reel-fed

Sheet markings:
Cylinder numbers: In top margin above vertical row 2, boxed
Marginal arrows: In centre, opposite rows 5/6 at both sides and at each side of vertical gutter
Colour register marks (crossed lines type):
No dot panes: Above and below vertical row 9 and large cross above vertical row 7 in top margin only
Dot panes: Above and below vertical row 4
Autotron marks: Vertical bars in order of traffic lights reading from left to right above vertical rows 6/7 on dot panes only
Perforation register marks: Vertical thick bar below vertical row 7 on dot panes only
Sheet values: Opposite rows 2/4 and 7/9 reading up at left and down at right
Traffic lights (boxed): In bottom margin below vertical row 2; also in same order reading up in gutter margin in row 2:
8½p. Gold, black, light new blue
10p. Gold, black, olive-green
11p. Gold, black, brownish grey
13p. Gold, chocolate, pale ochre

Quantities Sold 8½p. 37,550,000; 10p. 8,260,000; 11p. 7,320,000; 13p. 6,780,000

Withdrawn 28.9.77

W329 Virgin and Child

W330 Angel with Crown

W331 Angel appearing to Shepherds

W332 The Three Kings

(Des. Enid Marx)

1976 (24 NOVEMBER). CHRISTMAS

The Christmas scenes are taken from 13th and 14th century English embroideries from a collection on show at the Victoria and Albert Museum. The design for the 6½p. is from the Clare Chasuble (1272–1294). That of the 8½p. is from a pair of panels (1340–1370) found in a chapel in Hampshire. That of the 11p. stamp is from one of three panels (1320–1340) from an alb, a part of an ecclesiastical vestment. The design on the 13p. came from the Butler-Bowden Cope (1330–1350), one of the finest surviving examples of English medieval embroidery.

One 4 mm. phosphor band at right

W349 (=S.G. 1018)	**W329**	6½p.	blue, bistre-yellow, brown and bright orange ..	15	15
		a.	Imperforate (pair)	£450	
"All-over" phosphor					
W350 (=S.G. 1019)	**W330**	8½p.	sage-green, yell, br-ochre, chestnut & olive-blk	20	20
W351 (=S.G. 1020)	**W331**	11p.	deep mag, brown-orge, new bl, blk & cinnamon	35	40
		a.	Uncoated paper	60·00	30·00
		b.	Hook on 3	2·50	
W352 (=S.G. 1021)	**W332**	13p.	bright pur, new bl, cinnamon, bronze-grn & olive-grey	40	40

First Day Cover (W349/52)	†	1·25
Presentation Pack (W349/52)	2·00	†
PHQ Cards (W349/52)	3·25	11·00

Listed Variety

Magenta hook on 3 of 1320
(also known displaced)
(No dot, R. 3/2)

W351*b*

Cylinder Numbers (Blocks of Six)

	Perforation	Type R*
Cyl. Nos.	No dot	Dot
6½p. 2A (blue)—1B (bistre-yellow)—1C (brown)—1D (bright orange)—P64 (phosphor)	1·25	1·25
2A (blue)—1B (bistre-yellow)—1C (brown)—1D (bright orange)	5·00	5·00
8½p. 1A (sage-green)—1B (yellow)—1C (brown-ochre)—1D (chestnut)—2E (olive-black)—P62 (phosphor)	5·00	5·00
1A (sage-green)—1B (yellow)—1C (brown-ochre)—1D (chestnut)—2E (olive-black)	1·50	1·50
11p. 2A (brown-orange)—1B (cinnamon)—1C (new blue)—1D (deep magenta)—1E (black)	2·40	2·40
13p. 1A (bright purple)—1B (new blue)—1C (cinnamon)—1D (bronze-green)—1E (olive-grey)—P65 inverted (phosphor) ..	5·00	5·00
1A (bright purple)—1B (new blue)—1C (cinnamon)—1D (bronze-green)—1E (olive-grey)	2·75	2·75

All the phosphor cylinder numbers are unsynchronised and liable to occur in any position. In the 8½p. value cylinder P62 also occurs inverted in the right-hand margin and in addition phosphor cylinder P65 was used and this occurs upright in the right-hand margin only. The same applies to the 11p. and 13p. values but in the 13p. this cylinder is also known inverted, appearing in the left-hand margin both on the cylinder block or elsewhere.

Sheet Details

Sheet size: 100 (2 panes 10 × 5).   Double pane reel-fed

Sheet markings:

Cylinder numbers: Opposite row 9 (6½p.) or 8/9 (others), left margin, boxed

Marginal arrows: In centre at top and bottom of each pane, except 11p. where there are no arrows in gutter margin

Colour register marks (crossed lines type):

No dot panes: Opposite rows 1/2 at both sides and large cross opposite row 7, left margin

Dot panes: Opposite rows 6/7 at both sides

Autotron marks: In order of traffic lights opposite rows 1/3 (6½p.) or 1/4 (others), left margin on dot panes only

Perforation register marks: Thick bar opposite row 3, right margin on dot panes

Sheet values: Above and below vertical rows 2/4 and 7/9 reading from left to right in top margin and from right to left (upside down) in bottom margin

Traffic lights (boxed): Opposite rows 8/9, right margin; also in same order reading from left to right in gutter margin in vertical row 2, except 6½p. where the order is bistre-yellow, brown, blue, bright orange:

6½p.   Brown, bistre-yellow, blue, bright orange

8½p.   Yellow, brown-ochre, sage-green, chestnut, olive-black

11p.   Brown-orange, cinnamon, new blue, deep magenta, black

13p.   New blue, cinnamon, bronze-green, bright purple, olive-grey

Colour designations seen: All reading up in right margin:

6½p.   "G4 ORANGE G3 BLUE G2 BROWN G1" (rows 1/3 on dot panes) and "YELLOW" (row 10 on no dot panes)

8½p.   "G5 BLACK G4 BROWN G3 GREEN G2 CREAM (?) G1 Y" (rows 1/4 on dot panes) and "ELLOW" (row 10 on no dot panes)

11p.   "G5 BLACK G4 RED G3 BLUE G2 STONE G1 Y" (rows 1/4 on dot panes) and "ELLOW" (row 10 on no dot panes)

13p.   "1 BLUE" (row 10 on no dot panes)

Quantities Sold   6½p. 217,910,000; 8½p. 94,070,000; 11p. 12,790,000; 13p. 11,080,000

Withdrawn   23.11.77 (6½p. sold out shortly before)

1976 (24 NOVEMBER).   COLLECTORS PACK 1976

WCP10 Comprises Nos. W328/49 (Sold at £2·90)   14·00

Withdrawn   23.11.77

W333 Lawn Tennis

W334 Table Tennis

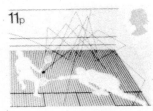

W335 Squash

(Des. Andrew Restall)

W336 Badminton

1977 (12 JANUARY).   RACKET SPORTS

Tennis, depicted on the 8½p. value, probably evolved in European monasteries around the 11th century but originated in its modern form in England and Henry VIII had a "Real Tennis" court built at Hampton Court in 1530. The Centenary of the Wimbledon Lawn Tennis Championships took place in 1977. Table Tennis, or Ping Pong, shown on the 10p., took root in the Victorian period in University common rooms and officers' messes. It was revived with proper rules after the First World War and it is appropriate that the World Table Tennis Championships were staged at the new National Exhibition Centre at Birmingham in 1977. Squash (11p.) developed in the 1870s from Fives, still played in some British public schools, using three walls. Squash is not a suitable subject for spectator sport but enjoys a great following as an indoor "keep fit" sport. Badminton (13p.) gets its name from the Duke of Beaufort's seat in Gloucestershire and developed from the children's game of battledore and shuttlecock around 1870 and was a great favourite with army officers in India. The Badminton Association was formed in 1893. This was the first special issue to be printed experimentally on phosphorised paper.

Phosphorised (fluorescent coated) paper

W353 (=S.G.1022)	**W333**	8½p. emerald-green, black, grey and bluish green	..	20	20
		a. Imperforate (horiz. pair)		£850	
		b. Extended centre line		2·50	
		c. Patch above hand		1·90	
W354 (=S.G.1023)	**W334**	10p. myrtle-green, black, grey-black and deep blue-green		30	30
W355 (=S.G.1024)	**W335**	11p. orange, pale yellow, black, slate-black and grey..		35	40
W356 (=S.G.1025)	**W336**	13p. brown, grey-black, grey and bright reddish violet		40	40
		a. Missing screening dots		2·25	

First Day Cover (W353/6)	†	1·40	
Presentation Pack (W353/6)	2·00	†	
PHQ Cards (W353/6)	6·00	9·00	

Listed Varieties

W353*b*
White centre-line extends through
serving line and off the edge of the
stamp
(No dot, R. 2/10)

W353*c*
Black patch above player's
right hand
(No dot, R. 7/6)

W356*a*
Screening dots missing at bottom of stamp by player's foot
(Dot, R. 10/1)

Cylinder Numbers (Blocks of Six)

Cyl. Nos.	Perforation Type R*	
	No dot	Dot
8½p. 1A (black)–3B (emerald-green)–2C (grey)–1D (bluish green) ..	1·50	1·50
10p. 1A (black)–1B (myrtle-green)–2C (grey-black)–1D (deep blue-green)	2·10	2·10
11p. 1A(black)–1B(paleyellow)–1C(grey)–1D(orange)–1E(slate-black)	2·50	2·50
13p. 2A (grey-black)–4B (brown)–1C (grey)–1D (bright reddish violet)	2·75	4·25*

Sheet Details

Sheet size: 100 (2 panes 10 × 5). Double pane reel-fed

Sheet markings:
Cylinder numbers: Opposite rows 8/9 (11p.) or 9 (others), left margin, boxed
Marginal arrows: In centre at top and bottom of each pane
Colour register marks (crossed lines type):
  No dot panes: Opposite rows 1/2 at both sides
  Dot panes: Opposite rows 6/8 (11p.) or 6/7 (others) at both sides and large cross opposite
  row 4, left margin
Autotron marks: In order of traffic lights opposite rows 1/3, left margin on dot panes only
Perforation register marks: Thick bar opposite rows 3/4 (11p.) or row 3 (others), right margin
  on dot panes
Quality control mark: Opposite row 10, left margin no dot pane on 13p. only
Sheet values: Above and below vertical rows 2/4 and 7/9 reading from left to right in top margin
  and from right to left (upside down) in bottom margin
Traffic lights (boxed): Opposite rows 8/9 (11p.) or 9 (others), right margin; also in same order
  reading from left to right in gutter margin in vertical rows 1/2 (11p.) or 2 (others):
  8½p. Emerald-green, grey, black, bluish green
  10p. Myrtle-green, grey-black, black, deep blue-green
  11p. Pale yellow, grey, orange, black, slate-black
  13p. Brown, grey, grey-black, bright reddish violet
Colour designations: None seen

Quantities Sold 8½p. 37,120,000; 10p. 8,240,000; 11p. 7,420,000; 13p. 6,790,000

Withdrawn Pack 11.1.78; others sold out 11.77

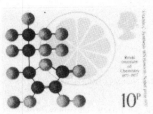

W337 Steroids—Conformation
Analysis

W338 Vitamin C—Synthesis

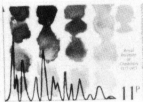

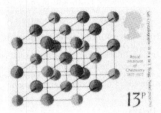

W339 Starch—Chromatography

W340 Salt—Crystallography

(Des. Jerzy Karo)

1977 (2 MARCH). ROYAL INSTITUTE OF CHEMISTRY CENTENARY

This issue is devoted to British achievements in chemistry and the stamps illustrate the work of Nobel prize winners. The 8½p. value concerns the work on conformational analysis by Professor Sir Derek Barton at the Imperial College which enabled the reproduction of complex natural substances in chemical plants. The 10p. refers to the work on Vitamic C by Sir Norman Haworth at Birmingham University which enabled the production of the first synthetic vitamin identical with that occurring in citrus fruits. The 11p. illustrates partition chromatography by which the components of a liquid or gas can be separated, identified and measured, this work being pioneered by Professors A. J. P. Martin and R. L. M. Synge. The 13p. shows crystallography, the X-ray photography of crystals, which was developed by the father and son team, Professors Sir William and Sir Lawrence Bragg.

"All-over" phosphor

W357 (=S.G.1029)	**W337**	8½p. rosine, new blue, olive-yellow, bright mauve, yellow-brown, black and gold..		20	20
		a. Imperforate (horiz. pair)		£850	
		b. Imperf. between stamp and bottom margin		£350	
		c. Dot over a of Barton		1·75	
W358 (=S.G.1030)	**W338**	10p. bright orange, rosine, new bl, bright bl, blk & gold		30	30
W359 (=S.G.1031)	**W339**	11p. rosine, greenish yell, new bl, deep vio, blk & gold		35	35
		a. Imperf. between stamp and bottom margin			
W360 (=S.G.1032)	**W340**	13p. new blue, bright green, black and gold		40	40

First Day Cover (W357/60)	..	..	..	†	1·40
Presentation Pack (W357/60)	..	..	..	2·40	†
PHQ Cards (W357/60)	..	..	..	6·00	9·00

Nos. W357*b* and W359*a* came from the lower parts of sheets which were only partly perforated in that they contained stamps showing indentation from the perforation pins so that no stamp in the sheets was completely devoid of perforations all round. However, in each case there was no sign of perforation indentations between the bottom row and the selvedge.

Listed Variety

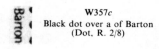

W357c
Black dot over a of Barton
(Dot, R. 2/8)

Cylinder Numbers (Blocks of Six)

	Cyl. Nos.	Perforation No dot	Type R* Dot
8½p.	2A (black)–1B (yellow-brown)–1C (olive-yellow)–1D (gold)–2E (new blue)–1F (bright mauve)–1G (rosine)–P62 (phosphor) ..	3·50	3·50
	2A (black)–1B (yellow-brown)–1C (olive-yellow)–1D (gold)–2E (new blue)–1F (bright mauve)–1G (rosine)	1·50	1·50
10p.	5A (black)–1B (bright orange)–1C (rosine)–1D (gold)–1E (new blue)–1F (bright blue)–P62 (phosphor)	2·10	2·10
	5A (black)–1B (bright orange)–1C (rosine)–1D (gold)–1E (new blue)–1F (bright blue)	4·00	4·00
11p.	3A (black)–1B (greenish yellow)–1C (rosine)–1D (gold)–1E (new blue)–1F (deep violet)	2·50	2·50
13p.	2A (black)–1B (bright green)–1C (new blue)–1D (gold) ..	2·75	2·75

The phosphor cylinder number P62 is unsynchronised and can occur in any position in the left-hand margin. The 8½p. is also known with the phosphor cylinder inverted so that the number appears inverted in the right-hand margin.

Sheet Details

Sheet size: 100 (2 panes 10 × 5). Double pane reel-fed

Sheet markings:
Cylinder numbers: Opposite rows 8/9, left margin, boxed
Marginal arrows: In centre at top and bottom of each pane
Colour register marks (crossed lines type):
No dot panes: Opposite rows 2/3 (13p.) or 1/3 (others) at both sides and large cross opposite row 7, left margin
Dot panes: Opposite rows 7/8 (13p.) or 6/8 (others) at both sides
Autotron marks: In order of traffic lights opposite rows 2/5 (13p.) or 1/5 (others), left margin, on dot panes only. 13p. has additional black bar above bright green bar
Perforation register marks: Thick bar opposite rows 3/4, right margin on dot panes
Sheet values: Above and below vertical rows 2/4 and 7/9 reading from left to right in top margin and from right to left (upside down) in bottom margin
Traffic lights (boxed): Opposite row 9 (13p.) or rows 8/9 (others), right margin; also in same order reading from left to right in gutter margin in vertical rows 2/3:
8½p. Yellow-brown, olive-yellow, rosine, new blue, bright mauve, black, gold
10p. Bright orange, rosine, new blue, bright blue, black, gold
11p. Greenish yellow, rosine, new blue, deep violet, black, gold
13p. Bright green, new blue, black, gold
Colour designations seen: 10p. "G3 LIGHT BLUE G2 RED" reading up opposite rows 7/9 right margin on no dot pane

Quantities Sold   8½p. 37,060,000; 10p. 9,360,000; 11p. 8,460,000; 13p. 7,860,000

Withdrawn   8½p. sold out 12.77; others withdrawn 1.3.78

W341

W342

W343

W344

The designs differ only in the decoration of the silver initials

(Des. Richard Guyatt)

1977 (11 MAY–15 JUNE (9p.)).   SILVER JUBILEE

This issue marks the 25th anniversary of the Queen's Accession to the throne. The design is reminiscent of that of the 1935 Silver Jubilee issue of the reign of King George V. The 9p. value was added later to meet a change in postal rates. The stamps remained on sale at post offices for about three months instead of the usual fortnight to ensure that supplies should be available during the extensive Jubilee Tour of the country made by the Queen, for which the Post Office issued special souvenir covers.

"All-over" phosphor

W361 (=S.G.1033)	W341	8½p. blackish grn, blk, silver, ol-grey & pale turq-grn		20	20
		a. Imperforate (pair)	£750		
		b. Imperf. between stamp and bottom margin ..			
W362 (=S.G.1034)	W341	9p. maroon, black, silver, olive-grey and lavender ..		25	25
		a. Imperf. between stamp and bottom margin ..			
W363 (=S.G.1035)	W342	10p. blackish blue, black, silver, olive-grey and ochre		25	30
		a. Imperforate (horiz. pair)			
W364 (=S.G.1036)	W343	11p. brown-purple, black, silver, olive-grey and rose-pink		30	35
		a. Imperforate (horiz. pair)	£1250		
W365 (=S.G.1037)	W344	13p. sepia, black, silver, olive-grey and bistre-yellow ..		40	40
		a. Imperforate (pair)	£1250		

First Day Covers (2) (W361/5)	†	1·75	
Souvenir Cover (W361, W363/5)*	†	3·00	
Presentation Pack (W361, W363/5)	1·75	†	
Souvenir Book (W361, W363/5) (Sold at £1·20) ..	4·00	†	
PHQ Cards (W361/5)	13·00	11·00	

First Day Covers with the set of four also exist with the 9p. added and postmarked again on 15 June and are scarce.

*Four special souvenir covers, one each for England, Northern Ireland, Scotland and Wales, were issued by the Post Office for use with special postmarks in 24 major towns included in the Queen's Royal Tour, which extended from 17 May to 11 August. They were issued bearing the four original values but after 15 June doubtless the 9p. value was added in many instances. The price is the same for any of these covers. The souvenir book is a 16-page booklet containing a history of the Queen's reign.

No. W362*a* occurred in the same circumstances as described in the note relating to Nos. W357*a* and W359*a*.

A quantity of the 9p. value was purchased from a sub-post office in Kingston on 9 June by a commercial firm which used them that day on circulars and they were duly postmarked with the Kingston upon Thames postmark and it is understood that they tried to obliterate the "9" by blue biro. Quite a number of post offices started selling this value on 13 June, the date of the increase in the first class postal rate.

Cylinder Numbers (Blocks of Six)

		Perforation	Type R*
	Cyl. Nos.	No dot	Dot
8½p. 2A (silver)–1B (pale turquoise-blue)–1C (olive-grey)–6D (blackish green)–1E (black)		1·50	1·50
9p. 2A (silver)–1B (lavender)–1C (olive-grey)–6D (maroon)–1E (blk) –P62 (phosphor)		5·00	5·00
2A (silver)–1B (lavender)–1C (olive-grey)–6D (maroon)–1E (blk)		1·75	1·75
10p. 1A (silver)–1B (ochre)–1C (olive-grey)–6D (blackish blue)–1E (brownish black)		1·75	1·75
11p. 2A (silver)–1B (rose-pink)–1C (olive-grey)–6D (brown-purple)– 1E (black)		2·10	2·10
13p. 2A (silver)–1B (bistre-yellow)–1C (olive-grey)–6D (sepia)–1E (black)		2·75	2·75

The phosphor cylinder numbers are P61 and P62 for the 9p., which are unsynchronised in the left margin, and P65 for the other values which is unsynchronised and upright in the right margin.

The ink cylinders 1B, 1C and 1D are common to all values. Cylinder 1E was used for the values and only the silver Cylinder 1A varies in the 10p. value.

Sheet Details

Sheet size: 100 (2 panes 10 × 5). Double pane reel-fed

Sheet markings:
   Cylinder numbers: Opposite rows 8/9, left margin, boxed
   Marginal arrows: In centre at top and bottom of sheet
   Colour register marks (crossed lines type):
      No dot panes: Opposite rows 1/2 at both sides
      Dot panes: Opposite rows 6/7 at both sides and large cross in circle opposite row 4, left margin
   Autotron marks: In order of traffic lights opposite rows 1/4, left margin, on dot panes only
   Perforation register marks: None
   Sheet values: Above and below vertical rows 2/4 and 7/9 reading from left to right in top margin and from right to left (upside down) in bottom margin
   Traffic lights (boxed): Opposite rows 8/9 (8½p., 11p.) or rows 3/4 (others), right margin; also in same order reading from left to right in gutter margin in vertical row 2:
      8½p. Pale turquoise-blue, olive-grey, blackish green, black, silver
      9p. Lavender, olive-grey, maroon, black, silver
      10p. Ochre, olive-grey, blackish blue, brownish black, silver
      11p. Rose-pink, olive-grey, brown-purple, black, silver
      13p. Bistre-yellow, olive-grey, sepia, black, silver
   Colour designations seen: Reading up in right margin, 8½p. "C5 SILVER C4 BLACK C3" opposite rows 1/3 on dot pane; 10p. "? C2 GREY ?" opposite rows 8/10 on no dot pane; 11p. "C4 BLACK C3" opposite row 1 on dot pane

Quantities Sold   8½p. 73,960,000; 9p. 42,620,000; 10p. 21,580,000; 11p. 19,380,000; 13p. 17,720,000

Withdrawn   8½p., 10p., 11p. 10.5.78; 13p. sold out shortly before; 9p. 14.6.78

W345   "Gathering of Nations"
(Des. Peter Murdoch)
(Printed in photogravure, with the inscription and pentagon lines recess-printed)

1977 (8 JUNE). COMMONWEALTH HEADS OF GOVERNMENT MEETING, LONDON

The summit conference in London of the Commonwealth Heads of Government is symbolised in a single stamp issue by a pattern of pentagons representing the individual countries and the five continents over which they are spread.

"All-over" phosphor

W366 (= S.G.1038)   **W345**   13p. black, blackish green, rose-carmine and silver   ..   30   35

First Day Cover (W366)	..	..	..	..	†	90
Presentation Pack (W366)	..	..	..	..	1·00	†
PHQ Card	..	..	..	..	..	3·00 3·50

At least two covers are known postmarked at Stevenage on 4 June 1977, the stamps having been pre-released over the counter the day before.
The PHQ card exists with the green (grey inner border) omitted. *Price* £300.

Cylinder Numbers (Blocks of Four)

	Cyl. Nos.	Perforation Type R*	
		No dot	Dot
13p. 1A (blackish green)–2B (silver)–1C (grey-black)–P61 (phosphor)		1·50	1·50
1A (blackish green)–2B (silver)–1C (grey-black) ..	.. ..	5·00	†

Sheet Details

Sheet size: 100 (2 panes 5 × 10). Double pane reel-fed

Sheet markings:
Cylinder numbers: In top margin above vertical row 2, boxed
Marginal arrows: In centre, opposite rows 5/6 at both sides and at each side of vertical gutter
Colour register marks (crossed lines type):
No dot panes: Above and below vertical rows 8/9, large cross above vertical row 4 and short vertical lines above vertical rows 3 and 4
Dot panes: Above and below vertical rows 3/4 with extra small cross above vertical row 4
Autotron marks: In order of cylinder numbers reading from left to right above vertical rows 6/7, on dot pane only
Additional markings: Grey-black photogravure bar opposite rows 5/6, left margin on no dot pane. Recess-printed black bar with rose-carmine extension at top in 4th row, left, right and gutter margins of both panes; also small recess dots in gutter margin of row 6
Sheet values: Opposite rows 2/4 and 7/9 reading up at left and down at right
Traffic lights (boxed): In bottom margin below vertical row 2 with separate box for grey-black, and similarly but in order of traffic lights in gutter margin in row 2:
13p. Silver, blackish green, grey-black
Colour designations seen: "SILVER C (?) BLACK" below vertical rows 8/9 on dot pane

Quantity Sold   13p. 8,560,000

Withdrawn   Stamp sold out 12.77, Pack 3.78

99

W346 Hedgehog

W347 Brown Hare

W348 Red Squirrel   W349 Otter   W350 Badger

The above were printed horizontally *se-tenant* throughout the sheet
(Des. Patrick Oxenham)

1977 (5 OCTOBER). BRITISH WILDLIFE

Some of Britain's best loved wild animals are featured in this issue which is designed to make children and adults more aware of the nation's wildlife heritage and the need to protect it.
"All-over" phosphor

W367 (= S.G.1039)	**W346**	9p. reddish brown, grey-black, pale lemon, bright turquoise-blue, bright magenta and gold	25	20
		a. Strip of 5. Nos. W367/71	1·40	1·50
		b. Imperforate (vert. pair)		
		c. Imperforate (horiz. pair, Nos. W367/8)		
W368 (= S.G.1040)	**W347**	9p. reddish brown, grey-black, pale lemon, bright turquoise-blue, bright magenta and blue	25	20
W369 (= S.G.1041)	**W348**	9p. reddish brown, grey-black, pale lemon, bright turquoise-blue, bright magenta and gold	25	20
		b. Berry on stem behind ear	1·50	
		c. Curved line below nut	1·50	
W370 (= S.G.1042)	**W349**	9p. reddish brown, grey-black, pale lemon, bright turquoise-blue, bright magenta and gold	25	20
		b. Broken e in Otter	1·90	
		c. Shortened whiskers	1·75	
		d. Grey-black hyphen after Otter	1·90	
W371 (= S.G.1043)	**W350**	9p. grey-black, reddish brown, pale lemon, bright turquoise-blue, bright magenta and gold	25	20

First Day Cover (W367/71)				†	2·00
Presentation Pack (W367/71)				2·00	†
PHQ Cards (W367/71)				4·00	4·25

Listed Varieties

W369b
Small berry on stem behind ear
(Dot, R. 7/3)

W369c
Curved line below nut
(Dot, R. 8/3)

W370b
Broken e
(Not dot, R. 8/9)

W370c
Shortened whiskers
(Dot, R. 7/9)

W370d
Hyphen added
(Dot, R. 9/9)

Cylinder Numbers (Blocks of Ten)

	Cyl. Nos.		Perforation Type R*
		No dot	Dot
9p.	1A (reddish brown)–1B (bright magenta)–1C (pale lemon)–1D		
	(bright turquoise-blue)–1E (grey-black)–1F (gold)	3·50	3·50

The phsophor cylinder number P62 appears inverted in bottom margin below vertical row 7.

Sheet Details

Sheet size: 100 (2 panes 5 × 10). Double pane reel-fed

Sheet markings:
Cylinder numbers: In top margin above vertical rows 2/3, boxed
Marginal arrows: In centre, opposite rows 5/6 at both sides only
Colour register marks (crossed lines type):
No dot panes: Above and below vertical rows 9/10
Dot panes: Above and below vertical rows 4/5 and large cross in circle in brown above vertical row 1
Autotron marks: In order of traffic lights reading from left to right above vertical rows 7/10, on dot pane only
Sheet values: Opposite rows 2/4 and 7/9 reading up at left and down at right
Traffic lights (boxed): Below vertical rows 7/8 (no dot) or rows 2/3 (dot), also in same order reading up in gutter margin in row 2:
9p. Gold, grey-black, reddish brown, bright turquoise-blue, pale lemon, bright magenta

Quantity Sold 9p. 12,284,000 of each design

Withdrawn Pack 4.10.78; Stamps sold out 4.78

"The Twelve Days of Christmas"
"On the twelfth day of Christmas, My true love sent to me—"

W351 "Three French Hens, Two
Turtle Doves and a Partridge
in a Pear Tree"

W352 "Six Geese a-laying, Five
Gold Rings, and Four Colly Birds"

W353 "Eight Maids a-milking,
Seven Swans a-swimming"

W354 "Ten Pipers piping,
Nine Drummers drumming"

W355 "Twelve Lords a-leaping,
Eleven Ladies dancing"

W356 "And a Partridge in a
Pear Tree"

Types **W351/5** were printed horizontally *se-tenant* within the sheet
(Des. David Gentleman)

1977 (23 NOVEMBER). CHRISTMAS

This popular carol originated as a parody by 13th century French minstrels poking fun at solemn chants celebrating Christmas. The English version dates from a 13th-century manuscript in the library of Trinity College, Cambridge. In Victorian times it was sung as a parlour game on Twelfth Night when the decorations were taken down and forfeits were often exacted from those who could not get the verses right or in the right order. It is a pity that the Post Office could not contrive to get the subjects in the right order on the strip of stamps.

One 4 mm. centre phosphor band

W372 (=S.G.1044)	**W351**	7p. slate, grey, bright yell-grn, new bl, rose-red & gold		15	15
		a. Strip of 5. Nos. W372/6		1·00	1·10
		ab. Imperforate (horiz. strip of 5. Nos. W372/6) ..		£900	
W373 (=S.G.1045)	**W352**	7p. slate, bright yellow-green, new blue and gold ..		15	15
		b. Break in outline of first goose		1·50	
W374 (=S.G.1046)	**W353**	7p. slate, grey, bright yell-grn, new bl, rose-red & gold		15	15

W375 (=S.G.1047)	**W354**	7p. slate, grey, bright yell-grn, new bl, rose-red & gold	15	15
W376 (=S.G.1048)	**W355**	7p. slate, grey, bright yell-grn, new bl, rose-red & gold	15	15

"All-over" phosphor

W377 (=S.G.1049)	**W356**	9p. pale brown, pale orange, bright emerald, pale greenish yellow, slate-black and gold	20	20
		a. Imperforate (pair) £750		

First Day Cover (W372/7)	.. ..	†	1·40
Presentation Pack (W372/7) ..		2·00	†
PHQ Cards (W372/7) ..	.. ..	3·25	4·00

We have seen a strip with an extra narrow band and a further faint narrow band to the left of the normal band on the first stamp, with two extra narrow bands right of the normal band on the fifth stamp and with an additional wide phosphor band to the left of the normal band on the third stamp. All these are evidently due to the malfunction of the phosphor doctor blade leaving the normal centre bands unaffected. Doubtless variations of this fault also exist.

Listed Variety

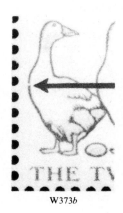

Left outline of first goose broken
(No dot, R. 8/2)

W373*b*

Cylinder Numbers
Blocks of Fifteen

	Perforation Type R*
Cyl. Nos.	No dot Dot
7p. 1A (slate)–1B (grey)–1C (bright yellow-green)–1D (new blue)–1E (rose-red)–1F (gold)–P62 (phosphor)	3·50 3·50

Blocks of Six

9p. 1A (slate-black)–1B (pale orange)–1C (pale greenish yellow)–1D (pale light brown)–1E (bright emerald)–1F (gold)–P66 (phosphor) .. ..   1·50   1·50

The phosphor cylinder numbers are synchronised on the cylinder blocks.

Sheet Details

Sheet size: 100 (2 panes 10 × 5). Double pane reel-fed

Sheet markings:
Cylinder numbers: Opposite rows 8/9, left margin, boxed
Marginal arrows: In centre at top and bottom of sheet
Colour register marks (crossed lines type):
No dot panes: Opposite rows 1/2 at both sides
Dot panes: Opposite rows 6/8 at both sides and large cross in circle opposite row 2, left margin
Autotron marks: In order of traffic lights opposite rows 2/5 and gutter margin, left margin on dot panes only
Sheet values: Above and below vertical rows 2/4 and 7/9 reading from left to right in top margin and from right to left (upside down) in bottom margin
Traffic lights (boxed): Opposite rows 8/9, right margin: also in same order reading from left to right in gutter margin in vertical row 2:
7p. Grey, bright yellow-green, new blue, rose-red, slate, gold
9p. Pale orange, pale greenish yellow, pale light brown, bright emerald, slate-black, gold

Quantities Sold   7p. 53,118,000 of each design; 9p. 111,230,000

Withdrawn   9p. sold out 11.78; others withdrawn 23.11.78

1977 (23 NOVEMBER).   COLLECTORS PACK 1977

WCP11 Comprises Nos. W353/77 (Sold at £2·68)   7·50
Withdrawn   22.11.78

W357 Oil
North Sea Production Platform

W358 Coal
Modern Pithead

W359 Natural Gas
Flame rising from the Sea

W360 Electricity
Nuclear Power Station and
Uranium Atom

(Des. Peter Murdoch)

1978 (25 JANUARY). ENERGY RESOURCES

This issue, featuring Britain's development of its oil, coal, natural gas and electricity resources, appears in the year during which North Sea oil and natural gas are coming ashore in large quantities for the first time. It also serves as a reminder of the need to conserve energy as there is only a short time to plan future energy supplies to meet the situation when the present supplies become insufficient for our needs.

"All-over" phosphor

W378 (=S.G.1050)	W357	9p.	deep green, orange-vermilion, grey-black, greenish yellow, rose-pink, new blue and silver	25	20
W379 (=S.G.1051)	W358	10½p.	light emerald-green, grey-black, red-brown, pale apple-green and silver	25	35
		a.	Retouch to left of C	2·75	
W380 (=S.G.1052)	W359	11p.	greenish blue, bright violet, violet-blue, blackish brown, grey-black and silver	35	40
W381 (=S.G.1053)	W360	13p.	orange-vermilion, grey-black, deep brown, greenish yellow, light brown, light blue and silver	40	40
		a.	Frame break at upper left	2·25	

First Day Cover (W378/81)	..	..	..	..	†	1·25
Presentation Pack (W378/81)	..	..	..	..	2·00	†
PHQ Cards (W378/81)	..	..	..	..	3·25	4·25

A cover has been reported inadvertently postmarked 25 January 1977 at MLO, Redhill.

105

Listed Varieties

W379a	W381a
Retouch to left of C	Frame break at upper left
(Dot, R. 8/10)	(No dot, R. 1/8)

Cylinder Numbers (Blocks of Six)

Cyl. Nos.	Perforation Type R*
	No dot Dot

9p. 2A (grey-black)–3B (rose-pink)–2C (deep brown)–2D (new
blue)–5E (orange-vermilion)–1F (silver)–2G (greenish yellow)–
P68 (phosphor) .. ..   4·00   4·00
2A (grey-black)–3B (rose-pink)–2C (deep brown)–2D (new
blue)–5E (orange-vermilion)–1F (silver)–2G (greenish yellow)   1·75   1·75
10½p. 2A (grey-black)–1B (pale apple-green)–1C (light emerald-green)–
1D (red-brown)–1E (slate-grey)–1F (silver)–P62 (phosphor) ..   1·75   1·75
2A (grey-black)–1B (pale apple-green)–1C (light emerald-green)–
1D (red-brown)–1E (slate-grey)–1F (silver) .. .. ..   5·00   5·00
11p. 3A (grey-black)–3B (violet-blue)–3C (bright violet)–2D (blackish
brown)–2E (greenish blue)–1F (silver)–P61 (phosphor) ..   2·40   2·40
3A (grey-black)–3B (violet-blue)–3C (bright violet)–2D (blackish
brown)–2E (greenish blue)–1F (silver) .. .. ..   †   5·00
13p. 2A (grey-black)–1B (deep brown)–2C (light brown)–1D (greenish yellow)–1E (orange-vermilion)–1F (silver)–1G (light blue)–
P68 (phosphor) .. ..   3·75   3·75
2A (grey-black)–1B (deep brown)–2C (light brown)–1D (green-
ish yellow)–1E (orange-vermilion)–1F (silver)–1G (light blue)..   2·75   2·75

All three phosphor cylinders employed are found with the cylinder numbers unsynchronised
in the top margin.

Sheet Details

Sheet size: 100 (2 panes 5 × 10). Double pane reel-fed

Sheet markings:
     Cylinder numbers: In top margin above vertical rows 2/3, boxed
     Marginal arrows: In centre, opposite rows 5/6 at both sides
     Colour register marks (crossed lines type):
         No dot panes: Above and below vertical rows 3/5 and large cross in circle above vertical
         row 9
         Dot panes: Above and below vertical rows 8/10
     Autotron marks: In order of traffic lights reading from left to right above vertical rows 4/7
     on dot panes only
     Sheet values: Opposite rows 2/4 and 7/9 reading up at left and down at right
     Traffic lights (boxed): In bottom margin below vertical rows 2/3 (9p., 10½p.) or rows 7/8 (11p.,
     13p.); also in same order reading up in gutter margin in row 2 (10½p.) or rows 2/3 (others):
         9p. Grey-black, silver, greenish yellow, orange-vermilion, new blue, deep brown, rose-pink
         10½p. Silver, grey-black, slate-grey, red-brown, light emerald-green, pale apple-green
         11p. Grey-black, silver, blackish brown, bright violet, violet-blue, greenish blue
         13p. Grey-black, silver, light blue, orange-vermilion, greenish yellow, light brown, deep brown
     Colour designations seen: 9p. "G6 BLACK" below vertical rows 5/6 and "G5 YELLOW G4
     RED G3" below vertical rows 9/10 on no dot pane; 11p. "PINK G2 DARK BLUE G1
     LIGHT BLUE" below vertical rows 1/3 on dot pane

Quantities Sold   9p. 42,270,000; 10½p. 10,630,000; 11p. 9,950,000; 13p. 9,340,000

Withdrawn   11p. sold out 12.78; others withdrawn 24.1.79

W361 The Tower of London   W362 Holyroodhouse

W363 Caernarvon Castle   W364 Hampton Court Palace

W365 Miniature Sheet
(Illustration reduced to three quarters actual size)
(Stamps des. Ronald Maddox. Miniature sheet des. Jeffery Matthews)

1978 (1 MARCH).   BRITISH ARCHITECTURE (HISTORIC BUILDINGS)

Continuing the British Architecture series, this set is devoted to historic Royal Palaces and Castles. The 9p. value marks the 900th anniversary of the Tower of London and features the White Tower, where the Crown Jewels are displayed. The north-west tower of Holyroodhouse, Edinburgh, shown on the 10½p., was built by James V (1513–1542). Caernarvon Castle (11p.) is noted for the establishment of the present line of Princes of Wales by King Edward I in 1284; other views of it are to be found on the issue devoted to the Investiture of the present Prince in 1969. The Great Gatehouse of Hampton Court Palace (13p.) was built in 1520. The Palace was given by Thomas Wolsey, Cardinal Archbishop of York, to King Henry VIII, who later rebuilt the Great Hall.

In issuing these four stamps as a miniature sheet to publicise the "London 1980" International Stamp Exhibition, the Post Office made philatelic history—as indicated by the inscription below the stamps. It was sold with a premium of 10p. for the benefit of the exhibition funds and the public swiftly responded as the entire printing was sold out within a few days.

"All-over" phosphor

W382 (= S.G.1054)	**W361**	9p.	black, olive-brown, new blue, bright green, light yellow-olive and rose-red	..	..	..	..	25	20
		a.	Bottom margin imperforate		..	..	..	£110	
		b.	Bite out of 9 ..	..	..	..	..	2·00	
		c.	Vertical line by P	..	..	..	..	1·50	
		d.	White spot on 9	..	..	..	..	1·50	
W383 (= S.G.1055)	**W362**	10½p.	black, brown-olive, orange-yellow, bright green, light yellow-olive and rose-red	..	..	..	25	30
		a.	Broken P	..	..	..	..	1·60	
		b.	Shortened serif to large 1	..	..	..	1·50	
W384 (= S.G.1056)	**W363**	11p.	black, brown-olive, violet-blue, bright green, light yellow-olive and dull blue ..	..	..	..	35	35
		a.	Joined fo	..	..	..	..	1·75	
W385 (= S.G.1057)	**W364**	13p.	black, orange-yell, lake-brn, bright green & light yellow-olive ..	..	..	..	40	40
		a.	Broken C in Court ..	..	..	..	..	2·10	

First Day Cover (W382/5)	..	..	..	..	†	1·25
Presentation Pack (W382/5)	..	..	..	..	2·00	†
PHQ Cards (W382/5)	..	..	..	..	3·00	3·50

WMS386 (= S.G.MS1058)	**W365**	Sheet size 121 × 89 mm. issued in folder (Sold at 53½p.)..	..	1·25	1·60
		a. Imperforate sheet			
		b. Light yellow-olive (Queen's head) omitted	..	£2500	
		c. Rose-red (Union Jack on 9p.) omitted	..	£1200	
		d. Orange-yellow omitted*	..	£1200	
		e. Phosphor omitted	..	£110	
		f. Break in sea wall	..	2·75	

First Day Cover (WMS386)	..	..	..	..	2·00

No. W382*a* came from the lower part of a sheet which was only partly perforated in that it contained stamps showing indentation from the perforation pins so that no stamp in the sheet was completely devoid of perforations all round.

The colours in the miniature sheet differ slightly in shade from those in the sheet stamps. It is probable that they were printed with the same colours but possibly in a different order and the impression would be different as the miniature sheets were printed on the Rembrandt press and the sheet stamps by the "Jumelle" machine.

We have seen a copy of the miniature sheet with the blue colour partially missing. Although the 9p. had all the new blue omitted it was only partially missing from the 11p. However, it was interesting to note that most of the blue wavy line border was omitted, showing that this was printed from the same cylinder.

*The effect of the missing orange-yellow is most noticeable on the 10½p. (spheres absent on towers) and around the roadway and arch on the 13p.

The miniature sheet is known used on cover postmarked 27 February, 1978, from Bethnal Green, Homerton, London.

Listed Varieties

W382b	**W382c**	**W382d**	**W383a**
Bite out of 9	Vertical line	White spot	Broken P
(No dot, R. 2/9)	(Dot, R. 1/5)	(Dot, R. 9/9)	(Dot, R. 5/1)

W383b	**W384a**	**W385a**
Shortened serif	Joined fo	Broken C
(Dot, R. 5/3)	(No dot, R. 5/2)	(No dot, R. 1/8)

Break in sea wall
(11p. Position 2)

WMS386f

Cylinder Numbers (Blocks of Six)

	Cyl. Nos.	Perforation No dot	Type R* Dot
9p.	2A (black)–1B (olive-brown)–2C (new blue)–1D (bright green)– 1E (light yellow-olive)–1F (rose-red)–P61 (phosphor)	1·75	1·75
10½p.	1A (black)–1B (brown–olive)–1C (orange-yellow)–2D (bright green)–1E (light yellow-olive)–1F (violet-blue)–P61 (phosphor)	1·90	1·90
11p.	2A (black)–1B (brown-olive)–1C (violet-blue)–1D (bright green) –1E (light yellow-olive)–1F (dull blue)–P61 (phosphor) ..	2·40	2·40
13p.	3A (black)–1B (orange-yellow)–1C (lake-brown)–1D (bright green)–1E (light yellow-olive)–P61 (phosphor)	2·75	2·75
	3A (black)–1B (orange-yellow)–1C (lake-brown)–1D (bright green)–1E (light yellow-olive)	3·25	3·25

Phosphor cylinder number P61 is synchronised on the cylinder number block in all values except the 13p.

Sheet Details

Sheet size: 100 (2 panes 10 × 5). Double pane reel-fed

Sheet markings:
Cylinder numbers: Opposite rows 8/9, left margin, boxed
Marginal arrows: In centre at top and bottom of sheet but on 11p. no dot pane the arrow
at bottom is one perforation to left of centre
Colour register marks (crossed lines type):
No dot panes: Opposite rows 6/7 at both sides and large cross in circle opposite row 2,
left margin
Dot panes: Not seen
Autotron marks: On dot panes but none seen
Sheet values: Above and below vertical rows 2/4 and 7/9 reading from left to right in top margin
and from right to left (upside down) in bottom margin
Traffic lights (boxed): Opposite row 9 (13p.) or rows 8/9 (others), right margin; also in reverse
order (9p., 13p.) or same order (others) reading from left to right in gutter margin in vertical
row 2:
9p.   Olive-brown, new blue, bright green, rose-red, black, light yellow-olive
10½p. Brown-olive, orange-yellow, bright green, violet-blue, black, light yellow-olive
11p.   Brown-olive, violet-blue, bright green, black, light yellow-olive
13p.   Orange-yellow, lake-brown, bright green, black, light yellow-olive
Colour designations seen: Reading up in right margin—10½p. "G6 COMMON (?) G5 BLACK
G4 MAUVE", opposite rows 1/4 and "G (?) GREEN G (?) ORANGE (?) G (?) STONE (?)
opposite rows 7/10, 13p. "G6 COMMON (?) G4 BLACK G3 GREEN G2 (?)" opposite rows
1/4.

Miniature Sheet

These were printed in sheets of nine miniature sheets on the Rembrandt press and perforated
15 × 14 by a Bickler machine. A reduced sized illustration of an uncut sheet appears on the next
page but naturally all the marginal markings shown were guillotined off. The cylinder numbers
employed were 2A–1B–1C–1D–2E–1F–1G–2H–1J. We are not aware of the phosphor cylinder
number.

Plating the Sheets

It is not too difficult to "plate" individual sheets by studying the brown curved lines at the
right of the white border surrounding the stamps, and in particular by counting the number of
incomplete lines at the top and bottom which appear to the left of the first continuous wavy
line.
We base our numbering system on the position in the uncut sheet, position 1 being R. 1/1,
position 2, R. 1/2 and so on.
The following positions can be identified simply by reckoning the number of incomplete lines
at top right in relation to the number at bottom right:

Lines at top	Lines at bottom	Position
1	1	8
1	1¼	3
1	2	2
2	2	6

The others require further tests for identification:

1¼	2	1, 5 or 9
2	1	4 or 7

To distinguish positions 1, 5 and 9 it is necessary to look at the hollows on the right formed
by the inner curved lines and check the number of short straight lines within them. There are
five hollows to each sheet:

Short straight lines in hollows	Position
5 (One in each hollow)	1
0 (All hollows empty)	5
2 (Upper line strong, lower one weak)	9

It only remains to distinguish positions 4 and 7. On position 7 the line at bottom is a little
shorter but a more obvious difference between the two is to be found by studying the bottom
left corner of the sheets. In position 4 the inner curved line is a full 1 mm. from the bottom
whereas in position 7 this line is almost joined to one at the bottom.

Several different systems for "plating" these sheets have been published but we feel that the characteristics described above are sufficient for identification without the need to introduce elaborate illustrations. They are taken from a pamphlet published by Mr. Andrey M. Roy and we express our thanks to him for permission to draw on this. (*"Plated" set of nine sheets price* £35.)

Quantities Sold   9p. 43,770,000; 10½p. 11,230,000; 11p. 10,850,000; 13p. 9,880,000;
Miniature Sheet 53½p. 2,520,000

Withdrawn   The minature sheet was sold out very soon after issue and the 9p. in 1.79; remainder withdrawn 28.2.79

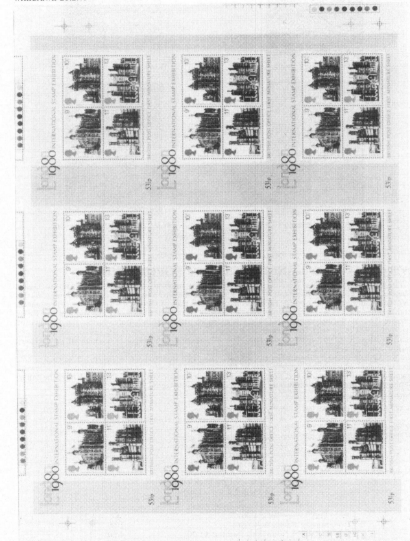

Photo: National Postal Museum   Uncut Sheet of 9 Miniature Sheets with Plate Markings

W366 State Coach

W367 St. Edward's Crown

W368 The Sovereign's Orb

W369 Imperial State Crown

(Des. Jeffery Matthews)

1978 (31 MAY).   25th ANNIVERSARY OF CORONATION

The Coronation Regalia was the subject chosen to celebrate the 25th anniversary of Queen Elizabeth's Coronation. The State Coach, shown on the 9p. value, was completed in 1762 for George III and has been used for each coronation since that of George IV. It is gilded throughout. Eight palm trees form its framework and the roof is surmounted with cherubs holding the Royal Crown. The St. Edward's Crown (10½p.) is worn by the sovereign only during the Coronation ceremony. Made in 1661 for Charles II, it is set with diamonds, emeralds, rubies, sapphires and pearls with a jewelled cross on the top. The Sovereign's Orb (11p.) is a globe of gold circled with a band of precious stones with a great amethyst set beneath a jewelled cross—symbolising the world dominated by the emblem of Christianity. The Imperial Crown (13p.) is worn for state occasions and was originally made for the Coronation of Queen Victoria. Its delicate framework is encrusted with diamonds and precious stones which include the Black Prince's Ruby, the Stuart Sapphire and drop pearls known as Queen Elizabeth's Ear-rings.

"All-over" phosphor

W387 (=S.G.1059)	W366	9p. gold and royal blue ..	..	..	..	20	20
		a. Cluster of white dots on at in Coronation			..	1·50	
W388 (=S.G.1060)	W367	10½p. gold and brown-lake	..	..	..	25	30
W389 (=S.G.1061)	W368	11p. gold and deep dull green ..	..	..	..	35	40
		a. Chunk missing from cross ..	..	..	..	1·90	
		b. Extra pearl on Orb ..	..	..	..	1·75	
		c. White retouch under "the Cor"	..	..	..	1·60	
W390 (=S.G.1062)	W369	13p. gold and reddish violet	..	..	..	40	40
		a. White spot on back of neck	..	..	..	1·90	
		b. Damaged a in Coronation ..	..	..	..	2·00	

First Day Cover (W387/90) ..	..	..	..	†	1·25
Presentation Pack (W387/90) ..	..	..	..	1·50	†
Souvenir Book (W387/90) (Sold at £1·20)	..	..	4·50	†
PHQ Cards (W387/90) ..	..	..	..	2·50	2·50

The souvenir book consists of a 16-page booklet illustrated with scenes from the Coronation.

Listed Varieties

W387*a*
Cluster of white dots over at
(Dot, R. 1/1)

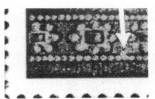

W389*b*
Extra pearl in band of Orb
(No dot, R. 3/6)

W389*a*
Chunk missing from cross
(No dot, R. 3/5)

W389*c*
White retouch under "the Cor"
(No dot, R. 4/5)

W390*b*
Damaged a in Coronation
(Dot, R. 6/8)

W390a
White spot on back of neck
(Dot, R. 5/10)

113

Cylinder Numbers (Blocks of Four)

	Cyl. Nos.	Perforation No dot	Type R* Dot
9p.	5A (royal blue)–2B (gold)–P62 (phosphor)	1·50	3·00*
10½p.	3A (brown-lake)–1B (gold)–P62 (phosphor)	1·75	1·75
11p.	6A (deep dull green)–2B (gold)	2·40	2·40
13p.	3A (reddish violet)–1B (gold)–P62 (phosphor)	2·75	2·75

Phosphor cylinder No. P62 appears to be synchronised on the cylinder block in the 9p., 10½p. and 13p. We have not seen a cylinder number in the top or bottom margin of the 11p. but Cyl. No. P69 has been reported as having been seen above vertical row 4 in the top margin.

The 9p. dot pane exists with the dot omitted after 2B but it is normally present. (*Price* £5)

Sheet Markings

Sheet size: 100 (2 panes 5 × 10). Double pane reel-fed

Sheet markings:

Cylinder numbers: In top margin above vertical row 2, boxed

Marginal arrows: In centre, opposite rows 5/6 at both sides

Colour register marks (crossed lines type):

No dot panes: above and below vertical row 10

Dot panes: Above and below vertical row 1 and also large cross in circle type above vertical row 9

Autotron marks: In order of traffic lights reading from left to right above vertical rows 7/8 on dot panes only

Perforation register marks: One short vertical line on either side of first extension hole in top and bottom margins in both panes (see illustration under General Notes). These were omitted at first and etched in by hand in bottom margin of 13p., being much finer lines

Sheet values: Opposite rows 2/4 and 7/9 reading up at left and down at right

Traffic lights (boxed): In bottom margin below vertical row 2; also in same order reading down in gutter margin in row 2:

9p. Gold, royal blue	11p. Gold, deep dull green
10½p. Gold, bronze-lake	13p. Gold, reddish violet

Quantities Sold   9p. 66,700,000; 10½p. 16,430,000; 11p. 15,200,000; 13p. 14,080,000

Withdrawn   30.5.79

W370 Shire Horse   **W371** Shetland Pony

W372 Welsh Pony   **W373** Thoroughbred
(Des. Patrick Oxenham)

1978 (5 JULY). HORSES

This issue marks the centenary of the Shire Horse Society of England and it was appropriate that Patrick Oxenham, the animal painter who also designed the Wildlife issue, should be invited to submit the designs. The Shire horse shown on the 9p. comes from a Gloucestershire farm close to the artist's home and is an old friend of his. The Shetland featured on the 10½p. is also a local pony. The Welsh pony (11p.) was from material supplied by the Welsh Pony Society and the Thoroughbred (13p.) was a composite taken from several sources to capture all the points of the breed.

"All-over" phosphor

W391 (=S.G.1063)	**W370**	9p.	black, pale reddish brown, grey-black, greenish yellow, light blue, vermilion and gold	25	30
		a.	Extra dot over i	1·50	
		b.	Black line on plough under horse	1·60	
W392 (=S.G.1064)	**W371**	10½p.	pale chestnut, magenta, brownish grey, greenish yellow, greenish blue, grey-black and gold	30	35
		a.	Imperf. between stamp and bottom margin		
		b.	Weak figures 10	1·75	
W393 (=S.G.1065)	**W372**	11p.	reddish brown, black, light green, greenish yellow, bistre, grey-black and gold	40	45
		a.	Large blob on hoof of left foreleg	2·00	
W394 (=S.G.1066)	**W373**	13p.	reddish brown, pale reddish brown, emerald, greenish yellow, grey-black and gold	45	50

First Day Cover (W391/4)					†	1·50
Presentation Pack (W391/4)					1·75	†
PHQ Cards (W391/4)					2·50	4·50

115

Listed Varieties

W391a
Extra dot over i
(No dot, R. 6/9)

W392b
Weak figures
(Dot, R. 3/5)

W393a
Blob on hoof
(No dot, R. 9/2)

W391b
Black line on plough
under horse
(No dot, R. 8/1)

Cylinder Numbers (Blocks of Six)

Cyl. Nos.	Perforation No dot	Type R* Dot
9p. 1A (grey-black)–1B (light blue)–1C (greenish yellow)–1D (vermilion)–1E (black)–1F (gold)–1G (pale reddish brown)–P62 (phosphor)	4·75*	3·50
1A (grey-black)–1B (light blue)–1C (greenish yellow)–1D (vermilion)–1E (black)–1F (gold)–1G (pale reddish brown) ..	3·00*	1·75
10½p. 1A (grey-black)–1B (greenish blue)–1C (greenish yellow)–1D (magenta)–1E (brownish grey)–1F (pale chestnut)–1G (gold) –P62 (phosphor)	2·75	2·75
1A (grey-black)–1B (greenish blue)–1C (greenish yellow)–1D (magenta)–1E (brownish grey)–1F (pale chestnut)–1G (gold) ..	2·10	2·10
11p. 1A (grey-black)–1B (light green)–1C (greenish yellow)–1D (bistre)–1E (black)–1F (reddish brown)–1G (gold)–P62 (phosphor)	4·75*	3·75
1A (grey-black)–1B (light green)–1C (greenish yellow)–1D (bistre) –1E (black)–1F (reddish brown)–1G (gold)	3·50*	2·75
13p. 2A (grey-black)–1B (emerald)–1C (greenish yellow)–1D (pale reddish brown)–1E (reddish brown)–1F (gold)	3·25	3·25

Phosphor cylinder number P62 is unsynchronised on the 9p., 10½p. and 11p. values. No cylinder number has been found at left or right on no dot sheets of the 13p. but phosphor No. P69 has been reported at left opposite row 4 on a dot sheet.

Sheet Details

Sheet size: 100 (2 panes 10 × 5). Double pane reel-fed

Sheet markings:
Cylinder numbers: Opposite rows 8/9, left margin, boxed
Marginal arrows: In centre at top and bottom of sheet
Colour register marks (crossed lines type):
No dot panes: Opposite rows 1/3 (13p.) or 2/3 (others) at both sides
Dot panes: Opposite rows 6/8 at both sides and large cross in circle opposite row 2, left margin

Autotron marks: In same order as traffic lights in left margin opposite rows 2/6 on dot panes only

Perforation register marks: None

Sheet values: Above and below vertical rows 2/4 and 7/9 reading from left to right in top margin and from right to left (upside down) in bottom margin

Traffic lights (boxed): Opposite rows 8/9, right margin; also in same order reading from left to right in gutter margin in vertical rows 1/2 (9p.), 2/3 (10½p., 11p.) or 2 (13p.):

9p.   Light blue, greenish yellow, vermilion, black, pale reddish brown, grey-black, gold

10½p. Greenish blue, greenish yellow, magenta, brownish grey, pale chestnut, grey-black, gold

11p.   Light green, greenish yellow, bistre, black, pale chestnut, grey-black, gold

13p.   Emerald, greenish yellow, pale reddish brown, reddish brown, grey-black, gold

Quantities Sold   9p. 48,470,000; 10½p. 12,490,000; 11p. 11,910,000; 13p. 10,940,000

Withdrawn   13p. sold out 3.79; others withdrawn 4.7.79

W374 "Penny-farthing" and   W375 1920 Touring Bicycles
       1884 Safety Bicycle

W376 Modern Small-wheel Bicycles   W377 1978 Road-racers

(Des. Fritz Wegner)

1978 (2 AUGUST). CENTENARIES OF CYCLISTS TOURING CLUB AND THE BRITISH CYCLING FEDERATION

In 1878 the world's first national cycling competitions took place and were organised by the newly-formed British Cycling Federation and the Bicycling Touring Club (later becoming the Cyclists Touring Club), which was set up to deal with the touring aspect. Roadracing became popular in the 1890s but with the advent of the motor car cycle racing was driven off the roads. However it was revived in 1942 by the annual 14-day Milk Race Tour of Britain organised on the lines of the Tour de France race.

France led the world in bicycle production until the outbreak of the Franco-Prussian war in 1870 when Britain gained supremacy and the industry was established in Coventry. In 1884 the low-built safety bicycle with chain drive to the rear wheel was developed and it attracted women to cycling, playing a large part in their emancipation. The wheel sizes later became standardised and in 1884 Dunlop patented the pneumatic-tyred safety bicycle. Thereafter there was little change in the basic design until Moulton introduced the open frame with 16-inch wheels in 1962.

"All-over" phosphor

W395 (=S.G.1067)	**W374**	9p.	brn, deep dull bl, rose-pk, pale ol, grey-blk, & gold	20	20
		a.	Imperforate (pair)	£300	
		b.	"Valve" on lady's rear wheel	1·60	
		c.	Black line in lady's front wheel	1·60	
W396 (=S.G.1068)	**W375**	10½p.	olive, pale yellow-orange, orange-vermilion, rose-red, light brown, grey-black and gold	25	35
		a.	Broken stay to mudguard of gent's rear wheel ..	1·40	
		b.	Short leg to n	1·75	
		c.	Chunk out of lady's chainguard	1·40	
		d.	Large gap in gent's cross-bar	2·25	
		e.	Large break in gent's front wheel	2·25	
W397 (=S.G.1069)	**W376**	11p.	orange-vermilion, greenish blue, light brown, pale greenish yellow, deep grey, grey-black and gold ..	35	35
W398 (=S.G.1070)	**W377**	13p.	new blue, orange-vermilion, light brown, olive-grey, grey-black and gold	40	40
		a.	Imperforate (pair)	£650	
		b.	Short leg to n	1·75	
		c.	Damaged P	1·75	
		d.	Broken g and white spot on blue shirt	2·25	
		e.	Broken y	1·75	
		f.	Break in blue cyclist's rear tyre tread	1·90	
		g.	Broken g	2·25	

First Day Cover (W395/8)	..	..	..	..	†	1·25
Presentation Pack (W395/8)	..	..	..	..	1·50	†
PHQ Cards (W395/8) ..	..	..	..	..	1·75	2·50

Listed Varieties

W395*b*
"Valve" on lady's rear wheel
(No dot, R. 7/7)

W395*c*
Black line in spokes of front wheel
(Dot, R. 10/1)

W396*a*
Broken stay to
mudguard
(No dot, R. 5/3)

W396*b*
Short leg to n
(No dot, R. 5/9)

W396*c*
Chunk out of chainguard
(Dot, R. 9/2)

W396d
Broken cross-bar
(Dot, R. 10/2)

W396e
Broken wheel
(Dot, R. 10/9)

W398b
Short leg to n
(No dot, R. 1/1)

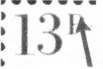

W398c
Damaged P
(No dot, R. 2/5)

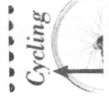

W398e
Broken y
(No dot, R. 5/10)

W398d
Broken g and white spot on shirt
(No dot, R. 5/5)

W398f
Break in tyre tread
(No dot, R. 6/4)

W398g
Broken g
(No dot, R. 10/5)

Cylinder Numbers (Blocks of Six)

	Cyl. Nos.	Perforation No dot	Type R* Dot
9p.	2A (grey-black)–1B (pale olive)–1C (rose-pink)–1D (deep dull blue)–1E (brown)–1F (gold)–P61 (phosphor)	1·50	2·75*
10½p.	4A (grey-black)–1B (pale yellow-orange)–2D (rose-red)–1E (olive)–1F (gold)–1G (light brown)	1·75	4·75*
	4A (grey-black)–1B (pale yellow-orange)–2D (rose-red)–1E (olive)–1F (gold)–1G (light brown)–P68 (phosphor)	4·00	7·00*
11p.	1A (grey-black)–1B (pale greenish yellow)–3C (light brown)–1D (greenish blue)–1E (orange-vermilion)–1F (gold)–1G (deep grey)	2·40	2·40
	1A (grey-black)–1B (pale greenish yellow)–3C (light brown)–1D (greenish blue)–1E (orange-vermilion)–1F (gold)–1G (deep grey)–P68 (phosphor)	5·50	5·50
13p.	1A (grey-black)–1B (light brown)–1C (new blue)–1D (orange-vermilion)–1E (olive-grey)–1F (gold)	2·75	2·75

Phosphor cylinder No. P61 is synchronised at row 8 on the cylinder block of the 9p. value and appears to be synchronised at row 6 on the 13p. value. Phosphor cylinder No. P68 is unsynchronised on the 10½p. and 11p. and on the 11p. it has been seen upright in the left margin but more frequently inverted in the right-hand margin.

Sheet Details

Sheet size: 100 (2 panes 10 × 5). Double pane reel-fed

Sheet markings:
Cylinder numbers: Opposite rows 8/9, left margin, boxed
Marginal arrows: In centre at top and bottom of sheet
Colour register marks (crossed lines type):
No dot panes: Opposite rows 1/2 (9p., 13p.) or 1/3 (others) at both sides
Dot panes: Opposite rows 6/7 (9p., 13p.) or 6/8 (others), at both sides and large cross in circle opposite row 2, left margin
Autotron marks: In same order as traffic lights in left margin opposite rows 2/6 on dot panes only
Sheet values: Above and below vertical rows 2/4 and 7/9 from left to right in top margin and from right to left (upside down) in bottom margin
Traffic lights (boxed): Opposite rows 8/9, right margin; also in same order reading from left to right in gutter margin in vertical row 2 (9p., 13p.) or rows 1/2 (others):
9p. Pale olive, rose-pink, deep dull blue, brown, grey-black, gold
10½p. Pale yellow-orange, orange-vermilion, rose-red, olive, light brown, grey-black, gold
11p. Pale greenish yellow, light brown, greenish blue, orange-vermilion, deep grey, grey-black, gold
13p. Light brown, new blue, orange-vermilion, olive-grey, grey-black, gold

Quantities Sold   9p. 44,990,000; 10½p. 12,760,000; 11p. 11,980,000; 13p. 10,980,000

Withdrawn   1.8.79

W378 Singing Carols round the
Christmas Tree

W379 The Waits

W380 18th-century Carol Singers

W381 "The Boar's Head Carol"

(Des. Faith Jaques)

1978 (22 NOVEMBER). CHRISTMAS

It was in the 19th century that Christmas celebrations, immortalised by Charles Dickens in his *Christmas Carol,* took on much of their present form, and the 7p. shows carol singing round a Christmas tree in Victorian times. The waits, depicted on the 9p. in a 19th-century scene, go back to medieval night watchmen, their original function being to sound a horn or play a tune to mark the hour. 18th-century carol singers appear on the 11p. and the 13p. shows a boar's head being carried on a platter and musicians dressed in late 16th-century costume. The tradition of eating a boar's head goes back to an ancient Yuletide ceremony and the carol is still sung at Queen's College, Oxford.

One 4 mm. centre phosphor band

W399 (= S.G.1071) **W378**	7p. bright grn, greenish yell, mag, new bl, blk & gold		20	20
	a. Imperforate (vert. pair) .. ..:	£300		
	b. Imperf. between stamp and bottom margin ..			
	c. Black mark on girl's shoe	2·25		
	d. "Bubble" flaw	2·25		
	e. Vertical scratch	2·40		
	f. Long diagonal scratch	2·75		
"All-over" phosphor				
W400 (=S.G.1072) **W379**	9p. mag, greenish yell, new bl, sage-grn, blk & gold		25	25
	a. Imperforate (horiz. pair)			
	b. Bottom side of collecting box missing	2·00		
	c. Ditto, Different position	2·00		
	d. Damaged foot to P	1·75		
W401 (=S.G.1073) **W380**	11p. mag, new bl, greenish yell, yellow-brn, blk & gold		30	35
	a. Imperforate (horiz. pair)			
W402 (=S.G.1074) **W381**	13p. salmon-pk, new bl, greenish yell, mag, blk & gold		35	35
	a. Damaged top to 1	1·75		
	b. Part of magenta garter missing	2·00		
	c. Broken outline on leg	2·50		

First Day Cover (W399/402)	†	1·00
Presentation Pack (W399/402)	1·40	†
PHQ Cards (W399/402)	1·75	3·50

Covers exist predated 21 November with the Royal Academy special handstamp 1978.

121

Listed Varieties

W399c
Black mark on girl's shoe
(No dot, R. 2/1)

W399d
Faint lines appearing as a
bubble from man's mouth
(No dot, R. 3/1)

W399e
Black scratch extending
to boy's hand
(No dot, R. 8/4)

W399f
Long diagonal scratch
(Dot, R. 1/10 only with 1F
gold cyl.)

W400b/c
Bottom side of collecting
box missing
(Var. a: Dot, R. 1/7)
(Var. b: Dot, R. 2/4)

W400d
Damaged foot to P
(Dot, R. 7/1)
For missing right half of serif
flaws see under "Minor con-
stant flaws"

W402a
Damaged top to 1
(Dot, R. 6/4)

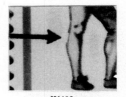

W402*b*
Part of magenta garter
missing from right leg
(Dot, R. 10/5)

W402*c*
Broken outline on leg
(No dot, R. 6/4)

Cylinder Numbers (Blocks of Six)

	Cyl. Nos.	Perforation No dot	Type R* Dot
7p.	1A (black)–1B (greenish yellow)–1C (bright green)–1D (magenta)–1E (new blue)–1F (gold)–P70 (phosphor)	2·50	2·50
	1A (black)–1B (greenish yellow)–1C (bright green)–1D (magenta)–1E (new blue)–1F (gold)	3·50	3·50
	1A (black)–1B (greenish yellow)–1C (bright green)–1D (magenta)–1E (new blue)–2F (gold)–P70 (phosphor)	1·50	1·50
	1A (black)–1B (greenish yellow)–1C (bright green)–1D (magenta)–1E (new blue)–2F (gold)	4·50	5·50
9p.	5A (black)–1B (greenish yellow)–1C (sage-green)–1D (magenta)–1E (new blue)–1F (gold)–P61 (phosphor)	1·75	1·75
	5A (black)–1B (greenish yellow)–1C (sage green)–1D (magenta)–1E (new blue)–1F (gold)	3·25	3·25
11p.	1A (black)–1B (greenish yellow)–2C (new blue)–1D (magenta)–1E (yellow-brown)–1F (gold)–P61 (phosphor)	2·10	2·10
13p.	1A (black)–1B (greenish yellow)–1C (salmon-pink)–1D (magenta)–1E (new blue)–1F (gold)–P61 (phosphor)	2·50	2·50

On the 7p. the phosphor cylinder P70 is without dot on both panes. In the other three values the P61 cylinder number has a dot on no dot panes and no dot on dot panes.

Sheet Details

Sheet size: 100 (2 panes 10 × 5). Double pane reel-fed

Sheet markings:
Cylinder numbers: Opposite rows 8/9, left margin, boxed
Marginal arrows: In centre at top and bottom of sheet
Colour register marks (crossed lines type):
No dot panes: Opposite rows 2/3 at both sides
Dot panes: Opposite rows 6/7 at both sides and large cross in circle opposite row 2, left margin
Autotron marks: In same order as traffic lights in left margin opposite rows 2/5 and gutter margin on dot panes only
Sheet values: Above and below vertical rows 2/4 and 7/9 reading from left to right in top margin and from right to left (upside down) in bottom margin
Traffic lights (boxed): Opposite rows 8/9, right margin; also in same order reading from left to right in gutter margin in vertical row 2:
7p. Greenish yellow, bright green, magenta, black, new blue, gold
9p. Greenish yellow, sage-green, magenta, black, new blue, gold
11p. Greenish yellow, new blue, magenta, black, yellow-brown, gold
13p. Greenish yellow, salmon-pink, magenta, black, new blue, gold

Quantities Sold   7p. 258,370,000; 9p. 119,400,000 11p. 19,480,000; 13p. 17,980,000

Withdrawn   21.11.79

1978 (22 NOVEMBER).   COLLECTORS PACK 1978

WCP12 Comprises Nos. W378/402 excluding WMS386 (Sold at £2·85)   9·00

Withdrawn   21.11.79

W382 Old English Sheepdog   **W383** Welsh Springer Spaniel

W384 West Highland Terrier   **W385** Irish Setter
(Des. Peter Barrett)

1979 (7 FEBRUARY).   BRITISH DOGS

This issue continues the popular animal theme which commenced with the 1977 Wildlife issue and was followed in 1978 by the stamps featuring horses. The date of issue coincided with the staging of Cruft's Dog Show. This annual event held under the auspices of the Kennel Club, is the most famous of its kind in the world. Favourite British breeds were chosen for the stamp designs which are the first from wildlife painter, Peter Barrett. The Welsh springer spaniel featured on the 10½p. is from the artist's 2½ year old pet spaniel "Charlie".

"All-over" phosphor

W403 (=S.G.1075)	**W382**	9p.	grey-black, sepia, turquoise-green, pale greenish yellow, pale greenish blue and grey	20	25
W404 (=S.G.1076)	**W383**	10½p.	grey-black, lake-brown, apple-green, pale greenish yellow, pale greenish blue and grey	30	35
		a.	Sliced top to P	1·50	
		b.	Sliced front to P	1·50	
		c.	Short serif to large 1	1·75	
		d.	Sliced loop to P	1·90	
W405 (=S.G.1077)	**W384**	11p.	grey-black, claret, yellowish green, pale greenish yellow, cobalt and grey	35	40
		a.	Imperforate (horiz. pair)		
		b.	Horizontal dark line	2·00	
W406 (=S.G.1078)	**W385**	13p.	grey-black, lake-brown, green, pale greenish yellow and deep turquoise-blue	40	40

First Day Cover (W403/6)	..	.. .. ..	†	1·25
Presentation Pack (W403/6)	..	.. .. ..	1·50	†
PHQ Cards (W403/6)	..	.. .. ..	3·50	3·50

Covers are known postmarked First Day of Issue in Paddington dated "7 February 1978" instead of 1979.

Listed Varieties

W404a	W404b	W404c
Sliced top to P	Sliced front to P	Short serif to large 1
(No dot, R. 8/1)	(No dot, R. 9/5)	(Dot, R. 1/3)

W404d	W405b
Sliced loop to P	Horizontal dark line
(Dot, R. 8/5)	to right of W
	(Dot, R. 3/8)

Cylinder Numbers (Blocks of Six)

	Cyl. Nos.	Perforation No dot	Type R* Dot
9p.	1A (grey-black)–1B (pale greenish yellow)–1C (turquoise-green)–1D (pale greenish blue)–1E (grey)–1F (sepia)–P61 (phosphor) ..	1·50	1·50
10½p.	2A (grey-black)–3B (pale greenish yellow)–2C (apple-green)–1D (pale greenish blue)–1E (lake-brown)–1F (grey)–P61 (phosphor)	3·50*	2·10
11p.	1A (grey-black)–1B (pale greenish yellow)–1C (yellowish green)–1D (cobalt)–1E (claret)–1F (grey)–P61 (phosphor) ..	2·40	2·40
	1A (grey-black)–1B (pale greenish yellow)–1C (yellowish green)–1D (cobalt)–1E (claret)–1F (grey)..	5·00	5·00
13p.	3A (grey-black)–1B (pale greenish yellow)–1C (green)–1D (deep turquoise-blue)–1E (lake-brown)–P61 (phosphor)	2.75	2·75

The phosphor cylinder number appears to be synchronised on the cylinder block.

Sheet Details

Sheet size: 100 (2 panes 10 × 5). Double pane reel-fed

Sheet markings:
Cylinder numbers: Opposite rows 8/9, left margin, boxed
Marginal arrows: In centre at top and bottom of sheet
Colour register marks (crossed lines type):
No dot panes: Opposite rows 2/3 (13p.) or 6/7 (others) at both sides and large cross in circle opposite row 2, left margin on 9p., 10½p. and 11p.
Dot panes: Opposite rows 6/7, left margin and rows 7/8, right margin (13p.) or rows 1/3 (others) at both sides and large cross in circle opposite row 2, left margin on 13p.
Autotron marks: In same order as traffic lights in left margin opposite rows 4/7 (9p., 10½p. and 11p.) or rows 2/4 (13p.) on dot panes only
Perforation register marks: Horizontal thin grey-black bar in right margin by lower perforation row of gutter margin on no dot panes (9p., 10½p. and 11p.) or dot pane (13p.)
Sheet values: Above and below vertical rows 2/4 and 7/9 reading from left to right in top margin and from right to left (upside down) in bottom margin
Traffic lights (boxed): Opposite rows 8/9, right margin; also in same order reading from left to right in gutter margin in vertical row 2:
9p. Pale greenish yellow, turquoise-green, pale greenish blue, grey, sepia, grey-black
10½p. Pale greenish yellow, apple-green, pale greenish blue, lake-brown, grey, grey-black
11p. Pale greenish yellow, yellowish green, cobalt, claret, grey, grey-black
13p. Pale greenish yellow, green, deep turquoise-blue, lake-brown, grey-black
Colour designations seen:
9p. "G6 BLACK G5 BROWN G4 GREY G" reading up at right, rows 1/4 on no dot sheets and "3 BLUE G2 GREEN G1 YELLOW" rows 8/10 on dot sheets
10½p. "G6 BLACK G5 GREY G4 BROWN G3 B" reading up at right, rows 1/4 on no dot sheets

11p. "G6 BLACK G5 GREY G4 RED G3" reading up at right, rows 1/4 on no dot sheets and "BLUE G2 GREEN G1 YELLOW" rows 8/10 on dot sheets

13p. "BLACK G5 BROWN G4 BLUE G3 GREEN G2 YELLOW G1" reading up at right, rows 1/6 on no dot sheets

Quantities Sold   9p. 49,790,000; 10½p. 15,010,000; 11p. 14,280,000; 13p. 13,930,000

Withdrawn   6.2.80

W386 Primrose

W387 Daffodil

W388 Bluebell

W389 Snowdrop

(Des. Peter Newcombe)

1979 (21 MARCH). SPRING WILD FLOWERS

Issued on the first day of Spring, this set features four of the popular early flowers of the country-side. Using their natural settings, the artist, Peter Newcombe has highlighted the change of the season with these, his first stamp designs. Until 1975 these flowers were unprotected by law but this situation changed with the introduction of the Conservation of Wild Creatures and Wild Plants Act whereby it is an offence to uproot any wild plant or to pick certain endangered species.

"All-over" phosphor

W407 (=S.G.1079)	**W386**	9p.	slate-black, deep brown, pale greenish yellow, deep olive, pale new blue and silver	20	20
			a. Imperforate (pair)	£400	
W408 (=S.G.1080)	**W387**	10½p.	greenish yellow, grey-green, steel-blue, slate-black, new blue and silver	30	35
			a. Imperforate (vert. pair)	£15.00	
			b. Imperf. between stamp and left-hand margin		
			c. Yellow petal flaw	1·75	
			d. Black blob in daffodil	1·60	
W409 (=S.G.1081)	**W388**	11p.	slate-black, deep brown, ultramarine, light greenish blue, pale greenish yellow and silver ..	35	40
			a. Imperforate (horiz. pair)	£1200	
			b. Vertical scratch	2·75	
W410 (=S.G.1082)	**W388**	13p.	slate-black, indigo, grey-green, sepia, ochre, & silver	35	40
			a. Imperforate (horiz. pair)	£750	

First Day Cover (W407/10)				†	1·25
Presentation Pack (W407/10)				1·50	†
PHQ Cards (W407/10)				1·50	3·50

Listed Varieties

W408*c*
Detached yellow petal
(Dot, R. 1/8)

W408*d*
Large black blob in
trumpet of daffodil
in foreground
(Dot, R. 5/6)

Long vertical black
scratch through
bluebell leaves to
margin (Dot, R. 10/8)

W409*b*

Cylinder Numbers (Blocks of Six)

	Cyl. Nos.	Perforation Type R*	
		No dot	Dot
9p.	5A (slate-black)–1B (pale greenish yellow)–1C (deep olive)–1D (pale new blue)–1E (deep brown)–1F (silver)–P61 (phosphor)..	1·50	1·50
10½p.	1A (slate-black)–1B (greenish yellow)–1C (grey-green)–2D (steel-blue)–1E (new blue)–1F (silver)–P61 (phosphor)	2·10	2·10
11p.	2A (slate-black)–1B (pale greenish yellow)–3C (light greenish-blue)–1D (ultramarine)–3E (deep brown)–1F (silver)–P61 (phosphor)	2·40	2·40
13p.	2A (slate-black)–1B (ochre)–1C (grey-green)–4D (indigo)–1E (sepia)–1F (silver)–P61 (phosphor	2·50	2·50

The above are with sheets orientated with head to left

The phosphor cylinder number appears to be synchronised on the cylinder block

Sheet Details

Sheet size: 100 (2 panes 5 × 10). Double pane reel-fed

Sheet markings:
Cylinder numbers: In top margin above vertical rows 2/3, boxed
Marginal arrows: In centre, opposite rows 5/6 at both sides
Colour register marks (crossed lines type):
  No dot panes: Above and below vertical rows 4/5 and also large cross in circle above vertical row 9
  Dot panes: Above and below vertical rows 9/10
Autotron marks: In reverse order of traffic lights reading from left to right above vertical rows 4/7 on dot panes only
Perforation register marks: Black bar below left gutter perforation row on no dot panes (10½p. and 11p.)
Sheet values: Opposite rows 2/4 and 7/9 reading up at left and down at right
Traffic lights (boxed): In bottom margin below vertical rows 2/3; also in same order reading down in gutter margin in row 2:
  9p.   Pale greenish yellow, deep olive, pale new blue, deep brown, slate-black, silver
  10½p. Greenish yellow, grey-green, steel-blue, new blue, slate-black, silver
  11p. Pale greenish yellow, light greenish blue, ultramarine, deep brown, slate-black, silver
  13p. Ochre, grey-green, indigo, sepia, slate-black, silver

Quantities Sold   9p. 50,010,000; 10½p. 15,080,000; 11p. 14,490,000; 13p. 13,980,000

Withdrawn   20.3.80

128

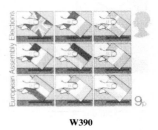

W390

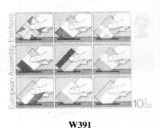

W391

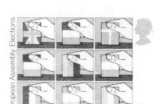

W392

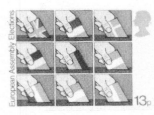

W393

The designs show hands placing the flags of the
member nations into the ballot boxes
(Des. Stafford Cliff)

1979 (9 MAY). FIRST DIRECT ELECTIONS TO THE EUROPEAN ASSEMBLY

The first direct elections to the European Assembly were commemorated by this issue. The flags as shown on the stamps are those of Britain, France, Denmark, Belgium, West Germany, Italy, Netherlands, Ireland and Luxembourg. These are the first stamp designs by Stafford Cliff.

Phosphorised (fluorescent coated) paper

W411 (= S.G.1083)	W390	9p.	grey-black, vermilion, cinnamon, pale greenish yellow, pale turquoise-green and dull ultramarine	20	20
		a.	Damaged ballot box	1·50	
W412 (= S.G.1084)	W391	10½p.	grey-black, vermilion, cinnamon, pale greenish yellow, dull ultramarine, pale turq-grn & chestnut	30	35
		a.	Incomplete stripe	1·50	
W413 (= S.G.1085)	W392	11p.	grey-black, vermilion, cinnamon, pale greenish yellow, dull ultramarine, pale turq-grn & grey-grn	35	40
W414 (= S.G.1086)	W393	13p.	grey-black, vermilion, cinnamon, pale greenish yellow, dull ultramarine, pale turq-grn & brn ..	35	40
		a.	Break in ribbon	2·75	
		b.	Broken r	1·90	

First Day Cover (W411/4)	†	1·25
Presentation Pack (W411/4)	1·50	†
PHQ Cards (W411/4)	1·60	3·50

129

Listed Varieties

W411*a*
Damage to ballot box
at bottom left
(No dot, R. 9/3)

W412*a*
Wedge shaped patch
of white below thumb
(No dot, R. 7/3)

W414*a*
Break in Queen's ribbon
(Dot, R. 6/9)

W414*b*
Broken r
(Dot, R. 8/7)

Cylinder Numbers (Blocks of Six)

	Cyl. Nos.	Perforation No dot	Type R* Dot
9p.	2A (grey-black)–1B (pale greenish yellow)–1C (dull ultramarine) –1D (pale turquoise-green)–1E (cinnamon)–1F (vermilion) ..	1·50	1·50
10½p.	1A (grey-black)–1B (pale greenish yellow)–1C (chestnut)–1D (dull ultramarine)–1E (pale turquoise-green)–1F (cinnamon)– 2G (vermilion)	5·50	5·50
	2A (grey-black)–1B (pale greenish yellow)–1C (chestnut)–1D (dull ultramarine)–1E (pale turquoise-green)–1F (cinnamon)–2G (vermilion)	2·10	2·10
11p.	1A (grey-black)–1B (pale greenish yellow)–1C (grey-green)–1D (dull ultramarine)–1E (pale turquoise-green)–1F (cinnamon) –2G (vermilion)	2·40	2·40
13p.	1A (grey-black)–1B (pale greenish yellow)–1C (brown)–1D (dull ultramarine)–1E (pale turquoise-green)–1F (cinnamon)–1G (vermilion)	2·50	2·50

Sheet Details

Sheet size: 100 (2 panes 10 × 5). Double pane reel-fed

Sheet markings:
Cylinder numbers: Opposite rows 8/9, left margin boxed
Marginal arrows: In centre at top and bottom of sheet
Colour register marks (crossed lines type):
  No dot panes: Opposite rows 6/7 at both sides and large cross in circle opposite row 2/1, left margin
  Dot panes: Opposite rows 1/2 at both sides
Autotron marks: In same order as traffic lights in left margin opposite rows 4/7 on dot panes only
Perforation register marks: Thick bar opposite lower gutter perforations, right margin on no dot panes only
Sheet values: Above and below vertical rows 2/4 and 7/9 reading from left to right in top margin and from right to left (upside down) in bottom margin

130

Traffic lights (boxed): Opposite rows 8/9, right margin, also in same order reading from left to right in gutter margin in vertical rows 2/3 (13p.) or row 2 (others)

9p.   Pale greenish yellow, grey-black, dull ultramarine, pale turquoise green, cinnamon, vermilion

10½p. Pale greenish yellow, grey-black, chestnut, dull ultramarine, pale turquoise green, cinnamon, vermilion

11p. Pale greenish yellow, grey-black, dull ultramarine, pale turquoise green, cinnamon, vermilion

13p. Pale greenish yellow, grey-black, brown, dull ultramarine, pale turquoise green, cinnamon, vermilion

Colour designations seen:

9p.   "G6 RED G5 FLESH G 4 GREEN G3 BLUE G2 BLACK G1" reading up at right, rows 1/5 on no dot sheets

11p. "G7 RED G6 FLESH G5 GREEN G4 BLUE G3 BACKGROUND G2 BLACK" reading up at right, rows 1/5 on no dot sheets

Quantities Sold   9p. 47,510,000; 10½p. 15,870,000; 11p. 15,400,000; 13p. 14,820,000

Withdrawn   8.5.80

W394 "Saddling 'Mahmoud'
for The Derby, 1936"
(Sir Alfred Munnings)

W395 "The Liverpool Great
National Steeple Chase, 1839"
(F. C. Turner)

W396 "The First Spring
Meeting, Newmarket, 1793"
(J. N. Sartorius)

W397 "Racing at Dorsett
Ferry, Windsor, 1684"
(Francis Barlow)

(Des. Stuart Rose)

131

1979 (6 JUNE). DERBY BICENTENARY

This issue, featuring horse racing paintings, commemorates the 200th Derby, which was first run on 4 May 1780 at Epsom Downs. The 10½p. is from an aquatint and shows the first Grand National at Aintree. Racing at Newmarket is featured on the 11p. and the 13p. has King Charles II shown watching the racing at Dorsett Ferry, Windsor, in 1684 from a painting by Francis Barlow.

"All-over" phosphor

W415 (=S.G.1087)	**W394**	9p.	light blue, red brown, rose-pink, pale greenish yellow, grey-black and gold	25	25
W416 (=S.G.1088)	**W395**	10½p.	bistre-yellow, slate-blue, salmon-pink, light blue, grey-black and gold	35	40
		a.	Brown spots	1·75	
W417 (=S.G.1089)	**W396**	11p.	rose, vermilion, pale greenish yellow, new blue, grey-black and gold	40	45
		a.	Short serif to first 1	1·75	
		b.	Yellow spot on horse	2·25	
W418 (=S.G.1090)	**W397**	13p.	bistre-yellow, rose, turquoise, grey-black and gold	45	45
		a.	Imperf. between stamp and bottom margin ..		
		b.	Missing serif at foot of 1	1·90	

First Day Cover (W415/8)	..	..	..	.. †	1·50
Presentation Pack (W415/8)	..	..	..	.. 1·75	†
PHQ Cards (W415/8	..	..	..	.. 1·60	2·75

The presentation pack contained an insert with cartoons specially commissioned from the artist Norman Thelwell.

Listed Varieties

W416*a*
Semi-circle of brown
spots over left tree
appearing as leaves
(Dot, R. 6/1)

W417*a*
Short serif to first
figure 1
(No dot, R. 4/5)

W417*b*
Large yellowish spot
on rear horse
(No dot, R. 8/2)

W418*b*
Bottom left serif to
1 of value missing
(No dot, R. 9/9)

Cylinder Numbers (Blocks of Six)

	Cyl. Nos.	Perforation No dot	Type R* Dot
9p.	1A (grey-black)–1B (pale greenish yellow)–1C (light blue)–1D (red-brown)–1E (gold)–1F (rose-pink)	1·75	1·75
	1A (grey-black)–1B (pale greenish yellow)–1C (light blue)–1D (red-brown)–1E (gold)–1F (rose-pink)–P61 (phosphor) ..	3·50	3·50
10½p.	2A (grey-black)–1B (bistre-yellow)–1C (light blue)–1D (salmon-pink)–1E (gold)–1F (slate-blue)–P61 (phosphor)	2·40	2·40
11p.	2A (grey-black)–1B (pale greenish yellow)–2C (new blue)–1D (rose)–1E (gold)–1F (vermilion)–P61 (phosphor)	6·50*	4·75
	2A (grey-black)–1B (pale greenish yellow)–2C (new blue)–1D (rose)–1E (gold)–1F (vermilion)	4·50*	2·75
13p.	1A (grey-black)–1B (bistre-yellow)–1C (turquoise)–2D (rose)–1E (gold)–P61 (phosphor)	5·00	5·00
	1A (grey-black)–1B (bistre-yellow)–1C (turquoise)–2D (rose)–1E (gold)	3·25	3·25

Phosphor cylinder No. P61 usually occurs opposite row 2 on both panes of the 9p. value. On the other values the phosphor number and inset appears to be synchronised at extreme top and bottom of the phosphor margin.

Sheet Details

Sheet size: 100 (2 panes 10 × 5). Double pane reel-fed

Sheet markings:
    Cylinder numbers: Opposite rows 8/9, left margin, boxed
    Marginal arrows: In centre at top and bottom of sheet
    Colour register marks (crossed lines type):
        No dot panes: Opposite rows 6/7 at both sides and cross in circle opposite row 2, left margin
        Dot panes: Opposite rows 1/3 at both sides
    Autotron marks: In same order as traffic lights in left margin opposite rows 4/7 on dot panes only
    Perforation register marks: Thick bar opposite lower gutter perforations, right margin on no dot panes only
    Sheet values: Above and below vertical rows 2/4 and 7/9 reading from left to right in top margin and from right to left (upside down) in bottom margin
    Traffic lights (boxed): Opposite row 9 (13p.) or rows 8/9 (others), right margin; also in same order reading from left to right in gutter margin in vertical row 2:
        9p.   Pale greenish yellow, light blue, red-brown, rose-pink, grey-black, gold
        10½p. Bistre-yellow, light blue, salmon-pink, slate-blue, grey-black, gold
        11p.   Pale greenish yellow, new blue, rose, vermilion, grey-black, gold
        13p.   Bistre-yellow, turquoise, rose, grey-black, gold

Quantities Sold   9p. 56,350,000; 10½p. 20,440,000; 11p. 19,880,000; 13p. 19,280,000

Withdrawn   5.6.80

W398 *The Tale of Peter Rabbit*
(Beatrix Potter)

W399 *The Wind in the Willows*
(Kenneth Grahame)

W400 *Winnie-the-Pooh*
(A. A. Milne)

W401 *Alice's Adventures in Wonderland*
(Lewis Carroll)

(Des. Edward Hughes)

1979 (11 JULY). INTERNATIONAL YEAR OF THE CHILD

The United Nations General Assembly, on the 20th anniversary of the Declaration of the Rights of the Child, chose 1979 as the International Year of the Child. This issue features designs taken from original illustrations in famous children's books. The characters shown on the 9p. are Peter Rabbit, Jemima Puddleduck and Squirrel Nutkin; on the 10½p. Toad of Toad Hall is in the foreground, with Mole, Rat and Mr. Badger in close support; the 11p. features Winnie-the-Pooh, Eeyore the donkey, Piglet and Christopher Robin; and the 13p. has Alice, the Mad Hatter and the Cheshire Cat.

"All-over" phosphor

W419 (= S.G.1091)	**W398**	9p.	deep bluish green, grey-black, bistre-brown, bright rose, greenish yellow and silver	35	20
			a. Broken bill	1·75	
			b. White patch on roof	1·90	
			c. Yellow patch above paw	1·75	
W420 (= S.G.1092)	**W399**	10½p.	dull ultramarine, grey-black, olive-brown, bright rose, yellow-orange, pale greenish yellow and silver	30	35
			a. Torn coat tail	2·00	
W421 (= S.G.1093)	**W400**	11p.	drab, grey-black, greenish yellow, new blue, yellow-orange, agate and silver	35	40
W422 (= S.G.1094)	**W401**	13p.	pale greenish yellow, grey-black, bright rose, deep bluish green, olive-brown, new blue and silver ..	40	40

First Day Cover* (W419/22) ..	..	..	..	†	1·25
Presentation Pack (W419/22) ..	..	..	..	2·00	†
PHQ Cards (W419/22) ..	..	..	..	1·60	2·25

Some stamps have been seen with thin dextrin gum which when seen under ultra violet light shows much of the fluorescence from the paper.

*Due to an industrial dispute affecting supplies of stamps, the issue date scheduled for 18 July was brought forward. An exceptional arrangement allowed collectors to obtain the 11 July first day cancellation on covers posted on or before 18 July.

Listed Varieties

W419*a*	W419*b*	W419*c*
Outline of duck's bill is incomplete (No dot, R. 8/8)	White patch on roof of shed at right (No dot, R. 9/2)	Large yellow patch above Rabbit's right paw (No dot, R. 5/1)

Large white gash
(tear) in Toad's coat tail
(No dot, R. 2/5)

W420*a*

Cylinder Numbers (Blocks of Six)

Cyl. Nos.	Perforation Type R*

	No dot	Dot
9p. 1A (grey-black)–1B (greenish yellow)–1C (deep bluish green)–1D (bright rose)–1E (bistre-brown)–1F (silver)–P61 (phosphor) ..	2·50	2·50
10½p. 1A (grey-black)–2B (pale greenish yellow)–1C (dull ultramarine)–1D (yellow-orange)–1E (bright rose)–1F (olive-brown)–1G (silver)	2·10	2·10
1A (grey-black)–2B (pale greenish yellow)–1C (dull ultramarine)–1D (yellow-orange)–1E (bright rose)–1F (olive-brown) –1G (silver)–P61 (phosphor).	†	10·00
11p. 1A (grey-black)–1B (greenish yellow)–1C (new blue)–1D (yellow-orange)–2E (agate)–1F (drab)–1G (silver)	2·40	2·40
13p. 1A (grey-black)–1B (greenish yellow)–1C (new blue)–1D (deep bluish green)–1E (bright rose)–1F (silver)–1G (olive-brown) ..	2·75	2·75

The above are with sheets orientated with head to left.
On the 9p. the P61 cylinder number has a dot on no dot panes and no dot on dot panes. The other values have an unsynchronised phosphor number. On the 10½p. it has been found upright in the left margin and inverted in the right-hand margin. P61 is inverted in the right margin on the other values.

Sheet Details

Sheet size: 100 (2 panes 5 × 10). Double pane reel-fed

Sheet markings:

Cylinder numbers: In top margin above vertical rows 2/3, boxed

Marginal arrows: In centre, opposite rows 5/6 at both sides

Colour register marks (crossed lines type):
    No dot panes: Above and below vertical rows 3/5 and cross in circle above vertical row 9
    Dot panes: Above and below vertical rows 8/10

Autotron marks: In order of traffic lights reading from left to right above vertical rows 4/7 on dot panes only

Perforation register marks: Thick bar below left gutter perforations on no dot panes only

Sheet values: Opposite rows 2/4 and 7/9 reading up at left and down at right

Traffic lights (boxed): In bottom margin below vertical row 2/3; also in same order reading up in gutter margin in row 2

9p.   Silver, grey-black, bistre-brown, bright rose, deep bluish green, greenish yellow

10½p. Silver, grey-black, olive-brown, bright rose, yellow-orange, dull ultramarine, pale greenish yellow

11p.   Silver, grey-black, drab, agate, yellow-orange, new blue, greenish yellow

13p.   Silver, grey-black, olive-brown, bright rose, deep bluish green, new blue, pale greenish yellow

Quantities Sold   9p. 54,990,000; 10½p. 18,950,000; 11p. 18,400,000; 13p. 17,960,000

Withdrawn   10.7.80

W402 Sir Rowland Hill

W403 Postman, *c* 1839

W404 London Postman, *c* 1839

W405 Victorian Lady and
Child with Letters, 1840

(Des. Eric Stemp)

1979 (22 AUGUST–24 OCTOBER (WMS427))   DEATH CENTENARY OF SIR ROWLAND HILL

This issue marks the centenary of the death of Sir Rowland Hill (1795-1879). His major postal reform was the introduction of Uniform Penny Postage, brought into effect on 10 January 1840. This meant that the charge for sending a letter if prepaid was 1d. per ½oz. anywhere in the British Isles or 2d. if unpaid. The new measures replaced the old system of charging postage by distance and the number of letter sheets carried.

The 11½p. shows the scarlet-uniformed Bellman of the General Post who rang in the London streets every evening to collect letters for the Night Mail serving destinations beyond the capital. The London Post had the blue-uniformed postmen shown on 13p., who carried letters within the capital. The 15p. serves to underline the popularity of the new system, when in 1840, more than twice as many letters were carried than in the previous year.

The miniature sheet issued on 24 October was delayed due to a change in postal tariffs. It was sold with a premium of 10p. for the benefit of the exhibition funds and like the 1978 sheet, WMS386, was sold out soon after issue.

"All-over" phosphor

W423 (= S.G.1095)	**W402**	10p.	grey-black, brown-ochre, myrtle-green, pale greenish yellow, rosine, bright blue and gold ..	25	25
W424 (= S.G.1096)	**W403**	11½p.	grey-black, brown-ochre, bright blue, rosine, bistre-brown, pale greenish yellow and gold ..	35	35
			a. Large dot on breeches	2·25	
			b. White chimney	1·75	
W425 (= S.G.1097)	**W404**	13p.	grey-black, brown-ochre, bright blue, rosine, bistre-brown, pale greenish yellow and gold ..	40	35
W426 (= S.G.1098)	**W405**	15p.	grey-black, brown-ochre, myrtle-green, bistre-brown, rosine, pale greenish yellow and gold ..	45	40
			a. Envelope incomplete	2·25	

First Day Cover (W423/6)	..	..	..	..	†	1·25
Presentation Pack (W423/6)	..	..	..	..	1·60	†
PHQ Cards (W423/6)	..	..	..	..	1·60	2·25

W406 Miniature Sheet
(*Illustration reduced to three quarters actual size*)

WMS427
(=S.G.MS1099)   **W406**   Sheet size 89 × 121mm. issued in pack with printed
card (sold at 59½p.) .. .. 1·10 1·25

a. Imperforate sheet	£1100	
b. Brown-ochre (15p. background, etc.) omitted ..	£950	
c. Gold (Queen's head) omitted	£225	
d. Brown-ochre, myrtle-green and gold omitted ..	£3000	
e. Bright blue (13p. background, etc.) omitted ..	£1100	
f. Myrtle-green (10p. background), 15p.) omitted	£1250	
g. Pale greenish yellow omitted	£160	
h. Rosine omitted	£650	
i. Bistre-brown omitted	£900	
j. Pale greenish yellow and phosphor omitted ..	£175	
k. Gold and phosphor omitted	£275	
l. Rosine and phosphor omitted	£750	
m. Phosphor omitted	45·00	

First Day Cover (WMS427)	..	..	..	..	1·25

The miniature sheet was pre-released at a Post Office in Hither Green, London on 17 October.

Listed Varieties

W424*a*
Large dot on breeches
(Dot, R. 2/2)

W424*b*
White chimney at
extreme right
(Dot, R. 10/8)

W426*a*
Envelope incomplete
(No dot, R. 8/7)

Cylinder Numbers (Blocks of Six)

	Cyl. Nos.	Perforation No dot	Type R* Dot
10p.	2A (grey-black)–1B (pale greenish yellow)–1C (brown-ochre) –1D (rosine)–1E (bright blue)–1F (myrtle-green)–1G (gold)–P65 (phosphor)	2·75	2·75
	2A (grey-black)–1B (pale greenish yellow)–1C (brown-ochre)– 1D (rosine)–1E (bright blue)–1F (myrtle-green)–1G (gold) ..	1·75	1·75
11½p.	2A (grey-black)–1B (pale greenish yellow)–2C (brown-ochre) –1D (rosine)–1E (bright blue)–1F (bistre-brown)–1G (gold) ..	2·40	4·25*
13p.	2A (grey-black)–1B (pale greenish yellow)–1C (brown-ochre) –1D (rosine)–3E (bright blue)–1F (bistre-brown)–1G (gold) ..	2·75	2·75
15p.	2A (grey-black)–1B (pale greenish yellow)–1C (brown-ochre) –1D (rosine)–1E (bistre-brown)–1F (myrtle-green)–1G (gold)– P65 (phosphor)	4·00	4·00
	2A (grey-black)–1B (pale greenish yellow)–1C (brown-ochre) –1D (rosine)–1E (bistre-brown)–1F (myrtle-green)–1G (gold) ..	3·25	3·25

The above are with sheets orientated with head to left.

On the 10p. and 15p. the phosphor cylinder No. P65 is unsynchronised and always appears inverted on cylinder blocks. The number is without dot on both panes. The 11½p. and 13p. have the number in the bottom margin only.

Sheet Details

Sheet size: 100 (2 panes 5 × 10). Double pane reel-fed

Sheet markings:
  Cylinder numbers: In top margin above vertical rows 2/3, boxed
  Marginal arrows: In centre, opposite rows 5/6 at both sides
  Colour register marks (crossed lines type):
    No dot panes: Above and below vertical rows 4/5 and cross in circle type above vertical row 9
    Dot panes: Above and below vertical rows 9/10
  Autotron marks: In order of traffic lights reading from left to right above vertical rows 4/7 on dot panes only
  Perforation register marks: Thick bar below left gutter perforation row on no dot panes only
  Sheet values: Opposite rows 2/4 and 7/9 reading up at left and down at right
  Traffic lights (boxed): In bottom margin below vertical rows 2/3; also in same order reading up in gutter margin in row 2:
  10p. Gold, grey-black, myrtle-green, bright blue, rosine, brown-ochre, pale greenish yellow
  11½p. Gold, grey-black, bistre-brown, bright blue, rosine, brown-ochre, pale greenish yellow
  13p. Gold, grey-black, bistre-brown, bright blue, rosine, brown-ochre, pale greenish yellow
  15p. Gold, grey-black, myrtle-green, bistre-brown, rosine, brown-ochre, pale greenish yellow

Miniature Sheet

Similar in size to the British Architecture sheet it was printed in sheets of nine on the Rembrandt press and perforated 15 × 14 on a Bickel machine. A reduced sized illustration of an uncut sheet appears following the next page but all the marginal markings shown were guillotined off. The cylinder numbers employed were 7A–1B–1C–4D–3E–1F–1G–1H. We are not aware of a phosphor cylinder number.

Plating the Sheets

Using a similar method to that adopted for the previous miniature sheet it is not difficult to "plate" the nine sheets. We base our numbering system on the position in the uncut printer's sheet of nine examples. Position 1 being R. 1/1, position 2, R. 1/2 and so on.

The first continuous brown horizontal wavy line above and below the white border surrounding the stamps forms hollows and crests. By counting the broken lines within two selected hollows it is possible to discover the position in the printer's sheet of individual miniature sheets. The lines at the top are in the first hollow, above the Queen's head on the 10p. and the lower hollow is above the word "SHEET". Note that totals marked with an * include one line that continues as a hair line, at right or left.

Lines at top	Lines at bottom	Position
3*	3	2
3	2	3
2	3*	4
2	3	5

The others require further tests for identification:

2	2	1, 6 or 9
3*	2	7 or 8

To distinguish positions 1, 6 and 9 it is necessary to look at the bottom left-hand corner of the white border and note the number of short lines that make up the first hollow above the letters "BR" of "BRITISH".

Lines at the bottom left

	Position
3 the last one ending in a hair line of dots	1
2 the first line is short and straight	6
2 curved lines	9

On position 6 there is a thickening of the brown lines at the lower right edge. The "T" of "SHEET" is weak in position 9.

It only remains to distinguish positions 7 and 8. On position 7 the five hollows at the top are completed by a short dash and four curved lines, each one getting longer from left to right. In position 8 the hollows are completed by five short and weak dashes also "T" of "SHEET" is weak.

We acknowledge the help of illustrations in a pamphlet published by Mr. Andrey M. Roy and we express our thanks to him for permission to draw on this.

(*"Plated" set of nine sheets price* £20.)

Quantities Sold   10p. 74,720,000; 11p. 18,210,000; 13p. 17,200,000; 15p. 18,470,000; Miniature Sheet 59½p. 5,230,000

Withdrawn   The miniature sheet was sold out soon after issue: remainder withdrawn 21.8.80

Photo : National Postal Museum

Uncut Sheet of 9 Miniature Sheets with Plate Markings

W407 Policeman on the Beat

W408 Policeman directing Traffic

W409 Mounted Policewoman
(Des. Brian Sanders)

W410 River Patrol Boat

1979 (26 SEPTEMBER). 150th ANNIVERSARY OF METROPOLITAN POLICE

In 1829 Sir Robert Peel, the then Home Secretary, brought in the Metropolitan Police Act which established a regular force for the metropolis. Before this, locally appointed constables and watchmen had performed the much-needed task of keeping law and order. The stamp designs feature the day-to-day duties carried out by members of the modern police force.

Phosphorised (fluorescent coated) paper

W428 (=S.G.1100)	W407 10p.	grey-black, red-brown, emerald, greenish yellow, bright blue and magenta	25	25
		a. Pale patch	1·50
		b. Extra cloud	1·75
		c. "Bird" on helmet	2·50
		d. Dark dots appear as a bird	2·00
W429 (=S.G.1101)	W408 11½p.	grey-black, bright-orange, purple-brown, ultramarine, greenish yellow and deep bluish green ..	30	35
W430 (=S.G.1102)	W409 13p.	grey-black, red-brown, magenta, olive-green, greenish yellow, and deep dull blue	35	40
		a. Faint railings	1·60
		b. White patch on trousers	1·60
W431 (=S.G.1103)	W410 15p.	grey-black, magenta, brown, slate-blue, deep brown, and greenish black	40	40
		a. Retouch on Queen's bust ··	2·75

First Day Cover (W428/31)	..	..	..	.. †	1·25
Presentation Pack (W428/31)	..	..	..	.. 1·50	†
PHQ Cards (W428/31) ..	..	..	..	.. 1·50	2·25

Listed Varieties

W428a
Loss of deep green
colour above fence
(Dot, R. 2/1)

W428b
Extra cloud under
Queen's silhouette
(No dot, R. 1/7)

W428c
Black dots above
helmet resemble a bird
(No dot, R. 3/1)

W428d
Dark screening dots
appear as a bird
above the trees
(No dot, R. 10/5)

W430a
Railings faint below
Queen's silhouette
(No dot, R. 7/5)

W430b
White patch on trousers
(No dot, R. 9/7)

W431a
Retouch on Queen's bust
(No dot, R. 5/7)

Cylinder Numbers (Blocks of Six)

Cyl. Nos.	Perforation No dot	Type R* Dot
10p. 2A (grey-black)–1B (greenish yellow)–1C (magenta)–2D (emerald)–1E (bright blue)–1F (red-brown)	1·75	1·75
11½p. 2A (grey-black)–1B (greenish yellow)–1C (bright orange)–1D (deep bluish green)–1E (ultramarine)–1F (purple-brown) ..	2·10	2·10
13p. 2A (grey-black)–1B (greenish yellow)–3C (magenta)–1D (olive-green)–1E (deep dull blue)–1F (red-brown)	2·50	2·50
15p. 2A (grey-black)–1B (greenish black)–1C (magenta)–1D (slate-blue)–1E (brown)–1F (deep brown)	2·75	2·75

Sheet Details

Sheet size: 100 (2 panes 10 × 5). Double pane reel-fed

Sheet markings:
Cylinder numbers: Opposite rows 8/9, left margin, boxed
Marginal arrows: In centre at top and bottom of sheet. On 13p. no dot pane top arrow is one perforation hole right of centre
Colour register marks (crossed lines type):
No dot panes: Opposite rows 6/7 at both sides and cross in circle opposite row 2, left margin
Dot panes: Opposite rows 1/2 at both sides
Autotron marks: In same order as traffic lights in left margin opposite rows 4/7 on dot panes only
Perforation register marks: Thick bar opposite lower gutter perforation row on no dot panes only
Sheet values: Above and below vertical rows 2/4 and 7/9 reading from left to right in top margin and from right to left (upside down) in bottom margin
Traffic lights (boxed): Opposite rows 8/9, right margin; also in same order reading from left to right in gutter margin in vertical row 2:
10p.   Greenish yellow, magenta, emerald, bright blue, red-brown, grey-black
11½p. Greenish yellow, bright orange, deep bluish green, ultramarine, purple-brown, grey-black
13p.   Greenish yellow, magenta, olive-green, deep dull blue, red-brown, grey-black
15p.   Greenish black, magenta, slate-blue, brown, deep brown, grey-black

Quantities Sold   10p. 50,870,000; 11½p. 17,190,000; 13p. 16,670,000; 15p. 16,170,000

Withdrawn   25.9.80

W411 The Three Kings

W412 Angel appearing to
the Shepherds

W413 The Nativity

W414 Mary and Joseph
travelling to Bethlehem

W415 The Annunciation

(Des. Fritz Wegner)

1979 (21 NOVEMBER).   CHRISTMAS

This issue features traditional scenes from the Nativity and were designed by Fritz Wegner, who is also responsible for the 1969 Christmas stamps.

One 4 mm. centre phosphor band

W432 (= S.G.1104) **W411** 8p. blue, grey-black, ochre, slate-violet and gold .. 20   20
    a. Imperforate (pair) £550
    b. Imperf. between stamp and bottom margin ..
    c. Black dot over tassels .. .. 2·00
    d. White patch on cloak .. .. 1·50

Phosphorised (fluorescent coated) paper

W433 (= S.G.1105) **W412** 10p. bright rose-red, grey-black, chestnut, chrome-yellow, deep violet and gold 25   25
    a. Imperf. between (vert. pair) £450
    b. Imperforate (pair) £600
    c. Imperf. between stamp and bottom margin ..
    d. Break in fold of angel's robe .. .. .. 1·75
    e. Diagonal scratch .. .. 1·75

W434 (= S.G.1106) **W413** 11½p. orange-vermilion, steel blue, drab grey-black, deep blue-green and gold 30   35
    a. Joseph's left eye missing .. .. .. 2·10

W435 (=S.G.1107)	**W414**	13p.	bright blue, orange-vermilion, bistre, grey-black and gold	..	..	40	40
			a. White patch on hind-leg	..	..	2·10	
			b. Diagonal dotted line	..	..	1·75	
W436 (=S.G.1108)	**W415**	15p.	orange-vermilion, blue, bistre, grey-black, green and gold	..	..	40	45

First Day Cover (W432/6)	†	1·40
Presentation Pack (W432/6)	1·75	†
PHQ Cards (W432/6)	1·60	2·25

Listed Varieties

W432c	**W432d**	**W433d**
Black blot over tassels of blanket (No dot, R. 4/1)	White patch on hem of King's cloak (Dot, R. 2/9)	Break in fold of Angel's robe (No dot, R. 2/1)

W433e	**W434a**	**W435a**	**W435b**
Scratch from Angel's robe to Shepherd's sleeve (No dot, R. 6/10)	White area over Joseph's left eye (Dot, R. 1/2)	White patch on donkey's left hind-leg (No dot, R. 7/7)	Diagonal dotted line from the point of Joseph's staff (Dot, R. 9/8)

Cylinder Numbers (Blocks of Six)

	Cyl. Nos.	Perforation Type R*	
		No dot	Dot
8p.	1A (grey-black)–1B (slate-violet)–1C (ochre)–1D (blue)–1E (gold)	1·50	1·50
	1A (grey-black)–1B (slate-violet)–1C (ochre)–1D (blue)–2E (gold)	1·50	1·50
10p.	2A (grey-black)–1B (chrome-yellow)–1C (bright rose-red)–1D (chestnut)–1E (deep violet)–1F (gold)	1·75	1·75
11½p.	1A (grey-black)–1B (drab)–1C (deep blue-green)–2D (steel blue)–1E (orange-vermilion)–1F (gold)	2·10	2·10
13p.	2A (grey-black)–1B (bistre)–1C (bright blue)–1D (orange-vermilion)–1E (gold)	2·75	2·75
15p.	2A (grey-black)–1B (bistre)–1C (green)–1D (blue)–1E (orange-vermilion)–1F (gold)	2·90	2·90

We are not aware of a phosphor cylinder number on the 8p.

Sheet Details

Sheet size: 100 (2 panes 10 × 5). Double pane reel-fed

Sheet markings:
Cylinder numbers: Opposite rows 8/9, left margin, boxed
Marginal arrows: In centre at top and bottom of sheet
Colour register marks (crossed lines type):
No dot panes: Opposite rows 6/7 at both sides and cross in circle opposite row 2, left margin
Dot panes: Opposite rows 1/2 at both sides
Autotron marks: In same order as traffic lights in left margin opposite rows 5/7 (8p.), 4/6 (13p.) or 4/7 (others) on dot panes only
Perforation register marks: Thick bar opposite lower gutter perforations, right margin on no dot panes only
Sheet values: Above and below vertical rows 2/4 and 7/9 reading from left to right in top margin and from right to left (upside down) in bottom margin
Traffic lights (boxed): Opposite row 9 (8p., 13p.) or rows 8/9 (others), right margin; also in same order reading from left to right in gutter margin in vertical row 2
8p.   Ochre, slate-violet, blue, grey-black, gold
10p.   Chrome-yellow, bright rose-red, chestnut, deep violet, grey-black, gold
11½p. Drab, deep blue-green, steel blue, orange-vermilion, grey-black, gold
13p.   Bistre, bright blue, orange-vermilion, grey-black, gold
15p.   Bistre, green, blue, orange-vermilion, grey-black, gold

Quantities Sold   8p.   304,780,000;   10p.   146,200,000;   11½p.   26,300,000;   13p.   25,450,000; 15p.   23,980,000

Withdrawn   20.11.80

1979 (21 NOVEMBER). COLLECTORS PACK 1979

WCP13 Comprises Nos. W403/36 excluding WMS427 (Sold at £4.09)   10·00

Withdrawn   20.11.80

W416 Kingfisher

W417 Dipper

W418 Moorhen

W419 Yellow Wagtails

(Des. Michael Warren)

1980 (16 JANUARY).   BRITISH BIRDS

This issue, featuring four popular British waterbirds, marks the centenary of the Wild Bird Protection Act of 1880.

Phosphorised (fluorescent coated) paper

W437 (= S.G.1109)	**W416**	10p.	bright blue, bright yellow-green, vermilion, pale greenish yellow, grey-black and gold	25	25
		a.	Short grey lines	1·75	
		b.	White nick from line at left	1·50	
		c.	Break in line right of tail	1·50	
		d.	White nick in grey line	1·50	
		e.	Break in line left of tail	1·50	
W438 (= S.G.1110)	**W417**	11½p.	sepia, grey-black, dull ultramarine, vermilion, grey-green, pale greenish yellow and gold ..	30	35
		a.	Short line	1·75	
W439 (= S.G.1111)	**W418**	13p.	emerald-green, grey-black, bright blue, vermilion, pale greenish yellow and gold	40	45
		a.	Broken line below bird's leg	2·00	
W440 (= S.G.1112)	**W419**	15p.	greenish-yellow, brown, light green, slate blue, grey-black, and gold	45	50
		a.	Claw and branch retouch	2·25	

First Day Cover (W437/40) ..	..	..	..	†	1·40
Presentation Pack (W437/40) ..	..	..	..	1·75	†
PHQ Cards (W437/40) ..	..	..	..	1·50	2·25

Listed Varieties

Normal   W437*a*
Grey lines at top are cut short
(No dot, R. 1/2)

W437*b*
White nick in thin wavy
line at left
(No dot, R. 1/9)

W437*c*
Break in blue wavy
line right of tail
(No dot, R. 4/7)

W437*d*
Nick out of grey
wavy line
(Dot, R. 1/3)

W437*e*
Break in blue wavy
line left of tail
(Dot, R. 4/1)

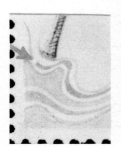

W438*a*
Thin blue line is
cut short at left
(Dot, R. 1/2)

W439*a*
Break in blue line
under bird's left leg
(No dot, R. 6/2)

W440*a*
Bird's claw and branch
retouched with fine
lines and dots
(No dot, R. 1/3)

Cylinder Numbers (Blocks of Six)

	Cyl. Nos.		Perforation Type R*	
			No dot	Dot
10p.	2A (grey-black)–1B (pale greenish yellow)–2C (bright blue)–1D (vermilion)–1E (bright yellow-green)–1F (gold) ..	.. ..	3·00*	3·00*

11½p. 2A (grey-black)–3B (bright blue)–1C (grey-green)–1D (vermilion)–1E (sepia)–1F (gold)–1G (pale greenish yellow)   ..   2·10   3·50*
13p. 4A (grey-black)–1B (pale greenish yellow)–1C (bright blue)–1D
(emerald-green)–2E (vermilion)–1F (gold)   ..   ..   ..   2·75   2·75
15p. 1A (grey-black)–1B (greenish yellow)–1C (slate-blue)–1D (light
green)–1E (brown)–1F (gold)   ..   ..   5·00*   3·25

The above are with sheets orientated with head to left.

Sheet Details

Sheet size: 100 (2 panes 5 × 10). Double pane reel-fed

Sheet markings:
Cylinder numbers: In top margin above vertical rows 2/3, boxed
Marginal arrows: In centre, opposite rows 5/6 at both sides
Colour register marks (crossed lines type):
No dot panes: Above and below vertical rows 4/5 and cross in circle type above vertical
row 9
Dot panes: Above and below vertical rows 9/10
Autotron marks: In order of traffic lights reading from left to right above vertical rows 4/7
on dot panes only
Perforation register marks: Thick bar below left gutter perforation row on no dot panes only
Sheet values: Opposite rows 2/4 and 7/9 reading up at left and down at right
Traffic lights (boxed): In bottom margin below vertical rows 2/3
10p. Gold, grey-black, bright yellow-green, vermilion, bright blue, pale greenish yellow
11½p. Gold, grey-black, pale greenish yellow, sepia, vermilion, grey-green, dull ultramarine
13p. Gold, grey-black, vermilion, emerald green, bright blue, pale greenish yellow
15p. Gold, grey-black, brown, light green, slate-blue, greenish yellow

Quantities Sold   12p. 47,177,000; 13½p. 11,811,000; 15p. 11,318,000; 17½p. 10,339,000

Withdrawn   15.1.81

W420 "Rocket" approaching
Moorish Arch, Liverpool

W421 First and
Second class Carriages
passing through
Olive Mount Cutting

W422 Third class
Carriage and Cattle
Truck crossing Chat Moss

W423 Horse-box and
Carriage Truck near
Bridgewater Canal

W424 Goods Truck and
Mail-coach at Manchester

Types **W420/4** were printed horizontally *se-tenant* within the sheet
(Des. David Gentleman)

1980 (12 MARCH).   150th ANNIVERSARY OF LIVERPOOL AND MANCHESTER RAILWAY

This issue commemorates the opening, in 1830, of the world's first train service to carry passengers and mail. The engine selected for this important service was George Stephenson's "Rocket" which was built in 1829. The stamps, issued in horizontal *se-tenant* strips, show a complete train of the period.

Phosphorised (fluorescent coated) paper

W441 (=S.G.1113)	**W420**	12p. lemon, light brown, rose-red, pale bl, & grey-blk	25	25
		a. Strip of 5 Nos. W441/5	1·50	1·60
		ab. Imperforate (horiz. strip of 5 Nos. W441/5)	.. £1200	
W442 (=S.G.1114)	**W421**	12p. rose-red, light brown, lemon pale blue & grey-blk	25	25

W443 (=S.G.1115)	**W422**	12p. pale blue, rose-red, lemon, light brn, & grey-blk	25	25
W444 (=S.G.1116)	**W423**	12p. light brown, lemon, rose-red, pale bl, & grey-blk	25	25
		b. Grey step	1·60	
W445 (=S.G.1117)	**W424**	12p. light brown, rose-red, pale blue, lemon & grey-blk	25	25
		b. Broken rail	1·60	

First Day Cover (W441/5)	†	1·50
Presentation Pack (W441/5)	2·00	†
PHQ Cards (W441/5)	1·75	2·50

Listed Varieties

W444*b*
Centre step of rail truck
filled in with grey dots
and large black dot above
(No dot, R. 8/4)

W445*b*
Break in rail beneath
mail-coach coupling
(No Dot, R. 1/5)

Cylinder Numbers (Blocks of Fifteen)

	Perforation	Type R*
Cyl. Nos.	No dot	Dot
12p. 1A (grey-black)–1B (lemon)–1C (rose-red)–1D (pale blue)–1E (light brown)	6·50*	5·50

Sheet Details

Sheet size: 100 (2 panes 10 × 5). Double pane reel-fed

Sheet markings:
  Cylinder numbers: Opposite rows 8/9, left margin, boxed
  Marginal arrows: In centre at top and bottom of sheet
  Colour register marks (crossed lines type):
    No dot panes: Opposite row 7 at both sides and cross in circle opposite row 2, left margin
    Dot panes: Opposite row 2 at both sides
  Autotron marks: In same order as traffic lights in left margin opposite rows 5/7 on dot panes only
  Perforation register marks: Thick bar opposite lower gutter perforations, right margin on no dot panes only
  Sheet values: Above and below vertical rows 2/4 and 7/9 reading from left to right in top margin and from right to left (upside down) in bottom margin
  Traffic lights (boxed): Opposite row 9, right margin
  12p. Lemon, rose-red, pale blue, light brown, grey-black

Quantity Sold   12p. 117,128,000

Withdrawn   11.3.81

152

INTERNATIONAL STAMP EXHIBITION

W425 Montage of London Buildings

W426 Miniature Sheet

(Illustration reduced to three quarters actual size)

(Des. Jeffery Matthews and eng. Geoffrey Holt.
Recess (miniature sheet border in photogravure))

1980 (9 APRIL—7 MAY (WMS448)). "LONDON 1980" INTERNATIONAL STAMP EXHIBITION

The International Philatelic Exhibition was held at Earls Court, London from 6—14 May. The stamp design features from left to right Westminster Abbey, Nelson's Column, Eros, The Post Office Tower, "Big Ben", St. Paul's Cathedral, the Tower of London and Tower Bridge.

During the printing of the stamp the die was re-cut resulting in the following two types. The stamp in the miniature sheet is always Type II.

TYPE I   TYPE II

Differences between the types:—

TYPE I. This is the original version. Top and bottom lines of shading in portrait oval broken. Hatched shading below left arm of Tower Bridge and hull of ship below right arm. Other points: Hatched shading on flag of Westminster Abbey, bottom right of Post Office Tower and archway of entrance to Westminster Abbey

TYPE II. (re-engraved). Lines in portrait oval unbroken. Solid shading on bridge and ship. Also solid shading on flag, Post Office Tower and archway.

Examples of both types are known in various shades of green. Such shades result from problems with the drying of the printed sheets on the press, but are not listed as similar colours can be easily induced.

Phosphorised (fluorescent coated) paper. Perf. 14½ × 14, (Type R*)

A. Type I

W446 (=S.G.1118)	**W425**	50p. agate ..	..	..	..	..	..	.. 1·25	1·25
		a. Solid blot above N ..		..	..	.. 3·75		
		b. Short line from top of frame		..	..	.. 2·75		
		c. Thin line from frame to clouds at right	..		.. 2·75		
		d. Heavy line to right of crown		..	..	.. 2·75		
		e. Diagonal scratch	..	..	..	..	.. 2·75	
		f. Mass of dots across portrait		..	..	.. 2·75		
		g. Thin line from frame at left		..	..	.. 2·75		

B. Type II

W447
(=S.G.1118Ea)   **W425**   50p. agate ..   ..   1·25   1·25

First Day Cover (W447)	..	..	..	..	†	1·25
Presentation Pack (W447)	..	..	..	.. 1·75	†	
PHQ Card	..	..	..	..	..	50	1·50

Supplies of Nos. W 446/7 were available on the first day of issue and therefore first day covers with No. W446 are not uncommon.

WMS448

(=S.G.MS1119) **W426**	Sheet size 90 × 123mm. (Type II) issued in pack· with printed card (sold at 75p.) .. .. .. 1·25	1·40
	a. Imperforate sheet £700	

> First Day Cover (WMS448) ..   ..   1·40

Listed Varieties

W446*a*
Solid blot above N
(R. 2/3)

W446*b*
Short line from
top of frame
(R. 2/4)

W446*c*
Thin line from
frame to clouds
(R. 2/5)

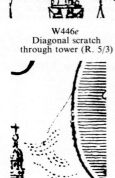

W446*e*
Diagonal scratch
through tower (R. 5/3)

W446*d*
Heavy line to
right of crown (R. 4/4)

W446*g*
Thin line from
frame at left (R. 5/5)

W446*f*
Mass of dots
across portrait (R. 5/4)

Nos. W446*b/g* are on the same pane. Five panes were printed by one rotation of the cylindrical plate. The panes were then guillotined into double-pane sheets. Varieties will be found on the right or left pane of a sheet, but not on both and we therefore give the stamp position in the pane.

Many of the ink blemishes found on stamps of this issue are not constant. An added difficulty in agreeing the position of the flaws is the absence of plate numbers on the five panes.

Sheet Details

Sheet Size: 50 (2 panes 5 × 5). Double pane reel-fed on the "Jumelle" machine

Sheet Markings:
Marginal arrows: At top and bottom of the gutter margin and in each of the two side margins where they are trimmed.

The only other marking on the sheet is a vertical thick bar in the colour of the stamp. This is opposite row 3 in the side and gutter margins usually being trimmed off at one side of the sheet. In the sequence of 5 panes there will be 5 bars. It is probable that in Type 1 minute dots engraved at the corners of the bar served to identify the panes. At the time of going to press we have seen the bar without dots and with 2 and 4 dots only.

In Type II the sheet markings were identical apart from dots *above* the bar in the vertical side margins. We illustrate these since the arrangement of the dots was probably used, by the printer, to identify particular panes.

Guide dots above bars–(Type II)

Miniature Sheet

The miniature sheet was printed by Harrison & Sons using continuous reels of paper. The frames are in a special screen which gives a variation in the size of the dots. This was done in order to achieve a more even etch on the larger tint background. The stamps were printed from a special recess cylinder of only 36 impressions. This, used in conjunction with the photogravure cylinder of 18 frames, printed large panes of 18 sheets which were then perforated, guillotined and sold in polythene covers with a card inscribed "Britain's Third Miniature Sheet". The card exists in cream or white and on the first printing the printers name is shown as "Harrisons". A later printing, on white card, was inscribed "Harrison" and a changed typeface to the figures in the second and third paragraphs.

A reconstruction of the original pair of uncut sheets of 18 by "plating" has not been achieved largely due to the absence of any distinguishing flaws in the frames and stamps.

Quantities Sold   50p. 24,997,000; Miniature Sheet 75p. 3,557,000

Withdrawn   8.4.81. No.WMS448 6.5.81

10^{1}_{2}P Buckingham Palace 12P The Albert Memorial 13^{1}_{2}P Royal Opera House

W427 Buckingham Palace   **W428** The Albert Memorial   **W429** Royal Opera House

15P Hampton Court 17^{1}_{2}P Kensington Palace

W430 Hampton Court   **W431** Kensington Palace

(Des. Sir Hugh Casson)

1980 (7 MAY).   LONDON LANDMARKS

The issue date coincided with the holding of the "London 1980" International Philatelic Exhibition. The designs are all based on water colours of famous London buildings.

Phosphorised (fluorescent coated) paper

W449 (= S.G.1120)	**W427**	10½p.	pale grey-blue, rosine, pale greenish yellow, yellowish green and silver ..	25	25
W450 (= S.G.1121)	**W428**	12p.	grey-black, bistre, rosine, yellowish green, pale greenish yellow and silver ..	30	30
		a.	Imperforate (vert. pair) ..	£500	
W451 (= S.G.1122)	**W429**	13½p.	grey-blk, pale salmon, pale ol-grn, slate-bl & silver	35	35
		a.	Imperforate (pair) ..	£500	
W452 (= S.G.1123)	**W430**	15p.	grey-black, pale salmon, slate-blue, dull yellowish green, olive-yellow and silver ..	40	45
		a.	Retouched H ..	2·00	
W453 (= S.G.1124)	**W431**	17½p.	grey, slate-blue, red-brown, sepia, yellowish green, pale greenish yellow and silver ..	50	55
		a.	Silver (Queen's head) omitted ..	£250	
		b.	Black dots by window ..	2·25	

First Day Cover (W449/53) ..	†	1·60
Presentation Pack (W449/53) ..	2·00	†
PHQ Cards (W449/53) ..	1·60	2·25

No. W453*a* came from a sheet of which seventeen examples were completely without the silver printing. Other stamps in the sheet showed traces of the silver and it is obvious that this error results from the previously known problem of the adherence of this ink. The head was previously printed in light yellow, as is now the normal practice for the use of these metallic inks.

Listed Varieties

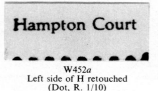

W452a
Left side of H retouched
(Dot, R. 1/10)

W453b
Black dots right of small
central window
(Dot, R. 4/4)

Cylinder Numbers (Blocks of Six)

	Cyl. Nos.	Perforation Type R*
		No dot	Dot

10½p. 2A (grey)–1B (pale greenish yellow)–1C (yellowish green)–1D
    (pale blue)–2E (silver)–1F (rosine) .. .. 1·75   1·75

12p. 1A (grey-black)–1B (yellowish green)–1C (pale greenish yel-
    low)–1D (bistre)–1E (silver)–1F (rosine) ..   2·10   2·50
    1A (grey-black)–1B (yellowish green)–1C (pale greenish yel-
    low)–1D (bistre)–2E (silver)–1F (rosine) ..   4·00   3·00

13½p. 1A (grey-black)–1B (pale salmon)–1C (pale olive-yellow)–1D
    (slate-blue)–2E (silver)   .. .. 2·40   2·40

15p. 2A (grey-black)–1B (pale salmon)–2C (olive-yellow)–1D (dull
    yellowish green)–2E (silver)–1F (slate-blue)   .. .. .. 2·75   2·75

17½p. 1A (grey)–1B (red-brown)–1C (pale greenish yellow)–1D (slate-
    blue)–2E (silver)–1F (sepia)–1G (yellowish green)   .. .. 3·50   3·50

The above are with sheets orientated with head to left.

Sheet Details

Sheet size: 100 (2 panes 5 × 10). Double pane reel-fed

Sheet markings:
    Cylinder numbers: In top margin above vertical rows 2/3, boxed
    Marginal arrows: In centre, opposite rows 5/6 at both sides
    Colour register marks (crossed lines type):
        No dot panes: Above and below vertical row 4 (13½p.) or rows 4/5 (others) also large cross
        in circle type above vertical row 9
        Dot panes: Above and below vertical row 9 (13½p.) or rows 9/10 (others)
    Autotron marks: In order of traffic lights reading from left to right above vertical rows 4/6
    (13½p.) or rows 4/7 (others on dot panes only)
    Perforation register marks: Thick bar below left gutter perforation row on no dot panes only
    Sheet values: Opposite rows 2/4 and 7/9 reading up at left and down at right
    Traffic lights (boxed): In bottom margin below vertical row 2 (13½p.) or rows 2/3 (others):
        10½p. Silver, grey, rosine, pale blue, pale greenish yellow, yellowish green
        12p. Silver, grey-black, rosine, bistre, pale greenish yellow, yellowish green
        13½p. Silver, grey-black, slate-blue, pale olive-yellow, pale salmon
        15p. Silver, grey-black, slate-blue, dull yellowish green, olive-yellow, pale salmon
        17½p. Silver, grey, yellowish green, sepia, slate-blue, pale greenish yellow, red-brown

Quantities Sold 10½p. 20,228,000; 12p. 48,242,000; 13½p. 12,557,000; 15p. 12,104,000; 17½p.
11,750,000

Withdrawn 6.5.81.

W432 Charlotte Brontë
(*Jane Eyre*)

W433 George Eliot
(*The Mill on the Floss*)

W434 Emily Brontë
(*Wuthering Heights*)

W435 Mrs. Gaskell
(*North and South*)

(Des. Barbara Brown)

1980 (9 JULY).   VICTORIAN WOMEN NOVELISTS ("EUROPA")

This issue honours four famous Victorian writers and features their portraits with background scenes from their novels. The C.E.P.T. emblem, incorporated in the designs of the 12p. and 13½p. values (first class inland and European postage rates) identifies the issue with the "famous people" theme chosen by the Conference of European Posts and Telecommunications for 1980 "Europa" stamps. The year 1980 marks the half-way point in the United Nations—sponsored "Decade for Women". The portraits of Charlotte Brontë and Mrs. Gaskell are from drawings by George Richmond, Emily Brontë's is from a painting by her brother, Branwell, and that of George Eliot is from a photograph by J. J. Mayall.

Phosphorised (fluorescent coated) paper

W454 (=S.G.1125)	**W432**	12p.	red-brown, bright rose, bright blue, greenish yellow, grey and gold ..	.. .. ..	30	25
			a. Missing P	..	22·00	
			b. Broken e	..	2·10	
			c. Circle and T incomplete	..	1·60	
W455 (=S.G.1126)	**W433**	13½p.	red-brown, dull vermilion, pale blue, pale greenish yellow, grey and gold	..	35	35
			a. Pale blue omitted	..	£900	
			b. Broken line in emblem	..	1·75	
			c. Retouched sleeve	..	2·00	
W456 (=S.G.1127)	**W434**	15p.	red-brown, vermilion, blue, lemon, grey and gold		40	45
			a. Eyebrow flaw	..	2·00	
W457 (=S.G.1128)	**W435**	17½p.	dull vermilion, slate-blue, ultramarine, pale greenish yellow, grey and gold	..	50	50
			a. Imperforate and slate-blue omitted (pair)	..	£850	

First Day Cover (W454/7)	†	1·40	
Presentation Pack (W454/7)	1·90	†	
PHQ Cards (W454/7)	1·50	2·00	

The 12p. value exists cancelled 8 July 1980 at Norwich, Norfolk.

It is understood that No. W454a occurred on a substantial part of the printing but that initially, the "P" was present.

159

Listed Varieties

W454a
Missing P in value
(No dot, R. 4/6)

W454b
Second e broken in Eyre
(No dot, R. 9/3)

W454c
Broken circle and
left arm of T missing
(Dot, R. 1/7)

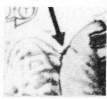

W455b
Broken line above C
(Dot, R. 1/3)

W455c
Sleeve retouch at left
(Dot, R. 8/1)

W456a
Nick in eyebrow
(No dot, R. 8/7)

Cylinder Numbers (Blocks of Six)

	Perforation	Type R*
Cyl. Nos.	No dot	Dot
12p. 4A (grey)–1B (bright blue)–1C (greenish yellow)–1D (red-brown)–1E (bright rose)–2F (gold)	2·10	2·10
13½p. 1A (grey)–1B (pale blue)–1C (pale greenish yellow)–1D (red-brown)–1E (dull vermilion)–2F (gold)	2·40	4·00*
15p. 2A (grey)–1B (blue)–1C (lemon)–1D (red-brown)–5E (vermilion)–2F (gold)	2·75	2·75
17½p. 4A (grey)–2B (slate-blue)–1C (pale greenish yellow)–2D (dull vermilion)–1E (ultramarine)–2F (gold)	3·50	3·50

Sheet Details

Sheet size: 100 (2 panes 10 × 5). Double pane reel-fed

Sheet markings:
Cylinder numbers: Opposite rows 8/9, left margin, boxed
Marginal arrows: In centre at top and bottom of sheet
Colour register marks (crossed lines type):
No dot panes: Opposite rows 6/7 at both sides and cross in circle opposite row 2, left margin
Dot panes: Opposite rows 1/2 at both sides
Autotron marks: In same order as traffic lights in left margin opposite rows 4/7 on dot panes only
Perforation register marks: Thick bar opposite lower gutter perforations, right margin on no dot panes only
Sheet values: Above and below vertical rows 2/4 and 7/9 reading from left to right in top margin and from right to left (upside down) in bottom margin
Traffic lights (boxed): Opposite rows 8/9, right margin
12p. Bright blue, greenish yellow, red-brown, bright rose, grey, gold
13½p. Pale blue, pale greenish yellow, red-brown, dull vermilion, grey, gold
15p. Blue, lemon, red-brown, vermilion, grey, gold
17½p. Slate-blue, pale greenish yellow, dull vermilion, ultramarine, grey, gold

Quantities Sold 12p. 46,296,000; 13½p. 11,274,000; 15p. 10,998,000; 17½p. 10,649,000
Withdrawn 8.7.81.

W436 Queen Elizabeth
the Queen Mother
(Des. Jeffery Matthews from a photograph by Norman Parkinson)

1980 (4 AUGUST). 80th BIRTHDAY OF QUEEN ELIZABETH THE QUEEN MOTHER

This is the first British postage stamp to be issued on the occasion of a royal birthday. Other royal stamp designs by Jeffrey Matthews include the two stamps marking the Silver Wedding anniversary of the Queen and Prince Philip in 1972 and the stamps in 1978 for the 25th Anniversary of the Queen's Coronation.

Phosphorised (fluorescent coated) paper

W458 (= S.G.1129)   **W436**   12p. bright rose, greenish yellow, new bl, grey and silver   35   35
           a. Imperforate (horiz. pair) £1200
           b. Break in side frame .   ..   .   1·75

First Day Cover (W458)	†	60
PHQ Card (W458)	50	90

The issue is known pre-released at Llandudno, Gwynedd, postmarked 29 July.

Listed Variety

W458*b*
Break in side frame
(No dot, R. 2/1)

Cylinder Numbers (Blocks of Six)

Cyl. Nos.	Perforation Type R*	
	No dot	Dot
12p. 1A (silver)–1B (greenish yellow)–1C (bright rose)–1D (new blue)–1E (grey)	3·50*	2·40

The above are with sheets orientated with head to left

Sheet Details

Sheet size: 100 (2 panes 5 × 10). Double pane reel-fed

Sheet markings:

Cylinder numbers: In top margin above vertical rows 2/3, boxed

Marginal arrows: In centre, opposite rows 5/6 at both sides

Colour register marks (crossed lines type):

No dot panes: Above and below vertical row 4 and also large cross in circle above vertical row 9

Dot panes: Above and below vertical row 9

Autotron marks: In order of traffic lights reading from left to right above vertical rows 4/7 on dot panes only

Perforation register marks: Thick bar below left gutter perforation row on no dot panes only

Sheet values: Opposite rows 2/4 and 7/9 reading up at left and down at right

Traffic lights (boxed): In bottom margin below vertical row 2

12p. Silver, grey, new blue, bright rose, greenish yellow

Quantity Sold   12p. 70,836,000

Withdrawn   3.8.81

W437 Sir Henry Wood

W438 Sir Thomas Beecham

W439 Sir Malcolm Sargent

W440 Sir John Barbirolli

(Des. Peter Gauld)

1980 (10 SEPTEMBER). BRITISH CONDUCTORS

This issue celebrates Britain's musical heritage and features four of the nation's most distinguished conductors. The 12p. shows Sir Henry Wood, who in 1895 founded London's Promenade Concerts. Sir Malcolm Sargent, shown on the 15p., carried on this work when Sir Henry died and he is remembered for this as well as his work with choirs. The 13½p. shows Sir Thomas Beecham who played a leading part in the revival of opera in England. He founded the London Philharmonic and Royal Philharmonic Orchestras. Sir John Barbirolli, conductor of the New York Philharmonic and Hallé Orchestras, is shown on the 17½p.

Phosphorised (fluorescent coated) paper

W459 (=S.G.1130)	**W437** 12p.	slate, rose-red, greenish yellow, bistre and gold ..	30	30
W460 (=S.G.1131)	**W438** 13½p.	grey-black, vermilion, greenish yellow, pale car-mine-rose and gold	35	40
W461 (=S.G.1132)	**W439** 15p.	grey-black, bright rose-red, greenish yellow, tur-quoise-green and gold	45	45
W462 (=S.G.1133)	**W440** 17½p.	black, bright rose-red, greenish yellow, dull violet-blue and gold	50	50
	a.	Fluorescent brightener omitted	2·50	

First Day Cover (W459/62)	..	..	..	..	†	1·40
Presentation Pack (W459/62)	..	..	..	..	1·90	†
PHQ Cards (W459/62)	..	..	..	..	1·60	2·25

No. W462*a* is printed on chalk surfaced paper but without the fluorescent additive.
All values are known on phosphorised paper with either a shiny ink surface which gives a photo-negative reflection or a matt surface without the negative effect.
The 12p. is known pre-released at Stockport, Cheshire, postmarked 9 September.

Cylinder Numbers (Blocks of Six)

	Cyl. Nos.	Perforation Type R*	
		No dot	Dot
12p.	2A (bistre)–1B (greenish yellow)–2C (rose-red)–1D (slate)–1E (gold)..	2·10	2·10
13½p.	1A (pale carmine-rose)–1B (greenish yellow)–3C (vermilion)–3D (grey-black)–1E (gold)	2·40	2·40
15p.	1A (turquoise-green)–2B (greenish yellow)–3C (bright rose-red)–1D (grey-black)–1E (gold)	3·25	3·25
17½p.	1A (dull violet-blue)–2B (greenish yellow)–2C (bright rose-red)–2D (black)–1E (gold)	3·50	3·50

The above are with sheets orientated with head to left

Sheet Details

Sheet size: 100 (2 panes 5 × 10). Double pane reel-fed
Sheet markings:
Cylinder numbers: In top margin above vertical rows 2/3, boxed
Marginal arrows: In centre, opposite rows 5/6 at both sides
Colour register marks (crossed lines type):
  No dot panes: Above and below vertical rows 4/5 and also large cross in circle type above vertical row 9
  Dot panes: Above and below vertical row 9
Autotron marks: In order of traffic lights reading from left to right above vertical rows 5/7 on dot panes only
Perforation register marks: Thick bar below left gutter perforations on no dot panes only except 13½p. value
Sheet values: Opposite rows 2/4 and 7/9 reading up at left and down at right
Traffic lights (boxed): In bottom margin below vertical row 2:
  12p. Gold, bistre, slate, rose-red, greenish yellow
  13½p. Gold, pale carmine-rose, grey-black, vermilion, greenish yellow
  15p. Gold, turquoise-green, grey-black, bright rose-red, greenish yellow
  17½p. Gold, dull violet-blue, black, bright rose-red, greenish yellow

Quantities Sold   12p. 45,144,000; 13½p. 10,477,000; 15p. 10,063,000; 17½p. 9,695,000

Withdrawn   10.9.81

W441 Athletics   **W442** Rugby Union

W443 Boxing   **W444** Cricket
(Des. Robert Goldsmith)
(Lithography by The House of Questa)

1980 (10 OCTOBER). BRITISH SPORTING CENTENARIES

Four centenaries in British Sport are marked by this issue. The 12p. value celebrates 100 years of the Amateur Athletics Association, which was founded in Oxford in April, 1880. The centenary of the Welsh Rugby Union, which was formed in Neath towards the end of the 1880–81 season, is marked by the 13½p. value. This stamp shows two international rugby players, one in the red shirt of Wales running in for a try, with a French opponent in pursuit. The 15p. value marks the formation of the Amateur Boxing Association in February, 1880. The 17½p. commemorates the first Test match against Australia played at the Oval in September 1880.

Phosphorised (fluorescent coated) paper. Comb perforation 14 × 14½.

W464 (= S.G.1134)	**W441**	12p.	pale new blue, greenish yellow, magenta, light brown, reddish purple and gold	30	30
		a.	Gold (Queen's head) omitted		
W465 (= S.G.1135)	**W442**	13½p.	pale new blue, olive yellow, bright purple, orange-vermilion, blackish lilac, and gold	35	40
W466 (= S.G.1136)	**W443**	15p.	pale new blue, greenish yellow, bright purple, chalky blue and gold	40	40
		a.	Imperf. between stamp and bottom margin	£150	
W467 (= S.G.1137)	**W444**	17½p.	pale new blue, greenish yellow, magenta, deep olive, grey brown and gold	50	55

First Day Cover (W464/7)	..	..	..	†	1·40
Presentation Pack (W464/7)	..	..	..	1·90	†
PHQ Cards (W464/7)	..	..	..	1·50	2·00

The 12p. is known pre-released at Salisbury, Wiltshire, postmarked 8 October. This was a Wednesday, which is normally the day chosen for the release of new commemoratives, but on this occasion the Post Office chose Friday, 10 October as an experiment.

No. W464*a* was caused by a paper fold.

Plate Numbers (Blocks of Four)

Colour order of plate nos.
12p. Pale new blue, greenish yellow, magenta, light brown, reddish purple, gold
13½p. Pale new blue, olive-yellow, bright purple, orange-vermilion, blackish lilac, gold
15p. Pale new blue, greenish yellow, bright purple, chalky blue, gold
17½p. Pale new blue, greenish yellow, magenta, deep olive, grey-brown, gold

	Plate Nos. (all No dot)				Perforation Type M
12p.	1A (×6)	..	..	..	1·50
	1B (×6)	..	..	..	1·50
	2A 1A 1A 1A 1A 1A	..	..	..	1·50
	2B 1B 1B 1B 1B 1B	..	..	..	1·50
	2A 1A 2A 1A 1A 1A	..	..	..	15·00
	2B 1B 2B 1B 1B 1B	..	..	..	15·00
	2A 1A 2A 2A 1A 1A	..	..	..	7·50
	2B 1B 2B 2B 1B 1B	..	..	..	7·50
	2A 2A 2A 2A 1A 1A	..	..	..	5·00
	2B 2B 2B 2B 1B 1B	..	..	..	5·00
13½p.	1A (×6)	..	..	..	1·75
	1B (×6)	..	..	..	1·75
	1A 1A 2A 1A 1A 1A	..	..	..	25·00
	1B 1B 2B 1B 1B 1B	..	..	..	25·00
15p.	1A (×5)	..	..	..	5·00
	1B (×5)	..	..	..	5·00
	1A 1A 1A 1A 2A	..	..	..	10·00
	1B 1B 1B 1B 2B	..	..	..	10·00
	2A 1A 1A 1A 1A	..	..	..	2·00
	2B 1B 1B 1B 1B	..	..	..	2·00
	2A 1A 2A 1A 1A	..	..	..	2·00
	2B 1B 2B 1B 1B	..	..	..	2·00
17½p.	1A (×6)	..	..	..	2·50
	1B (×6)	..	..	..	2·50
	1A 1A 1A 1A 2A 1A	..	..	..	2·50
	1B 1B 1B 1B 2B 1B	..	..	..	2·50
	1A 1A 1A 1A 3A 1A	..	..	..	5·00
	1B 1B 1B 1B 3B 1B	..	..	..	4·00

Sheet Details

Sheet size: 100 (2 panes 5 × 10). Double pane sheet-fed with "A" pane at top and "B" pane below
Sheet markings:
Plate numbers: In bottom margin below vertical rows 1/2
Marginal arrows: "W" shaped in centre, opposite rows 5/6 at both sides
Sheet values: Opposite rows 2/4 and 7/9 reading up at both sides
Imprint: In bottom margin below vertical rows 9/10
Traffic lights: In the form of Questa logo opposite row 1, right margin. For order of colours see
under "Plate Numbers" above

Quantities Sold 12p. 45,787,000; 13½p. 11,008,000; 15p. 10,229,000; 17½p. 9,910,000

Withdrawn 9.10.81

W445 Christmas Tree with
Decorations

W446 Candles and Ivy

W447 Mistletoe Spray
and Apples

W448 Paper Chains with
Crown and Bell

W449 Holly Wreath and
Decorations

(Des. Jeffery Matthews)

1980 (19 NOVEMBER). CHRISTMAS

This issue depicts traditional Christmas decorations.

One 4mm. centre phosphor band

W468 (=S.G.1138)	**W445**	10p.	black, turquoise-green, greenish yellow, vermilion, and blue	25	25
			a. Imperforate (horiz. pair)		
			b. Broken branch above left-hand bird's head	1·40	
			c. Broken bauble	1·50	

Phosphorised (fluorescent coated) paper

W469 (=S.G.1139)	**W446**	12p.	grey, magenta, rose-red, greenish grey, and pale orange	30	35
			a. Bottom margin imperforate		
			b. Break in outline of first small candle	1·75	
W470 (=S.G.1140)	**W447**	13½p.	grey-black, dull yellow-green, brown, greenish yellow, and pale olive-bistre	35	40
			a. Severed string above upper right apple	2·10	
W471 (=S.G.1141)	**W448**	15p.	grey-black, bistre-yellow, bright orange, magenta and new blue	40	45
W472 (=S.G.1142)	**W449**	17½p.	black, vermilion, dull yellowish green, and greenish yellow	45	50
			a. Break in outline of ribbon	2·75	

166

First Day Cover (W468/72)	..	..	..	..	†	1·60
Presentation Pack (W468/72)	..	..	..	..	2·00	†
PHQ Cards (W468/72)	..	..	..	..	..	1·60	2·00

The 12p. value exists cancelled 13 November 1980, Sussex Coast.

Listed Varieties

W468b
Broken branch above
left-hand bird's head
(No dot, R. 3/3)

W468c
Broken bauble
(Dot, R. 9/8)

W469b
Break in left-hand outline
of first small candle
(Dot, R. 9/7)

W470a
Severed string above
upper right apple
(No dot, R. 3/2)

W472a
Break in outline of ribbon
(No dot, R. 4/5)

167

W   1980.   Christmas and Collectors Pack

Cylinder Numbers (Blocks of Six)

Cyl. Nos.	Perforation No dot	Type R* Dot
10p. 1A (blue)–1B (greenish yellow)–1C (turquoise green)–1D (vermilion)–1E (black)	3·00	3·00
2A (blue)–1B (greenish yellow)–1C (turquoise-green)–1D (vermilion)–1E (black)	1·75	1·75
12p. 1A (rose-red)–1B (pale orange)–1C (magenta)–1D (greenish grey)–1E (grey)	2·10	2·10
13½p. 1A (pale olive-bistre)–1B (greenish yellow)–1C (dull yellow-green)–1D (grey-black)–1E (brown)	2·40	2·40
15p. 1A (bright orange)–1B (bistre-yellow)–1C (magenta)–1D (new blue)–1E (grey-black)	2·75	2·75
17½p. 1A (dull yellowish green)–1B (greenish yellow)–1C (vermilion)–1D (black)	3·25	3·25

Phosphor cylinder No. P73 occurs in the left margin and appears to be synchronised at row 4 on the no dot pane and at row 7 on the dot pane.

Sheet Details

Sheet size: 100 (2 panes 10 × 5). Double pane reel-fed

Sheet markings:
Cylinder numbers: Opposite row 8/9, left margin, boxed
Marginal arrows: In centre at top and bottom of sheet
Colour register marks (crossed lines type):
No dot panes: Opposite rows 6/7 at both sides and cross in circle opposite row 2, left margin
Dot panes: Opposite row 2 at both sides
Autotron marks: In same order as traffic lights in left margin opposite rows 4/5 and gutter margin (17½p.) or 4/6 (others) on dot panes only
Perforation register marks: Thick bar opposite lower gutter perforations, right margin on no dot panes only
Sheet values: Above and below vertical rows 2/4 and 7/9 reading from left to right in top margin and from right to left (upside down) in bottom margin
Traffic lights (boxed): Opposite row 9, right margin
10p. Greenish yellow, turquoise-green, blue, vermilion, black
12p. Pale orange, magenta, rose-red, greenish grey, grey
13½p. Greenish yellow, dull yellow-green, pale olive-bistre, brown, grey-black
15p. Bistre-yellow, bright orange, magenta, new blue, grey-black
17½p. Greenish yellow, vermilion, dull yellowish green, black

Quantities Sold   10½p. 277,875,000; 12p. 142,673,000; 13½p. 18,188,000; 15p. 17,525,000; 17½p. 16,225,000

Withdrawn   18.11.81

1980 (19 NOVEMBER).   COLLECTORS PACK 1980

WCP14 Comprises Nos. W437/72 excluding WMS448 (Sold at £5.22)   15·00

Withdrawn   18.11.81

W450 Saint Valentines Day

W451 Morris Dancers

W452 Lammastide

W453 Medieval Mummers

(Des. Fritz Wegner)

1981 (6 FEBRUARY).   FOLKLORE ("EUROPA")

This issue features four traditional folklore scenes. The 14p. stamp commemorates Saint Valentines Day and shows a heart surrounded by flowers, cherubs and lovebirds. The 18p. design was taken from a 16th century window now at Leigh Manor, Shropshire and consists of three Morris Dancers in traditional costume. The 14p. and 18p. stamps also include the "EUROPA" emblem in their design as folklore was chosen by the Conference of European Posts and Telecommunications as the 1981 "EUROPA" theme. The 22p. stamp shows two people in 18th century dress, traditional wheatsheaf and fruit, all of which appeared in the ancient harvest festival of Lammastide. Four Medieval Mummers appear on the 25p. value; the design for this stamp was taken from a 14th century manuscript.

Phosphorised (fluorescent coated) paper

W473 (= S.G.1143)	**W450**	14p.	cerise, green, yellow-orange, salmon pink, black, gold	..	35	35
		a.	Missing leaf ..	..	2·00	
		b.	Sliced wing tip	..	1·90	
W474 (= S.G.1144)	**W451**	18p.	dull ultramine, lemon, lake-brown, bright green, black, gold	..	45	50
W475 (= S.G.1145)	**W452**	22p.	chrome-yellow, rosine, brown, new blue, black, gold	..	60	60
W476 (= S.G.1146)	**W453**	25p.	bright, blue, red-brown, bright rose-red, greenish yellow, black, gold ..	..	65	70

First Day Cover (W473/6)	..	..	..	†	2·00
Presentation Pack (W473/6)	..	..	..	2·25	†
PHQ Cards (W473/6)	..	..	..	1·50	2·00

169

Listed Variety

W473a
Missing leaf at left
(No dot, R. 10/6)

W473b
Sliced top to upper wing tip
(Dot, R. 8/2)

Cylinder Numbers (Blocks of Six)

Cyl. Nos.	Perforation Type R*	
	No dot	Dot
14p. 1A (black)–1B (yellow-orange)–1C (cerise)–1D (green)–1E (salmon pink)–1F (gold)	2·40	3·50*
18p. 1A (black)–1B (lemon)–1C (bright green)–1D (dull ultramarine)–1E (lake-brown)–1F (gold)	3·25	3·25
22p. 1A (black)–1B (chrome-yellow)–1C (brown)–1D (new blue)–2E (rosine)–1F (gold)	4·25	4·25
25p. 1A (black)–1B (greenish yellow)–1C (red-brown)–1D (bright blue)–1E (bright rose-red)–1F (gold)	4·50	4·50

Sheet Details

Sheet size: 100 (2 panes 10 × 5). Double pane reel-fed

Sheet markings:
Cylinder numbers: Opposite rows 8/9, left margin, boxed
Marginal arrows: In centre at top and bottom of sheet
Colour register marks (crossed lines type):
No dot panes: Opposite rows 6/7 at both sides and cross in circle opposite row 2, left margin
Dot panes: Opposite rows 1/3 at both sides
Autotron marks: In same order as traffic lights in left margin opposite rows 4/7 on dot panes only
Perforation register marks: Thick bar opposite lower gutter perforations, right margin on no dot panes only
Sheet values: Above and below vertical rows 2/4 and 7/9 reading from left to right in top margin and from right to left (upside down) in bottom margin
Traffic lights (boxed): Opposite rows 8/9, right margin
14p. Yellow-orange, cerise, green, salmon pink, black, gold
18p. Lemon, bright green, dull ultramarine, lake-brown, black, gold
22p. Chrome-yellow, brown, new blue, rosine, black, gold
25p. Greenish yellow, red-brown, bright blue, bright rose-red, black, gold

Quantities Sold   14p. 47,496,000; 18p. 11,548,000; 22p. 11,252,000; 25p. 10,861,000

Withdrawn   5.2.82

W454 Blind Man with Guide Dog   W455 Hands Spelling "Deaf" in Sign Language

W456 Disabled Man in Wheelchair   W457 Disabled Artist Painting with Foot

(Des. John Gibbs)

1981 (25 MARCH).   INTERNATIONAL YEAR OF DISABLED PEOPLE

The United Nations General Assembly chose 1981 as International Year of Disabled People. To commemorate this the Post Office issued a special set of four stamps, each stamp featuring a method of combating a disability. These are the first stamp designs by John Gibbs.

Phosphorised (fluorescent coated) paper

W477 (=S.G.1147)	**W454**	14p.	drab, greenish yellow, bright rose-red, dull purple, deep dull blue and silver	35	35
			a. Break in right frame	2·25	
			b. Grey patch on shoe	2·25	
			c. Dotted line across right foreleg	2·00	
W478 (=S.G.1148)	**W455**	18p.	deep blue-green, bright orange, dull vermilion, grey-black, and silver	45	50
			a. Break in left frame	2·25	
			b. Smear by hand	2·00	
W479 (=S.G.1149)	**W456**	22p.	brown-ochre, rosine, purple-brown, greenish blue, black and silver	60	60
W480 (=S.G.1150)	**W457**	25p.	vermilion, lemon, pale salmon, olive brown, new blue, black and silver	65	70
			a. Brown disturbance	2·75	
			b. Diagonal line	2·50	
			c. Red scratch	2·25	
			d. Nick in paintbrush	2·50	

First Day Cover (W477/80)	†	2·00
Presentation Pack (W477/80)	2·25	†
PHQ Cards (W477/80)	1·50	2·25

The 14p. value was pre-released at a Bethnal Green Post Office, London E. on the 10 March 1981.

Listed Varieties

W477a
Break in frame
(No dot, R. 1/3)

W477b
Dark spot on right shoe
(No dot, R. 3/1)

W477c
Dotted line across right foreleg
(Dot R. 7/8)

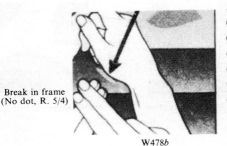

Break in frame
(No dot, R. 5/4)

Smear by second
right hand from top
(No dot, R. 6/3)

W478a   W478b

W480a
Brown disturbance across stamp
below frame extends to R. 1/2
(Dot, R. 1/1)

W480b
Diagonal line in green of
rainbow (Dot, R. 1/2)

W480c
Red scratch on foot
(Dot, R. 1/8)

W480d
White nick in left side
of paintbrush handle
(Dot, R. 5/10)

Cylinder Numbers (Blocks of Six)

	Cyl. Nos.	Perforation Type R*	
		No dot	Dot
14p.	2A (dull purple)–1B (greenish yellow)–1C (bright rose-red)–1D (deep dull blue)–1E (silver)–1F (drab)	2·40	2·40
18p.	1A (grey-black)–1B (bright orange)–1C (dull vermilion)–1D (deep blue green)–1E (silver)	3·25	3·25
22p.	1A (black)–1B (brown-ochre)–1C (rosine)–1D (greenish blue)– 1E (silver)–1F (purple-brown)	4·25	4·25
25p.	2A (black)–1B (lemon)–1C (vermilion)–1D (new blue)–1E (silver)–1F (olive-brown)–1G (pale salmon)..	4·50	4·50

Sheet Details

Sheet size: 100 (2 panes 10 × 5). Double pane reel-fed

Sheet markings:
  Cylinder numbers: Opposite rows 8/9, left margin, boxed
  Marginal arrows: In centre at top and bottom of sheet
  Colour register marks (crossed lines type):
    No dot panes: Opposite rows 6/7 at both sides and cross in circle opposite row 2, left margin
    Dot panes: Opposite rows 1/3 at both sides
  Autotron marks: In same order as traffic lights in left margin opposite rows 4/7 on dot panes only
  Perforation register marks: Thick bar opposite lower gutter perforations, right margin on no dot panes only
  Sheet values: Above and below vertical rows 2/4 and 7/9 reading from left to right in top margin and from right to left (upside down) in bottom margin
  Traffic lights (boxed): Opposite rows 8/9, right margin
    14p. Greenish yellow, bright rose-red, deep dull blue, drab, dull purple, silver
    18p. Bright orange, dull vermilion, deep blue green, grey-black, silver
    22p. Brown-ochre, rosine, greenish blue, purple-brown, black, silver
    25p. Lemon, vermilion, new blue, olive-brown, pale salmon, black, silver

Quantities Sold   14p. 43,061,000; 18p. 10,466,000; 22p. 10,037,000; 25p. 9,688,000

Withdrawn   24.2.82

W458 Small Tortoiseshell

W459 Large Blue

W460 Peacock   **W461** Chequered Skipper

(Des. Gordon Beningfield)

1981 (13 MAY).   BRITISH BUTTERFLIES

This set, marking 1981 as Butterfly Year features four well known butterflies. Changes in the environment coupled with the popular use of chemicals to kill insect pests all assist to diminish the butterfly numbers year by year. Probably the Large Blue shown on the 18p. is already extinct in the British Isles but it can still be found in many parts of Europe. Likewise the Chequered Skipper shown on the 25p. can only be seen in parts of Scotland. The two butterflies featured on the 14p. and 22p. are still seen in country districts and town gardens.

Phosphorised (fluorescent coated) paper

W481 (=S.G.1151)	**W458**	14p.	black, greenish yellow, yellow-green, bright-rose, bright blue, emerald and gold	35	35
		a.	Imperforate (pair)	£950	
W482 (=S.G.1152)	**W459**	18p.	black, greenish yellow, dull yellowish-green, bright mauve, bright blue, bright green and gold . .	50	50
		a.	Large spot on corn	2·00	
		b.	Pale curved scratch	2·25	
		c.	Indent above Large Blue	2·50	
		ca.	Retouched state	2·00	
		d.	Extra spot	1·75	
W483 (=S.G.1153)	**W460**	22p.	black, greenish yellow, bronze-green, rosine, ultramarine, light green and gold	60	65
W484 (=S.G.1154)	**W461**	25p.	black, greenish yellow, bronze-green, bright rose-red, ultramarine, bright emerald and gold . .	70	75
		a.	Retouch above wing-tip	2·75	

First Day Cover (W481/4)	. .	. .	. .	. .	†	2·00
Presentation Pack (W481/4)	. .	. .	. .	. .	2·50	†
PHQ Cards (W481/4) . .	. .	. .	. .	. .	1·50	2·40

Listed Varieties

W482a
Large spot on corn
(No. dot, R. 8/1)

W482b
Curved scratch
(Dot, R. 2/10)

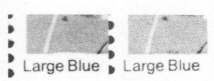

W482c   W482ca
Indent above inscription and retouched state
(Dot, R. 10/3)

W482d   Normal
Extra White Spot
(Dot, R. 10/8)

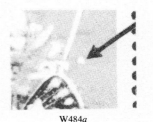

Retouch above wing-tip
(Dot, R. 6/6)

W484a

Cylinder Numbers (Blocks of Six)

	Perforation	Type R*
Cyl. Nos.	No dot	Dot
14p. 1A (black)–1B (greenish yellow)–2C (yellow-green)–1D (bright rose)–1E (bright blue)–1F (emerald)–1G (gold)	2·40	2·40
18p. 1A (black)–1B (greenish yellow)–2C (dull yellowish green)–1D (bright mauve)–1E (bright blue)–1F (bright green)–1G (gold)..	3·50	3·50
22p. 1A (black)–1B (greenish yellow)–1C (bronze-green)–1D (rosine) –1E (ultramarine)–1F (light green)–1G (gold)	4·25	4·25
25p. 1A (black)–1B (greenish yellow)–1C (bronze-green)–1D (bright rose-red)–1E (ultramarine)–1F (bright emerald)–1G (gold) ..	5·00	5·00

The above are with sheets orientated with head to left.

175

Sheet Details

Sheet size: 100 (2 panes 5 × 10). Double pane reel-fed

Sheet markings:

Cylinder numbers: In top margin above vertical rows 2/3, boxed

Marginal arrows: In centre, opposite rows 5/6 at both sides

Colour register marks (crossed lines type):

No dot panes: Above and below vertical rows 4/5 and also cross in circle above vertical row 9

Dot panes: Above and below vertical rows 8/10

Autotron marks: In order of traffic lights reading from left to right above vertical rows 4/7 on dot panes only

Perforation register marks: One short vertical line on either side of first extension hole in top and bottom margins in both panes (see illustration under General Notes) also thick bar below left gutter perforation row on no dot panes only

Sheet values: Opposite rows 2/4 and 7/9 reading up at left and down at right

Traffic lights (boxed): In bottom margin below vertical rows 2/3

14p. Gold, black, emerald, bright blue, bright rose, yellow-green, greenish yellow

18p. Gold, black, bright green, bright blue, bright mauve, dull yellowish-green, greenish-yellow

22p. Gold, black, light green, ultramarine, rosine, bronze-green, greenish yellow

25p. Gold, black, bright emerald, ultramarine, bright rose-red, bronze-green, greenish-yellow

Quantities Sold   14p. 45,936,000; 18p. 11,161,000; 22p. 10,656,000; 25p. 10,262,000

Withdrawn   12.5.82

W462 Glenfinnan, Scotland

W463 Derwentwater, England

W464 Stackpole Head, Wales

W465 Giant's Causeway,
Northern Ireland

W466 St. Kilda, Scotland

(Des. Michael Fairclough)

1981 (24 JUNE).   NATIONAL TRUST

This issue marked the 50th anniversary of the National Trust for Scotland. The 14p. depicts Loch Shiel in the Scottish Highlands. The tower shown in the foreground stands 64 feet high and was erected in 1815 by Alexander McDonald, 10th chieftain of Glenaladale. The 18p. features Derwentwater, much admired by William Wordsworth. The 20p. shows the limestone cliffs of Stackpole Head in Dyfed. The famous Giant's Causeway shown on the 22p. was, according to Irish mythology, built by the giant Finn MacCool in order to reach Scotland. St. Kilda, depicted on the 25p., was bequeathed to the National Trust in 1957.

Phosphorised (fluorescent coated) paper

W485 (=S.G.1155)	W462	14p.	lilac, dull blue, reddish brown, bistre-yellow, black and gold	40	40
W486 (=S.G.1156)	W463	18p.	bottle-green, bright blue, brown, bistre-yellow, black and gold	50	55
W487 (=S.G.1157)	W464	20p.	deep turquoise-blue, dull blue, greenish yellow, reddish brown, black and gold	55	60
W488 (=S.G.1158)	W465	22p.	chrome-yellow, reddish brown, new blue, yellow-brown, black and gold	60	60
W489 (=S.G.1159)	W466	25p.	ultramarine, new blue, olive-green, olive-grey and gold	65	70

W   1981.   Royal Wedding

First Day Cover (W485/9)	..	..	..	..	†	2·50
Presentation Pack (W485/9)	..	..	..	..	2·75	†
PHQ Cards (W485/9)	..	..	..	..	2·10	2·50

Cylinder Numbers (Blocks of Six)

	Cyl. Nos.	Perforation No dot	Type R* Dot
14p.	2A (black)–1B (bistre-yellow)–1C (reddish brown)–1D (dull blue)–1E (gold)–1F (lilac)	2·75	2·75
18p.	2A (black)–1B (bistre-yellow)–2C (brown)–1D (bright blue)–1E (gold)–3F (bottle green)	3·50	3·50
20p.	2A (black)–2B (greenish yellow)–1C (reddish brown)–2D (dull blue)–1E (gold)–2F (deep turquoise blue)	4·00	4·00
22p.	1A (black)–2B (chrome-yellow)–1C (reddish brown)–1D (new blue)–1E (gold)–1F (yellow-brown)	4·25	4·25
25p.	1A (olive-grey)–1B (olive-green)–1C (new blue)–1D (ultramarine)–1E (gold)	4·50	4·50

Sheet Details

Sheet size: 100 (2 panes 10 × 5). Double pane reel-fed

Sheet markings:
Cylinder numbers: Opposite rows 8/9, left margin, boxed
Marginal arrows: In centre at top and bottom of sheet
Colour register marks (crossed lines type):
No dot panes: Opposite rows 6/7 at both sides and cross in circle opposite row 2, left margin
Dot panes: Opposite rows 1/2 at both sides
Autotron marks: In same order as traffic lights in left margin opposite rows 4/7 or rows 4/6 (25p.) on dot panes only
Perforation register marks: Thick bar opposite lower gutter perforations, right margin on no dot panes only
Sheet values: Above and below vertical rows 2/4 and 7/9 reading from left to right in top margin and from right to left (upside down) in bottom margin
Traffic lights (boxed): Opposite row 9 (25p.) or rows 8/9 (others), right margin
14p. Bistre-yellow, reddish-brown, dull blue, lilac, black, gold
18p. Bistre-yellow, brown, bright blue, bottle green, black, gold
20p. Greenish yellow, reddish brown, dull blue, deep turquoise-blue, black, gold
22p. Chrome-yellow, reddish brown, new blue, yellow-brown, black, gold
25p. Olive-green, new blue, ultramarine, olive-grey gold

Quantities Sold   14p. 43,308,000; 18p. 10,498,000; 20p. 12,427,000; 22p. 9,920,000; 25p. 9,561,000

Withdrawn   23.6.82

W467 Prince Charles
and Lady Diana Spencer
(Des. Jeffery Matthews from photograph by Lord Snowdon)

1981 (22 JULY). ROYAL WEDDING

The stamps commemorate the marriage of HRH The Prince of Wales to the Lady Diana Spencer at St. Paul's Cathedral, London, on 29 July 1981. The design is from a photograph taken specially for the official souvenir book *The Royal Wedding*.

Phosphorised (fluorescent coated) paper

W490 (=S.G.1160)	**W467**	14p.	grey-black, greenish yellow, bright rose-red, ultramarine, pale blue, blue and silver	35	35
W491 (=S.G.1161)	**W467**	25p.	drab, greenish yellow, bright rose-red, ultramarine, grey-brown, grey-black and silver ..	90	90

First Day Cover (W490/1)	†	2·00
Presentation Pack (W490/1)	1·75	†
Souvenir Book (W490/1)	4·50	†
PHQ Cards (W490/1)	1·10	2·25

The souvenir book was a 12-page illustrated booklet with a set of mint stamps in a sachet attached to the front cover.

Cylinder Numbers (Blocks of Six)

	Cyl. Nos.	Perforation Type R* No dot	Dot
14p.	2A (grey-black)–1B (greenish yellow)–2C (bright rose-red)—2D (ultramarine)–1E (pale blue)–1F (blue)–1G (silver)	2·40	2·40
25p.	1A (drab)–1B (greenish yellow)–2C (bright rose-red)–2D (ultramarine)–1E (grey -brown)–2F (black)–1G (silver)	—	15·00
	1A (drab)–1B (greenish yellow)–2C (bright rose-red)–2D (ultramarine)–1E (grey-brown)–5F (black)–1G (silver)	6·50	6·50

The above are with sheets orientated with head to left.

Sheet Details

Sheet size: 100 (2 panes 5 × 10). Double pane reel-fed

Sheet markings:
Cylinder numbers: In top margin above vertical rows 2/3, boxed
Marginal arrows: In centre, opposite rows 5/6 at both sides
Colour register marks (crossed lines type):
No dot panes: Above and below vertical rows 4/5 and also large cross in circle above vertical row 9
Dot panes: Above and below vertical rows 8/10
Autotron marks: In order of traffic lights reading from left to right above vertical rows 4/7 on dot panes only
Perforation register marks: Thick bar below left gutter perforation row on no dot panes only
Sheet values: Opposite rows 2/4 and 7/9 reading up at left and down at right
Traffic lights (boxed): In bottom margin below vertical rows 2/3
14p. Grey-black, greenish yellow, bright rose-red, ultramarine, pale blue, blue, silver
25p. Drab, greenish yellow, bright rose-red, ultramarine, grey brown, grey-black, silver

Quantities Sold   14p. 87,040,000; 25p. 24,875,000

Withdrawn   Pack, sold out 9.81; remainder 21.7.82

W468 "Expeditions"   W469 "Skills"

W470 "Service"   W471 "Recreation"

(Des. Philip Sharland)

(Lithography by John Waddington Ltd.)

1981 (12 AUGUST). 25th ANNIVERSARY OF DUKE OF EDINBURGH'S AWARD SCHEME

Begun in 1956 as an experimental project, the Duke of Edinburgh's Award Scheme was set up to provide personal achievement, community involvement, adventure and a widening of leisure interests for young people between the ages of 14 and 25. There are three levels of award, bronze, silver and gold.

This was the first Post Office special stamp issue printed by John Waddington Ltd.

Phosphorised (fluorescent coated) paper. Comb perforation 14

W492 (=S.G.1162)	**W468**	14p.	greenish yellow, magenta, pale new blue, black, emerald and silver	35	35
W493 (=S.G.1163)	**W469**	18p.	greenish yellow, magenta, pale new blue, black, cobalt and gold	50	50
W494 (=S.G.1164)	**W470**	22p.	greenish yellow, magenta, pale new blue, black, red-orange and gold	60	60
W495 (=S.G.1165)	**W471**	25p.	bright orange, mauve, pale new blue, black, flesh and bronze	70	70

First Day Cover (W492/5)	..	..	..	.. †	1·90
Presentation Pack (W492/5)	..	..	..	.. 2·50	†
PHQ Cards (W492/5) ..	..	..	..	.. 1·75	2·25

Plate Numbers (Blocks of Four)

Colour order of plate nos.

14p. Greenish yellow, magenta, pale new blue, black, emerald, silver
18p. Greenish yellow, magenta, pale new blue, black, cobalt, gold
22p. Greenish yellow, magenta, pale new blue, black, red-orange, gold
25p. Bright orange, mauve, pale new blue, black, flesh, bronze

	Plate Nos.					Perforation Type N†	
						No dot	Dot
14p.	1A–1B–1C–1D–1E–1F	..	..	..	..	5·00	5·00
	1A–2B–1C–1D–1E–1F	..	..	..	..	8·00	12·00
	2A–2B–1C–1D–1E–1F	..	..	..	..	8·00	8·00
	3A–3B–2C–2D–2E–2F	..	..	..	..	8·00	8·00
	3A–3B–2C–2D–3E–2F	..	..	..	..	5·00	5·00
	3A–3B–2C–3D–3E–2F	..	..	..	..	8·00	8·00
	3A–3B–2C–3D–4E–2F	..	..	..	..	1·75	1·75
	4A–4B–3C–4D–5E–3F	..	..	..	..	5·00	5·00
	4A–5B–3C–4D–6E–4F	..	..	..	..	5·00	5·00
	5A–6B–3C–4D–7E–5F	..	..	..	..	5·00	5·00
	5A–6B–3C–5D–8E–5F	..	..	..	..	8·00	12·00
18p.	1A–1B–1C–1D–1E–1F	..	..	..	..	8·00	8·00
	1A–2B–1C–1D–1E–1F	..	..	..	..	5·00	5·00
	1A–2B–1C–1D–2E–1F	..	..	..	..	15·00	15·00
	1A–3B–1C–1D–2E–1F	..	..	..	..	10·00	10·00
	1A–3B–1C–1D–3E–1F	..	..	..	..	2·50	2·50
	1A–3B–2C–1D–3E–1F	..	..	..	..	15·00	15·00
22p.	1A–1B–1C–1D–1E–1F	..	..	..	..	7·50	7·50
	1A–2B–3C–2D–2E–1F	..	..	..	..	6·00	6·00
	1A–2B–3C–2D–2E–2F	..	..	..	..	10·00	5·00
	1A–2B–3C–2D–3E–2F	..	..	..	:.	10·00	10·00
	1A–3B–3C–2D–3E–2F	..	..	..	..	3·00	3·00
25p.	1A–3B–1C–1D–1E–1F	..	..	..	..	6·00	6·00
	1A–3B–1C–1D–2E–1F	..	..	..	..	3·50	7·50
	2A–4B–2C–2D–3E–1F	..	..	..	..	35·00	35·00
	2A–4B–2C–2D–4E–2F	..	..	..	..	8·00	8·00

† The perforation characteristics of this perforator are as follows:

	Top margin	Bottom margin	Left margin	Right margin
No dot pane	Perforated through	Imperforate	Imperforate	Perforated through
Dot pane	Imperforate	Perforated through	Imperforate	Perforated through

Sheet Details

Sheet size: 100 (2 panes 10 × 5). Double pane sheet-fed

Sheet markings:
Plate numbers: Opposite rows 4/5, left margin, boxed with Waddington logo above
Marginal arrows: In centre at top and bottom of sheet
Sheet values: Above and below vertical rows 2/4 and 7/9 reading from left to right in top margin and from right to left (upside down) in bottom margin
Traffic lights: Opposite row 8, right margin
14p. Greenish yellow, magenta, pale new blue, black, emerald and silver
18p. Greenish yellow, magenta, pale new blue, cobalt and gold
22p. Greenish yellow, magenta, pale new blue, black, red-orange and gold
25p. Bright orange, mauve, pale new blue, black, flesh and bronze

Quantities Sold   14p. 43,174,000; 18p. 10,292,000; 22p. 9,989,000; 25p. 9,519,000

Withdrawn   11.8.82

W472 Cockle-Dredging

W473 Hauling Trawl

W474 Lobster Potting

W475 Hoisting Seine Net

(Des. Brian Sanders)

1981 (23 SEPTEMBER).   FISHING INDUSTRY

This issue features the important contribution of Britain's fishermen to the national economy. Organisations in the fishing industry designated 1981 as Fishermen's Year and the stamps also commemorate the centenary of the Royal National Mission to Deep Sea Fishermen, a voluntary organisation which provides a social service for both fishermen and their families. The 14p. shows a hydraulic dredge used to wash cockles from the sand. Fishermen hauling in a trawl net are shown on the 18p. The 22p. depicts a fisherman baiting the lobster pots with freshly killed fish. A seine net used for catching surface schooling fish (herring) is shown on the 25p. Brian Sanders, the designer, was also responsible for the 1979 Police issue.

Phosphorised (fluorescent coated) paper

W496 (=S.G.1166)	**W472**	14p.	slate, greenish yellow, magenta, new blue, orange-brown, olive-grey and bronze-green	35	35
		a.	Blue flaw	2·00	
W497 (=S.G.1167)	**W473**	18p.	slate, greenish yellow, bright crimson, ultramarine, black and greenish slate	50	50
		a.	Retouched sleeve	2·25	
W498 (=S.G.1168)	**W474**	22p.	grey, greenish yellow, bright rose, dull ultramarine, reddish lilac and black	60	60
		a.	Gap in lobster basket	2·75	
		b.	Patch on frame of lobster basket	2·75	
		c.	Yellow patch on hood	3·25	
W499 (=S.G.1169)	**W475**	25p.	grey, greenish yellow, bright rose, cobalt, and black	70	65
		a.	Black spot on cabin	3·00	

First Day Cover (W496/9)	..	.. ..	†	1·90
Presentation Pack (W496/9)	..	.. ..	2·50	†
PHQ Cards (W496/9)	..	.. ..	2·10	2·25

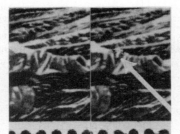

W496*a* Blue flaw (Dot. R. 1/6)	W497*a* Retouched sleeve appears as a flame by glove (Dot. R. 6/9)	W498*a* Gap in lobster basket (Dot. R. 5/5)

W498*b* Patch on frame of lobster basket (Dot. R. 8/7)	W498*c* Yellow patch on hood (Dot. R. 8/8)	W499*a* Black spot on cabin (No dot. R. 9/1)

Cylinder Number (Blocks of Six)

	Cyl. Nos.	Perforation Type R*	
		No dot	Dot
14p.	2A (slate)–1B (greenish yellow)–1C (magenta)–1D (new blue)–1E (orange-brown)–1F (olive-grey)–1G (bronze-green)	2·40	2·40
18p.	1A (slate)–1B (greenish yellow)–2C (bright crimson)–1D (ultramarine)–1E (black)–1F (greenish slate)	3·50	3·50
22p.	1A (grey)–1B (greenish yellow)–1C (bright rose)–1D (dull ultramarine)–1E (reddish lilac)–1F (black)	4·25	4·25
25p.	1A (grey)–1B (greenish yellow)–1C (bright rose)–1D (cobalt)–1E (black)	5·00	5·00

Sheet Details

Sheet size: 100 (2 panes 10 × 5). Double pane reel-fed

Sheet markings:
 Cylinder numbers: Opposite rows 8/9, left margin, boxed
 Marginal arrows: In centre at top and bottom of sheet
 Colour register marks (crossed lines type):
  No dot panes: Opposite rows 6/7 at both sides and cross in circle opposite row 2, left margin
  Dot panes: Opposite rows 1/3 (14p.), 1/2 (18p., 22p.) and rows 2/3 (25p.) at both sides
 Autotron marks: In same order as traffic lights in left margin opposite rows 4/6 (25p.) or rows 4/7 (others)
 Perforation register marks: Thick bar opposite lower gutter perforations, right margin on no dot panes only
 Sheet values: Above and below vertical rows 2/4 and 7/9 reading from left to right in top margin and from right to left (upside down) in bottom margin

Traffic lights (boxed): Opposite row 8, right margin (25p.) or rows 8/9 (others):
14p. Greenish yellow, magenta, new blue, orange-brown, olive-grey, bronze-green, slate
18p. Greenish yellow, bright crimson, ultramarine, black, greenish slate, slate
22p. Greenish yellow, bright rose, dull ultramarine, reddish lilac, black, grey
25p. Greenish yellow, bright rose, cobalt, black, grey

Quantities Sold   14p. 42,311,000; 18p. 9,790,000; 22p. 9,492,000; 25p. 9,143,000

Withdrawn   22.9.82

W476 Father Christmas
(Des. Samantha Brown)

W477 Jesus Christ
(Des. Tracy Jenkins)

W478 Flying Angel
(Des. Lucinda Blackmore)

W479 Joseph and Mary
arriving at Bethlehem
(Des. Stephen Moore)

W480 Three Kings
approaching Bethlehem
(Des. Sophie Sharp)

1981 (18 NOVEMBER).   CHRISTMAS

The designs are from paintings by children who were winners of a competition organised by the *Blue Peter* television programme in conjunction with the Post Office. The names and ages of the artists are shown on the stamps. In 1966 two six year old children were responsible for the designs of the first Post Office Christmas stamps.

One 4mm. phosphor band

W500 (=S.G.1170)	**W476** 11½p.	ultramarine, black, red, olive-bistre, bright green and gold	30	30
	b.	Imperf. between stamp and bottom margin ..	£375	

Phosphorised (fluorescent coated) paper

W501 (=S.G.1171)	**W477** 14p.	bistre-yellow, bright magenta, blue, greenish blue, bright green, black and gold	35	40
W502 (=S.G.1172)	**W478** 18p.	pale blue-green, bistre-yellow, bright magenta, ultramarine, black and gold	45	50
W503 (=S.G.1173)	**W479** 22p.	deep turquoise-blue, lemon, magenta, black and gold	60	60
	a.	Breaks in bottom frame	3·00	
W504 (=S.G.1174)	**W480** 25p.	royal blue, lemon, bright magenta, black and gold	65	70

First Day Cover (W500/04)	..	..	..	..	†	2·40
Presentation Pack (W500/04)	..	..	..	..	2·75	†
PHQ Cards (W500/04) ..	..	..	..	..	2·10	2·25

Listed Variety

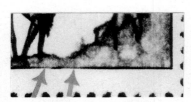

W503*a*
Two breaks in bottom frame
(No dot, R. 2/3)

Cylinder Numbers (Blocks of Six)

Cyl. Nos.	Perforation No dot	Type R* Dot
11½p. 1A (black)–1B (olive-bistre)–2C (red)–1D (ultramarine)–1E (gold)–1F (bright green)	2·10	†
1A (black)–1B (olive-bistre)–2C (red)–1D (ultramarine)–1E (gold)–1F (bright green)–P76 (phosphor)	†	2·10
1A (black)–1B (olive-bistre)–3C (red)–1D (ultramarine)–1E (gold)–1F (bright green)	3·00	†
1A (black)–1B (olive-bistre)–3C (red)–1D (ultramarine)–1E (gold)–1F (bright green)–P76 (phosphor)	†	3·00
14p. 2A (black)–1B (bistre-yellow)–1C (bright magenta)–1D (greenish blue)–1E (gold)–1F (blue)–1G (bright green)	2·40	2·40
18p. 1A (ultramarine)–2B (bistre-yellow)–1C (bright magenta)–3D (pale blue-green)–1E (gold)–1F (black)	3·25	3·25
22p. 2A (black)–3B (lemon)–3C (magenta)–3D (deep turquoise-blue)–1E (gold)	4·25	4·25
25p. 1A (black)–1B (lemon)–1C (bright magenta)–1D (royal blue)–1E (gold)	4·50	4·50

Phosphor cylinder No. P76 has been found on dot panes only in the left margin opposite row 10.

Sheet Details

Sheet size: 100 (2 panes 10 × 5). Double pane reel-fed

Sheet markings:
   Cylinder numbers: Opposite rows 8/9, left margin, boxed
   Marginal arrows: In centre at top and bottom of sheet
   Colour register marks (crossed lines type):
      No dot panes: Opposite rows 6/7 at both sides and cross in circle opposite row 2 left margin
      Dot panes: Opposite rows 1/3 (14p.) and 2/3 (others)
   Autotron marks: In same order as traffic lights in left margin opposite rows 4/7 (11½p., 14p., 18p.)
      and 5/7 (22p., 25p.) on dot panes only
   Perforation register marks: Thick bar opposite lower gutter perforations, right margin (11½p.,
      14p., 22p.) on no dot panes only
   Sheet values: Above and below vertical rows 2/4 and 7/9 reading from left to right in top margin
      and from right to left (upside down) in bottom margin
   Traffic lights (boxed): Opposite row 9 (25p.) and 8/9 (others), right margin
      11½p.   Olive-bistre, red, ultramarine, bright green, black, gold
      14p.   Bistre-yellow, bright magenta, greenish blue, blue, bright green, black, gold
      18p.   Bistre-yellow, bright magenta, ultramarine, pale blue-green, black, gold
      22p.   Lemon, magenta, deep turquoise-blue, black, gold
      25p.   Lemon, bright magenta, royal blue, black, gold

Quantities Sold   11½p. 276,077,000; 14p. 144,621,000; 18p. 17,630,000; 22p. 16,867,000;
      25p. 15,026,000

Withdrawn   17.11.82

1981 (18 NOVEMBER).   COLLECTORS PACK 1981
WCP14 Comprises Nos. W473/504 (Sold at £6.71½)   22·00

Withdrawn   17.11.82

W481 Charles Darwin and
Giant Tortoises

W482 Darwin and
Marine Iguanas

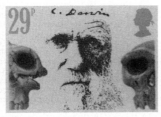

W483 Darwin, Cactus Ground Finch
and Large Ground Finch

W484 Darwin and
Prehistoric Skulls

(Des. David Gentleman)

1982 (10 FEBRUARY).   DEATH CENTENARY OF CHARLES DARWIN

This issue commemorates the English naturalist, Charles Robert Darwin (1809–82). Born in Shrewsbury, he became one of the leading pioneers of experimental biology. He journeyed round the world in the *Beagle* (1831–36) spending sometime studying creatures of the Pacific Islands in particular the Galapagos Archipelago off the coast of Ecuador. Three of the stamps depict species which led him to formulate his theory of evolution which was eventually published in the *Origin of Species* (1859). The 29p. stamp reflects the development of mankind; one of the skulls shown reported to be 1.7 million years old.

Phosphorised (fluorescent coated) paper

W505 (=S.G.1175)	**W481** 15½p.	dull purple, drab, bistre, black and grey-black	..		35	35
W506 (=S.G.1176)	**W482** 19½p.	violet-grey, bistre-yellow, slate-black, red-brown, grey-black and black	..	.. .. ..	55	60
W507 (=S.G.1177)	**W483** 26p.	sage green, bistre-yellow, orange, chalky blue, grey-black, red-brown and black ..	..	..	65	70
W508 (=S.G.1178)	**W484** 29p.	grey-brown, yellow-brown, brown-ochre, black and grey-black	..	.. .. ..	70	75

First Day Cover (W505/8)	..	..	..	.. †	2·25
Presentation Pack (W505/8)	..		..	.. 2·75	†
PHQ Cards (W505/8)	..	..	..	.. 2·50	4·00

The Post Office adopted a slightly larger size presentation pack for this and succeeding issues. It contained an information sheet about the issue which folded vertically instead of horizontally.

Cylinder Numbers (Blocks of Six)

	Perforation Type R*
	No dot Dot

15½p. 1A (dull purple)–1B (drab)–1C (bistre)–1D (black)–1E (grey-black) ..   ..   2·40   2·40

19½p. 1A (violet-grey)–1B (bistre-yellow)–2C (slate-black)–1D (red-brown)–1E (grey-black)–2F (black)   ..   ..   ..   4·00   4·00

26p. 1A (sage green)–1B (bistre-yellow)–1C (orange)–1D (chalky-blue)–1E (grey-black)–1F (red-brown)–1G (black) ..   4·50   4·50

29p. 1A (grey-brown)–1B (yellow-brown)–1C (brown-ochre)–1D (black)–1E (grey-black)   ..   ..   5·00   5·00

Sheet Details

Sheet size: 100 (2 panes 10 × 5). Double pane reel-fed

Sheet markings:
Cylinder numbers: Opposite rows 8/9, left margin, boxed with Harrison logo opposite row 10
Marginal arrows: In centre at top and bottom of sheet
Colour register marks (crossed lines type):
No dot panes: Opposite rows 6/7 at both sides and cross in circle opposite row 2, left margin
Dot panes: Opposite rows 1/2 (26p.) or 2/3 (others) at both sides
Autotron marks: In same order as traffic lights in left margin opposite rows 4/7 or in reverse traffic light order (19½p.) on dot panes only
Perforation register marks: Thick bar opposite lower gutter perforations, right margin on no dot panes only
Sheet values: Above and below vertical rows 2/4 and 7/9 reading from left to right in top margin and from right to left (upside down in bottom margin)
Traffic lights (boxed): Opposite rows 8/9 (19½p., 26p.) or row 9 (others) right margin
15½p. Dull purple, grey-black, black, bistre, drab
19½p. Violet-grey, grey-black, black, red-brown, slate-black, bistre-yellow
26p. Bistre-yellow, orange, chalky blue, grey-black, red-brown, black, sage green
29p. Grey-brown, black, grey-black, brown-ochre, yellow-brown

Quantities Sold   15½p. 40,637,400; 19½p. 9,361,400; 26p. 8,975,600; 29p. 8,674,800

Withdrawn   10.2.83

W485 Boys' Brigade   **W486** Girls' Brigade

W487 Boy Scout   **W488** Girl Guide
Movement   Movement

(Des. Brian Saunders)

1982 (24 MARCH).   YOUTH ORGANISATIONS

This issue commemorates the 75th anniversary of the Boy Scout Movement and the 125th birth anniversary of Lord Baden-Powell. The 15½p. depicts band members of the Boys' Brigade, which was founded by William Alexander Smith in 1883. The Girls' Brigade was formed by the amalgamation of three different girls' organisations in 1965. The Scouting movement was founded by Robert Baden-Powell and the first scout camp was held in 1907 on Brownsea Island, Dorset. Following the publication of *Scouting for Boys* the Girl Guide movement gained recognition and was organised by Baden-Powell's sister, Agnes. The Girl Guides were named after the famous Queen Victoria's Own Corps of Guides.

Phosphorised (fluorescent coated) paper

W509 (=S.G.1179)	**W485** 15½p.	gold, greenish yellow, pale orange, mauve, dull blue and grey-black ..	.. ..	35	35
W510 (=S.G.1180)	**W486** 19½p.	gold, greenish yellow, pale orange, bright rose, deep ultramarine, olive-bistre and grey-black ..		60	65
		a. Red stain on drum		3·00	
W511 (=S.G.1181)	**W487** 26p.	gold, greenish yellow, olive-sepia, rosine, deep blue, deep dull green, and grey-black		80	85
		a. Large red spot on flag		3·50	
W512 (=S.G.1182)	**W488** 29p.	gold, yellow, dull orange, cerise, dull ultramarine, chestnut and grey-black		90	90
		a. Point of star omitted		4·00	

First Day Cover (W509/12)	..	..	..	..	†	2·60
Presentation Pack (W509/12)	..	..	..	..	3·25	†
PHQ Cards (W509/12)	..	..	..	..	2·50	5·00

Listed Varieties

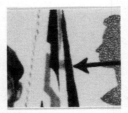

W510*a*	W511*a*	W512*a*
Red stain on drum	Large red spot	Point of star
(Dot, R. 5/6)	on flag	omitted
	(No dot, R. 1/4)	(No dot, R. 1/2)

Cylinder Numbers (Blocks of Six)

	Cyl. Nos.	Perforation No dot	Type R* Dot
15½p.	1A (gold)–1B (greenish yellow)–1C (pale orange)–1D (mauve)–2E (dull blue)–1F (grey-black)	2·40	2·40
19½p.	1A (gold)–1B (greenish yellow)–1C (pale orange)–1D (bright rose)–5E (deep ultramarine)–1F (olive-bistre)–1G (grey-black)	4·25	4·25
26p.	1A (gold)–1B (greenish yellow)–1C (olive-sepia)–1D (rosine)–1E (deep blue)–1F (deep dull green)–1G (grey-black)	5·50	5·50
29p.	1A (gold)–1B (yellow)–1C (dull orange)–1D (cerise)–1E (dull ultramarine)–1F (chestnut)–1G (grey-black)	6·50	6·50

Sheet Details

Sheet size: 100 (2 panes 5 × 10). Double pane reel-fed

Sheet markings:
  Cylinder numbers: In top margin above vertical rows 2/3 boxed. Harrison logo above vertical row 1
  Marginal arrows: In centre, opposite rows 5/6 at both sides
  Colour register marks (crossed lines type):
    No dot panes: Above and below vertical rows 4/5 and cross in circle type above vertical row 9
    Dot panes: Above and below vertical rows 8/10
  Autotron marks: In order of traffic lights reading from left to right above vertical rows 4/7 on dot panes only
  Perforation register marks: Thick bar below left gutter perforation row on no dot panes only
  Sheet values: Opposite rows 2/4 and 7/9 reading up at left and down at right
  Traffic lights (boxed): In bottom margin below vertical rows 2/3
    15½p. Gold, grey-black, dull blue, bright rose, pale orange, greenish yellow
    19½p. Gold, grey-black, olive-bistre, deep ultramarine, bright rose, pale orange, greenish yellow
    26p. Gold, grey-black, deep dull green, deep blue, rosine, olive-sepia, greenish yellow
    29p. Gold, grey-black, chestnut, dull ultramarine, cerise, dull orange, yellow

Quantities Sold   15½p. 40,169,000; 19½p. 9,234,500; 26p. 8,669,000; 29p. 8,361,900

Withdrawn   24.3.83

W489 Ballerina

W490 "Harlequin"

W491 "Hamlet"

W492 Opera Singer

(Des. Adrian George)

1982 (28 APRIL).   BRITISH THEATRE ("EUROPA")

The history of the British theatre and the 1982 "Europa" theme of "Historical Events" was commemorated with this issue. The stamps feature aspects of the performing arts and each value includes the CEPT Europa symbol. The 15½p. depicts ballet and 1982 marked the 250th anniversary of the first Theatre Royal, Covent Garden. A harlequin is shown on the 19½p. representing pantomine. The 26p. features stage drama with the Prince of Denmark from Shakespeare's *Hamlet* contemplating a skull and saying "Alas poor Yorick". Opera is represented on the 29p. with a singer in period costume.

Phosphorised (fluorescent coated) paper

W513 (=S.G.1183)	**W489** 15½p.	carmine-lake, greenish blue, greenish yellow, grey-black, bottle green and silver	35	35
W514 (=S.G.1184)	**W490** 19½p.	rosine, new blue, greenish yellow, black, ultramarine and silver	60	70
W515 (=S.G.1185)	**W491** 26p.	carmine-red, bright rose-red, greenish yellow, black, dull ultramarine, lake-brown and silver . .	85	90
	a.	Scratch in front of skull	3·50	
	b.	Falling tooth	3·50	
W516 (=S.G.1186)	**W492** 29p.	rose-red, greenish yellow, bright blue, grey-black and silver	90	1·00

First Day Cover (W513/6)	. .	. .	. .	. .	†	2·60
Presentation Pack (W513/6)	. .	. .	. .	. .	3·00	†
PHQ Cards (W513/6)	. .	. .	. .	. .	2·50	4·00

Listed Varieties

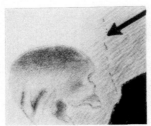

W515a
Scratch in front of
skull
(No dot, R. 2/8)

W515b
White patch in shading
resembles a falling tooth
(Dot, R. 1/1)

Cylinder Numbers (Blocks of Six)

	Perforation	Type R*
Cyl. Nos.	No dot	Dot
15½p. 1A (bottle green)–1B (greenish yellow)–2C (carmine-lake)–1D (greenish blue)–1E (silver)–1F (grey-black)	2·40	2·40
19½p. 1A (ultramarine)–1B (greenish yellow)–2C (rosine)–2D (new blue)–1E (silver)–1F (black)	4·25	4·25
26p. 1A (lake-brown)–1B (greenish yellow)–1C (bright rose-red)–1D (carmine-red)–1E (silver)–1F (dull ultramarine)–1G (black) ..	6·00	6·00
29p. 2A (rose-red)–1B (greenish yellow)–1C (bright blue)–1D (grey-black)–1E (silver)	6·50	6·50

Sheet Details

Sheet size: 100 (2 panes 5 × 10). Double pane reel-fed

Sheet markings:
   Cylinder numbers: In top margin above vertical rows 2/3 boxed. Harrison logo above vertical
   row 1
   Marginal arrows: In centre, opposite rows 5/6 at both sides
   Colour register marks (crossed lines type):
      No dot panes: Above and below vertical rows 4/5 and cross in circle type above vertical row 9
      Dot panes: Above and below rows 8/10 (26p.) or 8/9 (others)
   Autotron marks: In order of traffic lights reading from left to right above vertical rows 4/6 (29p.)
      or 4/7 (others) on dot panes only. Usually solid colour the 15½p. bottle green marking was hand
      engraved with short diagonal lines above vertical row 5
   Perforation register marks: Thick bar below left gutter perforation row on no dot panes only
   Sheet values: Opposite rows 2/4 and 7/9 reading up at left and down at right
   Traffic lights (boxed): In bottom margin below vertical rows 2/3
      15½p. Silver, grey-black, bottle green, greenish blue, carmine-lake, greenish yellow
      19½p. Silver, black, ultramarine, new blue, rosine, greenish yellow
      26p. Silver, lake-brown, black, dull ultramarine, carmine-red, bright rose-red, greenish
         yellow
      29p. Silver, grey-black, bright blue, rose-red, greenish yellow

Quantities Sold   15½p. 41,492,200; 19½p. 9,222,900; 26p. 8,740,000; 29p. 7,811,800

Withdrawn   28.4.83

W493 Henry VIII
and *Mary Rose*

| **W494** Admiral Blake and *Triumph* | **W495** Lord Nelson and H.M.S. *Victory* |

W496 Lord Fisher and H.M.S. *Dreadnought*   **W497** Viscount Cunningham and H.M.S. *Warspite*

(Des. Marjorie Saynor and eng. Czeslaw Slania)
(Printed in photogravure with ships and waves recess-printed in black)

1982 (16 JUNE).   MARITIME HERITAGE

Issued as a tribute to Britain's maritime and naval tradition, these stamps feature famous ships and personalities associated with them. The year 1982 was designated "Maritime England Year" by the English Tourist Board and marked the occasion of the Bicentenary of the Livery Grant by the City of London to the Worshipful Company of Shipwrights. One notable event in the year was the raising of the hull of the *Mary Rose*. This 600 ton vessel, named for King Henry VIII sister, was the flagship of the Lord High Admiral. She was completed in 1510 and was later refitted with heavy cannon placed to fire from gunports specially cut in the hull; the first ship in the British Navy so equipped. She keeled over and sank with the loss of most of the 700 men aboard while awaiting the French invasion fleet off Spithead. Admiral Blake (19½p.) fought with the Commonwealth Navy against the Dutch when the English Channel was threatened. H.M.S. *Victory* (24p.) is preserved at Portsmouth. The 26p. shows Admiral Fisher who is credited with the *Dreadnought*; prototype of the modern battleship. Admiral Cunningham (29p.) was outstanding as a commander in World War II and his flagship was the first of its kind to be fuelled only by oil.

Phosphorised (fluorescent coated) paper

W517 (=S.G.1187)	W493 15½p.	black, lemon, bright rose, pale-orange, ultramarine, grey	35	35
W518 (=S.G.1188)	W494 19½p.	black, greenish yellow, bright rose-red, pale orange, ultramarine, grey	50	60
W519 (=S.G.1189)	W495 24p.	black, orange-yellow, bright rose-red, lake-brown, deep ultramarine, grey	55	60
W520 (=S.G.1190)	W496 26p.	black, orange-yellow, bright rose, lemon, ultramarine, grey	65	70
		a. Imperforate (pair)		
		b. Retouched face	3·75	
W521 (=S.G.1191)	W497 29p.	black, olive-yellow, bright rose, orange-yellow, ultramarine, grey	75	80
		a. Retouch on eyebrow	2·50	
		b. Thinned line	3·00	

First Day Cover (W 517/21)	..	..	..	.. † 3·00
Presentation Pack (W517/21)	..	..	..	.. 3·25 †
PHQ Cards (W517/21) ..	..	..	..	.. 3·00 5·50

Listed Varieties

W520*b*	W521*a*	W521*b*
Retouched face	Retouch on eyebrow	Thinned line
(No dot, R. 8/10)	(No dot, R. 8/1)	(No dot, R. 5/4)

Cylinder Numbers (Blocks of Six)

	Perforation	Type R*
Cyl. Nos.	No dot	Dot
15½p. 1A (black)–1B (lemon)–1C (bright rose)–1D (pale orange)–1E (ultramarine)–1F (grey)	2·40	2·40
19½p. 1A (black)–1B (greenish yellow)–1C (bright rose-red)–1D (pale orange)–1E (ultramarine)–1F (grey)	3·50	3·50
24p. 2A (black)–1B (orange-yellow)–1C (bright rose-red)–1D (lake brown)–2E (deep ultramarine)–1F (grey)	4·00	4·00
26p. 1A (black)–1B (orange-yellow)–1C (bright rose)–1D (lemon)–1E (ultramarine)–1F (grey)	4·50	4·50
29p. 1A (black)–1B (olive-yellow)–1C (bright rose)–1D (orange-yellow)–1E (ultramarine)–1F (grey).	5·25	5·25

Sheet Details

Sheet size: 100 (2 panes 10 × 5). Double pane reel-fed

Sheet markings:
    Cylinder numbers: Opposite rows 8/9, left margin, boxed with Harrison logo opposite row 10
    Marginal arrows: In centre at top and bottom of sheet
    Colour register marks (crossed lines type):
        No dot panes: Opposite rows 6/7 at both sides and cross in circle opposite row 2, left margin
        Dot panes: Opposite rows 1/3 (29p.) and 2/3 (others) at both sides

193

W 1982. British Textiles

Autotron marks: In same order as traffic lights in left margin opposite rows 4/7 on dot panes only
Additional black horizontal bar hand-engraved (29p.) and photo-etched (others) in vertical row 4 on no dot panes only and a recess printed horizontal bar in vertical rows 4/5 in top, gutter and bottom margins on both panes in all values. Bars in the top and bottom margins are sometimes trimmed but when complete are shown with a horizontal row of up to six guide dots. These dots were engraved at the left side of the bar and are nearly always visible in the gutter margin position. The autotron marks were for adjusting the registration of the intaglio unit and the dots to identify individual panes.
Perforation register marks: Thick bar opposite lower gutter perforations, right margin on no dot panes only
Sheet values: Above and below vertical rows 2/4 and 7/9 reading from left to right in top margin and from right to left (upside down in bottom margin)
Traffic lights (boxed): Opposite rows 8/9, right margin
  15½p. Lemon, bright rose, pale orange, ultramarine, black, grey
  19½p. Greenish yellow, bright rose-red, pale orange, ultramarine, black, grey
  24p. Orange-yellow, bright rose-red, lake-brown, deep ultramarine, black, grey
  26p. Orange-yellow, bright rose, lemon, ultramarine, black, grey
  29p. Olive-yellow, bright rose, orange-yellow, ultramarine, black, grey

Quantities Sold 15½p. 43,768,700; 19½p. 10,559,500; 24p. 11,839,000; 26p. 9,694,100; 29p. 8,823,900

Withdrawn 16.6.83

W498 "Strawberry
Thief" (William Morris)

W499 Untitled
(Steiner and Co)

W500 "Cherry
Orchard" (Paul Nash)

W501 "Chevron"
(Andrew Foster)

(Des. Peter Hatch Partnership)

1982 (23 JULY). BRITISH TEXTILES

This issue celebrates the British textile industry and the 250th anniversary of the birth of Sir Richard Arkwright who developed the yarn spinning-frame. This invention was a major step from producing material by hand-operated machinery. The stamps feature fabric designs from 1883. The first of these is by William Morris, noted for many interior decoration designs of the Victorian period. The Art Noveau influence is evident in the scarlet tulip design of 1906 (19½p.). Abstract patterns are represented by the 26p. showing a design commissioned by Cresta silks (1929). The 29p. shows an example of screen-printed furnishing cotton called Chevron (1949).

Phosphorised (fluorescent coated) paper

W522 (=S.G.1192)	**W498** 15½p.	blue, olive-yellow, rosine, deep blue-green, bistre and Prussian blue	35	35
		a. Imperforate (horiz. pair)	£950	
W523 (=S.G.1193)	**W499** 19½p.	olive-grey, greenish yellow, bright magenta, dull green, yellow-brown and black	70	65
		a. Imperforate (vert. pair)	£1500	
		b. "Caterpillar" flaw	4·00	
W524 (=S.G.1194)	**W500** 26p.	bright scarlet, dull mauve, dull ultramarine and bright carmine	70	65
		a. Horizontal white scratch	4·00	
W525 (=S.G.1195)	**W501** 29p.	bronze-green, orange-yellow, turquoise-green, stone, chestnut and sage green	80	75
		a. Dark blemish above Queen's head	5·00	

First Day Cover (W522/5)	..	..	..	..	†	2·25
Presentation Pack (W522/5)	..	..	..	..	3·00	†
PHQ Cards (W522/5)	..	..	..	..	2·50	4·00

Listed Varieties

W523*b*
"Caterpillar" flaw
(Dot, R. 3/4)

W524*a*
Horizontal white scratch
(Dot, R. 2/7)

Dark blemish above
Queen's head
(Dot, R. 2/5)

W525*a*

Cylinder Numbers (Blocks of Six)

Cyl. Nos.	Perforation No dot	Type R* Dot
15½p. 2A (blue)–1B (olive-yellow)–1C (rosine)–1D (deep blue-green)–1E (bistre)–1F (Prussian blue)	2·40	2·40
19½p. 1A (olive-grey)–1B (greenish yellow)–1C (bright magenta)–1D (dull green)–1E (yellow-brown)–1F (black)	5·00	5·00
26p. 1A (bright scarlet)–1B (dull mauve)–1C (dull ultramarine)–1E (bright carmine)	5·25	5·25
29p. 1A (bronze-green)–1B (orange-yellow)–1C (turquoise-green)–1D (stone)–1E (chestnut)–1F (sage green)	5·50	5·50

The above are with sheets orientated with head to left.

Sheet Details

Sheet size: (2 panes 5 × 10). Double pane reel-fed

Sheet markings:
Cylinder numbers: In top margin above vertical row 2 (26p.) or 2/3 (others) boxed. Harrison logo above row 1
Marginal arrows: In centre, opposite rows 5/6 at both sides
Colour register marks (crossed lines type):
No dot panes: Above and below vertical rows 3/5 (19½p.) or 3/4 (others) and also cross in circle above vertical row 9
Dot panes: Above and below vertical rows 8/10
Autotron marks: In order of traffic lights reading from left to right above vertical rows 5/7 on dot panes only (26p.) or 4/7 (others) on dot panes only
Perforation register marks: Thick bars in bottom margin below the left gutter and right corner perforation rows on both panes
Sheet values: Opposite rows 2/4 and 7/9 reading up at left and down at right
Traffic lights (boxed): In bottom margin below vertical row 2 (26p.) or 2/3 (others)
15½p. Blue, Prussian blue, bistre, deep blue-green, rosine, olive-yellow
19½p. Olive-grey, black, yellow-brown, dull green, bright magenta, greenish yellow
26p.   Bright scarlet, bright carmine, dull ultramarine, dull mauve
29p.   Bronze-green, sage green, chestnut, stone, turquoise-green, orange-yellow

Quantities Sold 40,144,500; 19½p. 9,236,100; 26p. 8,732,600; 29p. 8,441,800

Withdrawn 23.7.83

W502 Development of
Communications

W503 Modern Technological Aids

(Des. Brian Delaney and Darrell Ireland)

1982 (8 SEPTEMBER).   INFORMATION TECHNOLOGY

An international conference was held in 1982 which was designated Information Technology Year supported by government and industry. The long designs, each in three parts, show progress in communciations and microelectronics. The 15½p. depicts Egyptian hieroglyphics, a Victorian period scene in the British Library and a modern word processor. The 26p. shows a Prestel viewdata set, communications satellite and a laser light pen used in shops to regulate stock control and sales.

Phosphorised (fluorescent coated) paper. Comb perforation 14 × 15

W526 (=S.G.1196)   **W502** 15½p. black, greenish yellow, bright rose-red, bistre-
brown, new blue, light ochre   45   50
    a. Imperforate (pair) £250
    b. Imperf. between stamp and right margin £350
    c. Retouch below display unit..   ..   ..   ..   2·40
W527 (=S.G.1197)   **W503** 26p. black, greenish yellow, bright rose-red, olive-
bistre, new blue, light olive-grey   80   85
    a. Imperforate (pair) £950

First Day Cover (W526/7)	†	1·50
Presentation Pack (W526/7)	1·75	†
PHQ Cards (W526/7)	1·50	3·00

Listed Variety

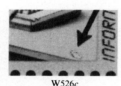

Retouch on table below
visual display unit
(No dot, R. 2/1)

W526*c*

Cylinder Numbers (Blocks of Four)

	Cyl. Nos.	Perforation Type R(A)	
		No dot	Dot
15½p.	2A (black)–1B (greenish yellow)–1C (bright rose-red)–2D (bistre-brown)–1E (new blue)–1F (light olive-grey)	2·25	2·25
26p.	1A (black)–1B (greenish yellow)–1C (bright rose-red)–2D (olive-bistre)–1E (new blue)–1F (light olive-grey)	4·00	4·00

Sheet Details

Sheet size: 60 (2 panes 3 × 10). Double pane reel-fed

Sheet markings:
    Cylinder numbers: In top margin above vertical rows 1/2, boxed. Harrison logo above vertical
       row 1
    Marginal arrows: In centre, two arrows opposite each gutter perforation row in top and bottom
       margins
    Colour register marks (crossed lines type):
       No dot panes: Below vertical rows 3 and 6 also cross in circle type opposite vertical row of
          perforations between rows 4/5, in bottom margin
       Dot panes: Above vertical rows 3 and 6
    Autotron marks: In order of traffic lights reading from left to right above vertical rows 4/5 on dot
       panes only
    Perforation register marks: Thick bar in bottom margin between vertical rows 3/4 on no dot panes
       only
    Sheet values: Opposite rows 2/4 and 7/9 reading up at left and down at right
    Traffic lights (boxed): In bottom margin below vertical rows 1/2
       15½p. Light ochre, black, new blue, bistre-brown, bright rose-red, greenish yellow
       26p.   Light olive-grey, black, new blue, olive-bistre, bright rose-red, greenish yellow

Quantities Sold   15½p. 33,174,960; 26p. 7,985,520

Withdrawn   8.9.83

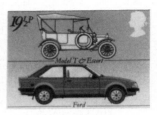

W504 Austin "Seven"
and "Metro"

W505 Ford "Model T"
and "Escort"

W506 Jaguar "SS1"
and "XJ6"

W507 Rolls-Royce
"Silver Ghost" and
"Silver Spirit"

(Des. Stanley Paine)
(Lithography by The House of Questa)

1982 (13 OCTOBER). BRITISH MOTOR INDUSTRY

Issued to highlight and promote British Industry this issue features modern cars and their famous vintage counterparts. The issue coincided with the staging of the British Motor Show, held in the National Exhibition Centre, Birmingham. This was the second occasion that the motor car has been features on a British stamp. The Jaguar and the 1966 "Mini" were depicted on the sixpence value of the British Technology series issued on 19 September 1966.

Phosphorised (fluorescent coated) paper. Comb perforation $14\frac{1}{2} \times 14$

W528 (=S.G.1198)	**W504** 15½p.	slate, orange-vermilion, bright orange, drab, yellow-green, olive-yellow, bluish grey and black		50	50
W529 (=S.G.1199)	**W505** 19½p.	slate, bright orange, olive-grey, rose-red, dull vermilion, grey and black		90	1·00
	a.	Imperforate between stamp and right margin ..		£450	
W530 (=S.G.1200)	**W506** 26p.	slate, red-brown, bright orange, turquoise-green, myrtle green, dull blue-green, grey and black ..		1·00	1·10
W531 (=S.G.1201)	**W507** 29p.	slate, bright orange, carmine-red, reddish purple, grey and black		1·25	1·25

First Day Cover (W528/31)	..	..	..	.. †	3·50
Presentation Pack (W528/31)	..	..	..	.. 4·25	†
PHQ Cards (W528/31)	..	..	..	.. 2·50	4·50

Plate Numbers (Blocks of Six)

Colour order of plate nos. following the Questa imprint
  15½p. Black, bluish grey, olive-yellow, yellow-green, drab, bright orange, orange-vermilion, slate
  19½p. Black, grey, dull vermilion, rose-red, olive-grey, bright orange, slate
  26p. Black, grey, dull blue-green, myrtle green, turquoise-green, bright orange, red-brown, slate
  29p. Black, grey, reddish purple, carmine-red, bright orange, slate

		Perf. Type M
15½p.	1A (×8)	10·00
	1B (×8)	10·00
	2A–1A–1A–1A–2A–1A–1A–1A	20·00
	2B–1B–1B–1B–2B–1B–1B–1B	20·00
	2A–1A–1A–1A–2A–2A–1A–1A	10·00
	2B–1B–1B–1B–2B–2B–1B–1B	10·00
	3A–2A–2A–2A–3A–3A–2A–2A	3·50
	3B–2B–2B–2B–3B–3B–2B–2B	3·50
19½p.	1A (×7)	10·00
	1B (×7)	10·00
	1A (×4)–2A–1A–1A	6·25
	1B (×4)–2B–1B–1B	6·25
26p.	1A (×8)	7·00
	1B (×8)	7·00
29p.	1A (×6)	9·00
	1B (×6)	9·00

Sheet Details

Sheet size: 100 (2 panes 10 × 5). Double pane sheets with "A" and "B" plate numbers

Sheet markings:
  Plate numbers: Opposite rows 8/9, left margin, arranged sideways in colour order as described following the imprint
  Marginal arrows: "W" shaped in centre, between vertical rows 5/6 in top and bottom margins
  Sheet values: Above and below vertical rows 2/4 and 7/9 reading from left to right in top margin and from right to left (upside down) in bottom margin
  Imprint: Opposite rows 9/10, left margin, arranged sideways reading up
  Traffic lights: Sideways in the form of Questa logo opposite row 9, right margin. For order of colours see under "Plate Numbers" above

Quantities Sold   15½p. 40,225,000; 19½p. 9,162,600; 26p. 8,762,500; 29p. 8,449,000

Withdrawn   13.10.83

W508 "While Shepherds
Watched"

W509 "The Holly   **W510** "I Saw Three
and the Ivy"   Ships"

W511 "We Three   **W512** "Good King
Kings"   Wenceslas"

(Des. Barbara Brown)

1982 (17 NOVEMBER). CHRISTMAS

This is the second Christmas series depicting scenes from famous carols. The first, designed by David Gentleman, appeared in 1973 and featured the traditional carol, "Good King Wenceslas". The 19½p. design represents the legend of the voyage made in 1162, between Milan and Cologne of the relics of the three Magi or Kings. The Magi are depicted on the 26p. value representing the Epiphany carol which was composed by Dr. J. H. Hopkins of Pennsylvania in about 1857.

One 4mm centre phosphor band

W532 (=S.G.1202) **W508** 12½p. black, greenish yellow, bright scarlet, steel blue,
red-brown and gold   30   30

Phosphorised (fluorescent coated) paper

W533 (=S.G.1203) **W509** 15½p. black, bistre-yellow, bright rose-red, bright blue,
bright green and gold   40   45
a. Fluorescent brightener omitted   ..   ..   ..   1·50
b. Missing serifs at top and base of large "1"   ..   2·00

W534 (=S.G.1204) **W510** 19½p. black, bistre-yellow, bright rose-red, dull blue,
deep brown and gold   60   65

200

W535 (=S.G.1205)   **W511**   26p.   black, bistre-yellow, bright magenta, bright blue,

                                        chocolate, gold and orange-red   60   65

W536 (=S.G.1206)   **W512**   29p.   black, bistre-yellow, magenta, bright-blue, chest-

                                        nut, gold and bright magenta   70   75

                                  a. Sliced "as" in Wenceslas   ..   ..   2·50

                                  b. Retouch to base of "2"   ..   ..   2·75

First Day Cover (W532/36)	†	2·50
Presentation Pack (W532/36)	3·25	†
PHQ Cards (W532/36)	3·00	4·00

No. W533*a* is printed on chalk surfaced paper but without the fluorescent additive.

Listed Varieties

W533*b*	W536*a*	W536*b*
Missing serifs at top and base of large "1" (Dot. R. 8/7)	Sliced "as" in Wenceslas (No dot. R. 10/2)	Retouch to base of "2" (Dot. R. 1/3)

Cylinder Numbers (Blocks of Six)

	Perforation No dot	Type R* Dot
One 4mm. centre phosphor band		
12½p. 2A (black)–1B (greenish yellow)–2C (bright scarlet)–1D (steel blue)–1E (red-brown)–1F (gold)–P77 (phosphor)	2·10	2·10
2A (black)–1B (greenish yellow)–2C (bright scarlet)–1D (steel blue)–1E (red-brown)–2F (gold)–P77 (phosphor)	4·50	4·50
2A (black)–1B (greenish yellow)–2C (bright scarlet)–1D (steel blue)–1E (red-brown)–2F (gold)	4·50	4·50
Phosphorised (fluorescent coated) paper		
15½p. 1A (black)–1B (bistre-yellow)–1C (bright rose-red)–1D (bright blue)–1E (bright green)–1F (gold)	2·75	2·75
19½p. 1A (black)–1B (bistre-yellow)–2C (bright rose-red)–1D (dull blue)–1E (deep brown)–1F (gold)	4·25	4·25
26p. 1A (black)–1B (bistre-yellow)–2C (bright magenta)–1D (bright blue)–1E (chocolate)–1F (gold)–1G (orange-red)	4·25	4·25
29p. 3A (black)–1B (bistre-yellow)–1C (magenta)–1D (bright blue)–2E (chestnut)–1F (gold)–2G (bright magenta)	5·00	5·00

Phosphor cylinder number P77 is synchronised at row 9 on the cylinder block but it has been seen opposite row 4 in the left margin on no dot panes showing the 2F (gold) cylinder number.

Sheet Details

Sheet size: 100 (2 panes 10 × 5). Double pane reel-fed

Sheet markings:
    Cylinder numbers: Opposite row 8/9, left margin, boxed with Harrison logo opposite row 10
    Marginal arrows: In centre at top and bottom of sheet
    Colour register marks (crossed lines type):
       No dot panes: Opposite rows 6/7 at both sides and cross in circle opposite row 2, left margin
       Dot panes: Opposite rows 1/2 at both sides
    Autotron marks: In same order as traffic lights in left margin opposite rows 4/7 on dot panes only
    Perforation register marks: Thick bar opposite lower gutter perforations, right margin on no dot
       panes only
    Sheet values: Above and below vertical rows 2/4 and 7/9 reading from left to right in top margin
       and from right to left (upside down) in bottom margin
    Traffic lights (boxed): Opposite rows 8/9, right margin
       12½p. Greenish yellow, bright scarlet, steel blue, red-brown, black, gold
       15½p. Bistre-yellow, bright rose-red, bright blue, black, bright green, gold
       19½p. Bistre-yellow, bright rose-red, dull blue, deep brown, black, gold
       26p. Bistre-yellow, bright magenta, bright blue, chocolate, black, orange-red, gold
       29p. Bistre-yellow, magenta, bright blue, chestnut, black, bright magenta, gold

Quantities Sold   12½p. 285,300,600; 15½p. 148,757,500; 19½p. 17,445,500; 26p. 16,241,600; 29p.
       14,867,800

Withdrawn   17.11.83

1982 (17 NOVEMBER).   COLLECTORS PACK 1982

WCP15 Comprises Nos. W505/36 (Sold at £7.63)   26·00

Withdrawn   17.11.83

W513 Salmon

W514 Pike

W515 Trout

W516 Perch

(Des. Alex Jardine)

1983 (26 JANUARY).   BRITISH RIVER FISHES

The popular theme of fauna and wildlife was continued with this issue which features well known river fish. The issue coincided with the 300th anniversary of the death of Izaac Walton, author and biographer who wrote *The Compleat Angler* in 1653. This work is considered one of the best books of its type dealing with the subject of angling.

Phosphorised (fluorescent coated) paper

W537 (=S.G.1207)	W513 15½p.	grey-black, bistre-yellow, bright purple, new blue and silver	35	35
W538 (=S.G.1208)	W514 19½p.	black, bistre-yellow, olive-bistre, deep claret, silver and deep bluish green	65	65
W539 (=S.G.1209)	W515 26p.	grey-black, bistre-yellow, chrome-yellow, magenta, silver and pale blue	60	65
		a. Extra "wavelet" and broken frame	3·50	
W540 (=S.G.1210)	W516 29p.	black, greenish yellow, bright carmine, new blue and silver	75	75
		a. Black spot on dorsal fin	3·50	

First Day Cover (W537/40)	†	2·50
Presentation Pack (W537/40)	3·25	†
PHQ Cards (W537/40)	2·50	4·50

A quantity of covers were inadvertently postmarked 26 January 1982 at Southend-on-Sea, Essex.

Listed Varieties

W539a	W540a
Extra "wavelet" and	Black spot on dorsal fin
broken frame	(Dot. R. 10/1)
(No dot. R. 4/8)	

Cylinder Numbers (Blocks of Six)

	Cyl. Nos.	Perforation No dot	Type R* Dot
15½p.	1A (grey-black)–1B (bistre-yellow)–1C (bright purple)–2D (new blue)–1E (silver)	2·40	2·40
19½p.	1A (black)–1B (bistre-yellow)–1C (olive-bistre)–1D (deep claret)–1E (silver)–1F (deep bluish green)	4·50	4·50
26p.	2A (grey-black)–1B (bistre-yellow)–1C (chrome-yellow)–3D (magenta)–1E (silver)–3F (pale blue)	4·25	4·25
29p.	1A (black)–1B (greenish yellow)–1C (bright carmine)–1D (new blue)–1E (silver)	5·25	5·25

Sheet Details

Sheet size: 100 (2 panes 10 × 5). Double pane reel-fed

Sheet markings:
Cylinder numbers: Opposite rows 8/9, left margin, boxed with Harrison logo opposite row 10
Marginal arrows: In centre at top and bottom of sheet
Colour register marks (crossed lines type):
No dot panes: Opposite rows 6/7 at both sides and cross in circle opposite row 2, left margin
Dot panes: Opposite rows 1/2 at both sides
Autotron marks: In same order as traffic lights in left margin opposite rows 4/7 on dot panes only
Perforation register marks: Thick bar opposite lower gutter perforations, right margin on no dot panes only
Sheet values: Above and below vertical rows 2/4 and 7/9 reading from left to right in top margin and from right to left (upside down) in bottom margin
Traffic lights (boxed): Opposite row 8 (15½p., 29p.) or rows 8/9 (others), right margin
15½p. Grey-black, bistre-yellow, bright purple, new blue, silver
19½p. Black, bistre-yellow, olive-bistre, deep claret, silver, deep bluish-green
26p. Grey-black, bistre-yellow, chrome-yellow, magenta, silver, pale blue
29p. Black, greenish yellow, bright carmine, new blue, silver

Quantities Sold   15½p. 38,353,600; 19½p. 7,957,400; 26p. 7,427,300; 29p. 7,093,400

Withdrawn   26.1.84

W517 Tropical
Island

W518 Desert

W519 Temperate
Farmland

W520 Mountain
Range

(Des. Donald Hamilton Fraser)

1983 (9 MARCH).   COMMONWEALTH DAY. GEOGRAPHICAL REGIONS

This issue marked Commonwealth Day on March 14. The designs symbolise the diversity of Commonwealth countries and the Queen's position as the head of the Commonwealth.

Phosphorised (fluorescent coated) paper

W541 (=S.G.1211)	**W517** 15½p.	greenish blue, greenish yellow, bright rose, light brown, grey-black, deep claret and silver	35	35
W542 (=S.G.1212)	**W518** 19½p.	bright lilac, greenish yellow, magenta, dull blue, grey-black, deep dull blue and silver	65	65
W543 (=S.G.1213)	**W519** 26p.	light blue, greenish yellow, bright magenta, new blue, grey-black, violet and silver	65	65
		a. Pale area in background	3·25	
W544 (=S.G.1214)	**W520** 29p.	dull violet-blue, reddish violet, slate lilac, new blue, myrtle green, black and silver	75	80
		a. Broken "4"	3·50	

First Day Cover (W541/44)	..	..	..	..	†	2·50
Presentation Pack (W541/44)	..	..	..	..	3·00	†
PHQ Cards (W541/44)	..	..	..	..	2·50	4·00

Listed Varieties

W543a	W544a
Pale area in	Broken "4"
background	(No dot. R. 3/9)
(Dot. R. 7/7)	

Cylinder Numbers (Blocks of Six)

	Cyl. Nos.	Perforation No dot	Type R* Dot
15½p.	2A (greenish blue)–1B (greenish yellow)–1C (bright rose)–1D (light brown)–1E (grey-black)–1F (deep claret)–1G (silver) ..	2·40	2·40
19½p.	1A (bright lilac)–1B (greenish yellow)–1C (magenta)–1D (dull blue)–1E (grey-black)–1F (deep dull blue)–1G (silver)	4·50	4·50
26p.	2A (light blue)–1B (greenish yellow)–1C (bright magenta)–1D (new blue)–1E (grey-black)–1F (violet)–1G (silver)	4·50	4·50
29p.	2A (dull violet-blue)–1B (reddish violet)–1C (slate-lilac)–1D (new blue)–2E (myrtle green)–2F (black)–1G (silver)	5·25	5·25

The above are with sheets orientated with head to left.

Sheet Details

Sheet size: 100 (2 panes 5 × 10). Double pane reel-fed

Sheet markings:
    Cylinder numbers: In top margin above vertical rows 2/3 boxed. Harrison logo above vertical row 1
    Marginal arrows: In centre, opposite rows 5/6 at both sides
    Colour register marks (crossed lines type):
      No dot panes: Above and below vertical rows 3/5 and cross in circle type above vertical row 9
      Dot panes: Above and below rows 8/10
    Autotron marks: In order of traffic lights reading from left to right above vertical rows 4/7 on dot panes only
    Perforation register marks: One short vertical line either side of first extension hole in top and bottom margins on both panes also thick bar below left gutter perforation row on no dot panes only
    Sheet values: Opposite rows 2/4 and 7/9 reading up at left and down at right
    Traffic lights (boxed): In bottom margin below vertical rows 2/3
      15½p.   Silver, deep claret, grey-black, light brown, greenish blue, bright rose, greenish yellow
      19½p.   Silver, deep dull blue, grey-black, magenta, dull blue, bright lilac, greenish yellow
      26p.   Silver, violet, grey-black, light blue, new blue, bright magenta, greenish yellow
      29p.   Silver, slate-lilac, black, myrtle green, new blue, dull violet-blue, reddish violet

Quantities Sold   15½p. 37,646,000; 19½p. 7,919,300; 26p. 7,385,900; 29p. 7,046,400

Withdrawn   9.3.84

W521 Humber Bridge

W522 Thames Flood
Barrier

W523 *Iolair* (oilfield
emergency support
vessel)

(Des. Michael Taylor)

1983 (25 MAY).   ENGINEERING ACHIEVEMENTS ("EUROPA")

The 1983 "Europa" theme was "Works of Human Genius" and this issue features notable British engineering achievements. The Humber Bridge, officially opened by the Queen in July 1981, has a span of 1,140 metres linking Hessle on the north bank with Barton-on-Humber on the south. The 20½p. shows the Thames Flood Barrier, one of the world's largest flood defence schemes. The support vessel for North Sea oil rigs *Iolair* (translated "Eagle" from Gaelic) was built by British Shipbuilders.

Phosphorised (fluorescent coated) paper

W545 (=S.G.1215)	**W521** 16p.	silver, orange-yellow, ultramarine, black and grey	50	45
	a.	Retouch on horizon	3·50	
W546 (=S.G.1216)	**W522** 20½p.	silver, greenish yellow, bright purple, blue, grey-black and grey	1·40	1·10
W547 (=S.G.1217)	**W523** 28p.	silver, lemon, bright rose-red, chestnut, dull ultramarine, black and grey	1·40	1·10

First Day Cover (W545/47)	..	..	†	2·50
Presentation Pack (W545/47)	..	..	3·25	†
PHQ Cards (W545/47)	..	..	2·50	3·75

Listed Variety

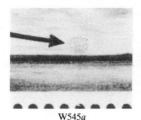

Retouch on horizon
(Dot. R. 1/2)

W545*a*

Cylinder Numbers (Blocks of Six)

	Perforation No dot	Type R* Dot
16p. 2A (silver)–1B (orange-yellow)–1C (ultramarine)–1D (black)– 1E (grey)	3·50	3·50
20½p. 3A (silver)–1B (greenish yellow)–2C (bright purple)–1D (blue)– 1E (grey-black)–1F (grey)	10·00	10·00
28p. 1A (silver)–1B (lemon)–2C (bright rose-red)–1D (chestnut)–2E (dull ultramarine)–1F (black)–1G (grey)	10·00	10·00

Sheet Details

Sheet size: 100 (2 panes 10 × 5). Double pane reel-fed

Sheet markings:
Cylinder numbers: Opposite rows 8/9, left margin, boxed with Harrison logo opposite row 10
Marginal arrows: In centre at top and bottom of sheet
Colour register marks (crossed lines type):
No dot panes: Opposite rows 6/8 (28p.) or 6/7 (others) at both sides and cross in circle opposite row 2, left margin
Dot panes: Opposite rows 1/2 at both sides
Autotron marks: In same order as traffic lights in left margin opposite rows 5/7 (16p.) or 4/7 (others) on dot panes only
Perforation register marks: Thick bar opposite lower gutter perforations, right margin on no dot panes only
Sheet values: Above and below vertical rows 2/4 and 7/9 reading from left to right in top margin and from right to left (upside down) in bottom margin
Traffic lights (boxed): Opposite row 9 (16p.) or rows 8/9 (others), right margin
16p. Orange-yellow, ultramarine, black, grey, silver
20½p. Greenish yellow, bright purple, blue, grey-black, grey, silver
28p. Lemon, bright rose-red, chestnut, dull ultramarine, black, grey, silver

Quantities Sold   16p. 39,498,300; 20½p. 8,365,000; 28p. 7,988,900

Withdrawn   25.5.84

W524 Musketeer
and Pikeman,
The Royal Scots
(1633)

W525 Fusilier and
Ensign, The Royal
Welch Fusiliers (mid-18th
century)

W526 Riflemen,
96th Rifles
(The Royal Green
Jackets) (1805)

W527 Sergeant
(khaki service
uniform) and
Guardsman (full
dress), The Irish
Guards (1900)
(Des. Eric Stemp)

W528 Paratroopers,
The Parachute Regiment
(1983)

1983 (6 JULY). BRITISH ARMY UNIFORMS

This issue commemorates the 350th anniversary of the raising of The Royal Scots, the senior infantry regiment of the line. The 16p. depicts a pikeman, forerunner of the Royal Scots, wearing the type of uniform designed to deflect musket balls. The redcoat shown on the 20½p. was chosen for distinction in the battlefield and was a synonym for the British soldier. In direct contrast to the redcoat are the green and khaki camouflage clothing shown on the other values. The designer, Eric Stemp, was also responsible for the stamps issued in 1979 commemorating Sir Rowland Hill.

Phosphorised (fluorescent coated) paper

W548 (=S.G.1218)	W524	16p.	black, buff, deep brown, slate-black, rose-red, gold and new blue	40	40
W549 (=S.G.1219)	W525	20½p.	black, buff, greenish yellow, slate-black, brown-rose, gold and bright blue	60	65
W550 (=S.G.1220)	W526	26p.	black, buff, slate-purple, green, bistre and gold	80	85
W551 (=S.G.1221)	W527	28p.	black, buff, light brown, grey, dull rose, gold and new blue	85	90
W552 (=S.G.1222)	W528	31p.	black, buff, olive-yellow, grey, deep magenta, gold, new blue	90	95

First Day Cover (W548/52)	..	..	..	..	†	3·25
Presentation Pack (W548/52)	..	..	..	..	4·25	†
PHQ Cards (W548/52) ..	..	..	..	..	3·75	5·00

Cylinder Numbers (Blocks of Six)

	Cyl. Nos.	Perforation No dot	Type R* Dot
16p.	1A (black)–1B (buff)–1C (deep brown)–1D (slate-black)–1E (rose-red)–1F (gold)–1G (new blue	2·75	2·75
20½p.	1A (black)–1B (buff)–1C (greenish yellow)–1D (slate-black)–2E (brown-rose)–1F (gold)–1G (bright blue)	4·25	4·25
26p.	1A (black)–1B (buff)–1C (slate-purple)–1D (green)–2E (bistre)–1F (gold)	5·50	5·50
28p.	1A (black)–1B (buff)–2C (light brown)–1D (grey)–3E (dull rose)–1F (gold)–1G (new blue)	6·00	6·00
31p.	1A (black)–1B (buff)–1C (olive-yellow)–1D (grey)–1E (deep magenta)–1F (gold)–1G (new blue)	6·50	6·50

The above are with sheets orientated with head to left.

Sheet Details

Sheet size: 100 (2 panes 5 × 10). Double pane reel-fed

Sheet markings:
Cylinder numbers: In top margin above vertical rows 2/3, boxed. Harrison logo above vertical row 1
Marginal arrows: In centre, opposite rows 5/6 at both sides
Colour register marks (crossed lines type):
No dot panes: Above and below vertical rows 3/4 (26p.) or 3/5 (others) and cross in circle above vertical row 9
Dot panes: Above and below vertical rows 9/10 (26p.) or 8/10 (others)
Autotron marks: In order of traffic lights reading from left to right above vertical rows 4/7 on dot panes only
Perforation register marks: Thick or thin bar below left gutter perforation row on dot panes only
Sheet values: Opposite rows 2/4 and 7/9 reading up at left and down at right
Traffic lights (boxed): In bottom margin below vertical rows 2/3
16p.   Gold, black, new blue, rose-red, slate-black, deep brown, buff
20½p.   Gold, black, bright blue, brown-rose, slate-black, greenish yellow, buff
26p.   Gold, black, bistre, green, slate-purple, buff
28p.   Gold, black, new blue, dull rose, grey, light brown, buff
31p.   Gold, black, new blue, deep magenta, grey, olive-yellow, buff

Quantities Sold   16p. 41,007,000; 20½p. 8,251,200; 26p. 10,235,400; 28p. 7,615,300; 31p. 7,323,700

Withdrawn   5.84

W529 20th-Century
Garden, Sissinghurst

W530 19th-Century
Garden, Biddulph Grange

W531 18th-Century
Garden, Blenheim

W532 17th-Century
Garden, Pitmedden

(Des. Liz Butler)
(Lithography by John Waddington Ltd.)

1983 (24 AUGUST). BRITISH GARDENS

This issue, featuring well known British gardens, also marked the bicentenary of the death of "Capability" Brown the landscape gardener. The garden shown on the 16p. was created by Vita Sackville-West and her husband, Sir Harold Nicolson after they purchased Sissinghurst Castle in 1930. The 20½p. shows the style of the formal garden which became popular in the 19th century. The pair of sphinx-style figures are placed at the entrance to a folly cottage. "Capability" Brown was responsible for landscaping the garden at Blenheim Palace where he widened the canal into a serpentine lake shown on the 28p. The 31p. depicts Pitmedden in Scotland, originally the work of Sir Alexander Seton. It is a fine example of a Tudor garden with formal water features and low-clipped hedges.

Phosphorised (fluorescent coated) paper. Comb perforation 14

W553 (=S.G.1223)	**W529** 16p.	greenish yellow, bright purple, new blue, black, bright green and silver	40 40
W554 (=S.G.1224)	**W530** 20½p.	greenish yellow, bright purple, new blue, black, bright green and silver	50 55
W555 (=S.G.1225)	**W531** 28p.	greenish yellow, bright purple, new blue, black, bright green and silver	80 90
W556 (=S.G.1226)	**W532** 31p.	greenish yellow, bright purple, new blue, black, bright green and silver	90 90

211

First Day Cover (W553/56)	..	..	..	..	†	2·75
Presentation Pack (W553/56)	..	..	..	..	3·50	†
PHQ Cards (W553/56) ..	..	..	..	..	2·50	4·00

Plate Numbers (Blocks of Six)

Colour order of plate nos. with sheets orientated head to left

All values. Greenish yellow, bright purple, new blue, black, bright green, silver

Plate Nos.					Perforation No dot	Type N† Dot
16p.	1A–1B–1C–1D–1E–1F	..	..	..	4·00	4·00
	1A–1B–1C–2D–1E–1F	..	..	..	10·00	10·00
	1A–1B–2C–2D–1E–1F	..	..	..	2·75	2·75
	1A–1B–2C–2D–1E–2F	..	..	..	5·00	5·00
20½p.	1A–1B–1C–1D–1E–1F	..	..	..	3·50	3·50
28p.	1A–1B–1C–1D–1E–1F	..	..	..	5·50	5·50
31p.	1A–1B–1C–1D–1E–1F	..	..	..	6·50	6·50

†The perforation characteristics of this perforator are as follows:

Vertical format stamps (bottom feed)

	Top margin	Bottom margin	Left margin	Right margin
No dot pane	Perforated through	Imperforate	Imperforate	Perforated through
Dot pane	Perforated through	Imperforate	Perforated through	Imperforate

The gutter margin is perforated through.

Sheet Details

Sheet size: 100 (2 panes 5 × 10). Double pane sheet-fed

Sheet Markings:
Plate numbers: Above vertical rows 2/3, top margin, boxed, with Waddington logo above vertical row 1
Marginal arrows: In centre, opposite rows 5/6 at both sides
Vertical positioning line: Printed in bright green
  No dot panes: Above and below vertical row 1
  Dot panes: Above and below vertical row 10
Sheet values: Opposite rows 2/4 and 7/9 reading up at left and down at right
Traffic lights: Below vertical row 2, bottom margin
  16p.   Silver, bright green, black, new blue, bright purple, greenish yellow
  20½p. Silver, bright green, black, new blue, bright purple, greenish yellow
  28p.   Silver, bright green, black, new blue, bright pruple, greenish yellow
  31p.   Silver, bright green, black, new blue, bright purple, greenish yellow

Quantities Sold   16p. 40,620,700; 20½p. 7,571,100; 28p. 7,062,100; 31p. 6,765,000

Withdrawn   23.8.84

W533 Merry-go-round

W534 Big Wheel,
Helter-skelter and
Performing Animals

W535 Side Shows   **W536** Early Produce Fair
(Des. Andrew Restall)

1983 (5 OCTOBER).   BRITISH FAIRS

The earliest record of fairs in Britain dates from Roman times. The 31p. depicts a typical scene showing livestock from one of the early fairs at which the local people would trade and barter their wares. The other values show the attractions of the modern fairground. The issue coincided with the 850th anniversary of St. Bartholomew's Fair which had to close in the mid 19th-century as it was felt that it was not in the public interest. The site of this once famous London fair is now Smithfield meat market.

Phosphorised (fluorescent coated) paper

W557 (=S.G.1227)	**W533** 16p.	grey-black, greenish yellow, orange-red, ochre and turquoise blue	40	40
W558 (=S.G.1228)	**W534** 20½p.	grey-black, yellow-ochre, yellow-orange, bright magenta, violet and black	50	55
	a.	Break in top of big wheel	2·75	
W559 (=S.G.1229)	**W535** 28p.	grey-black, bistre-yellow, orange-red, violet and yellow-brown	80	90
W560 (=S.G.1230)	**W536** 31p.	grey-black, greenish yellow, red, deep turquoise-green, slate-violet and brown	90	90

First Day Cover (W557/60)						†	2·75
Presentation Pack (W557/60)						3·50	†
PHQ Cards (W557/60)						2·50	4·00

Listed Variety

Break in top of big wheel
(Dot. R. 6/3)

W558*a*

213

Cylinder Numbers (Blocks of Six)

	Perforation	Type R*
Cyl. Nos.	No dot	Dot
16p. 1A (grey-black)–1B (greenish yellow)–1C (orange-red)–1D		
(ochre)–1E (turquoise-blue)	2·75	2·75
20½p. 1A (grey-black)–1B (yellow-ochre)–1C (yellow-orange)–1D		
(bright magenta)–1E (violet)–1F (black)	3·50	3·50
28p. 1A (grey-black)–1B (bistre-yellow)–1C (orange-red)–1D		
(violet)–1E (yellow-brown)	5·50	5·50
31p. 1A (grey-black)–1B (greenish yellow)–1C (red)–1D (deep		
turquoise-green)–1E (slate-violet)–1F (brown)	6·25	6·25

Sheet Details

Sheet size: 100 (2 panes 10 × 5). Double pane reel-fed

Sheet markings:
 Cylinder numbers: Opposite rows 8/9, left margin, boxed with Harrison logo opposite row 10
 Marginal arrows: In centre at top and bottom of sheet
 Colour register marks (crossed lines type):
  No dot panes: Opposite rows 7/8 at both sides and cross in circle opposite row 2, left margin
  Dot panes: Opposite rows 2/3 at both sides
 Autotron marks: In same order as traffic lights in left margin opposite rows 4/6 (16p., 28p.) or 4/7
  (others) on dot panes only
 Perforation register marks: Thin bar opposite lower gutter perforations, right margin on no dot
  panes only
 Sheet values: Above and below vertical rows 2/4 and 7/9 reading from left to right in top margin
  and from right to left (upside down) in bottom margin
 Traffic lights (boxed): Opposite row 9 (16p., 28p.) or rows 8/9 (others), right margin
  16p. Greenish yellow, orange-red, ochre, turquoise-blue, grey-black
  20½p. Yellow-ochre, yellow-orange, bright magenta, violet, black, grey-black
  28p. Bistre-yellow, orange-red, violet, grey-black, yellow-brown
  31p. Greenish-yellow, red, deep turquoise-green, slate-violet, brown, grey-black

Quantities Sold 16p. 38,000,300; 20½p. 7,938,600; 28p. 7,442,000; 31p. 7,113,400

Withdrawn 4.10.84

W537 "Christmas Post"
(pillar-box)

W538 "The Three Kings"
(chimney pots)

W539 "World at Peace"
(Dove and Blackbird)

W540 "Light of Christmas"
(street lamp)

W541 "Christmas Dove"
(hedge sculpture)

(Des. Tony Meeuwissen)

1983 (16 NOVEMBER).   CHRISTMAS

Each design includes a dove to symbolise the theme of "Peace on Earth".

One 4mm. phosphor band at left

W561 (=S.G.1231) W537 12½p. black, greenish yellow, bright rose-red, bright blue, gold and grey-black	30	30
a. Imperforate (horiz. pair)	£750	

Phosphorised (advanced coated) paper

W562 (=S.G.1232) W538 16p. black, greenish yellow, bright rose, pale new blue, gold and brown-purple	45	45
a. Imperforate (pair)	£850	
b. Imperforate between stamp and bottom margin ..	£450	

Phosphorised (fluorescent coated) paper

W563 (=S.G.1233) W539 20½p. black, greenish yellow, bright rose, new blue, gold and blue	60	60
a. Curved line from umbrella to blackbird's claw ..	5·00	
W564 (=S.G.1234) W540 28p. black, lemon, bright carmine, bluish violet, gold, deep turquoise-green and purple	90	90

W565 (=S.G.1235) **W541** 31p. black, greenish yellow, bright rose, new blue, gold,
green and brown-olive   95   90
     a. Large snowflake   ..   ..   3·25
     b. Missing left wing   ..   ..   3·50

First Day Cover (W561/5)	†	2·75
Presentation Pack (W561/5) ..	3·50	†
PHQ Cards (W561/5)	3·00	4·50

Listed Varieties

 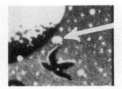 

W563*a*   W565*a*   W565*b*
Curved line from   Large snowflake   Missing left wing
umbrella to   (Dot. R. 1/1)   (Dot. R. 9/4)
blackbird's claw
(No Dot. R. 3/9)

Cylinder Numbers (Blocks of Six)

	Cyl. Nos.	Perforation No dot	Type R* Dot

One 4mm. phosphor band at left

12½p. 1A (black)–1B (greenish yellow)–1C (bright rose-red)–1D
(bright blue)–1E (gold)–1F (grey-black)–P78 (phosphor) ..   2·10   2·10
      1A (black)–1B (greenish yellow)–1C (bright rose-red)–1D (bright
blue)–2E (gold)–1F (grey-black)–P78 (phosphor) .   ..   ..   10·00   10·00
      1A (black)–1B (greenish yellow)–2C (bright rose-red)–1D
(bright blue)–1E (gold)–1F (grey-black)–P78 (phosphor) ..   5·00   5·00

Phosphorised paper

16p. 1A (black)–1B (greenish yellow)–1C (bright rose)–3D (pale new
blue)–1E (gold)–1F (brown-purple)   ..   ..   3·25   3·25
20½p. 1A (black)–1B (greenish yellow)–1C (bright rose)–2D (new
blue)–1E (gold)–1F (blue) ..   ..   4·25   4·25
28p. 2A (black)–1B (lemon)–3C (bright carmine)–1D (bluish violet)–
1E (gold)–1F (deep turquoise-green)–1G (purple)   ..   ..   6·25   6·25
31p. 2A (black)–1B (greenish yellow)–1C (bright rose)–1D (new
blue)–1E (gold)–1F (green)–1G (brown-olive) ..   ..   ..   6·50   6·50

Sheet Details

Sheet size: 100 (2 panes 10 × 5). Double pane reel-fed

Sheet markings:
   Cylinder numbers: Opposite rows 8/9, left margin, boxed with Harrison logo opposite row 10
   Marginal arrows: In centre at top and bottom of sheet
   Colour register marks (crossed lines type):
     No dot panes: Opposite rows 6/8 (28p., 31p.) or 7/8 (others) at both sides and cross in circle
     opposite row 2, left margin
     Dot panes: Opposite rows 1/3 (28p., 31p.) or 2/3 (others) at both sides
   Autotron marks: In same order as traffic lights in left margin opposite rows 4/7 on dot panes only
   Perforation register marks: Thin bar opposite lower gutter perforations, right margin on no dot
   panes only
   Sheet values: Above and below vertical rows 2/4 and 7/9 reading from left to right in top margin
   and from right to left (upside down) in bottom margin

Traffic lights (boxed): Opposite rows 8/9, right margin
12½p. Greenish yellow, bright rose-red, bright blue, black, grey-black, gold
16p. Greenish yellow, bright rose, pale new blue, brown-purple, black, gold
20½p. Greenish yellow, bright rose, new blue, black, blue, gold
28p. Lemon, bright carmine, bluish violet, black, deep turquoise-green, purple, gold
31p. Greenish yellow, bright rose, new blue, black, green, brown-olive, gold

Quantities Sold   12½p. 289,209,100; 16p. 150,863,200; 20½p. 16,798,600; 28p. 15,709,200; 31p. 13,985,900

Withdrawn   15.11.84

1983 (16 NOVEMBER).   COLLECTORS PACK 1983
WCP16 Comprises Nos. W537/65 (Sold at £7.25)   38·00

Withdrawn   15.11.84

W542 Arms of the College of Arms

W543 Arms of King Richard III

W544 Arms of the Earl Marshal of England

W545 Arms of the City of London

(Des. Jeffery Matthews)

1984 (17 JANUARY). HERALDRY

The College of Arms was founded by Richard III in the City of London where it still functions. This issue marked the 500th anniversary of the College which deals with heraldry, ceremonial peerage law and succession to titles. The 28p. features the arms of the Earl Marshal who presides over the College's officers-of-arms.

These stamps were the first to be issued by the Post Office in a square format.

Phosphorised (fluorescent coated) paper. Comb perforation 14½

W566 (=S.G.1236)	W542 16p.	black, chrome-yellow, reddish brown, scarlet-vermilion, bright blue and grey-black	40 40
W567 (=S.G.1237)	W543 20½p.	black, chrome-yellow, rosine, bright blue and grey-black	60 70
W568 (=S.G.1238)	W544 28p.	black, chrome-yellow, brown, rosine, bright blue, dull green and grey-black	80 90
W569 (=S.G.1239)	W545 31p.	black, chrome-yellow, rosine, bright blue and grey-black	85 90

First Day Cover (W566/9)	†	2·75
Presentation Pack (W566/9)	3·50	†
PHQ Cards (W566/9)	2·50	5·00

Cylinder Numbers (Blocks of Six)

Cyl. Nos.	Perforation No dot	Type R* Dot
16p. 1A (black)–1B (chrome-yellow)–1C (reddish brown)–2D (scarlet-vermilion)–1E (bright blue)–3F (grey-black)	2·75	2·75
20½p. 1A (black)–1B (chrome-yellow)–1C (rosine)–1D (bright blue)–3E (grey-black)	4·25	4·25
28p. 1A (black)–2B (chrome-yellow)–1C (brown)–1D (rosine)–1E (bright blue)–1F (dull green)–1G (grey-black)	5·75	5·75
1A (black)–2B (chrome-yellow)–1C (brown)–1D (rosine)–1E (bright blue)–1F (dull green)–3G (grey-black)	5·50	5·50
31p. 1A (black)–1B (chrome-yellow)–1C (rosine)–1D (bright blue)–2E (grey-black)	6·00	6·00

Sheet Details

Sheet size: 100 (2 panes 5 × 10). Double pane reel-fed

Sheet markings:
Cylinder numbers: Opposite rows 8/9 (16p., 28p.) or 9 (others), left margin, boxed with Harrison logo opposite row 10
Marginal arrows: In gutter margin opposite rows 5/6
Colour register marks (crossed lines type):
No dot panes: At both sides opposite rows 7/8 (16p., 20½p.), 6/8 (28p.) or 7 (31p.) and cross in circle (trimmed) in top left margin
Dot panes: At both sides opposite rows 2/3 (16p., 20½p.), 1/3 (28p.) or 2 (31p.) and cross in circle (trimmed) at bottom left margin
Autotron marks: In same order as traffic lights in left margin opposite rows 4/7 on dot panes only. Usually solid colour the 28p. dull green marking was hand engraved with close diagonal lines opposite row 7
Perforation register marks: Thin bar in right margin opposite first perforation row on no dot panes only
Sheet values: Above and below vertical rows 2/4 and 7/9 reading from left to right in top margin and from right to left (upside down) in bottom margin
Traffic lights (boxed): Opposite rows 8/9 (28p.) or 9 (others); right margin
16p. Chrome-yellow, reddish brown, scarlet-vermilion, bright blue, grey-black, black
20½p. Chrome-yellow, rosine, bright blue, grey-black, black
28p. Chrome-yellow, brown, rosine, bright blue, dull green, grey-black, black
31p. Chrome-yellow, rosine, bright blue, grey-black, black

Quantities Sold. 16p. 37,716,800; 20½p. 7,550,300; 28p. 6,895,500; 31p. 6,615,300

Withdrawn 16.1.85

W546 Highland Cow

W547 Chillingham Wild Bull

W548 Hereford Bull

W549 Welsh Black Bull

W550 Irish Moiled Cow

(Des. Barry Driscoll)

1984 (6 MARCH).   BRITISH CATTLE

This issue coincided with the centenary of the Highland Cattle Society and the bicentenary of the Royal Highland and Agricultural Society of Scotland, which organised the first Royal Highland Show in 1822 at Edinburgh. The 16p. shows the Highland Cow which can withstand severe weather conditions. It is an international breed famed for hardiness and adaptability. The 20½p. features the Chillingham Bull, a wild species which have remained uncrossed with domestic cattle. It has been in Chillingham Park, Northumberland, for over 700 years. In contrast the world famous Hereford is a direct result of selective breeding (26p.). The Welsh Black, known in Wales since the Celtic period, is able to survive in difficult conditions. The 31p. shows the Irish Moiled Cow which takes its name from the Irish word "Mael" meaning hornless.

Phosphorised (fluorescent coated)) paper

W570 (=S.G.1240)	**W546**	16p.	grey-black, bistre-yellow, rosine, yellow-orange, new blue and pale drab	40	40
W571 (=S.G.1241)	**W547**	20½p.	grey-black, greenish yellow, magenta, bistre, dull blue-green, pale drab and light green	65	65
W572 (=S.G.1242)	**W548**	26p.	black, chrome-yellow, rosine, reddish brown, new blue and pale drab	70	65
W573 (=S.G.1243)	**W549**	28p.	black, greenish yellow, bright carmine, orange-brown, deep dull blue and pale drab	85	85

W574 (=S.G.1244)   **W550**   31p.   grey-black, bistre-yellow, rosine, red-brown, light
blue and pale drab   90   90

First Day Cover (W570/4) .. .. †	3·25
Presentation Pack (W570/4) .. .. 4·00	†
PHQ Cards (W570/4) .. .. 3·00	5·00

The 28p. value is known postmarked 3 March 1984 at Ludlow, Salop.

Miscut Pane. Part of the printing of the 16p. had the sheets miscut so that the bottom pane
appeared at the top and vice versa. See under General Notes (page 7). (*Price for gutter pair showing
sheet margin inscription* £60).

Cylinder Numbers (Blocks of Six)

	Cyl. Nos.	Perforation No dot	Type R* Dot
16p.	1A (grey-black)–1B (bistre-yellow)–1C (rosine)–1D (yellow-orange)–1E (new blue)–1F (pale drab)	2·75	2·75
20½p.	3A (grey-black)–1B (greenish yellow)–2C (magenta)–1D (bistre)–1E (dull blue-green)–1F (pale drab)–1G (light green) ..	4·50	4·50
26p.	1A (black)–1B (chrome-yellow)–3C (rosine)–1D (reddish brown)–2E (new blue)–1F (pale drab)	5·00	5·00
28p.	3A (black)–2B (greenish yellow)–1C (bright carmine)–2D (orange-brown)–2E (deep dull blue)–1F (pale drab)	6·00	6·00
31p.	3A (grey-black)–2B (bistre-yellow)–2C (rosine)–2D (red-brown)–2E (light blue)—1F (pale drab)	6·50	6·50

Sheet Details

Sheet size: 100 (2 panes 10 × 5). Double pane reel-fed

Sheet markings:
   Cylinder numbers: Opposite row 8/9, left margin, boxed with Harrison logo opposite row 10
   Marginal arrows: In centre at top and bottom of sheet
   Colour register marks (crossed lines type):
      No dot panes: Opposite rows 7/8 at both sides and cross in circle opposite row 2, left margin
      Dot panes: Opposite rows 1/3 (20½p.) or 2/3 (others) at both sides
   Autotron marks: In same order as traffic lights in left margin opposite rows 4/7 on dot panes only
   Perforation register marks: Thin bar opposite lower gutter perforations, right margin on no dot
      panes only
   Sheet values: Above and below vertical rows 2/4 and 7/9 reading from left to right in top margin
      and from right to left (upside down) in bottom margin
   Traffic lights (boxed): Opposite rows 8/9, right margin
      16p.   Bistre-yellow, rosine, yellow-orange, new blue, grey-black, pale drab
      20½p. Greenish yellow, magenta, bistre, dull blue-green, light green, grey-black, pale drab
      26p.   Chrome-yellow, rosine, reddish brown, new blue, black, pale drab
      28p.   Greenish yellow, bright carmine, orange-brown, deep dull blue, black, pale drab
      31p.   Bistre-yellow, rosine, red-brown, light blue, grey-black, pale drab

Quantities Sold   16p. 36,572,900; 20½p. 7,211,300; 26p. 6,729,400; 28p. 6,626,300; 31p. 6,356,800

Withdrawn 5.3.85

W551 Garden Festival Hall,
Liverpool

W552 Milburngate
Centre, Durham

W553 Bush House,
Bristol

W554 Commercial Street
Development, Perth

(Des. Ronald Maddox and Trickett and Webb Ltd.)

1984 (10 APRIL).   URBAN RENEWAL

This issue coincided with the 150th anniversaries of the Royal Institute of British Architects and of the Chartered Institute of Building. The 16p. commemorated the opening of the Festival Hall in Liverpool which was the venue of the first International Gardens Festival in Britain. The 20½p. features a shopping centre and older buildings on the banks of the River Wear in Durham. A renovated area of derelict dockland became the site of Bush House and the Arnolfini Arts Centre shown on the 28p. The 31p. shows houses built at different heights and angles to resemble the traditional style on the bank of the River Tay in Perth.

Phosphorised (fluorescent coated) paper

W575 (=S.G.1245)	**W551** 16p.	bright emerald, greenish yellow, cerise, steel blue, black, silver and flesh ..	..	40	40
		a. Spot on lawn ..	..	2·25	
W576 (=S.G.1246)	**W552** 20½p.	bright orange, greenish yellow, deep dull blue, yellowish green, azure, black and silver ..	..	65	60
		a. Imperforate (horiz. pair) ..	..	£1000	
W577 (=S.G.1247)	**W553** 28p.	rosine, greenish yellow, Prussian blue, pale blue-green, black and silver	..	85	85
W578 (=S.G.1248)	**W554** 31p.	blue, greenish yellow, cerise, grey-blue, bright green, black and silver ..	..	90	90
		a. Imperforate (vert. pair) ..	..	£1000	
		b. Retouch on side window ..	..	3·00	

First Day Cover (W575/8)	..	†	2·90
Presentation Pack (W575/8)	..	3·25	†
PHQ Cards (W575/8)	..	2·50	4·25

Miscut Pane. Part of the printing of the 28p. had the sheets miscut so that the bottom pane appeared at the top and vice versa. See under General Notes (page 7). (*Price for gutter pair showing sheet margin inscription* £20).

221

Listed Varieties

W575a
Spot on lawn
(Dot. R. 3/1)

W578b
Retouch on side window
(Dot. R. 2/10)

Cylinder Numbers (Blocks of Six)

	Cyl. Nos.	Perforation No dot	Type R* Dot
16p.	1A (bright emerald)–1B (greenish yellow)–1C (cerise)–1D (steel blue)–1E (black)–1F (silver)–1G (flesh)	2·75	2·75
20½p.	1A (bright orange)–1B (greenish yellow)–1C (deep dull blue)–1D (yellowish green)–1E (azure)–1F (black)–1G (silver)	4·50	4·50
28p.	2A (rosine)–1B (greenish yellow)–2C (Prussian blue)–2D (pale blue-green)–2E (black)–1F (silver)	6·00	6·00
31p.	1A (blue)–1B (greenish yellow)–1C (cerise)–1D (grey-blue)–1E (bright green)–1F (black)–1G (silver)	6·50	6·50

Sheet Details

Sheet size: 100 (2 panes 10 × 5). Double pane reel-fed

Sheet markings:
Cylinder numbers: Opposite rows 8/9, left margin, boxed with Harrison logo opposite row 10
Marginal arrows: In centre at top and bottom of sheet
Colour register marks (crossed lines type):
  No dot panes: Opposite rows 7/8 (28p.) or rows 6/8 (others) at both sides and cross in circle opposite row 2, left margin
  Dot panes: Opposite rows 2/3 (28p.) or rows 1/3 (others) at both sides
Autotron marks: In same order as traffic lights in left margin opposite rows 4/7 on dot panes only
Perforation register marks: Thin bar opposite lower gutter perforations, right margin on no dot panes only
Sheet values: Above and below vertical rows 2/4 and 7/9 reading from left to right in top margin and from right to left (upside down) in bottom margin
Traffic lights (boxed):Opposite rows 8/9, right margin
  16p.   Greenish yellow, cerise, steel blue, bright emerald, flesh, black, silver
  20½p. Greenish yellow, bright orange, deep dull blue, yellowish green, azure, black, silver
  28p.   Greenish yellow, rosine, Prussian blue, pale blue-green, black, silver
  31p.   Greenish yellow, cerise, grey-blue, bright green, blue, black, silver

Quantities Sold   16p. 37,237,000; 20½p. 6,998,600; 28p. 6,507,500; 31p. 6,177,600

Withdrawn   10.4.85

W555 C.E.P.T. 25th
Anniversary Logo
(Des. Jacky Larriviere)

W556 Abduction of Europa
(Des. Fritz Wegner)

Types **W555/6** were printed horizontally *se-tenant* within the sheet

1984 (15 MAY).   "EUROPA"

This issue commemorated the 25th anniversary of the Conference of European Posts and Telecommunications and the holding of the second direct elections to the European Parliament. Type **W556** shows the god Zeus who took the form of a bull to abduct Europa, daughter of the King of Tyre. He carried her to the Island of Crete where Zeus resumed human form and later she gave birth to their son, Minos. The Minoan civilisation is historically associated with the beginning of European culture.

Phosphorised (fluorescent coated) paper

W579 (=S.G.1249)	**W555** 16p.	greenish slate, deep blue and gold	..	..	40	40
		a. Pair. Nos. W579/80 ..	.. .. ..	..	90	1·00
W580 (=S.G.1250)	**W556** 16p.	greenish slate, deep blue, black and gold		..	40	40
W581 (=S.G.1251)	**W555** 20½p.	Venetian red, deep magenta and gold	..		55	60
		a. Pair. Nos. W581/2 ..	.. ..	..	1·25	1·40
W582 (=S.G.1252)	**W556** 20½p.	Venetian red, deep magenta, black and gold		..	55	60

First Day Cover (W579/82)	..	..	..	†	2·25
Presentation Pack (W579/82)	..	..	..	2·90	†
PHQ Cards (W579/82)	..	..	..	2·50	4·25

Cylinder Numbers (Blocks of Four)

Cyl. Nos.	Perforation Type R*	
	No dot	Dot
16p. 1A (greenish slate)–2B (deep blue)–1C (black)–1D (gold) ..	2·25	2·25
20½p. 3A (Venetian red)–2B (deep magenta)–1C (black)–1D (gold) ..	3·25	3·25

Sheet Details

Sheet size: 100 (2 panes 10 × 5). Double pane reel-fed

Sheet markings:
Cylinder numbers: Opposite row 9, left margin, boxed with Harrison logo opposite row 10
Marginal arrows: In centre at top and bottom of sheet
Colour register marks (crossed lines type):
   No dot panes: Opposite rows 7/8 at both sides and cross in circle opposite row 2, left margin
   Dot panes: Opposite row 2 at both sides
Autotron marks: In same order as traffic lights in left margin opposite gutter margin and rows 6/7 on dot panes only
Perforation register marks: Thin bar opposite lower gutter perforations, right margin on no dot panes only
Sheet values: Above and below vertical rows 2/4 and 7/9 reading from left to right in top margin and from right to left (upside down) in bottom margin
Traffic lights (boxed): Opposite row 9, right margin
   16p. Greenish slate, deep blue, black, gold
   20½p. Venetian red, deep magenta, black, gold

W   1984.   London Economic Summit Conference

Quantities Sold   16p. 45,236,300 pairs; 20½p. 10,679,200 pairs
Withdrawn   14.5.85

W557 Lancaster House
(Des. Paul Hogarth)

1984 (5 JUNE).   LONDON ECONOMIC SUMMIT CONFERENCE

The summit conference was held at Lancaster House from 7 to 9 June. It was the first occasion since 1977 that the conference had been held in London. Flags of the seven participating nations are shown on the stamp.

Phosphorised (fluorescent coated) paper

W583 (=S.G.1253)   **W557** 31p.   black, reddish lilac, bistre-yellow, brown-ochre, rosine, bright blue and silver   80   85

First Day Cover (W583) .. .. † 2·00		
PHQ Card (W583) .. .. 50 1·50		

Cylinder Numbers (Blocks of Six)

	Cyl. Nos.	Perforation No dot	Type R* Dot
31p. 1A (silver)–1B (bistre-yellow)–1C (brown-ochre)–1D (black)– 1E (rosine)–1F (bright blue)–1G (reddish lilac)		5·50	5·50

The above are with sheets orientated with head to left.

Sheet Details

Sheet size: 100 (2 panes 5 × 10). Double pane reel-fed

Sheet markings:
  Cylinder numbers: In top margin above vertical rows 2/3, boxed. Harrison logo above vertical row 1
  Marginal arrows: In centre, opposite rows 5/6 at both sides
  Colour register marks (crossed lines type):
    No dot pane: Above and below vertical rows 3/4 and cross in circle type above vertical row 9
    Dot pane: Above and below rows 8/10
  Autotron marks: In order of traffic lights reading from left to right above vertical rows 4/7 on dot pane only
  Perforation register marks: Thin bar below left gutter perforation row on dot pane only
  Sheet values: Opposite rows 2/4 and 7/9 reading up at left and down at right
  Traffic lights (boxed): In bottom margin below vertical rows 2/3
    31p. Silver, reddish lilac, bright blue, rosine, black, brown-ochre and bistre-yellow

Quantity Sold   31p. 8,145,600

Withdrawn   4.6.85

W558 View of Earth from "Apollo 11"

W559 Navigational Chart of English Channel

W560 Greenwich Observatory

W561 Sir George Airy's Transit Telescope

(Des. Howard Waller)

(Lithography by The House of Questa)

1984 (26 JUNE). CENTENARY OF GREENWICH MERIDIAN

This issue commemorates the centenary of Greenwich Mean Time (GMT), officially recognised at an international conference held in Washington. Since 1880 GMT had been the legal standard in Britain, but other countries had their own systems. The conference, attended by delegates from 25 countries, accepted the Greenwich meridian line and this became the zero of longitude. The telescope shown on the 31p. was installed in the Royal Observatory in 1850. It was designed by the Astronomer Royal, Sir George Airy and it was regularly used until 1954 to make accurate observations of the solar system.

Phosphorised (fluorescent coated) paper. Comb perforation $14 \times 14\frac{1}{2}$

W584 (=S.G.1254)	**W558**	16p.	new blue, greenish yellow, magenta, black, scarlet and blue-black	40	40
W585 (=S.G.1255)	**W559**	20½p.	olive-sepia, light brown, pale buff, black and scarlet..	60	60
W586 (=S.G.1256)	**W560**	28p.	new blue, greenish yellow, scarlet, black and bright purple..	90	80
W587 (=S.G.1257)	**W561**	31p.	deep blue, cobalt, scarlet and black	95	90

First Day Cover (W584/7)	..	..	..	..	†	2·50
Presentation Pack (W584/7)	..	..	..	..	3·25	†
PHQ Cards (W584/7)	..	..	..	..	2·50	5·50

Plate Numbers (Blocks of Six)

Colour order of plate nos. following the Questa imprint:

16p. New blue, greenish yellow, magenta, black, scarlet, blue-black
20½p. Olive-sepia, light brown, pale buff, black, scarlet
28p. New blue, greenish yellow, scarlet, black, bright purple
31p. Deep blue, cobalt, scarlet, black

	Plate Nos. (all No dot)						Perforation Type M
16p.	1A (×6)	..	..	..	..	..	3·25
	1B (×6)	..	..	..	..	..	3·25
	1A–1A–1A–2A–1A–1A	..	..	..	..	10·00
	1B–1B–1B–2B–1B–1B	..	..	..	..	3·50
	2A–2A–2A–3A–2A–2A	..	..	..	..	3·50
	2B–2B–2B–3B–2B–2B	..	..	..	..	3·50
	2A–2A–3A–3A–2A–2A	..	..	..	..	5·00
	2B–2B–3B–3B–2B–2B	..	..	..	..	10·00
	2A–2A–3A–3A–2A–3A	..	..	..	..	2·75
	2B–2B–3B–3B–2B–3B	..	..	..	..	2·75
20½p.	1A (×5)	..	..	..	..	..	4·25
	1B (×5)	..	..	..	..	..	4·25
28p.	1A (×5)	..	..	..	..	..	6·25
	1B (×5)	..	..	..	..	..	6·25
31p.	1A (×4)	..	..	..	..	..	6·50
	1B (×4)	..	..	..	..	..	6·50

Sheet Details

Sheet size: 100 (2 panes 5 × 10). Double pane sheets with "A" and "B" plate numbers

Sheet markings:
Plate numbers: In top margin above vertical rows 2/3
Marginal arrows: "W" shaped in centre, opposite rows 5/6 at both sides
Sheet values: Opposite rows 2/4 and 7/9 reading up at left and down at right
Imprint: In top margin above vertical rows 1/2
Traffic lights: In the form of Questa logo below vertical row 2, bottom margin
For order of colours see under "Plate Numbers" above

Quantities Sold   16p. 36,238,700; 20½p. 7,066,100; 28p. 6,485,600; 31p. 6,189,200

Withdrawn   25.6.85

W562 Bath Mail Coach, 1784

W563 Attack on Exeter
Mail, 1816

W564 Norwich Mail in
Thunderstorm, 1827

W565 Holyhead and Liverpool
Mails leaving London, 1828

W566 Edinburgh Mail
Snowbound, 1831

The above were printed together, *se-tenant*, in horizontal strips of 5 throughout the sheet

(Des. Keith Bassford and Stanley Paine. Eng. Czeslaw Slania)

(Recess printed in black with Queen's head, value and background tint printed in photogravure)

1984 (31 JULY).   THE ROYAL MAIL

This issue marked the bicentenary of the first mail coach run from Bath and Bristol to London. The first run took place on 2 August 1784 and was the idea of John Palmer, manager of theatres in Bath and Bristol. The mail was protected on its journey by an armed guard being the only Post Office employee on board the mail coach. The quicker service offered by the railways had, by 1846, replaced the era of the horse-drawn mail coach.

Phosphorised (fluorescent coated) paper

W588 (=S.G.1258)	W562	16p. pale stone, black, grey-black and bright scarlet ..	40	40
		a. Strip of 5. Nos. W588/92	2·25	2·25
W589 (=S.G.1259)	W563	16p. pale stone, black, grey-black and bright scarlet ..	40	40
W590 (=S.G.1260)	W564	16p. pale stone, black, grey-black and bright scarlet ..	40	40
W591 (=S.G.1261)	W565	16p. pale stone, black, grey-black and bright scarlet ..	40	40
W592 (=S.G.1262)	W566	16p. pale stone, black, grey-black and bright scarlet ..	40	40

227

First Day Cover (W588/92)	..	..	..	..	†	2·25
Presentation Pack (W588/92)	..	..	..	..	3·00	†
Souvenir Book (W588/92) (Sold at £1.50)		..	..	5·50	†
PHQ Cards (W588/92) ..	..	..	..	..	3·00	4·00

The souvenir book is a 24-page illustrated booklet with a set of mint stamps in a sachet attached to the front cover.

Cylinder Numbers (Blocks of Ten)

	Cyl. Nos.	Perforation Type R*
		No dot Dot
16p. 1A (grey-black)–1B (bright scarlet)	.. ..	5·00 5·00

Sheet Details

Sheet size: 100 (2 panes 10 × 5). Double pane reel-fed

Sheet markings:
Cylinder numbers: Opposite row 9, left margin, boxed with Harrison logo opposite row 10
Marginal arrows: In centre at top and bottom of sheet
Colour register marks (crossed lines type):
No dot panes: Opposite row 7 at both sides and cross in circle opposite row 2, left margin
Dot panes: Opposite row 2 at both sides
Autotron marks: In same order as traffic lights in left margin opposite central gutter margin and row 6 on dot panes only
Additional horizontal bars: Grey-black photogravure bar in gutter margin, vertical row 4 on no dot pane. Recess printed bar in black with up to six guide dots to right on both panes in gutter margin and either top or bottom margin between vertical rows 4/5. The bar and marker dots at either the top or bottom of the pane may occur trimmed. The dots were used to identify individual panes
Perforation register marks: Thin bar opposite lower gutter perforations, right margin on no dot panes only
Sheet values: Above and below vertical rows 2/4 and 7/9 reading from left to right in top margin and from right to left (upside-down) in bottom margin
Traffic lights (boxed): Opposite row 9, right margin
16p. Bright scarlet, grey-black

Quantities Sold   16p. 12,130,540 of each design

Withdrawn   30.7.85

W567 Nigerian Clinic

W568 Violinist and Acropolis,
Athens

W569 Building Project,
Sri Lanka

W570 British Council Library,
Middle East

(Des. Newell and Sorrell Design Ltd.)

1984 (25 SEPTEMBER).   50th ANNIVERSARY OF THE BRITISH COUNCIL

This issue marked the 50th anniversary of the British Council. The aim of the Council is to promote in overseas countries an understanding of Britian, by means of cultural exchanges. The 17p. shows the theme of education for development and the 22p. illustrates promotion of the arts with the score of Sir Michael Tippett's, "The Midsummer Marriage" as a background to the design. A British training manual forms the background of the 31p. and the 34p. shows the work of the Council in promoting British books in overseas library services. The background is an extract from the Oxford English Dictionary.

Phosphorised (advanced coated) paper

W593 (=S.G.1263)   W567 17p. grey-green, greenish yellow, bright purple, dull
blue, black, pale green, and yellow-green   40   40

Phosphorised (fluorescent coated) paper

W594 (=S.G.1264)   W568 22p. crimson, greenish yellow, bright rose-red, dull
green, black, pale drab and slate-purple   60   65
  a. Black screening omitted from violin chin-rest   ..   3·00
W595 (=S.G.1265)   W569 31p. sepia, olive-bistre, red, black, pale stone and
olive-brown   90   1·00
W596 (=S.G.1266)   W570 34p. steel blue, yellow, rose-red, new blue, black, azure
and pale blue   95   1·00

First Day Cover (W593/6)	..	..	..	..	†	2·75
Presentation Pack (W593/6)	..	..	..	..	3·50	†
PHQ Cards (W593/6)	..	..	..	..	2·50	4·00

The 17p value exists postmarked 7 September 1984 in London.

W   1984.   British Council

Listed Variety

Black screening omitted
from violin chin-rest
(Dot. R. 3/5)

Normal   W594*a*

Cylinder Numbers (Blocks of Six)

	Cyl. Nos.	Perforation No dot	Type R* Dot
17p.	1A (grey-green)–1B (greenish yellow)–1C (bright purple)–3D (dull blue)–1E (black)–1F (pale green)–1G (yellow-green) ..	2·75	2·75
22p.	1A (crimson)–1B (greenish yellow)–2C (bright rose-red)–1D (dull green)–2E (black)–1F (pale drab)–1G (slate-purple) ..	4·25	4·25
31p.	1A (sepia)–1B (olive-bistre)–1C (red)–1D (black)–1E (pale stone)–1F (olive-brown)	6·25	6·25
34p.	1A (steel blue)–1B (yellow)–1C (rose-red)–1D (new blue)–1E (black)–1F (azure)–1G (pale blue)	6·50	6·50

Sheet Details

Sheet Size: 100 (2 panes 10 × 5). Double pane reel-fed

Sheet markings:
Cylinder numbers: Opposite rows 8/9, left margin, boxed with Harrison logo opposite row 10
Marginal arrows: In centre at top and bottom of sheet
Colour register marks (crossed lines type):
No dot panes: Opposite rows 7/8 at both sides and cross in circle opposite row 2, left margin
Dot panes: Opposite rows 2/3 at both sides
Autotron marks: In same order as traffic lights in left margin opposite rows 4/7 on dot panes only
Perforation register marks: Thin bar opposite first row and lower gutter perforation, right margin,
on both panes
Sheet values: Above and below vertical rows 2/4 and 7/9 reading from left to right in top margin
and from right to left (upside down) in bottom margin
Traffic lights (boxed): Opposite rows 8/9, right margin
17p. Greenish yellow, bright purple, dull blue, black, pale green, yellow-green, grey-green
22p. Greenish yellow, bright rose-red, dull green, black, pale drab, slate-purple, crimson
31p. Olive-bistre, red, black, pale stone, olive-brown, sepia
34p. Yellow, rose-red, new blue, black, pale blue, azure, steel blue

Quantities Sold   17p. 36,543,700; 22p. 7,882,400; 31p. 7,339,800; 34p. 7,036,500

Withdrawn   24.9.85

230

W571 "Holy Family"

W572 "Arrival in Bethlehem"   W573 "Shepherd and Lamb"

W574 "Virgin and Child"   W575 "Offering of Frankincense"

(Des. Yvonne Gilbert)

1984 (20 NOVEMBER). CHRISTMAS

This issue features traditional religious scenes from the Nativity and were the first stamps designed, for the Post Office, by Yvonne Gilbert. As a special offer the 13p. value was issued in panes of twenty in a Christmas booklet at a discount rate of £2.30.

One 4mm. phosphor band at right

W597 (=S.G.1267)	**W571**	13p.	pale cream, grey-black, bistre-yellow, magenta, red-brown and lake-brown	30	30

Phosphorised (advanced coated) paper

W598 (=S.G.1268)	**W572**	17p.	pale cream, grey-black, yellow, magenta, dull blue and deep dull blue	40	45
		a.	Dark spot on Joseph's left sleeve	2·25	
		b.	Cluster of dots over donkey's right eye	2·75	

Phosphorised (fluorescent coated) paper

W599 (=S.G.1269)	**W573**	22p.	pale cream, grey-black, olive-yellow, bright magenta, bright blue and brownish grey	55	55
W600 (=S.G.1270)	**W574**	31p.	pale cream, grey-black, bistre-yellow, magenta, dull blue and light brown	1·00	1·00
W601 (=S.G.1271)	**W575**	34p.	pale cream, olive-grey, bistre-yellow, magenta, turquoise-green and brown-olive	1·00	1·00
		a.	Extra jewel	3·00	

231

First Day Cover (W597/601) .. .. †	3·00
Presentation Pack (W597/601).. .. .. .. 3·75	†
PHQ Cards (W597/601) .. .. 3·00	4·25

One 4mm. phosphor band at right. Underprint as Type (4) multiple double lined star in blue
W602 (= S.G.1267 Eu) **W571** 13p. pale cream, grey-black, bistre-yellow, magenta,
red-brown and lake-brown   50

No. W602 is printed with the underprint *over* the gum from 1984 Christmas booklet pane No.
WP603.

Listed Varieties

W598a
Dark spot on Joseph's
left sleeve (Dot, R. 9/2)

W598b
Cluster of dots over donkey's
right eye appearing as flies
(Dot, R. 10/7)

W601a
Pink flaw appears as an extra
jewel on Magi's coat
(Dot, R. 8/5)

Type (4)
Underprint from 1984 Christmas
booklet pane No. WP603

Cylinder Numbers (Blocks of Six)

	Cyl. Nos.	Perforation No dot	Type R* Dot
One 4mm. phosphor band at right			
13p. 1A (lake-brown)–1B (bistre-yellow)–1C (magenta)–1D (red-brown)–1E (grey-black)–3 (pale cream)–P80 (phosphor) ..		6·00	6·00
1A (Lake-brown)–1B (bistre-yellow)–1C (magenta)–1D (red-brown)–1E (grey-black)–P80 (phosphor)		4·00	4·00
1A (lake-brown)–1B (bistre-yellow)–1C (magenta)–1D (red-brown)–1E (grey-black)		2·10	2·10
Phosphorised paper			
17p. 1A (deep dull blue)–1B (yellow)–3C (magenta)–1D (dull blue)–3E (grey-black)–3 (pale cream)		2·75	2·75
22p. 1A (brownish grey)–1B (olive-yellow)–1C (bright magenta)–1D (bright blue)–2E (grey-black)		4·00	4·00
31p. 1A (light brown)–1B (bistre-yellow)–1C (magenta)–1D (dull blue)–3E (grey-black)–3 (pale cream)		7·00	7·00
34p. 1A (brown-olive)-1B (bistre-yellow)–1C (magenta)–1D (turquoise-green)–1E (olive-grey)–3 (pale cream)		7·00	7·00

W 1984. Christmas

Phosphor cylinder No. P80 occurs in the left margin opposite row 9 but on part of the printing the phosphor cylinder was not synchronised. The cylinder employed to print the pale cream background occurs with and without dot but it is difficult to detect in some instances. This cylinder number appears to have been omitted from part of the 13p. printing.

Sheet Details

Sheet size: 100 (2 panes 10 × 5). Double pane reel-fed

Sheet markings:
  Cylinder numbers: Opposite rows 8/9 (13p., 22p.) or rows 8/10 (others), left margin, boxed with Harrison logo opposite row 10
  Marginal arrows: In centre at top and bottom of sheet
  Colour register marks (crossed lines type):
    No dot panes: Opposite rows 7/8 at both sides and cross in circle opposite row 2, left margin
    Dot panes: Opposite rows 2/3 at both sides
  Autotron marks: In same order as traffic lights in left margin opposite rows 5/7 on dot panes only
  Perforation register marks: Thin bar, hand engraved on 13p. or photo-etched (others), opposite lower gutter perforations, right margin on no dot panes only
  Sheet values: Above and below vertical rows 2/4 and 7/9 reading from left to right in top margin and from right to left (upside down) in bottom margin
  Traffic lights (boxed): Opposite row 9, right margin
    13p. Bistre-yellow, magenta, red-brown, grey-black, lake-brown
    17p. Yellow, magenta, dull blue, grey-black, deep dull blue
    22p. Olive-yellow, bright magenta, bright blue, grey-black, brownish grey
    31p. Bistre-yellow, magenta, dull blue, grey-black, light brown
    34p. Bistre-yellow, magenta, turquoise-green, olive-grey, brown-olive

Quantities Sold 13p. 251,570,800*; 17p. 148,837,700; 22p. 16,367,400; 31p. 14,675,600; 34p. 12,686,000
*Excludes 120,000,000 stamps issued in booklets

Withdrawn 19.11.85

FOLDED BOOKLET PANE

WP603
(Actual size 413 × 60 mm.)

Pane of twenty 13p. stamps with one 4mm. phosphor band and underprint as Type (4) printed over the gum in blue.
The binding margin is always at left as the right-hand margin is guillotined off.

Pane WP603. From Christmas £2·60 Booklet No. FX7 (sold at a discount rate of £2·30).

		Perf. Type E
WP603	(containing No. W602 × 20) (20.11.84)	10·00
WP603A	Miscut. As illustrated but cutting line in centre of margin	22·00

These panes have grey-black cutting lines and are folded four times between vertical rows 2/3, 4/5, 6/7 and 8/9.

Booklet Cylinder Numbers
Perforation as Type RE

Pane No.	Cyl. Nos. reading up (all No dot)	Perf. Type E
WP603	B2A (lake-brown)–B1B (bistre-yellow)–B1C (magenta)–B1D (red-brown)– B2E (grey-black)–P79 (phosphor)	12·00
WP603	B2A (lake-brown)–B1B (bistre-yellow)–B1C (magenta)–B1D (red-brown)– B2E (grey-black)	14·00
WP603	P79 (phosphor)	14·00
WP603A	Miscut. Pair of booklets showing complete cyl. no. .. .. .. *pair*	90·00

The phosphor cylinder No. P79 was unsynchronised and can be found printed over different ink cylinder numbers in addition to panes without other numbers.

233

Sheet Make-up
The stamps were printed by Harrison on the Jumelle press. The uncut sheet had one column of 22 horizontal rows with 10 stamps in each row, therefore each primary sheet produced 11 booklet panes. The cylinder numbers are sideways reading up and boxed. The blue star underprint was printed *over* the gum on the Albert press.

Withdrawn   24.12.84

1984. £2·60 Christmas Booklet (sold at a discount rate of £2·30)

Type FX7
(*Illustration reduced to ⅔ actual size*)
Des. Yvonne Gilbert

The sheet make-up was twenty-two horizontal rows of ten stamps in each.

Cover. Printed in red-orange and light brown

Composition. One pane of twenty Christmas stamps. No. W602: Pane WP603 (20 × 13p. one 4 mm. band (to right) with multiple double lined blue star underprint, folded four times and with left selvedge only

Type FX7 *The Nativity*

FX7 (September 1984) (20.11.84)		6,195,825	10·00
a. Miscut ..	.. ..		22·00

Withdrawn   24.12.84

1984 (20 NOVEMBER).   COLLECTORS PACK 1984
WCP17 Comprises Nos. W566/601 (Sold at £8·76)   36·00

Withdrawn   19.11.85

1984 (20 NOVEMBER).   ROYAL MAIL SPECIAL STAMPS YEARBOOK 1984
WYB1 Comprises Nos. W566/601 (Sold at £14·95)   55.00
The book contained 32 pages, with hardback covers and slip case.

Sold Out   Soon after issue

W576 "The Flying Scotsman"

W577 "The Golden Arrow"

W578 "The Cheltenham Flyer"

W579 "The Royal Scot"

W580 "The Cornish Riviera"

(Des. Terence Cuneo)

1985 (22 JANUARY).   FAMOUS TRAINS

Issued as a tribute to the age of the steam locomotive this set also marked the 150th anniversary of the founding of the Great Western Railway. Between 1923 and 1947 there were four groups which were amalgamated on 1 January 1948 to form British Rail. It was the element of competition between the four groups; the Great Western (GWR), the London and North Eastern (LNER), the London Midland and Scottish (LMSR) and the Southern (SR) which achieved high standards of service after the First World War. The world's first 70 m.p.h. service was credited, in 1932, to the Cheltenham Flyer (29p.).

Phosphorised (advanced coated) paper

W604 (= S.G.1272) **W576**	17p. black, lemon, magenta, dull blue, grey-black and gold	70	75
	a. Imperforate (pair)	£1750	
W605 (= S.G.1273) **W577**	22p. black, greenish yellow, bright rose, deep dull blue, grey-black and gold	85	85
	a. Short R	4·25	
W606 (= S.G.1274) **W578**	29p. black, greenish yellow, magenta, blue, grey-black and gold	1·25	1·25
W607 (= S.G.1275) **W579**	31p. black, bistre-yellow, bright magenta, new blue, slate-black and gold	1·25	1·25
W608 (= S.G.1276) **W580**	34p. black, greenish yellow, bright rose, blue, slate-black and gold	1·40	1·40

235

W   1985.   Trains

First Day Cover (W604/08)	..	..	..	..	† 7·50
Presentation Pack (W604/08)	..	..	..	..	6·25 †
PHQ Cards (W604/08) ..	..	..	..	3·50	11·00

Listed Variety

W605*a*
Short first "R" in "ARROW"
(No dot, R. 6/7)

Cylinder Numbers (Blocks of Six)

	Cyl. Nos.	Perforation No dot	Type R* Dot
17p.	1A (black)–1B (lemon)–1C (magenta)–3D (dull blue)–1E (grey-black)–1F (gold)	5·00	5·00
22p.	1A (black)–1B (greenish yellow)–2C (bright rose)–1D (deep dull blue)–1E (grey-black)–1F (gold)	6·00	6·00
29p.	1A (black)–2B (greenish yellow)–3C (magenta)–1D (blue)–2E (grey-black)–1F (gold)	9·00	9·00
31p.	1A (black)–1B (bistre-yellow)–3C (bright magenta)–2D (new blue)–3E (slate-black)–1F (gold)	9·50	9·50
34p.	1A (black)–1B (greenish yellow)–2C (bright rose)–3D (blue)–2E (slate-black)–1F (gold)	10·00	10·00

Sheet Details

Sheet size: 100 (2 panes 10 × 5). Double pane reel-fed

Sheet markings:
Cylinder numbers: Opposite rows 8/9, left margin, boxed with Harrison logo opposite row 10
Marginal arrows: In centre at top and bottom of sheet
Colour register marks (crossed lines type):
No dot panes: Opposite rows 6/8 at both sides and cross in circle opposite row 2, left margin
Dot panes: Opposite rows 1/3 at both sides
Autotron marks: In same order as traffic lights in left margin opposite rows 4/7 on dot panes only
Perforation register marks: Thin bar opposite lower gutter perforations, right margin on no dot panes only
Positioning lines: In vertical rows 1 and 10 in gutter margin and at top and bottom of sheet
Sheet values: Above and below vertical rows 2/4 and 7/9 reading from left to right in top margin and from right to left (upside down) in bottom margin
Traffic lights (boxed): Opposite rows 8/9, right margin
17p. Lemon, magenta, dull blue, grey-black, black, gold
22p. Greenish yellow, bright rose, deep dull blue, grey-black, black, gold
29p. Greenish yellow, magenta, blue, grey-black, black, gold
31p. Bistre-yellow, bright magenta, new blue, slate-black, black, gold
34p. Greenish yellow, bright rose, blue, slate-black, black, gold

Quantities Sold   17p. 37,698,600; 22p. 7,916,200; 29p. 7,472,200; 31p. 7,314,900; 34p. 7,050,500

Withdrawn   21.1.86, Pack sold out 10.85

Buff Tailed Bumble Bee

W581 Buff-tailed
Bumble Bee

Seven Spotted Ladybird

W582 Seven-spotted
Ladybird

Wart-Biter Bush-Cricket

W583 Wart-biter
Bush-cricket

Stag Beetle

W584 Stag Beetle

Emperor Dragonfly

W585 Emperor Dragonfly

(Des. Gordon Beningfield)

1985 (12 MARCH).   INSECTS

The centenaries of the Royal Entomological Society of London's Royal Charter and the Selbourne Society coincided with this issue. The 17p. features the bee and the buff-tailed variety is the British form. The ladybird shown on the 22p. is a common insect in Britain with over forty different species. The Wart-biter cricket derives its name from Scandinavian legend that the insect could act as a wart cure. Although it is seen on the Continent it is rare in Britain. The aggressive appearance of the Stag beetle discourages predators. The loss of woodlands, its breeding ground, has reduced its numbers considerably. The 34p. shows the Emperor dragonfly which is still fairly common in this country. For a similar set showing Butterflies see the 1981 issue by the same designer.

Phosphorised (advanced coated) paper

W609 (= S.G.1277)	W581	17p. black, greenish yellow, magenta, blue, azure, gold and slate-black	50	55
W610 (= S.G.1278)	W582	22p. black, greenish yellow, bright rose-red, dull blue-green, slate-black and gold	65	65
W611 (= S.G.1279)	W583	29p. black, greenish yellow, bright rose, greenish blue, black, gold and bistre-yellow	85	85
W612 (= S.G.1280)	W584	31p. black, greenish yellow, rose, pale new blue, black and gold	1·00	1·00
W613 (= S.G.1281)	W585	34p. black, greenish yellow, magenta, greenish blue, grey-black and gold	1·00	1·00

First Day Cover (W609/13)	..	..	..	†	4·25
Presentation Pack (W609/13)	..	..	..	4·75	†
PHQ Cards (W609/13)	..	..	..	2·75	5·50

Cylinder Numbers (Blocks of Six)

	Cyl. Nos.	Perforation No dot	Type R* Dot
17p.	2A (black)–1B (greenish yellow)–1C (magenta)–1D (blue)–1E (azure)–1F (gold)–1G (slate-black)	3·50	3·50
22p.	1A (black)–1B (greenish yellow)–2C (bright rose-red)–1D (dull blue-green)–1E (slate-black)–1F (gold)	4·50	4·50
29p.	1A (black)–1B (greenish yellow)–1C (bright rose)–1D (greenish blue)–1E (grey-black)–1F (gold)–1G (bistre-yellow)	6·00	6·00
31p.	1A (black)–1B (greenish yellow)–1C (rose)–1D (pale new blue)–1E (black)–1F (gold)..	7·00	7·00
34p.	2A (black)–3B (greenish yellow)–1C (magenta)–1D (greenish blue)–1E (grey-black)–1F (gold)	7·25	7·25

Sheet Details

Sheet size: 100 (2 panes 5 × 10). Double pane reel-fed

Sheet markings:
Cylinder numbers: In top margin above vertical rows 2/3, boxed. Harrison logo above vertical row 1.
Marginal arrows: In centre, opposite rows 5/6 at both sides
Colour register marks (crossed lines type):
No dot panes: Above and below vertical rows 3/5 and cross in circle type above vertical row 9
Dot panes: Above and below rows 8/10
Autotron marks: In order of traffic lights reading from left to right above vertical rows 4/8 (17p. and 29p.) or 4/7 (others)
Perforation register marks: One short vertical line either side of first extension hole in top and bottom margins on both panes also thin bar below left gutter perforation row on no dot panes only
Positioning lines: In horizontal rows 1 and 10 in gutter margin and at each corner on no dot panes or at top and bottom in left margin of dot panes
Sheet values: Opposite rows 2/4 and 7/9 reading up at left and down at right
Traffic lights (boxed): In bottom margin below vertical rows 2/3
17p. Gold, black, slate-black, azure, blue, magenta, greenish yellow
22p. Gold, black, slate-black, dull blue-green, bright rose-red, greenish yellow
29p. Gold, black, bistre-yellow, grey-black, greenish blue, bright rose, greenish yellow
31p. Gold, black (2), pale new blue, rose, greenish yellow
34p. Gold, black, grey-black, greenish blue, magenta, greenish yellow

Quantities Sold   17p, 39,534,200; 22p. 7,812,500; 29p. 9,495,200; 31p. 7,223,900; 34p. 6,932,600

Withdrawn 11.3.86

WATER·MUSIC
George Frideric Handel

W586 "Water Music"
(George Frideric Handel)

THE·PLANETS·SUITE
Gustav Holst

W587 "The Planets" Suite
(Gustav Holst)

THE·FIRST·CUCKOO
Frederick Delius

W588 "The First Cuckoo"
(Frederick Delius)

SEA·PICTURES
Edward Elgar

W589 "Sea Pictures"
(Edward Elgar)

(Des. Wilson McLean)

1985 (14 MAY). BRITISH COMPOSERS ("EUROPA")

The theme of music was selected for the CEPT issues of 1985 and the issue coincided with the 300th anniversary of the birth of George Frideric Handel. His music is featured on the first value which depicts a water reflection. The 22p. features Holst's "The Planets" suite which was composed at St. Paul's Girls School where he taught music. Delius was born in Yorkshire and he became famous for his music related to the countryside. In contrast the 34p. shows waves and a sea bird's wing to symbolise Elgar's "Sea Pictures". His other works were very patriotic including "Pomp and Circumstance" and the "Enigma Variations". By a curious coincidence the last three named composers all died in 1934.

Phosphorised (advanced coated) paper. Comb perforation $14 \times 14\frac{1}{2}$

W614 (= S.G.1282)	**W586**	17p.	black, bright yellow-green, deep magenta, new blue, grey-black and gold	..	..	..	40	40
		a.	Imperforate (vert. pair)	..	..	..		
		b.	Missing hyphen (dot)	..	..	..	3·00	
W615 (= S.G.1283)	**W587**	22p.	black, greenish yellow, bright magenta, new blue, grey-black and gold	..	..	..	65	65
W616 (= S.G.1284)	**W588**	31p.	black, greenish yellow, magenta, greenish blue, grey-black and gold	..	..	..	1·00	1·00
W617 (= S.G.1285)	**W589**	34p.	black, olive-yellow, bistre, turquoise-blue, slate and gold	..	..	..	1·00	1·00

First Day Cover (W614/17)	..	..	†	3·75
Presentation Pack (614/17)	..	..	3·50	†
PHQ Cards (W614/17) ..	..	..	2·50	5·25

The 17p. is known postmarked at Liverpool on 7 May 1985 having been pre-released one week early.

Listed Variety

W614*b*
Missing hyphen (dot) between
"SEVENTEEN" and "PENCE"
(Dot, R.1/5)

Cylinder Numbers (Blocks of Six)

	Cyl. Nos.	Perforation No dot	Type R* Dot
17p.	2A (black)–1B (bright yellow-green)–1C (deep magenta)–1D (new blue)–2E (grey-black)–1F (gold)	2·75	2·75
22p.	1A (black)–1B (greenish yellow)–4C (bright magenta)–1D (new blue)–1E (grey-black)–1F (gold)	4·50	4·50
31p.	1A (black)–2B (greenish yellow)–1C (magenta)–2D (greenish blue)–1E (grey-black)–1F (gold)	7·00	†
34p.	1A (black)–1B (olive-yellow)–1C (bistre)–1D (turquoise-blue)–1E (slate)–1F (gold)	7·25	7·25

Cylinder blocks of the 31p. exist only without dot as the dot sheets were found to be faulty and were not issued.

Sheet Details

Sheet size: 100 (2 panes 5 × 10). Double pane reel-fed

Sheet markings:
Cylinder numbers: Opposite rows 8/9, left margin, boxed with Harrison logo opposite row 10
Marginal arrows: In gutter margin opposite rows 5/6
Colour register marks (crossed lines type):
No dot panes: At both sides opposite row 7 and cross in circle opposite row 6, left margin
Dot panes: At both sides opposite row 2
Autotron marks: In same order as traffic lights in left margin opposite rows 4/7 on dot panes only
Perforation register marks: Thin bar in right margin opposite first perforation row on no dot panes only. One short horizontal line above and below bottom perforation row extension holes in left and right margin of 22p. no dot pane
Sheet values: Above and below vertical rows 2/4 and 7/9 reading from left to right in top margin and from right to left (upside down) in bottom margin
Traffic lights (boxed): Opposite row 9, right margin
17p. Bright yellow-green, deep magenta, new blue, grey-black, black, gold
22p. Greenish yellow, bright magenta, new blue, grey-black, black, gold
31p. Greenish yellow, magenta, greenish blue, grey-black, black, gold
34p. Olive-yellow, bistre, turquoise-blue, slate, black, gold

Quantities Sold   17p. 36,849,700; 22p. 7,805,800; 31p. 7,148,700; 34p. 6,806,100

Withdrawn 17.6.86

W590 R.N.L.I. Lifeboat and
Signal Flags

W591 Beachy Head Lighthouse
and Chart

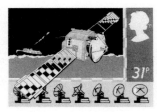

W592 "Marecs A" Communications Satellite and Dish Aerials

W593 Buoys

(Des. Newell and Sorrell Design Ltd.)

(Lithography by John Waddington Ltd.)

1985 (18 JUNE).   SAFETY AT SEA

It was appropriate that this issue appeared following the 11th conference of the International Association of Lighthouse Authorities at Brighton. It was the first occasion that the event had been held in Britain. Founded in 1957, the IALA represented 85 lighthouse authorities worldwide. The issue also marked the bicentenary of the invention of the unimmersible lifeboat by Lionel Lukin and the 50th anniversary of radar. The 17p. shows an "Oakley" Class lifeboat and alphabetical flags of the international code of signals. Beachy Head lighthouse (22p.) took two years to build and was brought into service in 1902 by Trinity House. The 31p. shows a European built satellite launched to provide a global transmission service of communications. In contrast the 34p. features a South Cardinal Class "I" buoy and Trinity House has been responsible for the development of a new IALA Buoyage System, designed to replace over thirty different systems used world-wide. The border design, common to each value, is similar to that found on Admiralty sea charts.

Phosphorised (fluorescent coated) paper. Comb perforation 14

W618 (= S.G.1286)	**W590**	17p.	black, azure, emerald, ultramarine, orange-yellow, vermilion, bright blue and chrome-yellow	40	40
		a.	Imperf. between stamp and bottom margin ..	£500	
W619 (= S.G.1287)	**W591**	22p.	black, azure, emerald, ultramarine, orange-yellow, vermilion, bright blue and chrome-yellow	65	65
W620 (= S.G.1288)	**W592**	31p.	black, azure, emerald, ultramarine, orange-yellow, vermilion, bright blue and chrome-yellow	1·00	1·00
W621 (= S.G.1289)	**W593**	34p.	black, azure, emerald, ultramarine, orange-yellow, vermilion, bright blue and chrome-yellow	1·00	1·00

First Day Cover (W618/21)	..	..	..	.. †	3·75
Presentation Pack (W618/21)	..	..	..	.. 3·50	†
PHQ Cards (W618/21)	..	..	..	.. 2·50	5·25

The 17p. is known postmarked at Lee Park, Havant on 10 June 1985. Further examples are known dated 11 and 12 June with attempts made to obliterate the date.

Plate Numbers (Blocks of Six)

Colour order of plate nos.

17, 22 and 34p. Black, azure, emerald ultramarine, orange-yellow, vermilion, bright blue, chrome-yellow

31p. Black, azure, emerald, ultramarine, orange-yellow, vermilion, bright blue

	Plate Nos.						Perforation No dot	Type N (R)† Dot
17p.	2A–2B–2C–2D–2E–2F–2G–2H	..	..	..	..	..	3·75	3·75
	2A–3B–2C–2D–2E–2F–3G–3H	..	..	..	..	..	2·75	2·75
	2A–3B–2C–2D–3E–2F–4G–4H	..	..	..	..	..	2·75	2·75
22p.	3A–3B–3C–3D–3E–3F–3G–3H	..	..	..	..	..	4·50	4·50
31p.	2A–2B–2C–2D–2E–2F–2G..	..	..	..	..	..	7·00	7·00
	2A–2B–2C–2D–2E–2F–3G..	..	..	..	..	..	15·00	7·00
34p	2A–2B–2C–2D–2E–2F–2G–2H	..	..	..	..	..	7·25	7·25

†The perforation characteristics of this perforator are as follows:

Horizontal format stamps (right-hand feed)

	Top margin	Bottom margin	Left margin	Right margin
No dot pane	Perforated through	Imperforate	Perforated through	Imperforate
Dot pane	Imperforate	Perforated through	Perforated through	Imperforate

Sheet Details

Sheet size: 100 (2 panes 10 × 5). Double pane sheet-fed

Sheet markings:
Plate numbers: Opposite rows 8/10, left margin, boxed with Waddington logo below
Marginal arrows: In centre at top and bottom of sheet
Sheet values: Above and below vertical rows 2/4 and 7/9 reading from left to right in top margin
   and from right to left (upside down) in bottom margin
Traffic lights: Opposite rows 8/9, right margin
   17p. Black, azure, emerald, ultramarine, orange-yellow, vermilion, bright blue, chrome-yellow
   22p. Black, azure, emerald, ultramarine, orange-yellow, vermilion, bright blue, chrome-yellow
   31p. Black, azure, emerald, ultramarine, orange-yellow, vermilion, bright blue
   34p. Black, azure, emerald, ultramarine, orange-yellow, vermilion, bright blue, chrome-yellow

Quantities Sold   17p. 36,372,000; 22p. 9,078,400; 31p. 7,057,400; 34p. 6,757,600

Withdrawn   17.6.86

W594 Datapost Motor-
cyclist, City of
London

W595 Rural Postbus

W596 Parcel Delivery
Service

W597 Town Letter
Delivery

(Des. Paul Hogarth)

1985 (30 JULY).   350 YEARS OF ROYAL MAIL SERVICE TO THE PUBLIC

This issue marked the 350th anniversary of the announcement, by King Charles I in 1635, that the Royal Mail could be used by all his subjects. The stamps depict different delivery services operated by the Post Office. The Datapost service (17p.) is for urgent sendings which require same day or overnight delivery. The stamp shows a red Datapost aircraft and a uniformed motorcyclist. The 22p. depicts a Royal Mail postbus which carries fare-paying passengers and mail in areas where there is restricted or no public transport.

Phosphorised (advanced coated) paper

W622 (= S.G.1290)	**W594**	17p.	black, greenish yellow, bright carmine, greenish blue, yellow-brown, grey-black and silver ..	40	40
			a. Imperforate on 3 sides (vert. pair)	£1250	
W623 (= S.G.1291)	**W595**	22p.	black, greenish yellow, cerise, steel blue, light green, grey-black and silver	65	65
W624 (= S.G.1292)	**W596**	31p.	black, greenish yellow, bright carmine, dull blue, drab, grey-black and silver	1·00	1·00
			a. Imperforate (vert. pair)	£1250	
W625 (= S.G.1293)	**W597**	34p.	black, greenish yellow, cerise, ultra-marine, light brown, grey-black and silver	1·00	1·00

First Day Cover (W622/5)	..	..	..	.. †	3·75
Presentation Pack (W622/5)	..	..	..	.. 3·50	†
PHQ Cards (W622/5) ..	..	..	..	.. 2·50	5·25

243

(5)

Phosphorised (advanced coated) paper. Underprint as type (5) multiple double-lined D in blue
W626 (= S.G.1290 Eu) **W594** 17p. black, greenish yellow, bright carmine, greenish
blue, yellow-brown, grey-black and silver   ..   65

The underprint is printed *over* the gum and comes from the £1·70 booklet (sold at £1·53). The
illustrated booklet cover shows a Datapost mail van and aircraft No. FT4

Cylinder Numbers (Blocks of Six)

	Cyl. Nos.	Perforation No dot	Type R* Dot
17p.	1A (black)–1B (greenish yellow)–1C (bright carmine)–1D (greenish blue)–1E (yellow-brown)–1F (grey-black)–1G (silver)	2·75	2·75
22p.	1A (black)–1B (greenish yellow)–1C (cerise)–1D (steel blue)–1E (light green)–2F (grey black)–1G (silver)	4·50	4·50
31p.	2A (black)–1B (greenish yellow)–1C (bright carmine)–1D (dull blue)–1E (drab)–1F (grey-black)–1G (silver)	7·00	7·00
34p.	2A (black)–1B (greenish yellow)–1C (cerise)–1D (ultramarine)–1E (light brown)–2F (grey-black)–1G (silver)	7·25	7·25

Sheet Details

Sheet size: 100 (2 panes 5 × 10). Double pane reel-fed

Sheet markings:
Cylinder numbers: In top margin above vertical rows 2/3, boxed. Harrison logo above vertical
row 1
Marginal arrows: In centre, opposite rows 5/6 at both sides
Colour register marks (crossed lines type):
No dot panes: Above and below vertical rows 4/5 and cross in circle above vertical row 9
Dot panes: Above and below vertical rows 8/10
Autotron marks: In order of traffic lights reading from left to right above vertical rows 4/7 on dot
panes only
Perforation register marks: Bar in bottom margin opposite last perforation row at right also
horizontal and vertical positioning lines in right margin at top and bottom on no dot panes.
These lines occur in the left margin on dot panes
Sheet values: Opposite rows 2/4 and 7/9 reading up at left and down at right
Traffic lights (boxed): In bottom margin below vertical rows 2/3
17p. Silver, grey-black, black, yellow-brown, greenish blue, bright carmine, greenish yellow
22p. Silver, grey-black, black, light green, steel blue, cerise, greenish yellow
31p. Silver, grey-black, black, drab, dull blue, bright carmine, greenish yellow
34p. Silver, black, grey-black, light brown, ultramarine, cerise, greenish yellow

Quantities Sold 17p. 36,318,300*; 22p. 7,682,100; 31p. 7,087,500; 34p. 6,772,700
*Excludes 50,576,500 stamps issued in booklets

Withdrawn 29.7.86

FOLDED BOOKLET PANE

WP627
(*Actual size* 213 × 60 mm.)

Pane of ten 17p. stamps on phosphorised (advanced coated) paper and double lined D (multiple) printed *over* the gum in blue.
The binding margin is always at the top of the pane.

Pane WP627. From £1·70 Booklet No. FT4 (sold at a discount rate of £1·53)

	Perf. Type E
WP627 (containing No. W626 × 10) (30.7.85)	7·00

These panes have black cutting lines and are folded twice between rows 1/2 and 3/4.

Booklet Cylinder Numbers

Single pane cylinder

		Perforation Type E	
		Left col.	Right col.
Pane No.	Cyl. Nos. reading up (No Dot)		
WP627 B3A (black)–B1B (greenish yellow)–B1C (bright carmine)–B1D (greenish blue)–B1E (yellow-brown)–B1F (grey-black)–B1G (silver)..		10·00*	10·00

Cylinder numbers were printed in both the right and left vertical margins of the printer's sheet. The cylinder number from the right column shows B and A of B3A with sliced tops to the letters.
*Examples of the cylinder pane from the left of the sheet show a minor constant flaw on stamps R.1/2 and 2/2. This consists of the absence of the back bumper to the taxi opposite "V" of "SERVICE".

Sheet Make-up

The stamps were printed by Harrison on the Jumelle press. The uncut printer's sheet contained 22 horizontal rows each with 10 stamps. The two columns of stamps (22 × 5) in the sheet, were printed tête-bêche giving 22 panes with a binding margin at the top.

£1·70 Booklet (sold at a discount rate of £1·53)

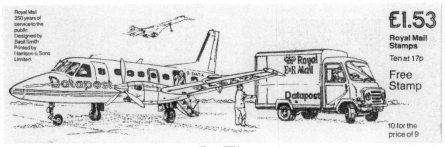

Type FT4
(*Illustration reduced to* ⅔ *actual size*)
Datapost Service. Des. Basil Smith

Royal Mail 350 Years of Service to the Public

Special Discount Booklet (sold at £1·53)

Cover. Printed in rosine and bright blue

Composition. One pane of ten stamps No. W626: Pane WP627 (10 × 17p. on phosphorised (advanced coated) paper with multiple double lined "D" underprint). Folded twice between rows 1/2 and 3/4 with selvedge at top only.

- *Type* FT4, *Royal Mail 350 Years of Service to the Public*

FT4 Datapost Service (September 1984) (30.7.85)   5,057,600   7·00

Withdrawn   31.8.85

W598 King Arthur and
Merlin

W599 Lady of the Lake

W600 Queen Guinevere
and Sir Lancelot

W601 Sir Galahad

(Des. Yvonne Gilbert)

1985 (3 SEPTEMBER).   ARTHURIAN LEGENDS

Sir Thomas Malory's epic work, *Le Morte D'Arthur*, was printed 500 years ago by William Caxton. The well-known British legend concerns the exploits of King Arthur and the Knights of the Round Table. The 17p. shows Arthur listening to Merlin the Magician who predicts that, Mordred the king's nephew, would be an adversary. On the 22p. the sword Excalibur is shown and the flight from Camelot by Guinevere and Lancelot is depicted on the 31p. In his quest for the Holy Grail, Sir Galahad is shown praying on the 34p.

Phosphorised (advanced coated) paper

W628 (= S.G.1294) **W598**	17p. grey-black, lemon, brown-lilac, ultramarine, grey-black and silver	40	40
	a. Imperforate (pair)	£1750	
W629 (= S.G.1295) **W599**	22p. black, lemon, brown-lilac, pale blue, grey-black, silver and grey-black	65	65
W630 (= S.G.1296) **W600**	31p. black, lemon, magenta, turquoise-blue, grey-black, silver and grey-black	1·00	1·00
W631 (= S.G.1297) **W601**	34p. grey, lemon, magenta, new blue, grey-black, silver and grey-black	1·00	1·00

First Day Cover (W627/30)	†	3·75
Presentation Pack (W627/30)	3·50	†
PHQ Cards (W627/30)	2·50	5·25

Cylinder Numbers (Blocks of Six)

	Cyl. Nos.	Perforation No dot	Type R* Dot
17p.	1A (grey-black)–1B (lemon)–1C (brown-lilac)–1D (ultramarine)–1E (grey-black)–1F (silver)	2·75	2·75
22p.	1A (black)–1B (lemon)–1C (brown-lilac)–1D (pale blue)–1E (grey-black)–1F (silver)–1G (grey-black)	4·50	4·50
	1A (black)–1B (lemon)–1C (brown-lilac)–1D (pale blue)–2E (grey-black)–1F (silver)–1G (grey-black)	35·00	35·00
31p.	1A (black)–1B (lemon)–1C (magenta)–1D (turquoise-blue)–1E (grey-black)–1F (silver)–1G (grey-black)	7·00	7·00
34p.	1A (grey)–1B (lemon)–1C (magenta)–1D (new blue)–1E (grey-black)–1F (silver)–1G (grey-black). . .. .. · ..	7·25	7·25

Sheet Details

Sheet size: 100 (2 panes 10 × 5). Double pane reel-fed

Sheet markings:
Cylinder numbers: Opposite rows 8/9, left margin, boxed with Harrison logo opposite row 10
Marginal arrows: In centre at top and bottom of sheet
Colour register marks (crossed lines type):
No dot panes: Opposite rows 7/8 (17p.) or rows 6/8 (others) at both sides and cross in circle opposite row 2, left margin
Dot panes: Opposite rows 2/3 (17p.) or rows 1/3 (others) at both sides
Autrotron marks: In same order as traffic lights in left margin opposite rows 4/7 on dot panes only
Perforation register marks: Thick bar opposite lower gutter perforations, right margin on no dot panes only
Positioning lines: In top margin above vertical rows 1 and 10 of 17p. and 31p. on no dot panes only
Sheet values: Above and below vertical rows 2/4 and 7/9 reading from left to right in top margin and from right to left (upside down) in bottom margin
Traffic lights (boxed): Opposite rows 8/9, right margin
17p. Lemon, brown-lilac, ultramarine, grey-black (2), silver
22p. Lemon, brown-lilac, pale blue, grey-black (2), black, silver
31p. Lemon, magenta, turquoise-blue, grey-black (2), black, silver
34p. Lemon, magenta, new blue, grey-black (2), grey, silver

Quantities Sold   17p. 37,582,500; 22p. 7,783,500; 31p. 7,272,100; 34p. 6,984,300

Withdrawn 2.9.86

W602 Peter Sellers
(Bill Brandt)

W603 David Niven
(Cornell Lucas)

W604 Charlie Chaplin
(Lord Snowdon)

W605 Vivien Leigh
(Angus McBean)

W606 Alfred Hitchcock
(Howard Coster)

(Des. Keith Bassford from portrait photographs)

1985 (8 OCTOBER).   BRITISH FILM YEAR

British Film Year ran from March to May the following year. This issue also marked the 150th anniversary of the invention of the positive to negative process by William Henry Fox. This technique enabled many copies to be made from a photographic negative. In 1896 the first projected film performance in Britain was shown at the Empire, a theatre, in Leicester Square, London. In the same year the first filmed news event in Britain was recorded at the boat race between the Oxford and Cambridge Universities.

Phosphorised (advanced coated) paper. Comb perforation 14½

W632 (= S.G.1298)	W602	17p. grey-black, olive-grey, gold and silver	..	..	40	40
W633 (= S.G.1229)	W603	22p. black, brown, gold and silver	..	..	..	70	70
W634 (= S.G.1300)	W604	29p. black, lavender, gold and silver	..	..	..	95	1·00
W635 (= S.G.1301)	W605	31p. black, pink, gold and silver	..	..	85	80
W636 (= S.G.1302)	W606	34p. black, greenish blue, gold and silver	..	..	95	1·00

First Day Cover (W632/6)	..	..	..	.. †	5·00
Presentation Pack (W632/6)	..	..	..	.. 4·25	†
Souvenir Book (W632/6) (Sold at £2)..	..	.. 6·50	†
PHQ Cards (632/6)	..	..	..	.. 2·75	5·75

The souvenir book is a 24-page illustrated booklet with a set of mint stamps in a sachet attached to the front cover.

Cylinder Numbers (Blocks of Four)

Cyl. Nos.	Perforation No dot	Type R* Dot
17p. 1A (grey-black)–1B (olive-grey)–1C (gold)–1D (silver)	2·00	2·00
22p. 1A (black)–1B (brown)–1C (gold)–1D (silver)	3·50	3·50
29p. 3A (black)–1B (lavender)–1C (gold)–1D (silver)	4·75	4·75
31p. 1A (black)–1B (pink)–1C (gold)–1D (silver)	4·25	4·25
34p. 2A (black)–1B (greenish blue)–1C (gold)–1D (silver)	4·75	4·75

Sheet Details

Sheet size: 100 (2 panes 5 × 10). Double pane reel-fed

Sheet markings:
Cylinder numbers: Opposite row 9, left margin, boxed with Harrison logo opposite row 10
Marginal arrows: In gutter margin opposite rows 5/6
Colour register marks (crossed lines type):
    No dot panes: At both sides opposite row 7 and cross in circle in left margin opposite rows 6/7
    Dot panes: Not examined
Autotron marks: Dot panes not examined
Perforation register marks: One short line either side of extension holes at bottom left and right
    on both panes and thick bar in right margin opposite first perforation row on no dot panes
Positioning lines: Above or below vertical rows 1 and 10
Sheet values: Above and below vertical rows 2/4 and 7/9 reading from left to right in top margin
    and from right to left (upside down) in bottom margin
Traffic lights (boxed): Opposite row 9, right margin
    17p. Olive-grey, grey-black, gold, silver
    22p. Brown, black, gold, silver
    29p. Lavender, black, gold, silver
    31p. Pink, black, gold, silver
    34p. Greenish blue, black, gold, silver

Quantities Sold   17p. 36,204,900; 22p. 7,740,300; 29p. 7,264,600; 31p. 7,122,300; 34p. 6,792,200

Withdrawn 7.10.86

W607 Principal Boy

W608 Genie

W609 Dame

W610 Good Fairy

W611 Pantomime Cat

(Des. Adrian George)

1985 (19 NOVEMBER).   CHRISTMAS

The designs by Adrian George, showing pantomime characters, were taken from crayon drawings and are overlaid with gold and silver stars. The same designer was responsible for the 1982 British Theatre stamps.

On 4 November the existing 13p. second class letter rate was reduced to 12p. This value was issued in sheets, booklet and a special Christmas folder but only the stamps from booklets had the double-lined star underprint (No. W642).

One 4 mm. phosphor band at right

W637 (= S.G.1303)	**W607**	12p.	new blue, greenish yellow, bright rose, gold, grey-black and silver	..	..	..	..	..	35	35
			a. Imperforate (pair) ..	..	..	..	..	£1250

Phosphorised (advanced coated) paper

W638 (= S.G.1304)	**W608**	17p.	emerald, greenish yellow, bright rose, new blue, black, gold and silver	..	..	..	..	45	50
			a. Imperforate (pair) ..	..	..	..	..	£1750
W639 (= S.G.1305)	**W609**	22p.	bright carmine, greenish yellow, pale new blue, grey, gold and silver	..	..	..	..	65	65

W   1985.   Christmas

W640 (= S.G.1306) **W610**	31p.	bright orange, lemon, rose, slate-purple, silver and gold	90 90
W641 (= S.G.1307) **W611**	34p.	bright reddish violet, bright blue, bright rose, black, grey-brown, gold and silver	1·00 1·00

First Day Cover (W637/41)	†	3·75
Presentation Pack (W637/41)	3·75	†
Christmas Folder (W637 × 50) (Sold at £6)	20·00	
PHQ Cards (W637/41)	2·75	5·50

The 17p. has a distinctive pattern on the gummed side as a paper coating machine was used to apply the gum. The excess gum was removed by a Meyer bar which left a vertical pattern on the back of the stamps. Other denominations had gum applied in the usual way.

The 17p. is also known postmarked London S.W. on 18 November 1985 having been pre-released on that day.

One 4 mm. phosphor band at right. Underprint as Type (4) multiple double lined star in blue
W642 (= S.G.1303Eu) **W607** 12p. new blue, greenish yellow, bright rose, gold, grey-black and silver 45

No. W642 is printed with the underprint *over* the gum from 1985 Christmas booklet pane No. WP643.

Cylinder Numbers (Blocks of Six)

	Cyl. Nos.	Perforation No dot	Type R* Dot
One 4 mm. phosphor band at right			
12p. 1A (new blue)–1B (greenish yellow)–1C (bright rose)–1D (gold)–1E (grey-black)–1F (silver)–P82 (phosphor)		2·40	2·40
Phosphorised (advanced coated) paper			
17p. 1A (emerald)–1B (greenish yellow)–1C (bright rose)–1D (new blue)–1E (black)–1F (gold)–1G (silver)		3·25	3·25
22p. 2A (bright carmine)–1B (greenish yellow)–1C (pale new blue)–1D (grey)–1E (gold)–1F (silver)		4·50	4·50
3A (bright carmine)–1B (greenish yellow)–1C (pale new blue)–1D (grey)–1E (gold)–1F (silver)		10·00	5·50
31p. 1A (bright orange)–1B (lemon)–2C (rose)–2D (slate-purple)–1E (silver)–1F (gold)		6·50	6·50
34p. 1A (bright reddish violet)–1B (bright blue)–1C (bright rose)–1D (black)–1E (grey-brown)–1F (gold)–1G (silver)		7·00	7·00

Sheet Details

Sheet size: 100 (2 panes 10 × 5). Double pane reel-fed

Sheet markings:
Cylinder numbers: Opposite rows 8/9, left margin, boxed with Harrison logo opposite row 10
Marginal arrows: In centre at top and bottom of sheet
Colour register marks (crossed lines type):
No dot panes: Opposite rows 6/8 (17p., 34p.) or 7/8 (others) at both sides and cross in circle opposite row 2, left margin
Dot panes: Opposite rows 1/3 (17p., 34p.) or 2/3 (others) at both sides
Autotron marks: In same order as traffic lights in left margin opposite rows 4/7 on dot panes only
Perforation register marks: Thin bar opposite lower gutter perforations, right margin on no dot panes only
Positioning lines: Between dot and no dot panes in vertical rows 1 and 10
Sheet values: Above and below vertical rows 2/4 and 7/9 reading from left to right in top margin and from right to left (upside down) in bottom margin
Traffic lights (boxed): Opposite rows 8/9, right margin
12p. Greenish yellow, bright rose, new blue, gold, grey-black, silver
17p. Greenish yellow, bright rose, new blue, black, emerald, gold, silver
22p. Greenish yellow, bright carmine, pale new blue, grey, gold, silver
31p. Lemon, rose, slate-purple, bright orange, silver, gold
34p. Bright blue, bright rose, black, grey-brown, gold, silver, bright reddish violet

Quantities Sold 12p. 284,590,600*; 17p. 150,799,500; 22p. 17,357,500; 31p. 14,786,000; 34p. 13,101,200
*Excludes 61,972,000 stamps issued in booklets

Withdrawn 18.11.86. Christmas folder 24.12.85

FOLDED BOOKLET PANE

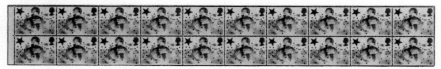

WP643
(Actual size 413 × 60 *mm.)*

Pane of twenty 12p. stamps with one 4 mm. phosphor band at right and underprint as type (4) printed *over* the gum in blue.

The binding margin is always at left as the right-hand margin is guillotined off.

Pane WP643. From Christmas £2·40 Booklet No. FX8

Perforation Type E

WP643   (containing No. W642 × 20) (19.11.85)   ..   ..   8·00

These panes have grey-black cutting lines and are folded four times between vertical rows 2/3, 4/5, 6/7 and 8/9.

Booklet Cylinder Numbers

Perforation as Type RE

Pane No.   Cyl. Nos. reading up (all No dot)   Perforation Type E

WP643 B2A (new blue)–B1B (greenish yellow)–B1C (bright rose)–B1D
(gold)–B1E (grey-black)–B1F (silver)–P83 (phosphor) ..   ..   11·00

Sheet Make-up

As for the Christmas booklet pane No. WP603.

Withdrawn 18.11.86

1985.   £2·40 Christmas Booklet

Type FX8
(Illustration reduced to $\frac{2}{3}$ size)

Des. Adrian George

The sheet make-up was twenty-two horizontal rows of ten stamps each.

Cover. Printed in bright blue and rose

Composition. One pane of twenty Christmas stamps No. W642: Pane WP643 (20 × 12p., one 4 mm. band at right with multiple double lined blue star underprint, folded four times between rows 2/3, 4/5, 6/7 and 8/9 with left selvedge only)

Type FX8, *The Pantomime*

FX8 (19.11.85)   3,105,950   8·00

Withdrawn 18.11.86

1985 (19 NOVEMBER). COLLECTORS PACK 1985

WCP 18 Comprises Nos. W604/25, W627/41 (Sold at £9·94)   38·00

Withdrawn 18.11.86

1985 (19 NOVEMBER). ROYAL MAIL SPECIAL STAMPS YEARBOOK 1985

WYB2 Comprises Nos. W604/25, W627/41 (Sold at £15·95)   65·00

This book contained 24 pages, with hardback covers and slip case.

Withdrawn 18.11.86

17 PENCE · INDUSTRY YEAR 1986

W612 Light Bulb and
North Sea Oil Drilling
Rig (Energy)

22 PENCE · INDUSTRY YEAR 1986

W613 Thermometer and
Pharmaceutical Laboratory
(Health)

31 PENCE · INDUSTRY YEAR 1986

W614 Garden Hoe and
Steelworks (Steel)

34 PENCE · INDUSTRY YEAR 1986

W615 Loaf of Bread
and Cornfield
(Agriculture)

(Des. Keith Bassford)

(Lithography by The House of Questa)

253

1986 (14 JANUARY).   INDUSTRY YEAR

Industry Year 1986 was initiated by the Royal Society for the Encouragement of Arts, Manufactures and Commerce. Each stamp design focuses attention on the varied contributions made by industry in Britain. It was the first occasion that the Post Office had commissioned stamps to be designed from photographic montages.

Phosphorised (fluorescent coated) paper. Comb perforation 14½ × 14

W644 (= S.G.1308)	**W612**	17p. gold, black, magenta, greenish yellow and new blue ..	.. ..	45	45
W645 (= S.G.1309)	**W613**	22p. gold, pale turquoise-green, black, magenta, greenish yellow and blue ..	.. .. ..	65	65
W646 (= S.G.1310)	**W614**	31p. gold, black, magenta, greenish yellow and new blue ..	.. ..	90	90
W647 (= S.G.1311)	**W615**	34p. gold, black, magenta, greenish yellow and new blue ..	.. ..	1·00	1·00

First Day Cover (W644/7)	.. ..	†	4·50
Presentation Pack (W644/7)	.. .. ..	3·25	†
PHQ Cards (W644/7) ..	.. .. ..	2·25	5·50

Plate Numbers (Blocks of Six)

Colour order of plate numbers following the Questa imprint:
17p. Gold, black, magenta, greenish yellow, new blue
22p. Gold, pale turquoise-green, black, magenta, greenish yellow, blue
31p. Gold, black, magenta, greenish yellow, new blue
34p. Gold, black, magenta, greenish yellow, new blue

	Plate Nos.							Perforation Type M*
17p.	1A (× 5)	..	..	..	..	..	..	3·25
	1B (× 5)	..	..	..	..	..	..	3·25
	2A–1A–1A–1A–1A..	..	..	..	..	..	..	8·00
	2B–1B–1B–1B–1B ..	..	..	..	..	..	..	8·00
	3A–2A–2A–2A–2A..	..	..	..	..	..	..	3·25
	3B–2B–2B–2B–2B ..	..	..	..	..	..	..	3·25
22p.	1A (× 6) ..	..	..	..	..	..	..	4·50
	1B (× 6) ..	..	..	..	..	..	..	4·50
31p.	1A (× 5) ..	..	..	..	..	..	..	6·25
	1B (× 5) ..	..	..	..	..	..	..	6·25
34p.	1A (× 5)	..	..	..	..	..	..	7·00
	1B (× 5)	..	..	..	..	..	..	7·00
	1A–1A–2A–1A–1A..	..	..	..	..	..	..	12·00
	1B–1B–2B–1B–1B ..	..	..	..	..	..	..	25·00
	2A–2A–3A–2A–2A..	..	..	..	..	..	..	12·00
	2B–2B–3B–2B–2B ..	..	..	..	..	..	..	50·00

*All sheet margins are perforated through except the left-hand margin which is imperforate.

Sheet Details

Sheet size: 100 (2 panes 10 × 5). Double pane sheets with "A" and "B" plate numbers

Sheet markings:
Plate numbers: Opposite rows 8/9, left margin, arranged sideways in colour order as described following the imprint
Marginal arrows: "W" shaped in centre, between vertical rows 5/6 in top and bottom margins
Sheet values: Above and below vertical rows 2/4 and 7/9 reading from left to right in top margin and from right to left (upside down) in bottom margin
Imprint: Opposite rows 9/10, left margin, arranged sideways reading up
Traffic lights: Sideways in the form of Questa logo opposite row 9, right margin, in same order as plate numbers reading up
17p. Gold, black, magenta, greenish yellow, new blue
22p. Gold, pale turquoise-green, black, magenta, greenish yellow, blue
31p. Gold, black, magenta, greenish yellow, new blue
34p. Gold, black, magenta, greenish yellow, new blue

Quantities Sold   17p. 35,414,400; 22p. 7,262,300; 31p. 6,275,800; 34p. 6,180,600

Withdrawn   13.1.87

W616 Dr. Edmond Halley
as Comet

W617 *Giotto* Spacecraft
approaching Comet

W618 "Maybe TWICE in a
lifetime"

W619 Comet orbiting Sun
and Planets

(Des. Ralph Steadman)

1986 (18 FEBRUARY).   HALLEY'S COMET

Dr. Edmond Halley (1656–1742) was not the discoverer of the Comet, but he was the first to calculate its orbit and return. It is probable that he saw the Comet in 1682 with the aid of a telescope from his home in Islington. He was England's second Astronomer Royal. Halley's Comet was first seen by Chinese astronomers in 240BC. It makes an appearance once in every 76 years and will not be visible again from Earth until AD2061. The 22p. shows the spacecraft which was launched by the European Space Agency named *Giotto* after the Italian artist, Giotto di Bondone. He used the Comet as a model for the Star of Bethlehem in his "Adoration of the Magi" after he saw it in 1301.

Phosphorised (advanced coated) paper

W648 (= S.G.1312)	W616	17p. black, bistre, rosine, blue, grey-black, gold and deep brown	..	..	..	..	45	45
		b. Short tail to 7	..	..	..	..	2·25	
W649 (= S.G.1313)	W617	22p. orange-vermilion, greenish yellow, bright purple, new blue, black and gold	..	..	..	65	70
W650 (= S.G.1314)	W618	31p. black, greenish yellow, bright purple, deep turquoise-blue, grey-black and gold	..	..	90	90
W651 (= S.G.1315)	W619	34p. deep turquoise-blue, greenish yellow, magenta, blue, black and gold	..	..	..	1·00	1·00
		a. Black spot on Earth	..	..	..	..	4·00	

First Day Cover (W648/51)	..	..	..	..	†	5·00
Presentation Pack (W648/51)	..	..	..	..	3·75	†
PHQ Cards (W648/51)	..	..	..	..	2·40	5·25

Listed Varieties

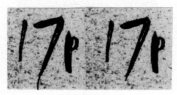

W648*b*
Short tail to 7
(No dot, R. 10/9)

W651*a*
Black spot on Earth
(Dot, R. 4/5)

W648*b* is best collected in a pair from the bottom right corner of the sheet. Other examples exist from both panes showing a tail slightly longer than normal.

Cylinder Numbers (Blocks of Six)

	Cyl. Nos.	Perforation No Dot	Type R* Dot
17p.	1A (black)–1B (bistre)–1C (rosine)–3D (blue)–1E (grey-black)–1F (gold)–1G (deep brown)	3·25	3·25
22p.	1A (orange-vermilion)–1B (greenish yellow)–2C (bright purple)–1D (new blue)–1E (black)–1F (gold)	4·50	4·50
31p.	1A (black)–1B (greenish yellow)–3C (bright purple)–1D (deep turquoise-blue)–1E (grey-black)–1F (gold)	6·25	6·25
34p.	1A (deep turquoise-blue)–1B (greenish yellow)–1C (magenta)–1D (blue)–1E (black)–1F (gold)	7·00	7·00

Sheet Details

Sheet size: 100 (2 panes 10 × 5). Double pane reel-fed

Sheet markings:
Cylinder numbers: Opposite rows 8/9, left margin, boxed with Harrison logo opposite row 10
Marginal arrows: In centre at top and bottom of sheet
Colour register marks (crossed lines type):
  No dot panes: Opposite rows 6/7 at both sides and cross in circle opposite row 2, left margin
  Dot panes: Opposite rows 1/3 at both sides
Autotron marks: In same order as traffic lights in left margin opposite rows 4/7 on dot panes only
Perforation register marks: Thin bar opposite lower gutter perforations, right margin on no dot panes only
Positioning lines: Between dot and no dot panes in vertical rows 1 and 10 and in gutter margins at both sides of the sheet on all panes
Sheet values: Above and below vertical rows 2/4 and 7/9 reading from left to right in top margin and from right to left (upside down) in bottom margin
Traffic lights (boxed): Opposite rows 8/9, right margin
  17p. Bistre, rosine, blue, grey-black, deep brown, black, gold
  22p. Greenish yellow, bright purple, new blue, black, orange-vermilion, gold
  31p. Greenish yellow, bright purple, deep turquoise-blue, grey-black, black, gold
  34p. Greenish yellow, magenta, blue, deep turquoise-blue, black, gold

Quantities Sold   17p. 35,571,800; 22p. 7,097,500; 31p. 6,430,100; 34p. 6,120,500

Withdrawn   17.2.87

W620 Queen Elizabeth II
in 1928, 1942 and 1952

W621 Queen Elizabeth II
in 1958, 1973 and 1982

Types **W620/1** were printed horizontally *se-tenant* within the sheets

(Des. Jeffery Matthews)

1986 (21 APRIL).   60th BIRTHDAY OF QUEEN ELIZABETH II

The six portraits of the Queen were specially selected to represent each decade of her life. The first portrait, from a photograph by Marcus Adams, shows the Queen as Princess Elizabeth when she was two years old. In the next portrait, by Cecil Beaton, she was heir presumptive to the throne, aged sixteen years. The well known portrait by Dorothy Wilding is the third portrait and shows the Queen as she was shortly after she succeeded to the throne on the death of her father, King George VI. On the second stamp the first portrait was taken at her birthday parade in 1958. The next portrait is less formal and depicts the Queen at the Badminton Horse Trials in 1973. The camera held by the Queen shows her keen interest in horses and equestrian events. The third portrait, taken by Lord Snowdon in 1982, shows the Queen wearing the same diadem as that in the Wilding photograph of 1952.

Phosphorised (advanced coated) paper

W652 (= S.G.1316)	**W620**	17p.	grey-black, turquoise-green, bright green, green and dull blue	..	..	..	45	45
			a. Pair. Nos. W652/53	..	..	..	1·25	1·25
W653 (= S.G.1317)	**W621**	17p.	grey-black, dull blue, greenish blue and indigo ..				45	45
W654 (= S.G.1318)	**W620**	34p.	grey-black, deep dull purple, yellow-orange and red ..	..	..	..	1·00	1·00
			a. Pair. Nos. W654/55	..	..	..	2·10	2·25
W655 (= S.G.1319)	**W621**	34p.	grey-black, olive-brown, yellow-brown, olive-grey and red	..	..	..	1·00	1·00

First Day Cover (W652/55) ..	..	†	4·50
Presentation Pack (W652/55) ..	..	4·25	†
Souvenir Book (W652/55) (Sold at £2)	..	6·50	†
PHQ Cards (W652/55) ..	..	2·40	5·50

The souvenir book is a special booklet, fully illustrated and containing a mint set of stamps.

Cylinder Numbers (Blocks of Six)

	Cyl. Nos.	Perforation No dot	Type R* Dot
17p.	2A (dull blue)–2B (green)–6C (grey-black)–1D (bright green)–2E (turquoise-green)–1F (greenish blue)–1G (indigo)	4·50	4·50
34p.	3A (red)–1B (olive–brown)–6C (grey-black)–1D (yellow-orange)–2E (deep dull purple)–1F (yellow-brown)–1G (olive-grey)	7·50	7·50

Sheet Details

Sheet size: 100 (2 panes 10 × 5). Double pane reel-fed

Sheet markings:
Cylinder numbers: Opposite rows 8/9, left margin, boxed with Harrison logo opposite row 10
Marginal arrows: In centre at top and bottom of sheet
Colour register marks (crossed lines type):
No dot panes: Not examined

257

Dot panes: Opposite rows 1/3 at both sides
Autotron marks: In same order as traffic lights in left margin opposite rows 4/7 on dot panes only
Positioning lines: Between dot and no dot panes in vertical row 1
Sheet values: Above and below vertical rows 2/4 and 7/9 reading from left to right in top margin
and from right to left (upside down) in bottom margin
Traffic lights (boxed): Opposite rows 8/9, right margin
    17p. Grey-black, bright green, turquoise-green, green, greenish blue, dull blue, indigo
    34p. Grey-black, yellow-orange, deep dull purple, red, yellow-brown, olive-brown, olive-grey

Quantities Sold   17p. 77,003,200 pairs; 34p. 16,459,100 pairs

Withdrawn   20.4.87

W622 Barn Owl

W623 Pine Marten

W624 Wild Cat

W625 Natterjack Toad

(Des. Ken Lilly)

1986 (20 MAY).   NATURE CONSERVATION ("EUROPA")

Each stamp is inscribed "Species at Risk" with the Europa symbol below the value. The theme was the protection of Nature and the environment and these stamps show just four British species which are at risk. The British Wildlife Appeal was launched with the aim of raising ten million pounds for nature conservation.

Phosphorised (advanced coated) paper. Comb perforation 14½ × 14

W656 (= S.G.1320)	**W622**	17p.	gold, greenish yellow, rose, yellow-brown, olive-grey, new blue and black	50	55
W657 (= S.G.1321)	**W623**	22p.	gold, greenish yellow, reddish brown, olive-yellow, turquoise-blue, grey-black and black ..	60	65
W658 (= S.G.1322)	**W624**	31p.	gold, bright yellow-green, magenta, light brown, ultramarine, olive-brown and black	1·10	1·10
W659 (= S.G.1323)	**W625**	34p.	gold, greenish yellow, bright rose-red, bright green, grey-black and black	1·10	1·10

First Day Cover (W656/59)	..	..	..	.. †	4·50
Presentation Pack (W656/59)	..	..	..	.. 4·00	†
PHQ Cards (W656/59)	..	..	..	.. 2·00	5·50

The 17p. value exists cancelled 15 May 1986 at Bideford, North Devon.
The 17p. and 31p. PHQ cards exist showing the inscriptions and value transposed and inverted. *Price for either card*, £300.

Cylinders Numbers (Blocks of Six)

		Cyl. Nos.	Perforation No dot	Type R* Dot
17p.	2A (gold)–1B (greenish yellow)–1C (rose)–1D (yellow-brown) –1E (olive-grey)–1F (new blue)–1G (black)		4·50	3·50
	2A (gold)–1B (greenish yellow)–2C (rose)–1D (yellow-brown) –1E (olive-grey)–1F (new blue)–1G (black)		3·50	3·50
22p.	1A (gold)–2B (greenish yellow)–2C (reddish brown)–1D (olive-yellow)–2E (turquoise-blue)–1F (grey-black)–1G (black) ..		4·25	4·25
31p.	1A (gold)–1B (bright yellow-green)–2C (magenta)–2D (light brown)–1E (ultramarine)–2F (olive-brown)–1G (black)		7·75	7·75
34p.	1A (gold)–1B (greenish yellow)–3C (bright rose-red)–1D (bright green)–3E (grey-black)––1F (black)		8·00	8·00

Sheet Details

Sheet size: 100 (2 panes 10 × 5). Double pane reel-fed

Sheet markings:
  Cylinder numbers: In top margin above vertical rows 2/3, boxed. Harrison logo above vertical row 1
  Marginal arrows: In gutter margin at centre of the sheet
  Colour register marks (crossed lines type):
    No dot panes: Above and below vertical rows 3/4 (34p.) or 3/5 (others) and cross in circle above vertical row 5
    Dot panes: Above and below vertical rows 8/10 (31p.) or 9/10 (others)
  Autotron marks: In same order as traffic lights in top margin above vertical rows 4/7 (22p., 31p.) on dot panes only, others not examined
  Perforation register marks: Thin bar in bottom margin opposite last perforation row (17p., 34p.) no dot panes only, others not examined
  Positioning lines: Long vertical line in left margin opposite rows 1 and 10 (17p.) no dot pane only. Short horizontal line in right margin opposite rows 1 and 10 in top and bottom perforation rows of no dot panes. Similar line on dot panes in right margin opposite rows 1 and 10
  Sheet values: Opposite rows 2/4 and 7/9 reading up at left and down at right
  Traffic lights (boxed): In bottom margin below vertical row 2 (34p.) or 2/3 (others)
    17p. Gold, black, new blue, olive-grey, yellow-brown, rose, greenish yellow
    22p. Gold, black, grey-black, turquoise-blue, olive-yellow, reddish brown, greenish yellow
    31p. Gold, black, olive-brown, ultramarine, light brown, magenta, yellow-green
    34p. Gold, black, grey-black, bright green, bright rose-red, greenish yellow

Quantities Sold   17p. 36,000,800; 22p. 7,135,800; 31p. 6,384,200; 34p. 6,022,000

Withdrawn   19.5.87

W626 Peasants working
in Fields

W627 Freemen working
at Town Trades

W628 Knight and
Retainers

W629 Lord at Banquet

(Des. Tayburn Design Consultancy)

1986 (17 JUNE).   900th ANNIVERSARY OF DOMESDAY BOOK

The original Domesday Book was written for William the Conqueror and was in two volumes. The peasants, as shown on the 17p. were dependent on their livelihood on the lord of the manor. The next value shows the freemen who managed to attain that status by purchase, apprenticeship or birth. Superior to this class were the knights who maintained numbers of retainers as depicted on the 31p. It is understood that he would allocate 40 days service a year to his feudal lord (34p.). At that time the King bestowed power to the lords in return for their allegiance, dues from the estate and when needed, military service.

Phosphorised (advanced coated) paper

W660 (= S.G.1324)	**W626**	17p. yellow-brown, vermilion, lemon, bright emerald, orange-brown, grey and brownish grey	45	50
W661 (= S.G.1325)	**W627**	22p. yellow-ochre, red, greenish blue, chestnut, grey-black and brownish grey	60	60
		a. Clipped corner to E	3·00	
W662 (= S.G.1326)	**W628**	31p. yellow-brown, vermilion, green, indian red, grey-black and brownish grey	90	90
W663 (= S.G.1327)	**W629**	34p. yellow-ochre, bright scarlet, grey-brown, new blue, lake-brown, grey-black and grey	95	95

First Day Cover (W660/3)	..	..	..	..	†	3·75
Presentation Pack (W660/3)	..	..	..	..	3·50	†
PHQ Cards (W660/3)	..	..	..	..	2·00	5·00

The 17p. value was inadvertently released two weeks before the official date and was postmarked in London W1 on 3 June 1986.

Listed Variety

W661*a*
Clipped corner of E in DOMESDAY
(No dot, R. 1/2)

Cylinder Numbers (Blocks of Six)

	Cyl. Nos.	Perforation No dot	Type R* Dot
17p.	1A (brownish grey)–1B (yellow-brown)–1C (vermilion–1D (lemon)–1E (bright emerald)–1F (orange-brown)–1G (grey) ..	3·25	3·25
22p.	1A (brownish grey)–1B (yellow-ochre)–1C (red)–1D (greenish blue)–1E (chestnut)–1F (grey-black)	4·25	4·25
31p.	1A (brownish grey)–2B (yellow-brown)–1C (vermilion)–1D (green)–1E (indian red)–1F (grey-black)	6·25	6·25
34p.	1A (grey)–2B (yellow-ochre)–1C (bright scarlet)–1D (grey-brown)–1E (new blue)–1F (lake-brown)–1G (grey-black) ..	6·75	6·75

Sheet Details

Sheet size: 100 (2 panes 10 × 5). Double pane reel-fed

Sheet markings:
Cylinder numbers: Opposite rows 8/9, left margin, boxed with Harrison logo opposite row 10
Marginal arrows: In centre at top and bottom of sheet
Colour register marks (crossed lines type):
    No dot panes: Opposite rows 6/8 at both sides and cross in circle opposite row 2, left margin
    Dot panes: Opposite rows 1/3 at both sides
Autotron marks: In same order as traffic lights in left margin opposite rows 4/7 on dot panes only
Perforation register marks: Thin bar opposite lower gutter perforations, right margin on no dot panes only
Positioning lines: Between dot and no dot panes in vertical rows 1 and 10 on all values
Sheet values: Above and below vertical rows 2/4 and 7/9 reading from left to right in top margin and from right to left (upside down) in bottom margin
Traffic lights (boxed): Opposite rows 8/9, right margin
    17p. Yellow-brown, vermilion, lemon, bright emerald, orange-brown, grey, brownish grey
    22p. Yellow-ochre, red, greenish blue, chestnut, grey-black, brownish grey
    31p. Yellow-brown, vermilion, green, indian red, grey-black, brownish grey
    34p. Yellow-ochre, bright scarlet, grey-brown, new blue, lake-brown, grey-black, grey

Quantities Sold   17p. 35,062,700; 22p. 7,018,700; 31p. 6,249,100; 34p. 5,917,000

Withdrawn   16.6.87

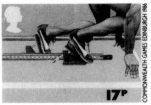

W630 Athletics

W631 Rowing

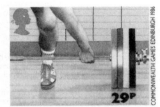

W632 Weightlifting

W633 Rifle Shooting

634 Hockey

(Des. Nick Cudworth)

1986 (15 JULY).   THIRTEENTH COMMONWEALTH GAMES

The 1986 Commonwealth Games were held in Edinburgh from 24 July to 2 August. The 34p.
value commemorates the centenary of the Hockey Association and to mark this event the sixth
World Hockey Cup for Men was staged in London from 4 to 19 October.

Phosphorised (advanced coated) paper

W664 (= S.G.1328)	**W630**	17p. black, greenish yellow, orange-vermilion, ultra-marine, chestnut and emerald		45	50
W665 (= S.G.1329)	**W631**	22p. black, lemon, scarlet, new blue, royal blue, chestnut and deep ultramarine		60	60
W666 (= S.G.1330)	**W632**	29p. grey-black, greenish yellow, scarlet, new blue, brown-ochre, brown-rose and pale chestnut ..		80	80
W667 (= S.G.1331)	**W633**	31p. black, greenish yellow, rose, blue, dull yellow-green, chestnut and yellow-green		1·00	1·00
W668 (= S.G.1332)	**W634**	34p. black, lemon, scarlet, bright blue, bright emerald, red-brown and vermilion		1·00	1·00
		a. Imperforate (pair)		£1250	
		b. Broken O		4·00	

First Day Cover (W664/8)	..	..	..	.. †	5·50
Presentation Pack (W664/8)	..	..	..	.. 4·50	†
PHQ Cards (W664/8) ..	..	..	..	.. 2·25	5·75

W   1986.   Commonwealth Games

The 17p. value was inadvertently released one week before the official date and was postmarked 8 July 1986 at Coventry. All four values were pre-released in Liverpool on 9 July 1986. First Day of Issue covers postmarked in Croydon, Surrey were dated "15 July 1985" in error.

Listed Variety

W668*b*
Broken O in HOCKEY
(Dot, R. 9/5)

Cylinder Numbers (Blocks of Six)

	Cyl. Nos.	Perforation No dot	Type R* Dot
17p.	3A (black)–2B (greenish yellow)–1C (orange-vermilion)–1D (ultramarine)–1E (chestnut)–3F (emerald)	3·25	3·25
22p.	2A (black)–1B (lemon)–1C (scarlet)–2D (new blue)–1E (royal blue)–1F (chestnut)–1G (deep ultramarine)	4·25	4·25
29p.	1A (grey-black)–1B (greenish yellow)–1C (scarlet)–1D (new blue)–1E (brown-ochre)–1F (brown-rose)–1G (pale chestnut) ..	5·50	5·50
31p.	1A (black)–1B (greenish yellow)–1C (rose)–2D (blue)–1E (dull yellow-green)–1F (chestnut)–1G (yellow-green) ..	7·00	7·00
34p.	2A (black)–1B (lemon)–1C (scarlet)–1D (bright blue)–1E (bright emerald)–1F (red-brown)–1G (vermilion)..	7·25	7·25

Sheet Details

Sheet size: 100 (panes 10 × 5). Double pane reel-fed

Sheet markings:
Cylinder numbers: Opposite rows 8/9, left margin, boxed with Harrison logo opposite row 10
Marginal arrows: In centre at top and bottom of sheet
Colour register marks (crossed lines type):
  No dot panes: Opposite rows 6/8 at both sides and cross in circle opposite row 2, left margin
  Dot panes: Opposite rows 1/3 at both sides
Autotron marks: In same order as traffic lights in left margin opposite rows 4/7 on dot panes only
Perforation register marks: Thin bar opposite lower gutter perforations, right margin on no dot panes only
Positioning lines: Between dot and no dot panes in vertical rows 1 and 10 on all values
Sheet values: Above and below vertical rows 2/4 and 7/9 reading from left to right in top margin and from right to left (upside down) in bottom margin
Traffic lights (boxed): Opposite rows 8/9, right margin
  17p. Greenish yellow, orange-vermilion, ultramarine, chestnut, emerald, black
  22p. Lemon, scarlet, new blue, royal blue, chestnut, black, deep ultramarine
  29p. Greenish yellow, scarlet, new blue, brown-ochre, brown-rose, grey-black, pale chestnut
  31p. Greenish yellow, rose, blue, dull yellow-green, chestnut, black, yellow-green
  34p. Lemon, scarlet, bright blue, bright emerald, red-brown, black, vermilion

Quantities Sold   17p. 35,087,400; 22p. 7,157,700; 29p. 6,372,200; 31p. 6,443,100; 34p. 6,087,000

Withdrawn   14.7.87

W635   **W636**
Prince Andrew and Miss Sarah Ferguson
(Des. Jeffery Matthews from photograph by Gene Nocon)

1986 (22 JULY). ROYAL WEDDING

The wedding of HRH Prince Andrew and Miss Sarah Ferguson took place on 23 July 1986 at Westminster Abbey. The design of the stamps was chosen from a photograph taken by a colleague of Prince Andrew. The bottom panel shows either wedding bells or Prince Andrew's rank of a Royal Navy Lieutenant.

One 4 mm. phosphor band at left
W669 (= S.G.1333) **W635**   12p. lake, greenish yellow, cerise, ultramarine, black
  and silver   40   40
  b. Pale scratch on collar   ..   ..   2·75
  c. Scratch retouched ..   ..   2·25

Phosphorised (advanced coated) paper
W670 (= S.G.1334) **W636**   17p. steel-blue, greenish yellow, cerise, ultramarine,
  black and gold   55   55
  a. Imperforate (pair) £850

First Day Cover (W669/70)	†	2·60
Presentation Pack (W669/70)	1·60	†
PHQ Cards (W669/70)	1·10	2·75

Listed Varieties

Pale scratch on collar
(No dot, R. 9/5)

W669*b*

The original flaw shows as a whitish scratch but in a later state grey screening dots were added to fill the pale area. Both flaws can be obtained in a plain gutter pair to show the variety with normal.

Cylinder Numbers (Blocks of Six)

Cyl. Nos.	Perforation No dot	Type R* Dot
One 4 mm. phosphor band at left		
12p. 2A (lake)–1B (greenish yellow)–1C (cerise)–1D (ultramarine)–1E (black)–1F (silver)–P84 (phosphor)	2·75	2·75

Phosphorised (advanced coated) paper
  17p.   1A (steel-blue)–1B (greenish yellow)–1C (cerise)–1D (ultra-
         marine)–1E (black)–1F (gold)   ..   ..   4·00   4·00

Sheet Details

Sheet size: 100 (2 panes 5 × 10). Double pane reel-fed

Sheet markings
  Cylinder numbers: In top margin above vertical rows 2/3, boxed. Harrison logo above vertical
    row 1
  Marginal arrows: In centre, opposite rows 5/6 at both sides
  Colour register marks (crossed lines type):
    No dot panes: Above and below vertical rows 3/4 and cross in circle above vertical row 9
    Dot panes: Above and below vertical rows 8/9
  Autotron marks: In order of traffic lights reading from left to right above vertical rows 4/7 on dot
    panes only
  Perforation register marks: Bar in bottom margin opposite first perforation row on no dot pane
    of 17p. only
  Positioning lines: In right margin opposite horizontal rows 1 and 10 on no dot panes and in left
    margin on dot panes
  Sheet values: Opposite rows 2/4 and 7/9 reading up at left and down at right
  Traffic lights (boxed): In bottom margin below vertical rows 2/3
    12p. Silver, lake, black, ultramarine, cerise, greenish yellow
    17p. Gold, steel-blue, black, ultramarine, cerise, greenish yellow

Quantities Sold   12p. 61,642,500; 17p. 59,684,400

Withdrawn   21.7.87

W637 Stylised Cross
on Ballot Paper

(Des. John Gibbs)

(Lithography by The House of Questa)

1986 (19 AUGUST).   COMMONWEALTH PARLIAMENTARY ASSOCIATION CONFERENCE

The conference was opened by the Queen and was attended by representatives from nearly fifty countries. The venue was Westminster Hall in London.

Phosphorised (advanced coated) paper. Comb perforation $14 \times 14\frac{1}{2}$
W671 (= S.G.1335)   **W637**   34p. pale grey-lilac, black, vermilion, yellow and ultramarine   95   1·00

First Day Cover (W671)	†	1·75
PHQ Card (W671)	55	1·75

Plate Numbers (Blocks of Six)

Colour order of plate numbers following the Questa imprint:
  Pale grey-lilac, black, vermilion, yellow, ultramarine

	Plate Nos. (all No dot)	Perforation Type M(B)*
34p. 1A (× 5)		6·75
1B (× 5)		6·75

*All sheet margins are perforated through except the bottom margin which is imperf.

Sheet Details

Sheet size: 100 (2 panes 5 × 10). Double pane sheets with "A" and "B" plate numbers

Sheet markings:
  Plate numbers: In top margin above vertical rows 2/3
  Marginal arrows: "W" shaped in centre, opposite rows 5/6 at both sides
  Sheet values: Opposite rows 2/4 and 7/9 reading up at left and down at right
  Imprint: In top margin above vertical rows 1/2
  Traffic lights: in the form of Questa logo below vertical row 2, bottom margin
    34p. Pale grey-lilac, black, vermilion, yellow, ultramarine

Quantity Sold   34p. 7,089,400

Withdrawn   18.8.87

W638 Lord Dowding and
Hawker "Hurricane"

W639 Lord Tedder and
Hawker "Typhoon"

W640 Lord Trenchard and
De Havilland "DH9A"

W641 Sir Arthur Harris
and Avro "Lancaster"

W642 Lord Portal and
De Havilland "Mosquito"

(Des. Brian Sanders)

1986 (16 SEPTEMBER). THE ROYAL AIR FORCE

This issue celebrates the history of the Royal Air Force and in particular the important decision, taken 50 years ago, to organise the RAF into Bomber, Fighter, Coastal and Training Commands. In 1918 the RAF had been formed by combining the Royal Flying Corps and the Royal Naval Air Service. The 29p. shows the "father of the RAF", Lord Trenchard and a famous bomber of the First World War. Other values depict famous commanders of the Second World War and the aircraft associated with them.

Phosphorised (advanced coated) paper. Comb perforation 14½

W672 (= S.G.1336) **W638**	17p.	pale blue, greenish yellow, bright rose, blue, black and grey-black	40	40
W673 (= S.G.1337) **W639**	22p.	pale turquoise-green, greenish yellow, magenta, new blue, black and grey-black	60	60
	a.	Face value omitted*	£400	
	b.	Queen's head omitted*	£400	
W674 (= S.G.1338) **W640**	29p.	pale drab, olive-yellow, magenta, blue, grey-black and black	80	80
W675 (= S.G.1339) **W641**	31p.	pale flesh, greenish yellow, magenta, ultramarine, black and grey-black	85	85
W676 (= S.G.1340) **W642**	34p.	buff, greenish yellow, magenta, blue, grey-black and black	90	90

First Day Cover (W672/6)					†	4·50
Presentation Pack (W672/6)					4·00	†
PHQ Cards (W672/6)					2·60	6·00

*Nos. W673*a*/*b* came from three consecutive sheets on which the stamps in the first vertical row were without the face value and those in the second vertical row the Queen's head.

Cylinder Numbers (Blocks of Six)

	Cyl. Nos.	Perforation No dot	Type R* Dot
17p.	1A (pale blue)–1B (greenish yellow)–3C (bright rose)–4D (blue)–1E (black)–1F (grey-black)	2·75	5·00
22p.	1A (pale turquoise-green)–1B (greenish yellow)–1C (magenta) –1D (new blue)–1E (black)–1F (grey-black)	4·25	4·25
29p.	1A (pale drab)–1B (olive-yellow)–1C (magenta)–1D (blue)–1E (grey-black)–1F (black)	5·50	5·50
31p.	1A (pale flesh)–1B (greenish yellow)–1C (magenta)–1D (ultramarine)–1E (black)–1F (grey-black)	6·00	9·00
34p.	1A (buff)–1B (greenish yellow)–1C (magenta)–1D (blue)–1E (grey-black)–1F (black)	6·50	6·50

Sheet Details

Sheet size: 100 (2 panes 5 × 10). Double pane reel-fed

Sheet markings:
Cylinder numbers: Opposite rows 8/9, left margin, boxed with Harrison logo opposite row 10
Marginal arrows: In gutter margin at centre of the sheet
Colour register marks (crossed lines type):
No dot panes: Opposite rows 7/8 at both sides and cross in circle opposite row 9 (31p.) or rows 6/7 (others)
Dot panes: Opposite rows 2/3 at both sides
Autotron marks: In same order as traffic lights in left margin opposite rows 4/7 on dot panes only
Perforation register marks: Thin bar in right margin opposite first perforation row on no dot panes only
Positioning lines: Long horizontal and short vertical lines between dot and no dot panes in vertical rows 1 and 10 on all values
Sheet values: Above and below vertical rows 2/4 and 7/9 reading from left to right in top margin and from right to left (upside down) in bottom margin
Traffic lights (boxed): Opposite row 9, right margin
17p. Greenish yellow, bright rose, blue, black, grey-black, pale blue
22p. Greenish yellow, magenta, new blue, grey-black, black, pale turquoise-green
29p. Olive-yellow, magenta, blue, grey-black, black, pale drab
31p. Greenish yellow, magenta, ultramarine, black, grey-black, pale flesh
34p. Greenish yellow, magenta, blue, black, grey-black, buff

Quantities Sold   17p. 35,497,000; 22p. 7,124,200; 29p. 6,343,200; 31p. 6,407,700; 34p. 6,056,000

Withdrawn   15.9.87

W643 The Glastonbury
Thorn

W644 The Tanad Valley
Plygain

W645 The Hebrides
Tribute

W646 The Dewsbury
Church Knell

W647 The Hereford
Boy Bishop

(Des. Lynda Gray)

1986 (18 NOVEMBER–2 DECEMBER (12p.)). CHRISTMAS

This issue features the customs and ancient legends of Christmas. The Glastonbury thorn still survives, but the original was destroyed in the 17th century. The ornate candles shown on the 18p. were carried at a Plygain or carol service. Almsgiving is the origin of the Hebrides Tribute when fish, caught on Christmas Day, was distributed among the poor people of the district. The 31p. depicts the bell-ringing custom when the bell is rung once for each year of Christ's life, ceasing at midnight on Christmas Eve. On the 34p. a mock bishop is being enthroned for the period of 6 to 28 December. This custom is at least a thousand years old, although it was suppressed several times. Choir boys carry out the enthroning on St. Nicholas Day and the "reign" ends on the day of the Feast of the Holy Innocents.

No. W677 which was issued in sheets without an underprint represented a discount of 1p. off the then second class postage rate and was available between 2 and 24 December. Additionally the 13p. value in the same design was issued in the Christmas folder at £4·30. This was a discount price and these stamps have an underprint on the reverse. The folder and the 12p. were issued on 2 December 1986.

269

One 4 mm. centre phosphor band

W677 (= S.G.1341) **W643**	12p.	gold, greenish yellow, vermilion, deep brown, emerald and deep blue	..	.. .. ..	45	40
W678 (= S.G.1342) **W643**	13p.	deep blue, greenish yellow, vermilion, deep brown, emerald and gold ..		.. .. ..	35	40

Phosphorised (advanced coated) paper

W679 (= S.G.1343) **W644**	18p.	myrtle green, yellow, vermilion, deep blue, black, reddish brown and gold ..		.. .. ..	50	50
W680 (= S.G.1344) **W645**	22p.	vermilion, olive-bistre, dull blue, deep brown, deep green and gold		.. .. ..	60	60
W681 (= S.G.1345) **W646**	31p.	deep brown, yellow, vermilion, violet, deep dull green, black and gold	..	.. .. ..	80	80
W682 (= S.G.1346) **W647**	34p.	violet, lemon, vermilion, deep dull blue, reddish brown and gold	..	.. .. ..	90	90

```
First Day Covers (2) (W677/82)      ..    ..    ..  †    5·00
Presentation Pack (W678/82) ..      ..    ..    .. 3·50  †
Christmas Folder (W683 × 36) (Sold at £4·30).   .. 17·00 †
PHQ Cards (W678/82) ..    ..    ..    ..    ..    .. 2·60  5·50
```

One 4·5 mm. phosphor band. Underprint as Type (4) multiple double-lined star in blue

W683 (= S.G.1342Eu) **W643**	13p.	deep blue, greenish yellow, vermilion, deep brown, emerald and gold (2.12) ..	.. ..	50

No. W683 was printed with the underprint *over* the gum from the Christmas folder. This contained a small sheet of 36 stamps (3 × 12) in double pane format and horizontal gutter margin between the two panes of 18. The sheets were numbered every second sheet both at top and bottom and both numbers should be the same. However, examples exist with different numbers due to the counters becoming unsynchronised. There is no premium for such sheets.

Cylinder Numbers (Blocks of Six)

		Perforation	Type R*
	Cyl. Nos.	No dot	Dot

One 4 mm. centre phosphor band

		Perforation No dot	Type R* Dot
12p.	1A (gold)–1B (greenish yellow)–1C (vermilion)–2D (deep brown)–1E (emerald)–2F (deep blue)–P86 (phosphor)	3·25	3·25
13p.	2A (deep blue)–1B (greenish yellow)–1C (vermilion)–2D (deep brown)–1E (emerald)–1F (gold)–P86 (phosphor)	2·40	2·40

Phosphorised (advanced coated) paper

		Perforation No dot	Type R* Dot
18p.	1A (myrtle green)–1B (yellow)–1C (vermilion)–1D (deep blue)–1E (black)–1F (reddish brown)–1G (gold).. ..	3·50	3·50
22p.	1A (vermilion)–1B (olive-bistre)–1C (dull blue)–1D (deep brown)–1E (deep green)–1F (gold)	4·25	4·25
31p.	1A (deep brown)–1B (yellow)–1C (vermilion)–1D (violet)–1E (deep dull green)–1F (black)–1G (gold)	5·50	5·50
34p.	1A (violet)–1B (lemon)–1C (vermilion)–1D (deep dull blue)–1E (reddish brown)–1F (gold)	6·50	6·50

Sheet Details

Sheet size: 100 (2 panes 10 × 5). Double pane reel-fed

Sheet markings:
Cylinder numbers: Opposite rows 8/9, left margin, boxed with Harrison logo opposite row 10
Marginal arrows: In centre at top and bottom of sheet
Colour register marks (crossed lines type):
  No dot panes: Opposite rows 7/8 at both sides and cross in circle opposite row 2, left margin
  Dot panes: Opposite rows 1/3 at both sides
Autotron marks: In same order as traffic lights in left margin opposite rows 3/7 (18p., 31p.) and 4/7 (others) on dot panes only
Perforation register marks: Bar opposite lower gutter perforations, right margin on dot panes only
Positioning lines: Between dot and no dot panes in vertical rows 1 and 10 on all values
Sheet values: Above and below vertical rows 2/4 and 7/9 reading from left to right in top margin and from right to left (upside down) in bottom margin
Traffic lights (boxed): Opposite rows 8/9, right margin
  12p. Greenish yellow, vermilion, deep blue, deep brown, emerald, gold
  13p. Greenish yellow, vermilion, deep blue, deep brown, emerald, gold

18p. Yellow, vermilion, deep blue, myrtle green, black, reddish brown, gold
22p. Olive-bistre, vermilion, dull blue, deep brown, deep green, gold
31p. Yellow, vermilion, violet, deep dull green, deep brown, black, gold
34p. Lemon, vermilion, deep dull blue, violet, reddish brown, gold

Quantities Sold 12p.   100,613,200;   13p.   164,743,600;   18p.   148,542,100;   22p.   16,635,800;
31p. 14,188,300; 34p. 12,359,100

Withdrawn   12p. 1.12.87, others 17.11.87

Christmas Sheets of 36 stamps (2 December 1986)
The 13p. value as **Type W643** was issued with 4·5 mm phosphor band in special Christmas folders. The price was £4·30 which meant a saving of 38p. and the stamps were printed on the reverse with double lined stars in blue. The sheets of 36 were in double panes of 18 stamps with a folded horizontal gutter margin. The folder had a cut-out window through which the stamps could be seen and to fit inside the small sheet was folded three times. The folders, which were printed by Moore & Matthes, were sold in polypropylene sachets.
The stamps were printed on the Jumelle machine on fluorescent coated paper with a phosphor band in a similar position to the sheet stamps. However, the width of the band was 4·5 mm as opposed to 4 mm. and the phosphor cylinder number (B65) was always trimmed off. It is known that the ink cylinder numbers were 2A, 1B, 1C, 1D, 1E, 1F but again they do not appear in the margin.

Sheet Details

Sheet size: 36 (2 panes 3 × 6). Reel-fed

Perforation register marks: Short horizontal lines at each side of the sheet between rows 3/4 and 9/10
Positioning lines: At the corners of the sheet at left, right or both sides
Gutter margin: This was perforated horizontally so that the sheet could be folded
Sheet numbers: In black and on every second sheet at top and bottom. Some examples have different numbers on the same sheet of 36
Traffic lights (boxed): Bottom margin below R.12/3
Gold, emerald, deep brown, deep blue, vermilion, greenish yellow

Quantity Printed   4,000,000

Withdrawn   24.12.86

1986 (18 NOVEMBER).   COLLECTORS PACK 1986

WCP19 Comprises Nos. W644/76, W678/82 (Sold at £10·32)   28·00

Withdrawn   17.11.87

1986 (18 NOVEMBER).   ROYAL MAIL SPECIAL STAMPS YEARBOOK 1986

WYB3 Comprises Nos. W644/82 (Sold at £15·95)   45·00
This book contained 32 pages, with hardback covers and slip case.

Withdrawn   17.11.87

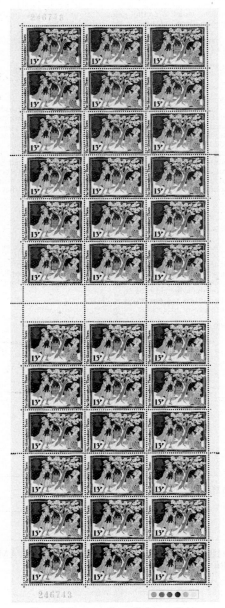

Sheet of 36 stamps from Christmas Folder

W648 North American
Blanket Flower

W649 Globe Thistle

W650 *Echeveria*

W651 Autumn Crocus

(Adapted by Jeffery Matthews)

1987 (20 JANUARY). FLOWER PHOTOGRAPHS BY ALFRED LAMMER

Black backgrounds were used to show the unusual shape and colours of the flower studies photographed by Alfred Lammer. The margins surrounding the designs are wider to allow for a strong enough signal for cancelling machines. A year date, at bottom left, appears on each value.

Phosphorised (advanced coated) paper. Comb perforation $14\frac{1}{2} \times 14$

W684 (= S.G.1347)	**W648**	18p. silver, greenish yellow, rosine, deep green and black..	45	45
W685 (= S.G.1348)	**W649**	22p. silver, greenish yellow, new blue, greenish blue and black	65	65
W686 (= S.G.1349)	**W650**	31p. silver, greenish yellow, scarlet, blue-green, deep green and black	90	90
		a. Imperforate (pair) ..	£1600	
W687 (= S.G.1350)	**W651**	34p. silver, greenish yellow, magenta, dull blue, deep green and black	1·00	1·00

First Day Cover (W684/7)	..	..	†	3·75
Presentation Pack (W684/7)	..	..	3·00	†
PHQ Cards (W684/7) ..	..	..	2·00	5·75

Cylinder Numbers (Blocks of Six)

	Cyl. Nos.	Perforation No dot	Type R* Dot
18p.	1A (silver)–1B (greenish yellow)–1C (rosine)–1D (deep green) –1E (black) ..	3·25	3·25
22p.	1A (silver)–1B (greenish yellow)–1C (new blue)–1D (greenish blue)–1E (black) ..	4·50	4·50
31p.	1A (silver)–1B (greenish yellow)–1C (scarlet)–1D (blue-green) –1E (deep green)–1F (black).	6·25	6·25
34p.	1A (silver)–1B (greenish yellow)–1C (magenta)–1D (dull blue) –1E (deep green)–1F (black).	7·00	7·00

W   1987.   Sir Isaac Newton

Sheet Details

Sheet size: 100 (2 panes 10 × 5). Double pane reel-fed

Sheet markings:
 Cylinder numbers: In top margin above vertical rows 2/3, boxed. Harrison logo above vertical row 1
 Marginal arrows: In gutter margin at centre of the sheet
 Colour register marks (crossed lines type):
  No dot panes: Above and below vertical row 3 (22p.) or 4/5 (others) and cross in circle above vertical row 2
  Dot panes: Above and below vertical row 7
 Autotron marks: In same order as traffic lights in top margin above vertical rows 4/6 (18p.), 3/5 (22p.) and 3/6 (others) on dot panes only
 Perforation register marks: Thin bar in top margin opposite last perforation row on no dot panes only
 Positioning lines: Between dot and no dot panes opposite horizontal rows 1 and 10, all values
 Sheet values: Opposite rows 2/4 and 7/9 reading up at left and down at right
 Traffic lights (boxed): In bottom margin below vertical row 2
  18p. Silver, black, deep green, rosine, greenish yellow
  22p. Silver, black, greenish blue, new blue, greenish yellow
  31p. Silver, black, deep green, blue-green, scarlet, greenish yellow
  34p. Silver, black, deep green, dull blue, magenta, greenish yellow

Withdrawn   19.1.88

Sir *ISAAC NEWTON* (1642-1727)

W652 *The Principia Mathematica*

Sir *ISAAC NEWTON* (1642-1727)

W653 *Motion of Bodies in Ellipses*

Sir *ISAAC NEWTON* (1642-1727)

W654 *Optick Treatise*

Sir *ISAAC NEWTON* (1642-1727)

W655 *The System of the World*

(Des. Sarah Godwin)

1987 (24 MARCH). SIR ISAAC NEWTON

This issue celebrates the 300th anniversary of the publication of Newton's *Mathematical Principles of Natural Philosophy* (*Philosophiae Naturalis Principia Mathematica*). Newton was born on Christmas Day, 1642 two months after the death of his father. He studied at Cambridge University from 1661, but lived at Woolsthorpe, Lincolnshire. Newton wrote the *Principia* at Cambridge, starting in March 1686 and it was published in 1687. He was knighted by Queen Anne at Cambridge in 1705 by which time he was Master of the Mint. Further editions of the *Principia* appeared in 1713 and 1726 and in the following year Newton died, aged 84 years. He was buried on 28 March 1727 at Westminster Abbey.

Phosphorised (advanced coated) paper

W688 (= S.G.1351)	**W652**	18p. black, greenish yellow, cerise, blue-green, grey-black and silver	45	45
W689 (= S.G.1352)	**W653**	22p. black, greenish yellow, bright orange, blue, bright emerald, silver and bluish violet	60	60
		a. White patch on Jupiter	3·00	
W690 (= S.G.1353)	**W654**	31p. black, greenish yellow, scarlet, new blue, bronze-green, silver and slate-green	85	85
		a. Yellow flaw on bottle	3·75	
W691 (= S.G.1354)	**W655**	34p. black, greenish yellow, red, bright blue, grey-black and silver	95	95
		a. Broken line at left	4·25	

First Day Cover (W688/91) ..	..	..	.. †	3·75
Presentation Pack (W688/91) ..	..	..	.. 3·00	†
PHQ Cards (W688/91) ..	..	..	.. 2·00	5·00

Listed Varieties

W689*a*	W690*a*	W691*a*
White patch on Jupiter (Dot, R. 4/7)	Angled yellow flaw below T of OPTICK (No dot, R. 4/5)	Broken circumference at left (Dot, R. 10/7)

Cylinder Numbers (Blocks of Six)

	Perforation	Type R*
Cyl. Nos.	No dot	Dot
18p. 1A (black)–1B (greenish yellow)–1C (cerise)–1D (blue-green)–1E (grey-black)–2F (silver)	3·25	3·25
22p. 1A (black)–1B (greenish yellow)–1C (bright orange)–1D (blue)–1E (bright emerald)–2F (silver)–1G (bluish violet) ..	4·25	4·25
31p. 1A (black)–1B (greenish yellow)–1C (scarlet)–1D (new blue)–1E (bronze-green)–2F (silver)–3G (slate-green)	6·00	6·00
34p. 1A (grey-black)–1B (greenish yellow)–1C (red)–1D (bright blue)–1E (grey-black)–2F (silver)	6·75	6·75

Sheet Details

Sheet size: 100 (2 panes 5 × 10). Double pane reel-fed

Sheet markings:
  Cylinder numbers: In top margin above vertical rows 2/3, boxed. Harrison logo above vertical row 1

Marginal arrows: In centre, opposite rows 5/6 at both sides
Colour register marks (crossed lines type):
  No dot panes: Above and below vertical rows 4/5 and cross in circle above vertical row 9
  Dot panes: Above and below vertical rows 8/10
Autotron marks: In order of traffic lights reading from left to right above vertical rows 4/7 (18p., 34p.) or 4/8 (others) on dot panes only
Perforation register marks: Bar in bottom margin opposite first gutter perforation row on no dot panes only
Positioning lines: Long vertical and short horizontal lines between no dot and dot panes in vertical margin seen at right on no dot and at left on dot panes
Sheet values: Opposite rows 2/4 and 7/9 reading up at left and down at right
Traffic lights (boxed): In bottom margin below vertical rows 2/3
  18p. Silver, black, grey-black, blue-green, cerise, greenish yellow
  22p. Silver, black, bluish violet, bright emerald, blue, bright orange, greenish yellow
  31p. Silver, black, slate-green, bronze-green, new blue, scarlet, greenish yellow
  34p. Silver, black, grey-black, bright blue, red, greenish yellow

Withdrawn   23.3.88

W656 Willis Faber and
Dumas Building, Ipswich

W657 Pompidou Centre,
Paris

W658 Staatsgalerie,
Stuttgart

W659 European Investment
Bank, Luxembourg

(Des. Brian Tattersfield)

1987 (12 MAY). BRITISH ARCHITECTS IN EUROPE ("EUROPA")

The Europa theme was Modern Arts, with the emphasis on architecture and on each stamp the title of the issue is set above the architects surname(s), locality of the building and Europa symbol. The 18p. shows a building which is predominately of glass and at the top there is a roof garden. An escalator, rather than lifts, serve each level. The Pompidou Centre brings to the fore the air conditioning system as shown on the 22p. The sculpture court is shown on the 31p. and the next value depicts the European Investment Bank which is circular in design and is built on the edge of a ravine.

Phosphorised (advanced coated) paper

W692 (= S.G.1355)	**W656**	18p.	black, bistre-yellow, cerise, bright blue, deep grey and grey-black	45	45
W693 (= S.G.1356)	**W657**	22p.	black, greenish yellow, carmine, bright blue, deep grey and grey-black	60	60
		b.	Blue line above escalator	3·75	
W694 (= S.G.1357)	**W658**	31p.	grey-black, bistre-yellow, cerise, bright blue, bright green, black and dull violet	85	85
		a.	Imperforate (horiz. pair) £1000		
W695 (= S.G.1358)	**W659**	34p.	black, greenish yellow, cerise, bright blue, deep grey and grey-black	95	95

First Day Cover (W692/5)	..	..	..	.. †	3·75
Presentation Pack (W692/5)	..	..	..	.. 3·25	†
PHQ Cards (W692/5) ..	..	..	..	.. 2·00	5·00

Listed Variety

W693*b*
Blue line above escalator canopy
(No dot, R. 6/7)

Cylinder Numbers (Blocks of Six)

	Cyl. Nos.	Perforation No dot	Type R* Dot
18p.	1A (black)–1B (bistre-yellow)–1C (cerise)–1D (bright blue)–3E (deep grey)–1F (grey-black)	3·25	3·25
22p.	1A (black)–1B (greenish yellow)–1C (carmine)–1D (bright blue)–1E (deep grey)–1F (grey-black)	4·25	4·25
31p.	3A (grey-black–1B (bistre-yellow)–1C (cerise)–1D (bright blue) –1E (bright green)–1F (black)–1G (dull violet)	6·00	6·00
34p.	1A (black)–1B (greenish yellow)–1C (cerise)–1D (bright blue) –4E (deep grey)–1F (grey-black)	6·75	6·75

Sheet Details

Sheet size: 100 (2 panes 10 × 5). Double pane reel-fed

Sheet markings:
    Cylinder numbers: Opposite rows 8/9, left margin, boxed with Harrison logo opposite row 10
    Marginal arrows: In centre at top and bottom of sheet
    Colour register marks (crossed lines type):
        No dot panes: Opposite row 7 (22p.) or 6/8 (others) at both sides and cross in circle opposite row 2, left margin
        Dot panes: Opposite rows 1/3 at both sides
    Autotron marks: In same order as traffic lights in left margin opposite rows 4/7 on dot panes only

Perforation register marks: Thin bar opposite upper gutter perforations, right margin on dot panes only

Positioning lines: Between dot and no dot panes in vertical rows 1 and 10 on all values

Sheet values: Above and below vertical rows 2/4 and 7/9 reading from left to right in top margin and from right to left (upside down) in bottom margin

Traffic lights (boxed): Opposite rows 8/9, right margin

   18p. Bistre-yellow, cerise, bright blue, deep grey, black, grey-black

   22p. Greenish yellow, carmine, bright blue, deep grey, black, grey-black

   31p. Bistre-yellow, cerise, bright blue, bright green, dull violet, grey-black, black

   34p. Greenish yellow, cerise, bright blue, deep grey, black, grey-black

Withdrawn   11.5.88

W660 Brigade Members
with Ashford Litter,
1887

W661 Bandaging Blitz
Victim, 1940

W662 Volunteer with
fainting girl, 1965

W663 Transport of
Transplant Organ by
Air Wing, 1987

(Des. Debbie Cook)

(Lithography by The House of Questa)

1987 (16 JUNE). ST. JOHN AMBULANCE

This set celebrates the centenary of the St. John Ambulance and the stamps show the changing society and transport over the past one hundred years. The Brigade's essential aim of training volunteers in first-aid has not changed since the formation of the Association in July 1877. In 1887 the St. John Ambulance Brigade was formed and in that year came their first major public duty when vast crowds attended Queen Victoria's Jubilee celebrations. During the Boer War of 1899–1902 members and supplies were sent to South Africa and in the First World War the St. John Ambulance had over 1,000 of their personnel killed and over 30,000 had seen service. Again by the outbreak of war in 1939 there were 10,000 instructors at work training new volunteers. By attending all major functions in peacetime they provide very important services and the 31p. shows one of these. Transport is a key role and St. John Ambulance Air Wing personnel are shown on the 34p. in their work of airlifting essential medical supplies, including human organs, for transplant surgery.

Phosphorised (advanced coated) paper. Comb perforation 14 × 14½.

W696 (= S.G.1359)	**W660**	18p.	new blue, greenish yellow, magenta, black, silver and pink	45	45
W697 (= S.G.1360)	**W661**	22p.	new blue, greenish yellow, magenta, black, silver and cobalt	60	60
W698 (= S.G.1361)	**W662**	31p.	new blue, greenish yellow, magenta, black, silver and bistre-brown	85	85
W699 (= S.G.1362)	**W663**	34p.	new blue, greenish yellow, magenta, black, silver and greenish grey	95	95

First Day Cover (W696/9)	..	..	..	..	†	3·75
Presentation Pack (W696/9)	..	..	..	3·00	†	
PHQ Cards (W696/9)	..	..	..	..	2·00	5·50

Plate Numbers (Blocks of Six)

Colour order of plate nos.
18p. New blue, greenish yellow, magenta, black, silver, pink
22p. New blue, greenish yellow, magenta, black, silver, cobalt
31p. New blue, greenish yellow, magenta, black, silver, bistre-brown
34p. New blue, greenish yellow, magenta, black, silver, greenish grey

	Plate Nos. (all No dot)	Perforation Type M
18p.	1A (×6)	3·25
	1B (×6)	3·25
	1A (×5)–2A	3·25
	1B (×5)–2B..	6·50
	1A (×5)–3A	25·00
	1B (×5)–3B..	25·00
	1A–1A–2A–1A–1A–3A	6·00
	1B–1B–2B–1B–1B–3B	6·00
	2A–2A–2A–2A–1A–3A	4·50
	2B–2B–2B–2B–1B–3B	4·50
	2A–2A–3A–2A–1A–3A	3·75
	2B–2B–3B–2B–1B–3B	3·75
22p.	1A (×6)	4·25
	1B (×6)	4·25
31p.	1A (×6)	6·00
	1B (×6)	6·00
34p.	1A (×6)	6·75
	1B (×6)	6·75

Sheet Details

Sheet size: 100 (2 panes 5 × 10). Double pane sheets with "A" and "B" plate numbers

Sheet markings:
Plate numbers: In top margin above vertical rows 2/3
Marginal arrows: "W" shaped in centre, opposite rows 5/6 at both sides
Sheet values: Opposite rows 2/4 and 7/9 reading up at left and down at right
Imprint: In top margin above vertical rows 1/2
Traffic lights: In the form of Questa logo below vertical row 2, bottom margin
For order of colours see under "Plate Numbers" above

Withdrawn 15.6.88

279

W664 Arms of the Lord
Lyon King of Arms

W665 Scottish Heraldic
Banner of Prince Charles

W666 Arms of Royal
Scottish Academy of Painting,
Sculpture and Architecture

W667 Arms of Royal
Society of Edinburgh

(Des. Jeffery Matthews)

1987 (21 JULY). SCOTTISH HERALDRY

This issue marks the 300th anniversary of the revival of the Order of the Thistle in 1687 by King James VII of Scotland and II of England. The most familiar insignia of the Order is the Star worn on the left breast and this is shown at the top left in each design. It also serves as the cap badge of the Scots Guards and badges of similar shape, but of different design, are worn by some other Scottish regiments. The 18p. shows the crown of Scotland and batons of the type carried by the Lord Lyon on ceremonial occasions. The 22p. depicts the banner used by the Sovereign's eldest son when in Scotland and the Queen bestowed the banner on Prince Charles in 1974. The 31p. and 34p. show the use of heraldry by modern-day societies and the square bearing the royal arms of Scotland is a special honour that can only be added with the consent of the Sovereign.

Phosphorised (advanced coated) paper. Comb perforation 14½

W700 (= S.G.1363)	**W664**	18p.	black, lemon, scarlet, blue, deep green, slate and brown	45	45
W701 (= S.G.1364)	**W665**	22p.	black, greenish yellow, carmine, new blue, deep green, grey and lake-brown	60	60
W702 (= S.G.1365)	**W666**	31p.	black, greenish yellow, scarlet, new blue, dull green, grey and grey-black	85	85
W703 (= S.G.1366)	**W667**	34p.	black, greenish yellow, scarlet, deep ultramarine, dull green, grey and yellow-brown	95	95

First Day Cover (W700/03)	..	..	..	..	†	3·75
Presentation Pack (W700/03)	..	..	..	..	3·00	†
PHQ Cards (W700/03) ..	..	..	..	..	2·00	5·00

Cylinder Numbers (Blocks of Six)

	Cyl. Nos.	Perforation No dot	Type R* Dot
18p.	1A (black)–1B (lemon)–1C (scarlet)–1D (blue)–1E (deep green) –1F (slate)–1G (brown)	3·25	3·25
22p.	1A (black)–1B (greenish yellow)–1C (carmine)–1D (new blue)–1E (deep green)–1F (grey)–1G (lake-brown)	4·25	4·25
31p.	1A (black)–1B (greenish yellow)–1C (scarlet)–1D (new blue)–2E (dull green)–1F (grey)–1G (grey-black)	6·00	6·00
34p.	1A (black)–1B (greenish yellow)–1C (scarlet)–1D (deep ultra- marine)–1E (dull green)–1F (grey)–1G (yellow-brown)	6·75	6·75

Sheet Details

Sheet size: 100 (2 panes 5 × 10). Double pane reel-fed

Sheet markings:
    Cylinder numbers: Opposite rows 8/9, left margin, boxed with Harrison logo opposite row 10
    Marginal arrows: In gutter margin opposite rows 5/6
    Colour register marks (crossed lines type):
        No dot panes: At both sides opposite rows 6/8 and cross in circle opposite row 9, left margin
        Dot panes: At both sides opposite rows 2/3
    Autotron marks: In same order as traffic lights in left margin opposite rows 4/7 on dot panes only
    Perforation register marks: Thin bar in right margin opposite first perforation row on no dot panes only
    Sheet values: Above and below vertical rows 2/4 and 7/9 reading from left to right in top margin and from right to left (upside down) in bottom margin
    Traffic lights (boxed): Opposite rows 8/9, right margin
        18p. Lemon, scarlet, blue, deep green, slate, brown, black
        22p. Greenish yellow, carmine, new blue, deep green, grey, lake-brown, black
        31p. Greenish yellow, scarlet, new blue, dull green, grey, grey-black, black
        34p. Greenish yellow, scarlet, deep ultramarine, dull green, grey, yellow-brown, black

Withdrawn 20.7.88

W668 Crystal Palace,
"Monarch of the Glen"
(Landseer) and Grace Darling

W669 *Great Eastern, Beeton's
Book of Household Management*
and Prince Albert

W670 Albert Memorial
Ballot Box and Disraeli

W671 Diamond Jubilee Emblem,
Newspaper Placard for Relief
of Mafeking and Morse Key

(Des. Mike Dempsey. Eng. Czeslaw Slania)

(Recess (values and background) and photogravure Harrison)

1987 (8 SEPTEMBER). VICTORIAN BRITAIN

The stamps mark the 150th anniversary of Queen Victoria's accession to the throne and the centenary of her Golden Jubilee. The portraits of Queen Victoria, at various stages of her long reign, are set against backgrounds that show the achievements, inventiveness, sentimentality and energy of this remarkable era. The 18p. whilst showing the venue of the 1851 Great Exhibition also includes Grace Darling, a heroine who rowed through a storm to rescue five survivors of a shipwreck. The 22p. features the book by Isabella Beeton which is still in print and the *Great Eastern* (18,918 tons). Launched in 1858, she was designed by Isambard Kingdom Brunel with an iron hull and was the largest ship to be built for 40 years. The Prince Consort is also shown on the 22p. Following his death in 1861 the Queen went into a period of seclusion. Disraeli encouraged the Queen's return to public life and the 31p. depicts him and the Albert Memorial in Kensington Gardens, London. The ballot box marks the introduction of secret ballots held for Parliamentary and local elections following the Ballot Act 1872. The 34p. shows the Diamond Jubilee portrait of the Queen and the special Jubilee emblem. At the close of the century and her reign, the Boer War was in progress and Marconi had transmitted the first wireless-telegraph message across the English Channel.

Phosphorised (advanced coated) paper

W704 (= S.G.1367)	**W668**	18p. pale stone, deep blue, lemon, rose, greenish blue, brown-ochre and grey-black	45	45
W705 (= S.G.1368)	**W669**	22p. pale stone, deep brown, lemon, rose, grey-black and brown-ochre	60	60
		a. Prince Consort vignette (part) in left margin ..		
		.. .. (*single with margin*) 35·00		

W706 (= S.G.1369) **W670**   31p. pale stone, deep lilac, lemon, cerise, brown-ochre,
                                greenish blue and grey-black 85   85
                                a. Re-entry showing frame and date doubled .. 4·50
                                b. Shading retouched above hair .. .. .. 4·25
                                c. Recut spire, shading etc. .. .. 4·50
                                d. Shading retouched and dot over tree .. .. 4·25
W707 (= S.G.1370) **W671**   34p. pale stone, myrtle-green, yellow-ochre, reddish
                                brown and brown-ochre 95   95

First Day Cover (W704/07) ..	.. .. ..	†	3·75
Presentation Pack (W704/07) ..	.. .. ..	.. 3·00	†
PHQ Cards (W704/07)	.. ..	.. 2·00	5·00

The 18p. is known postmarked at Bow, East London on 3 September 1987.

Listed Varieties

W705*a*

No. W705*a* shows only a small part of the Prince Consort vignette in the margin at left. A test row of impressions from the recess plate picked up ink residue during printing. It is understood that a few sheets were affected; one variety per horizontal row. It is probable that in future issues any test row will be positioned beyond the trimmed margin of the sheets. (*Price for cylinder block of six, includes 3 varieties,* £125).

W706*a*
Year and frames at top show
doubling
(Pl. 6, R. 8/7)

W706*b*
Retouched shading between
hair and frame
(Pl. 6, R. 9/6)

W706c

This variety, which adjoins Nos. W706b and d, shows recut lines in various parts of the design. The shading and Disraeli's face have been retouched while the Memorial has been partly recut ‑particularly the small spire at right. This is vertical instead of leaning to left and a small figure 3 on its side replaces the squiggle over the left spire. There is also a large spot in the 1 of 31p. which is not illustrated
(Pl. 6, R. 9/7)

W706d

Spot over the tree appears as an early bird and shading retouched behind Disraeli. The inner frame is damaged and several states are known but in these the spot appears to be constant
(Pl. 6, R. 9/8)

Cylinder Numbers (Blocks of Six)

	Cyl. Nos.	Perforation No dot	Type R* Dot
18p.	1A (lemon)–1B (rose)–1C (greenish blue)–1D (brown-ochre)–2E (grey-black)	3·25	3·25
22p.	1A (lemon)–1B (rose)–1C (grey-black)–1D (brown-ochre) ..	4·25	4·25
31p.	1A (lemon)–2B (cerise)–2C (brown-ochre)–1D (greenish blue) –3E (grey black)	6·00	6·00
34p.	1A (yellow-ochre)–1B (reddish brown)–2C (brown-ochre) ..	6·75	6·75

Sheet Details

Sheet size: 100 (2 panes 10 × 5). Double pane reel-fed

Sheet markings:
Cylinder numbers: Opposite rows 8/9, left margin, boxed with Harrison logo opposite row 10
Marginal arrows: In centre at top and bottom of sheet
Colour register marks (crossed lines type):
   No dot panes: At both sides opposite row 7 and cross in circle opposite row 2, left margin
   Dot panes: At both sides opposite row 2

Autotron marks: In same order as traffic lights in left margin opposite rows 4/7 (31p.), gutter/7 (34p.) and others not examined. Additional black horizontal bar photo-etched in vertical row 4 of the gutter margin on no dot panes. In addition and on both panes an additional bar recess printed in the colour of the value between vertical rows 4/5 in central gutter and at top and bottom of the sheet. Occasionally they are trimmed but a horizontal row of up to six dots to the right of the bar indicates the plate sequence to the printer.

Perforation register marks: Thick bar opposite lower gutter perforations, right margin on no dot panes only

Positioning lines: Long horizontal or short vertical lines in vertical rows 1 or 10 on dot panes

Sheet values: Above and below vertical rows 2/4 and 7/9 reading from left to right in top margin and from right to left (upside-down) in bottom margin

Traffic lights (boxed): Opposite row 9, right margin

18p. Lemon, rose, greenish blue, grey-black, brown-ochre
22p. Lemon, rose, grey-black, brown-ochre
31p. Lemon, cerise, greenish blue, grey-black, brown-ochre
34p. Yellow-ochre, reddish brown, brown-ochre

Withdrawn   7.9.88

W672 Pot by Bernard Leach

W673 Pot by Elizabeth Fritsch

W674 Pot by Lucie Rie

W675 Pot by Hans Coper

(Des. Tony Evans)

1987 (13 OCTOBER).   STUDIO POTTERY

The centenary of the birth of Bernard Leach and the renaissance of British studio pottery is commemorated by this issue showing distinctive pottery. Leach died at the age of 92 and was famed for his work in teaching and writing books on pottery. The 18p. depicts one of his pots which shows the oriental influence of his friend, Shoji Hamada the Japanese potter. The 26p. shows the geometric design on a pot made by Elizabeth Fritsch. She built the pots instead of using the wheel. The work of Viennese-born Lucie Rie is depicted on the 31p. which shows the delicate fine line pattern and high glaze of her pots. She worked with the late Hans Coper and together exerted an important influence on studio pottery design after the Second World War.

Phosphorised (advanced coated) paper. Comb perforation $14\frac{1}{2} \times 14$

W708 (= S.G.1371)	**W672**	18p. gold, lemon, light red-brown, chestnut, light grey and black	30 35
W709 (= S.G.1372)	**W673**	26p. blue over silver, yellow-orange, bright purple, lavender, bluish violet, grey-brown and black ..	40 45
W710 (= S.G.1373)	**W674**	31p. rose-lilac over silver, greenish yellow, cerise, new blue, grey-lilac and black	50 55
W711 (= S.G.1374)	**W675**	34p. copper, yellow-brown, reddish brown, grey-lilac and black	55 60

First Day Cover (W708/11)	†	3·50
Presentation Pack (W708/11)	2·00	†
Pack also exists with a Hafnia '87 insert card.		
PHQ Cards (W708/11)	1·10	4·50

At the international stamp exhibition, Hafnia '87 in Copenhagen, Denmark presentation packs were available from the British Post Office stand with a special insert card stating that the pack had been assembled at the exhibition.

Cylinder Numbers (Blocks of Six)

	Cyl. Nos.	Perforation No dot	Type R* Dot
18p.	1A (gold)–1B (lemon)–1C (light red-brown)–1D (chestnut)–1E (light grey)–3F (black)	2·10	2·10
26p.	1A (blue over silver)–1B (yellow-orange)–1C (bright purple)–1D (lavender)–1E (bluish violet)–1F (grey-brown)–2G (black) ..	2·75	2·75
31p.	1A (rose-lilac over silver)–1B (greenish yellow)–2C (cerise)–1D (new blue)–1E (grey-lilac)–2F (black)	3·50	3·50
34p.	1A (copper)–1B (yellow-brown)–1C (reddish brown)–1D (grey-lilac)–2E (black)	4·00	4·00

Sheet Details

Sheet markings:
   Cylinder numbers: In top margin above vertical row 2 (34p.) or rows 2/3 (others), boxed.
   Harrison logo above vertical row 1
   Marginal arrows: In gutter margin at centre of the sheet
   Colour register marks (crossed lines type):
      No dot panes: Above and below vertical row 4
      Dot panes: Above and below vertical row 9 and cross in circle type above vertical rows 1/2
   Autotron marks: In order of traffic lights reading from left to right above vertical rows 4/7 on dot panes only
   Perforation register marks: Thick bar in bottom margin opposite last perforation row on no dot panes only
   Positioning lines: Long vertical and short horizontal lines between no dot and dot panes in vertical margin seen at right on no dot and at left on dot panes
   Sheet values: Opposite rows 2/4 and 7/9 reading up at left and down at right
   Traffic lights (boxed): In bottom margin below vertical rows 2/3 (26p.) or row 2 (others)
      18p. Gold, black, light grey, chestnut, light red-brown, lemon
      26p. Blue over silver, black, grey-brown, bluish violet, lavender, bright purple, yellow-orange
      31p. Rose-lilac over silver, black, grey-lilac, new blue, cerise, greenish yellow
      34p. Copper, black, grey-lilac, reddish brown, yellow-brown

W676 Decorating the
Christmas Tree

W677 Waiting for
Father Christmas

W678 Sleeping Child and
Father Christmas in Sleigh

W679 Child reading

W680 Child playing
Recorder and Snowman

· (Des. Michael Foreman)

1987 (17 NOVEMBER).   CHRISTMAS

The theme of this set is the magic of Christmas as seen through the eyes of a young child.
The 13p. shows the child selecting decorations for the Christmas tree, a custom that comes from the middle ages revived by Prince Albert in the 19th century. Christmas Eve, and the child gazes expectantly out of the window on the 18p. stamp. Lights in the church indicate a service is in progress. Christmas night on the 26p. shows the child asleep and the toys delivered by Father Christmas. The 31p. features the child on Christmas morning reading a new book and the opened presents. Christmas afternoon on the 34p. and the snowman peers through the window as the child learns to play the new recorder.
There was no Christmas stamp booklet but the folder contained the 13p. with the multiple double-lined star underprint in blue. For the first time on special stamps, the new phosphor ink was used. Under ultra-violet light it is very faint compared to the ink it replaced.

One 4·5 mm. phosphor band (to left of centre)
W712 (= S.G.1375)   **W676**   13p. gold, greenish yellow, rose, greenish blue and
                                   black.   20   25

Phosphorised (advanced coated) paper

W713 (= S.G.1376)	**W677**	18p.	gold, greenish yellow, bright purple, greenish blue, bright blue and black	30	35
W714 (= S.G.1377)	**W678**	26p.	gold, greenish yellow, bright purple, new blue, bright blue and black	40	45
W715 (= S.G.1378)	**W679**	31p.	gold, greenish yellow, scarlet, bright magenta, dull rose, greenish blue and black	50	55
W716 (= S.G.1379)	**W680**	34p.	gold, greenish yellow, dull rose, greenish blue, bright blue and black	55	60

First Day Cover (W712/16)	.. †	3·50
Presentation Pack (W712/16)	.. 2·10	†
Christmas Folder (W717 × 36) (Sold at £4·60).	.. 7·00	†
PHQ Cards (W712/16)	.. 1·10	4·75

One 4·5 mm phosphor band. Underprint as Type (4) multiple-double star in blue

W717 (= S.G.1375Eu)	**W676**	13p.	gold, greenish yellow, rose, greenish blue and black..	30

No. W717 was printed with the underprint *over* the gum from the Christmas folder. The sheet of 36 stamps (3 × 12) was printed in the same format as the 1986 Christmas sheet on the Jumelle press.

Cylinder Numbers (Blocks of Six)

	Cyl. Nos.	Perforation No dot	Type R* Dot
One 4·5 mm. phosphor band			
13p. 1A (gold)–1B (greenish yellow)–1C (rose)–2D (greenish blue)–1E (black)–P87 (phosphor)		1·40	1·40
Phosphorised (advanced coated) paper			
18p. 1A (gold)–1B (greenish yellow)–2C (bright purple)–1D (greenish blue)–2E (bright blue)–2F (black)		2·10	2·10
26p. 1A (gold)–1B (greenish yellow)–1C (bright purple)–1D (new blue)–1E (bright blue)–1F (black)		2·75	2·75
31p. 1A (gold)–1B (greenish yellow)–1C (scarlet)–1D (bright magenta)–1E (dull rose)–2F (greenish blue)–1G (black) ..		3·50	3·50
34p. 1A (gold)–1B (greenish yellow)–1C (dull rose)–1D (greenish blue)–1E (bright blue)–1F (black)		4·00	4·00

Sheet Details

Sheet size: 100 (2 panes 10 × 5). Double pane reel-fed

Sheet markings:
Cylinder numbers: Opposite rows 8/9, left margin, boxed with Harrison logo opposite row 10
Marginal arrows: In centre at top and bottom of sheet
Colour register marks (crossed lines type):
No dot panes: Opposite row 7 (13p.) or 6/7 (others) at both sides and cross in circle opposite row 2, left margin
Dot panes: Opposite rows 1/2 at both sides
Autotron marks: In same order as traffic lights in left margin opposite rows 6/8 (13p.) and 5/8 (others) on dot panes only
Perforation register marks: Thick bar opposite lower gutter perforations, right margin on no dot panes only
Positioning lines: Between dot and no dot panes in vertical rows 1 and 10 on all values
Sheet values: Above and below vertical rows 2/4 and 7/9 reading from left to right in top margin and from right to left (upside down) in bottom margin
Traffic lights (boxed): Opposite row 9 (13p.) or rows 8/9 (others), right margin
13p. Greenish yellow, rose, greenish blue, black, gold
18p. Greenish yellow, bright purple, greenish blue, bright blue, black, gold
26p. Greenish yellow, bright purple, new blue, bright blue, black, gold
31p. Greenish yellow, scarlet, bright magenta, dull rose, greenish blue, black, gold
34p. Greenish yellow, dull rose, greenish blue, bright blue, black, gold

Christmas Sheets of 36 stamps

Issued on 17 November 1987 this was as No. W712 but with the addition of the underprint on the gum side. Following the successful introduction of the sheet in a Christmas folder in 1986, the pattern was followed. The notes below No. W683 apply here. The folder was sold at £4·60 which meant a saving of just 8p. on the total face value of the stamps (36 @ 13p. each). There were no cylinder numbers on the issued sheets.

1987 (17 NOVEMBER).   COLLECTORS PACK 1987

WCP20 Comprises Nos. W684/716 (Sold at £9·28)   14·00

1987 (17 NOVEMBER).   ROYAL MAIL SPECIAL STAMPS
YEARBOOK 1987

WYB4 Comprises Nos. W684/716 (Sold at £15·95)   24·00
This book contained 32 pages, with hardback covers and slip case.

W681 Bull-rout
(Jonathan Couch)

W682 Yellow Waterlily
(Major Joshua Swatkin)

W683 Bewick's Swan
(Edward Lear)

W684 *Morchella esculenta*
(James Sowerby)

(Des. Edward Hughes)

1988 (19 JANUARY).   BICENTENARY OF LINNEAN SOCIETY

The Linnean Society was named after the famous Swedish naturalist, Carl Linne (1707–1778) also known as Carl Linnaeus, the inventor of the system by which finds in the natural world are named. He recognised that every living thing belongs to a particular family and accordingly gave a Latin name to this with a further Latin name describing the traits and the section of the family from which it comes. The Linnean Society was formed in London, ten years after the death of Linnaeus. Some great names in biology have been members, including Sir Joseph Banks, Charles Darwin and Alfred Russell Wallace. The society is the world's oldest existing learned body which is devoted to natural history and biology.

Phosphorised (advanced coated) paper

W718 (= S.G.1380)	**W681**	18p.	grey-black, stone, orange-yellow, bright purple, olive-bistre and gold	30	35
W719 (= S.G.1381)	**W682**	26p.	black, stone, bistre-yellow, dull orange, greenish blue, gold and pale bistre	40	45
W720 (= S.G.1382)	**W683**	31p.	black, stone, greenish yellow, rose-red, deep blue, gold and olive-bistre	50	55
		a.	Imperforate (horiz. pair) £1250		
W721 (= S.G.1383)	**W684**	34p.	black, stone, yellow, pale bistre, olive-grey, gold and olive-bistre	55	60

First Day Cover (W718/21) ..	..	..	.. †	3·25
Presentation Pack (W718/21) ..	..	..	.. 2·00	†
PHQ Cards (W718/21) ..	..	..	.. 1·10	4·50

Cylinder Numbers (Blocks of Six)

	Cyl. Nos.	Perforation No dot	Type R* Dot
18p.	1A (grey-black)–1B (stone)–1C (orange-yellow)–1D (bright purple)–1E (olive-bistre)–1F (gold)	2·10	2·10
26p.	3A (black)–1B (stone)–1C (bistre-yellow)–1D (dull orange)–1E (greenish blue)–1F (gold)–1G (pale bistre)	2·75	2·75
31p.	1A (black)–1B (stone)–1C (greenish yellow)–1D (rose-red)–1E (deep blue)–1F (gold)–1G (olive-bistre)	3·50	3·50
34p.	2A (black)–1B (stone)–1C (yellow)–2D (pale bistre)–1E (olive-grey)–1F (gold)–1G (olive-bistre)	4·00	4·00

Sheet Details

Sheet size: 100 (2 panes 10 × 5). Double pane reel-fed

Sheet markings:
Cylinder numbers: Opposite rows 8/9, left margin, boxed with Harrison logo opposite row 10
Marginal arrows: In centre at top and bottom of sheet
Colour register marks (crossed lines type):
No dot panes: Opposite rows 6/8 at both sides and cross in circle opposite row 2
Dot panes: Opposite rows 1/3 at both sides
Autotron marks: In same order as traffic lights in left margin opposite rows 4/7 (18p.) and 3/7 (others) on no dot panes only
Perforation register marks: Thick bar opposite horizontal perforation row 4, right margin on no dot panes only
Positioning lines: Between dot and no dot panes in vertical rows 1 and 10 on all values
Sheet values: Above and below vertical rows 2/4 and 7/9 reading from left to right in top margin and from right to left (upside down) in bottom margin
Traffic lights (boxed): Opposite rows 8/9, right margin
18p. Stone, orange-yellow, bright purple, olive-bistre, grey-black, gold
26p. Stone, bistre-yellow, dull orange, greenish blue, pale bistre, black, gold
31p. Stone, greenish yellow, rose-red, deep blue, olive-bistre, black, gold
34p. Stone, yellow, pale bistre, olive-grey, olive-bistre, black, gold

ꞓilliam Morgan. ꞓyficithydd y Beibl
Cymraeg cyntaf 1588.
Translator of the first complete Bible into
the ꞓelsh language 1588.

ꞓilliam Salesbury. Prif gyficithydd y
Testament Newydd Cymraeg 1567.
Principal translator of the New Testament
into the ꞓelsh language 1567.

W685 Revd. William
Morgan (Bible
translator, 1588)

W686 William Salesbury
(New Testament
translator, 1567)

Richard Davies. Sgogydd a chyd-gyficithydd
y Testament Newydd Cymraeg 1567.
Motivator and part translator of the New
Testament into the ꞓelsh language 1567.

Richard Parry. Golygydd y cyficithiad
diwygiedig o'r Beibl Cymraeg 1620.
Editor of the revised version of the ꞓelsh
language Bible 1620.

W687 Bishop Richard
Davies (New Testament
translator, 1567)

W688 Bishop Richard
Parry (editor of Revised
Welsh Bible, 1620)

(Des. Keith Bowen)

1988 (1 MARCH). THE WELSH BIBLE

This issue celebrates the 400 years since the first Bible in Welsh was completed by William Morgan, later Bishop of St. Asaph. It was made possible by the passing of an Act in Parliament which decreed the translation of the Bible into Welsh. The 18p. shows Bishop William Morgan who took ten years to complete the first translation of the Bible. It was an enormous volume which was revised in 1620. Both the 26p. and 31p. depict translators of the New Testament, but it was Bishop Richard Davies who was instrumental in persuading Parliament to allow the passing of the Act and he later continued the work of William Salesbury. It fell to Bishop Richard Parry (34p.) to edit the revised version of the original Welsh Bible and in 1630 the "Little Bible" appeared. This popular version made William Morgan's earlier work available to everyone.

Phosphorised (advanced coated) paper. Comb perforation $14\frac{1}{2} \times 14$

W722 (= S.G.1384)	**W685**	18p. grey-black, greenish yellow, cerise, blue, black and emerald..	30	35
W723 (= S.G.1385)	**W686**	26p. grey-black, yellow, bright rose-red, turquoise-blue, black and orange	40	45
		a. Reddish spot in background	1·60	
W724 (= S.G.1386)	**W687**	31p. black, chrome-yellow, carmine, new blue, grey-black and blue	50	55
		a. Lines across writing tablet	2·00	
W725 (= S.G.1387)	**W688**	34p. grey-black, greenish yellow, cerise, turquoise-green, black and bright violet	55	60

First Day Cover (W722/5)	..	..	..	.. †	3·00
Presentation Pack (W722/5)	..	..	..	.. 2·00	†
PHQ Cards (W722/5) ..	..	..	..	.. 90	4·50

Listed Varieties

W723*a*
Reddish spot in background
above right shoulder
(Dot, R. 10/10)

W724*a*
Grey lines across the
writing tablet
(Dot, R. 9/1)

Cylinder Numbers (Blocks of Six)

	Cyl. Nos.	Perforation No dot	Type R* Dot
18p.	3A (grey-black)–1B (greenish yellow)–4C (cerise)–1D (blue)–2E (black)–1F (emerald)	2·10	2·10
26p.	2A (grey-black)–1B (yellow)–4C (bright rose-red)–1D (turquoise-blue)–2E (black)–1F (orange)	2·75	2·75
31p.	2A (black)–1B (chrome-yellow)–1C (carmine)–1D (new blue)–1E (grey-black)–1F (blue)	3·50	3·50
34p.	1A (grey-black)–2B (greenish yellow)–2C (cerise)–1D (turquoise-green)–2E (black)–1F (bright violet)	3·75	3·75

Sheet Details

Sheet size: 100 (2 panes 10 × 5). Double pane reel-fed

Sheet markings:
Cylinder numbers: In top margin above vertical rows 2/3, boxed. Harrison logo above vertical row 1
Marginal arrows: In gutter margin opposite rows 5/6
Colour register marks (crossed lines type):
No dot panes: Above and below vertical row 4
Dot panes: Above and below vertical row 9 and cross in circle type above vertical rows 1/2
Autotron marks: In order of traffic lights reading from left to right above vertical rows 4/7 on dot panes only
Perforation register marks: Thick bar in bottom margin opposite last perforation row on no dot panes only
Positioning lines: Long vertical and short horizontal lines between no dot and dot panes in vertical margin seen at right on no dot and at left on dot panes
Sheet values: Opposite rows 2/4 and 7/9 reading up at left and down at right
Traffic lights (boxed): In bottom margin below vertical row 2
18p. Grey-black, emerald, black, blue, cerise, greenish yellow
26p. Grey-black, orange, black, turquoise-blue, bright rose-red, yellow
31p. Grey-black, blue, black, new blue, carmine, chrome-yellow
34p. Grey-black, bright violet, black, turquoise-green, cerise, greenish yellow

W689 Gymnastics   **W690** Downhill
                                    Ski-ing

W691 Tennis   **W692** Football

(Des. Jake Sutton)

1988 (22 MARCH).   SPORT ORGANIZATIONS

The centenary of the British Amateur Gymnastics Association is marked by the 18p. showing a
girl exercising on a beam. As a tribute to the Ski Club of Great Britain the 26p. was issued in the
same year as the birth centenary of Sir Alfred Lunn, the man responsible for the first world
championships. The centenaries of the Lawn Tennis Association and the Football League are
represented by the other values.

Phosphorised (advanced coated) paper. Comb perforation $14\frac{1}{2}$

W726 (= S.G.1388)	**W689**	18p.	violet-blue, greenish yellow, rosine, bright rose, new blue and silver..	30	35
W727 (= S.G.1389)	**W690**	26p.	violet-blue, greenish yellow, vermilion, carmine, yellow-orange and silver	40	45
W728 (= S.G.1390)	**W691**	31p.	violet-blue, greenish yellow, rose, blue, pale greenish blue, silver and bright orange	50	55
			a. Orange pocket on skirt	1·90	
W729 (= S.G.1391)	**W692**	34p.	violet-blue, greenish yellow, vermilion, blue, bright emerald, silver and pink	55	60

First Day Cover (W726/9)	..	..	..	.. †	3·00	
Presentation Pack (W726/9)	..	..	..	.. 2·00	†	
PHQ Cards (W726/9)	..	..	..	.. 90	4·50	

Listed Variety

W728*a*

Orange patch on skirt
appears as a pocket
(No dot, R. 5/4)

Cylinder Numbers (Blocks of Six)

	Cyl. Nos.	Perforation No dot	Type R* Dot
18p.	1A (violet-blue)–1B (greenish yellow)–1C (rosine)–1D (bright rose)–1E (new blue)–1F (silver)	2·10	2·10
26p.	1A (violet-blue)–1B (greenish yellow)–1C (vermilion)–1D (carmine)–1E (yellow-orange)–1F (silver)..	2·75	2·75
31p.	1A (violet-blue)–1B (greenish yellow)–1C (rose)–1D (blue)–2E (pale greenish blue)–1F (silver)–1G (bright orange)	3·50	3·50
34p.	1A (violet-blue)–1B (greenish yellow)–1C (vermillion)–1D (blue)–2E (bright emerald)–1F (silver)–1G (pink)	3·75	3·75

Sheet Details

Sheet size: 100 (2 panes 5 × 10). Double pane reel-fed

Sheet markings:
Cylinder numbers: Opposite rows 8/9, left margin, boxed with Harrison logo printed in violet-blue, opposite row 10
Marginal arrows: In gutter margin opposite rows 5/6 in violet-blue
Colour register marks (crossed lines type):
No dot panes: Opposite rows 7/8 at both sides
Dot panes: Opposite rows 2/3 at both sides
Autotron marks: In same order as traffic lights in left margin opposite rows 3/7 (31p. and 34p.) or rows 4/7 (others) on dot panes only
Perforation register marks: Thick bar opposite first horizontal perforation row, right margin on no dot panes only. On the 31p. the bar was etched by hand and appears patchy. All were printed in violet-blue
Positioning lines: Between dot and no dot panes in vertical rows 1 and 10 on all values in violet-blue
Sheet values: In violet-blue above and below rows 2/4 and 7/9 reading from left to right in top margin and from right to left (upside down) in bottom margin
Traffic lights (boxed): Opposite row 9 (18p. and 26p.) or rows 8/9 (others), right margin
18p. Greenish yellow, rosine, violet-blue, bright rose, new blue, silver
26p. Greenish yellow, vermilion, violet-blue, carmine, yellow-orange, silver
31p. Greenish yellow, rose, violet-blue, blue, pale greenish blue, bright orange, silver
34p. Greenish yellow, vermilion, violet-blue, blue, bright emerald, pink, silver

W693 *Mallard* and Mailbags
on Pick-up Arms

W694 Loading Transatlantic
Mail on Liner *Queen Elizabeth*

W695 Glasgow Tram No. 1173
and Pillar Box

W696 Imperial Airways Handley
Page "HP24" and Airmail Van

(Des. Mike Dempsey)

1988 (10 MAY). TRANSPORT AND COMMUNICATIONS ("EUROPA")

The theme chosen by the CEPT was "Means of Transport and Communications" and each design is shown in a travel poster style of the nineteen thirties. The 18p. shows the *Mallard* which set a world speed record of 126 m.p.h. for steam power on 6 July 1938. In the same year the liner, *Queen Elizabeth* was launched and at 83,763 tons was the largest liner ever built. The tram depicted on the 31p. entered service in 1938 and offered luxury travel for 65 passengers. A letter being posted on the first stage of the journey is shown. At its height the Glasgow tramway network had over 1,000 cars using the 150 miles of route. Tram no. 1173 is preserved in Glasgow's Museum of Transport, Kelvin Hall. Although the speed of the Handley Page "HP24" was a modest 110 m.p.h. it served regular routes to Europe, India, South Africa and far outposts of the British Empire from 1924. Blue Royal Mail vans carried the airmail to Croydon Airport as shown on the 34p.

Phosphorised (advanced coated) paper

W730 (= S.G.1392)	**W693**	18p.	brown, yellow, rose-red, dull blue, deep brown, reddish violet and black	30	35
W731 (= S.G.1393)	**W694**	26p.	brown, yellow, orange-vermilion, dull blue, violet-blue, bright emerald and black	40	45
W732 (= S.G.1394)	**W695**	31p.	brown, yellow-orange, carmine, dull purple, violet-blue, bright green and black	50	55
W733 (= S.G.1395)	**W696**	34p.	brown, orange-yellow, carmine-rose, bluish violet, bright blue, sepia and black	55	60
		a.	Black blemish opposite Queen's chin	1·75	

First Day Cover (W730/3)	..	..	..	.. † 3·00
Presentation Pack (W730/3)	..	..	..	.. 2·00 †
PHQ Cards (W730/3)	..	..	..	.. 90 4·50

Listed Variety

W733*a*

Black blemish opposite
the Queen's chin
(No dot, R. 7/7)

Cylinder Numbers (Blocks of Six)

	Cyl. Nos.	Perforation No dot	Type R* Dot
18p.	1A (brown)–2B (yellow)–2C (rose-red)–3D (dull blue)–1E (deep brown)–1F (reddish violet)–2G (black)	2·10	2·10
26p.	1A (brown)–1B (yellow)–1C (orange-vermilion)–1D (dull blue) –1E (violet-blue)–1F (bright emerald)–1G (black).	2·75	2·75
31p.	1A (brown)–1B (yellow-orange)–1C (carmine)–1D (dull purple) –1E (violet-blue)–1F (bright green)–1G (black)		
34p.	1A (brown)–1B (orange-yellow)–1C (carmine-rose)–1D (bluish violet)–1E (bright blue) –1F (sepia)–1G (black)	3·75	3·75

Sheet Details

Sheet size: 100 (2 panes 10 × 5). Double pane reel-fed

Sheet markings:
Cylinder numbers: Opposite rows 8/9, left margin, boxed with Harrison logo opposite row 10
Marginal arrows: In centre at top and bottom of sheet
Colour register marks (crossed lines type):
No dot panes: Opposite rows 6/7 at both sides and cross in circle opposite row 2
Dot panes: Opposite rows 1/2 at both sides
Autotron marks: In same order as traffic lights in left margin opposite rows 3/7 on dot panes only
Perforation register marks: Thick bar opposite horizontal perforation row 4, right margin on no dot panes only
Positioning lines: Between dot and no dot panes in vertical rows 1 and 10 on all values
Sheet values: Above and below vertical rows 2/4 and 7/9 reading from left to right in top margin and from right to left (upside down) in bottom margin
Traffic lights (boxed): Opposite rows 8/9, right margin
18p. Yellow, rose-red, dull blue, deep brown, reddish violet, black, brown
26p. Yellow, orange-vermilion, dull blue, violet-blue, bright emerald, black, brown
31p. Yellow-orange, carmine, dull purple, violet-blue, bright green, black, brown
34p. Orange-yellow, carmine-rose, bluish violet, bright blue, sepia, black, brown

APPENDIX I

Perforators

For ease of reference the perforation types described below are shown here in tabular form and the characteristics given relate to the sheet viewed with the stamps the right way up. Vertical format stamps are invariably printed sideways and pass through the perforators sideways but obviously the characteristics are different when the sheet is viewed with the stamps the right way up.

The identification of a particular perforation type from a cylinder block can easily be established by referring to this table in conjunction with the perforation types given under "Cylinder Numbers" in Section W.

I. HORIZONTAL FORMAT STAMPS

Perforation Type	Top margin	Bottom margin	Left margin	Right margin
Type A (T) *(top feed)*	Imperforate	Perforated through	Single extension hole	Single extension hole
Type G (L) *(left feed)*	Perforated through	Perforated through	Imperforate	Perforated through
Type M *left feed*	Perforated through	Perforated through	Imperforate	Perforated through
Type R*	Perforated through	Perforated through	Single extension hole	Single extension hole
Type R* (X)	Single extension hole	Single extension hole	Perforated through	Perforated through
Type R (A)	Single extension hole	Single extension hole	Imperforate	Imperforate

II. VERTICAL FORMAT STAMPS

Perforation Type	Top margin	Bottom margin	Left margin	Right margin
Type A (T) *(head to left)*	Single extension hole	Single extension hole	Perforated through	Imperforate
Type A (T) *(head to right)*	Single extension hole	Single extension hole	Imperforate	Perforated through
Type A *(head to right)*	Perforated through	Imperforate	Single extension hole	Single extension hole
Type M *(top feed)*	Imperforate	Perforated through	Perforated through	Perforated through
Type R* *(head to left)*	Single extension hole	Single extension hole	Perforated through	Perforated through

Description of Sheet and Reel-fed Perforators

Type A (T). Grover sheet-fed machines employing a two-row comb (Types A or A (T)) where a few sheets are fed at a time so that the rate of output is comparatively low. At first it was used for single pane sheet-fed issues but when larger quantities were required, starting with the 1971 2½p. Christmas, it was also used for double pane reel-fed issues which require guide holes. The position of the guide holes employed for some issues to the 1973 Christmas set, are given under "Sheet Details" in Section W.

Vertical format stamps are printed sideways with the head to left with the exception of the 1972 Royal Silver Wedding issue printed on the Rembrandt press which have the head to right.

The perforations in the no dot and dot panes are the same.

Type A. This is as Type A (T) but with bottom feed and its only use in the Special issues was on the 1972 3p. Royal Silver Wedding issue printed on the "Jumelle" machine.

Type G (L). Vertical single-row comb. Sheet-fed.

No dot panes—

Top margin	Perforated through
Bottom margin	Perforated through
Left margin	Imperforate
Right margin	Perforated through
Guide holes	None

APPENDIX I   Perforators—Special Issues

The top and bottom margins are sometimes not completely perforated through.
This left feed perforator was used by Bradbury, Wilkinson for the 1973 Inigo Jones and Parliamentary Conference issues.

Type M. Horizontal Comb. Sheet-fed
This was used for issues printed by Questa. These panes have a narrow perforated gutter. The "A" pane was printed first, followed by "B" pane.

Types N and N(R). Vertical comb. Sheet-fed
This perforator was used by Waddington for the 1981 Duke of Edinburgh's Award, 1983 British Gardens and 1985 Safety at Sea issues. The panes have a gutter margin which is identical in size to the Harrison issues. Perforation characteristics are given after the listings.

Type R* (X). Horizontal rotary cylinder. Reel-fed

No dot and dot panes—

	Top margin	A single extension hole
	Bottom margin	A single extension hole
	Left margin	Perforated through
	Right margin	Perforated through
	Guide holes	None

This was used exclusively for an extra emergency supply of the 1973 3p. Christmas on paper with gum arabic. These stamps have no inter-pane gutter and were printed sideways in the reel and passed through the rotary perforator. It has the characteristics of Type R* but turned sideways.

Type R*. Horizontal rotary cylinder. Reel-fed.

No dot and dot panes

Top margin	Perforated through
Inter-pane gutter	Perforated through
Bottom margin	Perforated through
Left margin	A single extension hole
Right margin	A single extension hole
Guide holes	None

Vertical format stamps are printed sideways with the head to left.
A German Kampf machine which is also a rotary cylinder and later became an integral part of the "Jumelle" press. This perforates in the reel as fast as the stamps are printed. It is the standard perforator used for the Special issues and high value Machin photogravure stamps which appear in Post Office sheets containing two panes of 50 stamps separated by an inter-pane gutter margin.

Type R(A). Horizontal rotary perforator. Reel-fed
First use of the APS machine was on the 1982 Technology issue in double panes (3 × 10) with vertical imperforate gutter margin.

Extension or Marker Pins
As with Type R for the Machin issues, extra pins were introduced on the perforating drum to help with the location of damaged pins and, whilst the extra extension holes are in theory liable to occur anywhere in the sheet margins, they are in practice to be found only at the corners or gutter margins. They are collectable items and worth a premium but are outside the scope of this catalogue since they are not representative of a different perforator.
They were first introduced with the 1973 Royal Wedding issue, where the extra extension holes appear in the right margin at fixed points of both no dot and dot sheets, either at perforation rows 12 and 1 of consecutive sheets or at the gutter margin in perforation rows 6 and 7, since each revolution of the perforating drum perforates an odd number of panes as is explained later. Thus the left margin would not be affected unless the perforating drum was inverted in relation to the ink cylinders, and this did not occur with this setting. This setting was used on all 1974 issues, the 1975 Charity stamp and the 1976 Telephone issue. Naturally with vertical format stamps one has to orientate the sheet through 90 degrees.
With the 1975 Turner issue the setting was changed so as to produce one extra extension hole at each side of both sheets, either immediately below the gutter, i.e. perforation row 7, or at the top corners, i.e. perforation row 1. This setting was used on all subsequent issues (except the 1976 Telephone stamps) up to and including the 1977 Chemistry issue.
Another setting was used on the following issues: 1977 Wildlife and Christmas and the 9p., 10½p. and 13p. values of the 1978 Energy. This gives one extra extension hole on the right-hand side only of the sheet either immediately above the gutter, i.e. perforation row 6, or at the bottom corner, i.e. perforation row 12. On the 9p., 11p. and 13p. values of the 1978 Christmas issue the perforating drum was inverted in relation to the ink cylinders, giving an extra extension hole on the left-hand side only of the sheet, either at the top corner, i.e. perforation row 1, or immediately below the gutter, i.e. perforation row 7. Extra extension holes have not been reported on the following issues: 1977 Silver Jubilee and Commonwealth Heads of Government, 1978 Energy (11p. value), Historic Buildings, Coronation, Horses, Cycling and Christmas (7p. value), 1979 Dogs, Wild Flowers, Elections and Horseracing.

APPENDIX I   Perforators—Special Issues

Unlike the Machin definitives, where the intersheet gutter is the height of one stamp and the no dot and dot sheets are printed side by side, in the Special Issues the gutter margins are not the height of a stamp, as explained under "Gutter Margins" in the General Notes to Section W, and the no dot and dot cylinders are placed one below the other.

Thus if an extra extension pin exists on the perforation drum on "perforation" pane 1 and this coincides with printed pane 1 at the start of a run, the extra extension hole will reappear seven panes later at pane 8, 15 etc. As the ratio of the perforating drum to the ink cylinders is seven panes to four, the exact sequence will recommence at sheet 15 with pane 29. This is demonstrated by the following diagram:—

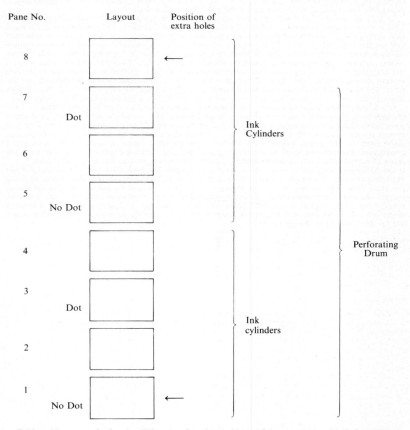

Pane No.	Layout	Position of extra holes

Taking this a stage further it will be seen that the positions of the extra extension holes will be as follows:—

No dot	Lower pane	Pane 1
Dot	Upper pane	Pane 8
Dot	Lower pane	Pane 15
No dot	Upper pane	Pane 22
No dot	Lower pane	Pane 29 etc.

The same sequence of occurrence may be applied for the repetition of such other perforating irregularities as bent or broken pins.

For this information we are indebted to a further article by Mr. F. D. Wild and one by Mr. P. Daniels, in the May 1978 issue of *Guidec*, published by The British Decimal Stamps Study Circle.

APPENDIX I   Perforators—Special Issues

In 1979 the marker pin reappeared on the International Year of the Child issue with the extension hole at both sides of the sheet, i.e., perforation rows 6 or 12. It occurs on the Police 13p. value but the other values of this set have been reported with a single extension hole at perforation rows 1 or 7 in the right margin only, these designs being in the horizontal format. This setting was continued for the 1979 Christmas issue up to and including the 1980 Railway stamp. The 50p. "London 1980" issue has been found with the extra extension holes in the top and bottom margins at perforation row 7. The issues following the "London 1980" stamp had the single extension holes in the right-hand margin, but the perforator was changed with the 1980 Conductors issue, which had the extra extension holes at both sides of the sheet at perforation rows 6 or 12. For stamps in horizontal format the perforation rows will be 1 or 7. This setting has been employed for all special issues, printed by Harrison, up to and including the 1982 British Textiles.

In 1982 the Swedish style APS machine was introduced to replace the German Kampf machine. This is a rotary type perforator with pins which are designed to pierce the paper from the printed side. Surplus paper is removed from the gummed side by blades which are set in rollers. It was used first on the 1982 Information Technology issue and had to be specially adapted for these stamps which were in a long format. The perforation type for this issue is Type R(A), but the following issues, perforated by this machine, reverted to the former Type R*. No extension holes were seen on the Information Technology issue but other issues had a single extension marker pin in the left margin, except for the 1984 "Europa" which is known with the extension hole at both sides of the pane. The German Kampf machine was brought back into use for the 1982 Christmas, 1983 British River Fishes and Commonwealth Day sets, although on the last issue no extension pin was noted.

It is likely that each special issue was perforated by either machine rather than both. During 1985 changes took place in the size and shape of special issues. The use of the APS perforator made it possible to make these changes and the first of these was the British Composers issue which was almost square with a perforation of $14 \times 14\frac{1}{2}$. The high speed cutting blades which grind perforated discs away as the paper passes over the male-pin cylinder meant a much more economical production. The previous method of matching male-pin and female-pinhole cylinders had been the cause of broken pins and the requirement for extension marker pins to locate the breakages.

On APS perforated special issues the marker pins appeared at both sides of the sheet and did not vary their position. They can be seen at the corner of a sheet, therefore cylinder blocks exist showing the extra hole opposite the bottom perforation row. They can also be found opposite the gutter margin although the position does not change according to the number of sheets printed. It will be noted from the listings that the APS perforator has a tendency to leave small areas of a sheet imperforate in error, but the incidence of broken pins has probably diminished to the point where the marker pins are no longer needed.

Further Reading

Mackay, James A. *British Stamps.* (1985. Longman Group Ltd, London.)

Pask, Brian and Peachey, Colin G. *Twenty Years of First Day Postmarks: The story and details of "First Day of Issue" Postmarks used by the British Post Office from 1963 to 1983.* (1983. British Postmark Society, Hemel Hempstead, Herts.)

Pearson, George R. *Special Event Postmarks of the United Kingdom.* (1984. 3rd Edn. British Postmark Society, London.)

Rigo de Righi, A. G. *The Stamp of Royalty; British Commonwealth Issues for Royal Occasions, 1935–1972.* (1973. The National Postal Museum, London.)

Rose, Stuart. *Royal Mail Stamps—A Survey of British Stamp Design.* (1980. Phaidon Press, Oxford.)

Whitney, J. T. *Collect British Postmarks.* (1987. 4th Edn. The Author, Benfleet, Essex.)

Wijman, J. J. *Postage Stamps of Great Britain and their History.* (1986. The Author, Netherlands.)

PHILATELIC PERIODICALS DEVOTED TO GREAT BRITAIN STAMPS AND POSTMARKS

The Bookmark (The GB Decimal Stamp Book Study Circle.)

British Philatelic Bulletin (From 1963) (The Post Office, London) (title was *Philatelic Bulletin,* 1963–83.)

British Postmark Bulletin (Fom 1971) (The Post Office, London) (title was *Postmark Bulletin,* 1971–84.)

British Postmark Society Quarterly Bulletin (From 1958) (British Postmark Society.)

Gibbons Stamp Monthly (*British Stamps* supplement from October 1981, January, April and July 1982, monthly since October 1982.)

Guidec (The British Decimal Stamps Study Circle.)

The GB Journal (From 1956) (The Great Britain Philatelic Society, London.)

The Philatelist/Philatelic Journal of Great Britain (From 1981) (The P.J.G.B., 1891–1980, was wholly devoted to Great Britain after March 1966.) (Robson Lowe Ltd., London.)

STANLEY GIBBONS UNIVERSAL
The complete collecting system.

If your collection include booklets, first day covers or presentation packs as well as stamps, you will undoubtedly have faced the problem as to how best to mount them all up. This problem is now solved – thanks to the Stanley Gibbons Universal System.

The advantage of the Universal is that it is based on a standard 22 ring binder with a choice of twelve different leaf formats; thus enabling stamps, covers, entires, booklets and presentation packs to be included either in the same album or in a series of matching albums. There are three different stamp albums, a cover album, a booklet album and a presentation pack album in the Universal range as well as extra binders and packs of leaves in all twelve formats.

The Universal Stamp Album
is available with either white unfaced, white faced or black faced leaves.

The Universal Cover Album
contains 13 leaves, 12 double pocket and 1 single pocket; the latter taking covers up to 8½in × 10½in.

The Universal Booklet Album
with six different leaf types available. Stitched, folded, "Prestige" and the latest "window" style booklets can be included in the same album.

The Universal Presentation Pack Album
Yes – presentation packs too can now be mounted alongside basic sets and covers – once again two different leaf formats are offered – single or double pocket.

All Universal Albums and binders
are available in a choice of dark red, deep blue or brown grained PVC, gold blocked on the spine and presented in a smart slip box.

For further details visit your favourite stamp shop or, in case of difficulty write to:

Stanley Gibbons Publications Ltd.,
5 Parkside,
Christchurch Road,
Ringwood, Hampshire BH24 3SH
Telephone 0425 472363

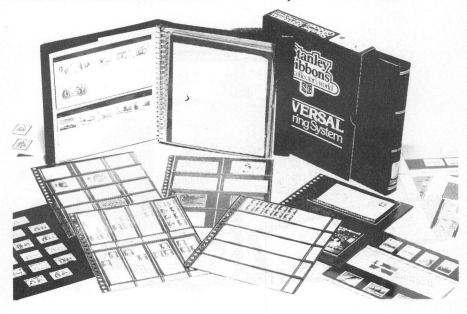

COVER ALBUMS

With cover collecting growing in popularity all the time we are proud to offer a comprehensive range of albums to meet the needs of first day cover collector and postal historian alike. All leaves have black card inserts to set off your covers to best advantage.

1. THE NEW PIONEER COVER ALBUM

A fully padded PVC Binder in a choice of black, green or red. Holds up to 40 covers in a high capacity, low priced album, ideal for the beginner.

2. THE PROTECTOR COVER ALBUM

The luxury padded binder comes in deep blue, brown or maroon with gold blocking on the spine and a secure 4-ring arch mechanism. The album contains 19 double and 1 single-pocket leaves, the former being specifically designed to house the current standard British Post Office first day covers. The leaves are made from 'Polyprotec' a material which does not crease or tear easily, will not degrade and offers considerable protection against heat and ultra violet light. Holds up to 78 covers.

3. THE MALVERN COVER ALBUM

Another great value album suitable for collectors at all levels. The 4-ring arch fitting binder contains 19 double-pocket leaves, 1 single-pocket leaves and holds up to 78 covers in all. Available in blue, green or red.

4. THE NEW CLASSIC COVER ALBUM

A compact de-luxe album with 20 crystal clear leaves offering full protection for up to 40 covers and two clear fly leaves to hold an index of notes. Available in black, red or blue and supplied in a protective slip box.

5. THE SG MAJOR COVER ALBUM

(Not illustrated)
A luxury album recommended for that really special collection. The fully padded, leather grained PVC binder has peg fittings and comes with 13 crystal clear leaves (12 double-pocket and 1 single pocket) and two clear fly leaves in which to insert notes. Available in dark red, deep blue or brown – the top of the range.

6. THE UNIVERSAL COVER ALBUM

The cover album which allows stamps, booklets and presentation packs to be housed all together – see page 303 for details.

STOCKBOOKS

We are pleased to announce that Stanley Gibbons are now offering a selected range of Lighthouse stockbooks in addition to the popular S.G. branded junior style. Fastbound with stout linen-hinged leaves, all come with glassine interleaving to ensure complete protection for your stamps and will give years of use.

1. Junior Stockbooks
With a bright full-colour, stamp design cover these stockbooks have white leaves with glassine strips and interleaving – ideal for the younger collector.

	Size (ins)	No. of Pages	No. of Strips
Item 2625	7½ × 5¼	8	48
Item 2659	8½ × 6⅝	8	48
Item 2650	11 × 8¾	8	72

2. Lighthouse Stockbooks
A variety of bright single colour covers with gold blocking on the front and spine.

	Size (ins)	No. of Pages	No. of Strips
Item 2649	7¾ × 5½	16	96
Item 2651	9 × 7	16	96
Item 2631	9 × 7	32	192

For further details visit your favourite stamp shop or, in case of difficulty, write to:

**Stanley Gibbons Publications Ltd.,
5 Parkside, Christchurch Road,
Ringwood, Hampshire BH24 3SH
Telephone 0425 472363**

The larger page size stockbooks feature a luxury leather look binding and have double glassine interleaving for even greater protection. NOTE the new 48-page stockbook (item 2662) has double linen hinged 'lay flat' leaves.

	Size (ins)	No. of Pages	No. of Strips
Item 2652	12 × 9	16	144
Item 2653	12 × 9	32	288
Item 2662	12 × 9	48	432

3. Two stylish stockbooks with binding as above but with black leaves and crystal clear strips. Double glassine interleaving.

Item 2664	12 × 9	16	144
Item 2665	12 × 9	32	288

4. A 'King Size' addition to the S.G. Stockbook range! Cover Specifications as above with 64 double linen-hinged leaves to ensure that the book lies absolutely flat when open. White leaves with glassine strips and double interleaving. Definitely the top of the range and a luxury stockbook any collector would be proud to own.

Item 2678	12 × 9	64	576

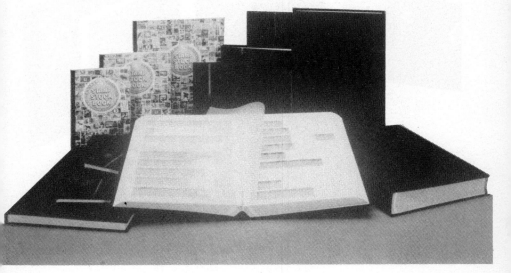

BLANK SPRINGBACK ALBUMS

These fine albums give the more advanced collector the freedom and flexibility he needs to arrange his collection exactly as he wants it.

All leaves are finely printed with a feint quadrille and most have side and centre markings to aid arrangement. Many have transparent interleaving to reduce friction between stamps and facing pages – interleaving sheets are available for those albums which are not supplied with this.

There are six very popular, value-for-money albums in the Stanley Gibbons springback range.

1. Tower (Item 0331) A choice of red, green, or black gold-blocked binder with 100 leaves of white cartridge 11⅛" × 9⅞". Boxed.

2. Senator Medium (Item 0384) A very popular 'first' blank leaved album for many years now. 50 leaves 10⅜" × 8¾", a choice of three binder colours; black, green or red.

3. Senator Standard (Item 0386) As the Senator Medium but with 100 larger sized leaves (11⅛" × 9⅞"). One of our best selling albums!

4. Simplex Medium (Item 3810) Fifty leaves of high quality cream paper with a subtle decorative border (10⅜" × 8¾"). Binder choice of green or red with gold blocking on the spine.

5. Simplex Standard (Item 3812) 100 larger sized leaves (11⅛" × 9⅞"), otherwise the same style as the Simplex Medium. Boxed. Popular with generations of stamp collectors!

6. Utile (Item 3821) 25 white cartridge special double linen-hinged transparent faced leaves (11⅛" × 9⅞") designed to lie flat when album is opened. Attractive binder in choice of green or red.

Transparent Interleaving Fine quality glazed transparent paper in packs of 100 sheets for Tower, Senator, Simplex or similar types of loose-leaf springback albums.

Item 3310 Standard size 11" × 9⅝".

Item 3311 Medium size 10" × 8⅛".

For further details visit your favourite stamp shop or, in case of difficulty, write to:

**Stanley Gibbons Publications Ltd.,
5 Parkside, Christchurch Road,
Ringwood, Hampshire BH24 3SH
Telephone 0425 472363**

PEG-FITTING
BLANK LOOSE-LEAF ALBUMS

Stanley Gibbons blank albums give you the freedom and flexibility you need to arrange your collection exactly as you want it.

All those items which can add real interest to a collection: shades, inverted watermarks, gum variations, cylinder blocks, unusual cancellations, etc. can be easily accommodated and there is no need to be frustrated by empty spaces perpetually reminding you of the stamps you do not have.

Peg-fitting albums represent the very peak of Stanley Gibbons range – albums which have stood the test of time from the Devon, now in its 30th year of production to the Philatelic which has been housing the great collections of the world for over a century!

The Devon
A strong elegant, large-capacity binder containing 100 fine quality cartridge leaves (10⅜ × 9¾ in.). Choice of maroon, green, black or blue. Ideal for collections where that extra capacity is required. Transparent interleaving available, boxed.

The Exeter
A quality binder in a choice of red, blue or green containing 40 leaves (10¼ × 9¾ in.) of fine white cartridge. All leaves are double linen-hinged with transparent facing so that leaves lie flat when the album is opened and damaging friction is minimised.

An illustrated colour brochure giving prices of these and all other Stanley Gibbons Publications Products is available by post from

Stanley Gibbons Publications Ltd.,
5 Parkside, Christchurch Road,
Ringwood, Hampshire BH24 3SH.
Telephone 0425 472363.

The Plymouth
Maroon, black, green or blue, a connoisseur's album in a strong matching slip-case. Supplied with 40 double linen-hinged leaves (10⅛ × 9¼ in.) with glassine facing for additional protection.

The Philatelic
The largest album in the Stanley Gibbons range, it not only accommodates more stamps per page than other albums but also allows sheets, blocks, etc., to be arranged and mounted on its 12⅞ × 10¼ in. leaves. Bound in handsome deep green cloth with leather corners and spine, supplied with 80 double linen-hinged, transparent faced leaves and presented in a sturdy deep green slip-case.

The Oriel
Supreme among luxury blank albums, the Oriel will enhance the very finest collection. Half bound in rich red leather with gold tooling, each album contains 50 superior gilt-edged double linen-hinged leaves (10⅛ × 9⅛ in.) with transparent facings and is supplied in a luxury matching slip-case.

The most prestigious home for your stamps.

Additional binders and leaves are available for all Stanley Gibbons peg-fitting albums.

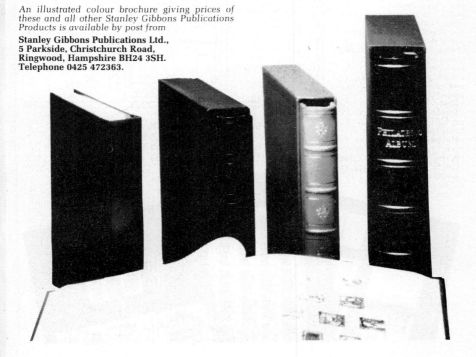

SAFE 'N' CLEAR

Stanley Gibbons Safe 'n' Clear leaves combine the versatility of blank leaves with the ease of use of a hingeless album – just slip the stamps into the strips and build a permanent collection or rearrange them instantly as required. Nine different leaf formats for singles, pairs, strips, blocks, gutter pairs or cylinder blocks and even early postal history and presentation packs – in fact a Safe 'n' Clear leaf for every need! There is also one to house stamps and covers of the same set on the same leaf. Stanley Gibbons Safe 'n' Clear is safe because the entire system is manufactured only from highest quality materials guaranteed to give maximum protection to stamps, covers and postal history. The leaves are of tough, matt board, colour fast and completely free of harmful chemicals. The crystal clear polyester strips contain no softeners, acids, solvents or plasticisers and offer substantial protection against ultra-violet light, humidity and friction. The bonding between strips and leaf is likewise chemically inert, ensuring the leaves will not warp or buckle under adverse conditions, whilst holding stamps and covers firmly in place. Stanley Gibbons Safe 'n' Clear leaves are 280 × 215 mm. The multi-punched holes are designed to fit a vast range of ring binders from 2 to 22 ring: Whatever the ring system Safe 'n' Clear is likely to fit it. Alternatively use the special Stanley Gibbons Safe 'n' Clear Album.

242mm

1 × 242mm strip Item 6001

119mm

2 × 119mm strips Item 6002

79mm

3 × 79mm strips Item 6003

58mm

4 × 58mm strips Item 6004

45mm

5 × 45mm strips Item 6005

37mm

6 × 37mm strips Item 6006

31mm

7 × 31mm strips Item 6007

27mm

8 × 27mm strips Item 6008

36mm
67mm
139mm

36/67/139mm strips Item 6009

Stanley Gibbons Publications Ltd.,
5 Parkside, Christchurch Road,
Ringwood, Hampshire BH24 3SH
Telephone 0425 472363